Travelling MAGICALLY

How to turn your journey into a life-changing experience

DR RIMA MORRELL

PIATKUS

PIATKUS

First published in Great Britain in 2008 by Piatkus Books

Copyright © 2008 by Rima Morrell

The moral right of the author has been asserted

A CIP catalogue record for this book
is available from the British Library

ISBN 978-0-7499-2818-6

Typeset in Minion by Palimpsest Book Production Limited,
Grangemouth, Stirlingshire
Printed in the UK by CPI William Clowes Beccles NR34 7TL

Papers used by Piatkus Books are natural, renewable and recyclable
products made from wood grown in sustainable forests and certified
in accordance with the rules of the Forest Stewardship Council.

Piatkus Books
An imprint of
Little, Brown Book Group
100 Victoria Embankment
London EC4Y 0DY

An Hachette Livre UK Company

www.hachettelivre.co.uk

www.piatkus.co.uk

To Dr Janez Drnovsek, *predsednik Republike Slovenije* 2002–7 (President of Slovenia 2002–7), whose pilgrim soul has climbed that last white mountain barred with snow . . . and to all those who help. We are all going to the same high place in our own way, in our own time and aiding others helps us to reach a higher point on our inner mountain.

About the author

Dr Rima Morrell was born in the Netherlands, and grew up in London, Indonesia and Australia. She gained a degree in anthropology from Cambridge University and a Ph.D. in geography at University College, London, where she specialised in Hawaiian culture and beliefs. A fellow of the Royal Geographic Society and Royal Anthropological Institute, she gives talks for various institutions including universities, the *Daily Telegraph* Travel Show and the British Museum. She is a member of the Doctor Healer network and the Scientific and Medical Network. Dr Morrell is the author of two previous books about Huna, the ancient wisdom of Hawaii. She can often be found in London or Scotland, or on her website: www.rimamorrell.com, where she offers consultations on magical travel, soulmates and other good stuff.

The author has made every effort to trace copyright owners. Where she has failed, she offers her apologies and undertakes to make proper acknowledgement where possible in reprints or on the accompanying website.

The recommendations given in this book are intended solely as education and information, and should not be taken as medical advice. It is necessary to consult your own doctor for medical advice before following any of the medical recommendations in this book. This book is not suitable for children.

Contents

PART 3: COMING HOME AGAIN   379

Acknowledgements

There has been so much help with this book. So many of you in so many places, at so many times. I only wish I could name you all here. Thank you all so much. Whenever I needed help, help was there. It was as if this voyage was meant to be. I have been blessed and I know that this is so I can be a blessing to others. For we are all travellers on our earth and help is the most important thing we can give, as we each climb our silver path into the magic.

Den does deserve particular thanks for being an exceptional ex-husband, and for enabling me to have the time and space to write. Together, we managed to keep our various projects, joint and separate, going and this is in no small measure due to his willingness to 'go the extra mile', often quite literally, when necessary; even while working as an emergency doctor in the north of Scotland. His determination is akin to that of his ancestor, the great explorer Sir Ernest Shackleton, who never gave up, even in extremely arduous conditions, so accomplishing the impossible. On the publishing side, many thanks to Antonia Hodgson of the Little, Brown Book Group for gracefully and efficiently shepherding the project through and Paola Ehrlich for great publicity. Thank you also to Judy Piatkus and Gill Edwards of Piatkus Books for the commission after a meeting where they wanted to know about the works I had written years ago, when the world was at a different point in understanding. Thank you too to Ann Napier of Cygnus Books for making the original connection.

I was inspired to write *Travelling Magically* in Mosman, NSW, Australia in a large, modern living room filled with Aboriginal art. The writing flowed easily and beautifully and the first version took just a couple of weeks. I was lucky enough to be able to take breaks in the garden outside, where cicadas chirped, vegetation frothed and an occasional plop was heard from the huge goldfish living under the round leaves skimming the surface of the dark pond. The garden on the south-east rim of the world where the Pacific ocean was a line of sharp blue, on the song of the morning.

Time moved on. And so did I. The following millennium, I would revise the book on the other side of the world, the north and west side. I would write at the dining table of our animal sanctuary on the Isle of Skye in the Inner Hebrides, sitting on the chair carved like a whale, looking out to the north-west. Paradise? No, even as the haze hovered above the expanse of ocean, the humps of the Hebridean Islands ranging along the blue horizon. A sense of connection? Yes, as the cream sheep inhabit our green croft like clouds, the chickens spread their wings in the sunshine and the cats dream next to my computer. A magical sense of connection? Yes, as the sunset falls, slowly and softly, delicately painting the sea in a palette of glowing colours and the pink islands rise into the air like isles of myth. Did I know how to experience this glorious feeling before I began to travel? Absolutely not. I believed that the realm of enchantment was in the land of children's fables about wizards and fairyland in my loft, and did not realize that it is a magical state that is always here, and that every moment provides the chance to accept it.

A question before we start. Henry David Thoreau said: 'Why do you stay here and live this mean toiling life when a glorious existence is possible for you? These same stars twinkle over fields other than these.' It is a good question. For we are all explorers. And now is the particular time. In the end, we each have a choice as to whether to leave or stay. In leaving, I found something greater than I ever thought possible. For magical travel brought me places, people and experiences beyond the sunrise. I would not have missed my journeys for the whole wide world. For my journeys brought me the world. A wonderful world.

FOREWORD

As a child I dreamed of travelling the world. In my twenties I set off on a journey that covered six continents and lasted five years. Now, many years later, if I were a dictator, I would decree that everyone had to travel, had to immerse themselves for a time in an unfamiliar culture where their language doesn't work and their skin is a different colour. The understanding this brings, the questioning of irrational prejudices, the realisation that the finest human values are universal (and commonly more abundant without your familiar culture) can only lead to the greater good of the world. It will, without doubt, lead to your greater good. You will return a more enlightened soul. You will have grown into yourself. In your new stature you will know your truths and values. You may find your path in life, your career, your partner. If you dream of travel, go. Don't hesitate. The hardest part is leaving. (The next hardest part is stopping.) Once you're on your way, however, more important than the 'where', 'when' or 'why' is the 'how'. It is this vital aspect that this book addresses in a unique way.

For the most part on my five-year journey I hitchhiked, camped and hostelled. My intention was to go to the offbeat places not mentioned in guidebooks or to visit the popular ones in the wrong season. I travelled alone for it seemed every day brought sufficient temporary companions or solitude, whatever I wanted. Times to share and learn, times to think. My route became a loose direction awaiting deflections by those who knew the land. The journey's essence became the going as much as the destination. From this book I see how this process came about, how I might have achieved Dr Morrell's 'golden realms' sooner with an awareness of her Five Principles. *Travelling Magically* would have taught me the profound benefits of meditation (though I fear I was not ready for the lesson at the time).

It would have shown me the key to drawing rewards out of frustration, finding calmness and inner strengths. What is as important as reality – indeed, perhaps more so – is our perception of reality. Changing our perception can transform our mood and the whole experience of a situation. As a mundane example I recall the first time I had to drink butter tea in Ladakh. I found it to be semi-congealed fat and salt and I could barely swallow a mouthful. Butter tea ceremonies became a dreaded ordeal. Then I began thinking of it not as tea but as soup. I grew to love butter soup.

This book is full of such keys to transforming your travels. It is also a brave book. Converse with any experienced traveller and they'll speak of 'amazing coincidences', synchronicities and philosophies of karma that may seem to defy belief. Such events happen all the time but they are the hardest things to convey to those who haven't experienced them personally. To talk of higher consciences, spirituality, sacredness, rhythms and vibrations too often evokes scepticism in others. Our vocabulary is inept, our indoctrination too rigid. Such concepts are beyond our definitions, our comfort zones, and this intimidates us. They should do the opposite: they should excite and console us, offer us hope for they represent what we yearn for beyond the humdrum mediocrity and narrowness of our 'civilised', safe circular path. Dr Morrell breaks new ground here confronting the physical and the metaphysical, showing you how to pack both your bag and your mind.

Many may find this book challenging, as is the nature of esoteric knowledge, but without it you will garner the least rewards from your journeys. Persist. Read it all, dip in and out, take from it what you can. It is an apprenticeship. It will save you 10,000 miles of frustrations and the trials of learning the hard way. It will smooth your passage and ensure that the outer journey becomes an inner one.

Alastair Scott

Alastair Scott is a travel writer, adventurer and photographer. He is the author of eight books, including *Tracks Across Alaska* and *Native Stranger.* www.alastair-scott.com

INTRODUCTION

Why travel this way?

Man was born free, but everywhere he is in chains
Jean-Jacques Rousseau

We all desire to leave our chains behind, but we don't know how. We all long for freedom but we don't know where it lies. Some of us seek religion or aspects of the spirit, others go out and explore new lands. The lure of travel is well known. It has been documented in poetry, books and films and is the subject of many individual and collective desires. This book focuses on how to travel, particularly through using your intuition – the best travel guide of all.

There are many tremendous travel books in the world, but this is the only one to help you find your true home. I wish I'd known the things I am now sharing with you when I started travelling. I wrestled with so many questions and situations, from 'who can I trust?' and 'when do I travel with other people?' to 'where do I go?' and even 'when do I have sex?' Most importantly, 'what did it all mean?' For your true home ultimately is in what you have learned, not where you have been. As far as I know, this is the only 'how-to-travel' guide – much needed considering travel is the world's biggest industry.

MAGICAL TRAVEL: THE FIVE PRINCIPLES

Let's look at the five principles of magical travel, and at how they differ from ordinary travel:

1. **First principle: Follow your intuition**
   Be prepared to travel solo – with your intuition as your travel guide.
2. **Second principle: Travel spontaneously**
   Go from place to place according to what feels right.
3. **Third principle: Go local**
   Leave the beaten track. Go local, travelling cheaply and ethically.
4. **Fourth principle: Allow the sacred**
   Prepare for mystical experiences, in sacred places and elsewhere.
5. **Fifth principle: Integrate your journey into your life**
   Make your magical experiences part of your everyday life.

There are five main distinctions between magical travel and ordinary travel. The first is choose the silver road of your intuition to travel, out of the many possible roads. We shall talk more about what your intuition is and how to follow it. For now, let's leave it as the road to your magic is an inner journey, which will always lead you to the best possible place in the outer world. You are prepared to travel alone. Even if it seems scary at the moment, there are plenty of tips to help you. The second is to travel in an unstructured way, according to where feels right at the time. You won't go to places because they are famous or other people say you should go there, but because it feels right for you. The third is often to leave the beaten track and explore the local culture, travel by local transport and so on. You will not go on organised tours and you will need relatively little money. The fourth is that you are encouraged to prepare for your own mystical experiences, for example in sacred places, which can lead you into states of bliss. The fifth difference is that you will learn techniques to integrate your experiences into your life. For your trip, unlike other trips, isn't disassociated from the rest of your life. Magical travel is your silvery portal into a new world.

By teaching you how to follow your intuition, not only your journey but your life will be transformed. Your intuition will lead you to a high world of freedom that lasts for far longer than your outer journey. In reviewing it, you may discover that some of your experiences actually provided 'tests' for you – lessons you needed to learn to make your life better. They may be simple, like 'you don't need money to be happy', or more profound, such as on the nature of reality. Through these lessons, you will be catapulted away from your familiar, plain grey life towards a life of light and excitement. Your experiences will crack you open and change you forever, even if you don't believe it's possible. That's what happened to me.

My story

> *Much have I travel'd in the realms of gold*
> *John Keats*

I was miserable when I set off alone to India, Nepal, Pakistan and Australia when I was 18. I had the next few years mapped out and was on my way to Cambridge University to study Anthropology after my gap year finished. I was an atheist because God simply wasn't a rational concept and there were so many bad things happening in the world. I certainly wasn't expecting my life to be transformed.

When I arrived in India I had an odd feeling of coming home. I suddenly knew I could go anywhere, do anything. My Lonely Planet guidebook was very useful, but the best guide proved to be my intuition. I was led to amazing places: a turret over the most sacred village in India, where elephants were being bathed at sunset in the lake below. Desert rides on camels and the most perfect powder snow in Kashmir. In Kathmandu, the capital of Nepal, my blood started to sing and zing, a feeling akin to falling in love. What I felt was magic. It was the magic of truly being at home for the first time. At home with myself.

What was going on? I had lost my belief in magic when I was a little girl and stopped writing about fairyland. But unknowingly I had followed four out of the five principles of travelling magically. I started alone, and while I met some great people along the way, I retained my freedom to make decisions, which I did by following my intuition. So I covered the first principle. I travelled in an unstructured way, going from mountain to city to desert according to what felt right, so fulfilling the second. I had left the beaten track and became fascinated by the local cultures, that was the third. To my surprise, I encountered some incredible mystical experiences, even though I didn't believe they were possible, that was the fourth. But I didn't know how to integrate them with my previous life experiences or philosophy. Thus I failed the final test, the fifth principle, integrating that journey into my life. I had to give up university because I became very sick with a tropical disease. Yet somehow an inner voice made me carry on. Even though I had no idea where it came from, and it made no sense to me, I knew it was important.

FOLLOWING INTUITION

> Straight path escapes the winding roads
> I leave home for the truth
> **Akiane**

It wasn't surprising that I had no idea where my intuition came from. For lessons in mainstream schooling did not teach me how to access it, nor did they acknowledge it existed. The downplaying and ignoring of our intuition may be the hardest thing about growing up in the West. Sociologist Emile Durkheim (1858–1917) said that we have lost meaning, a state of disconnection that he termed anomie. Unlike smaller-scale societies, we work hard, play hard, travel a lot, but often don't know the people around us and feel empty inside. We don't know what it's all for. Do you recognise this state?

If you are like most people, others will have decided what you will do with your life. You are born into a family, a society, and your role is merely to live the life you were born for, whether you are a check-out person in a supermarket or a barrister. You have been formed to fit a shape that is probably not appropriate for the essential you; you have been told that your hopes and your dreams are not significant. Most people are simply going through the motions and escaping from the humdrum reality of their lives through drink, drugs, the Internet and other media. Yet in truth there is a reason and a purpose to everything that happens to us. We do need to be free to find it, and travelling magically provides the opportunity. For your free time, even if it is only an afternoon of a weekend trip, will help you realise who you are, the essential you. Your best guide is always – you.

Luckily one mistake I didn't usually make in the hard years that followed my magical trip was to deny my intuition. As I was on the right path to begin with, I didn't need to change it and eventually got back to Cambridge to finish my degree in Anthropology. I learned about other cultures and belief systems, and focused on local and tribal ones. I studied alternative economic systems, shamanism, art around the world and topics such as development, the East–West divide and medical anthropology. Then I travelled around the islands of the Pacific and finally completed a Ph.D. on Hawaiian language and culture, for which my first degree was perfect preparation. My intuition led me better than 'I' ever could have. Most importantly I realised that everything – even my years of illness – has a purpose. I believe in God, although not a fatherly God – God to me is more of a sense of connection. And I got over many fears, including death. I don't believe in miracles, I *know* miracles because I regularly experience them.

I still travel magically. In the USA, I have been led, quite unknowingly, from pow-wow to pow-wow, in a way I could never have planned. Each was in full swing, the cloaked dancers moving in synchrony, their feather headdresses shining in the sunlight. I have bent and picked up a lump of jade, seals barking nearby, next to a glittering sea on the only beach in the world where the rainforest and glaciers fringe the coral reef. I have fallen in love in some amazing places. I have hung out in faraway bars and danced at Polynesian festivals where I was the only Westerner. I love my work, which has developed as a direct result of my finding my truth. So my seemingly going off-track actually led to me being on track. For my intuition always knew, even when I didn't. My life is now rich and full and I reached this ledge of light by following the five silvery principles of magical travel.

WHO IS THIS BOOK FOR – AND NOT FOR?

....

We shall not travel, but we make the road
Helen Friedlander

We are all special. And all it takes to use this book is the ability to dream and the courage to let go and take the first step. You don't even need money, but you do need a bit of time – even if only a weekend. This book is for gap-year students, for career-breakers, and for the elderly. It's for those off on their big OE (overseas experience), it's for empty nesters. It's for weekenders and it's for flashpackers – those used to going to destinations fast. This book is for 'backpackers' (people who travel cheaply, often with backpacks) as well as those used to travelling more expensively and less expansively. It's for a fortnight, a year or a lifetime. It's for all those who want more in their life – more love, more meaning, more people you click with, more memories, more fizz. For ultimately we can make our dreams reality. All of us. No one is ever in our way but ourselves.

Not everyone will choose this book, and that's fine too. It's not a post-colonial diatribe, of the kind beloved by so many academics. There are indeed numerous problems in the world, but the way to change them is by changing yourself; then you will instinctively make the right decisions. But if you would rather focus on the problems – and analyse them on a mental level – then this book is not for you. Nor is it for you if you have an addiction such as drugs or alcohol, in which case seek help. Otherwise your addiction will block your magical experiences. If you are on anti-depressants, try and get off them (in conjunction with medical advice), so that your true feelings can come through. Nor is this book for those running away from situations such as debts or custody cases – deal with them first. And you don't need it if your life is already full of myth, meaning and magic, which is probably only likely if you're a native of a traditional society. This book is also not for those who don't want it, like Will and Lisa.

Will and Lisa

A journey is like marriage
The way to be wrong is think you control it
John Steinbeck

Will and Lisa, married for ten years, look forward to their annual holiday abroad. They have decided where they are going before they leave the country, booked the accommodation and car hire in advance and agreed on their excursions. They stick to the same old circuits and meet the same people. The biggest surprise might be the hotel plumbing not working as well as it should. When they return they show off their memorabilia and slot back into their familiar life as if they'd never left. When their suntans fade, they have their photos and dinner-party conversations to sustain them.

There is so much *more* they could be experiencing, but like tourists who look at an iceberg (nine-tenths of which is under the surface) they will never see the rest. When they have a sense of something (and they do), they don't talk about it, even to each other; they 'act like they're happy' as Lisa calls it, and carry on with their trip. They do exactly the same at home, so the trip is an extension of their life. By working so hard to stay in control they have not exposed themselves to other ways of doing things. Their travel could change their job and their character and bring out their potential. It could expose them to experiences that they would never have at home. It could transform them into people they have never known. But Will and Lisa would rather stay the same and stay safe, and not open the door. That's okay.

But what if you *do* choose to open the door and allow some change into your life?

Opening the door

....

There upon the beach the ugly houses stand:
Come and see my shining palace built upon the sand!
Edna St Vincent Millay

This beautiful quote was on the door of the dorm room of anthropologist Margaret Mead, when she was in college. In later years she went on to help us redefine many of our familiar notions.

By leaving your familiar land and drawing in new experiences like iron filings to a magnet, you are ready to find a new world. By the end of the book you will know what to do – cheaply, easily and spontaneously – to restore meaning to your life. For in the end, what is there to lose but your chains? And you will certainly have a very memorable trip that is far more than a holiday – whether it takes a weekend or a lifetime.

Magical travel opens new doors, not only to other countries and other cultures, but to the most important journey of all, the journey inside yourself. Within you lie the realms of silver and gold. They are the home of your deep knowing and your sense of peace and rightness. They are your core, the true home of your soul. Your journey morphs into alchemy as you are guided on the most important one of all – your life path.

How this book works

....

Teach us the road to travel and we will not depart from it forever
Satank, Kiowa

The book is divided into three sections: 'Before you go', 'When you're there' and 'Coming home again'. Even though some of the advice, such as 'when do you come home?' is only relevant for those on a longer journey, the inner wisdom applies whatever the length of your trip. The book consists of stories, some from my early magical travel experiences, some from others. Where people are published or otherwise well-known, so they are already in the public domain, I use their full name, otherwise I use first names, which have sometimes been changed. Yet the point of the book isn't in the stories, it is in what lies below the stories. For the book works on an intuitive, as well as a mental level.

For example, every chapter is discrete, and the book can be read straight through or by going to the relevant parts according to where you are on your journey. As you open this book you may find you are drawn to one section rather than another. Follow your intuition – this book does not have to be read in chronological order. It can be used as and when you need it. The references, including websites and suggestions for further reading, can be found in the Resources section at the end. I would recommend dipping into it as you please. Over 80 per cent of travel resources now are web-based, so for those of you so far unfamiliar with the web, why not try a course? Your local library or college often offers inexpensive ones, even free for the 'silver surfers' amongst you. Remember that not all websites are independent, indeed most travel websites are sponsored. Be aware of their limitations and always trust your own intuition above all else.

Unusually for a travel book today, I include references to books. The range is wide, from travel and guidebooks, to the odd academic text, to personal stories of awakening. If you wish, you can bring them on your trip according to the particular qualities you would like to gain – such as the ability to relax or to be open to mystical experiences. This is why I have arranged them according to chapter. I don't for a moment expect you to agree with every part of every book, they are selected to stimulate and illuminate. For reasons of variety, I tend to mention only one book by a particular writer.

The astute reader will notice many references to India. Perhaps that's because of the power of place – if every place has its own vibration, then India's is particularly intense, and it magnetises people. If you would rather go to Uganda then great. Take the Indian examples and apply them to your experience in Africa. The principles are universal. India is merely the crucible boiling them into worldly form for so many.

This book is an interactive tool and I would love to hear about your travel experiences. Some of them will be put up on the website accompanying the book (www.rimamorrell.com), where you can find some photographs of my early travel experiences. I have not been paid for any recommendations in this book. But one thing's for sure, things change, so please look at the website for any additional recommendations.

Thank you for choosing to travel magically, it's time to start moving.

PART 1

Before you go

The moment one definitely commits oneself, then Providence moves too. All sorts of things occur to help one that would never otherwise have occurred. A whole stream of events issues from the decision, raising in one's favour all manner of unforeseen incidents and meetings and material assistance, which no man could have dreamed would have come his way. I learned a deep respect for one of Goethe's couplets: Whatever you can do, or dream you can do, begin it. Boldness has genius, power, and magic in it! Begin it now.
William Hutchinson Murray

CHAPTER 1

Travelling with intuition

He has his invitation from all the spheres
In new eastern horizons, in light and more light
Rabindranath Tagore

Travelling always takes you from one place to another. Travelling magically teaches you the silver road to magical travel. The high road that spirals ever upwards. You now have an opportunity to discover worlds of glory, worlds of wonder. For we do not have to go to heaven to find them, they are already here. Magical travel is the road to your heart. Your heart will take you home.

But we are not usually taught how to hear our heart. So let's look at the best way to listen. We will then explore four concepts to help us tread that silver path. They are intuition, the Higher Self, the journey of the soul and vibration. You certainly don't have to agree with them – at this point or ever – but it's useful to be aware of what they are at least. For as you travel magically these concepts may be useful to help you 'make sense' of your new experiences, as the English language is often lacking. Then we'll finish by looking at the power of the sacred, we'll look at when and how to visit sacred places in the middle section of the book. So let's look for our 'new road to travel'. It begins and ends with your heart.

HEARING YOUR HEART

....

> *'Does a man's heart always help him?'* the boy asked the
> alchemist.
> *'Mostly just the hearts of those who are trying to live out their
> destinies.'*
> **Paulo Coelho**

Does your heart hear a call from far away? Do you know what it is? For just as Western culture does not teach us to contact our intuition, so it does not teach us to contact the heart. Western culture values the mind, whereas more traditional cultures value the heart. In travelling magically, we get in touch with our heart. For when we try to live out our destiny, we will be helped.

We must begin by identifying the unchained melody. The call to travel is an old one, a mythic one. Joseph Campbell, mythology professor and writer, said that the hero must venture forth from the world of 'commonsense consciousness into a region of supernatural wonder. There he encounters fabulous forces . . . after a fierce battle, he wins a decisive victory over the powers of darkness. Then he returns from his mysterious adventure with the gift of knowledge of fire, which he bestows on his fellow man.' That 'knowledge of fire' is your sacred knowledge, which may be found by travelling afar. Your journey is, on one level, a mythic quest.

Much of our great literature concerns the theme of the quest. From the voyages of Odysseus to Maui's quest for fire. As you travel magically, you will become a hero. For you are launching yourself on a journey that transmutes lead into gold. You must go through the fire, allow your base metal to be burnt away and reconnect to your golden core. You choose certain veins – beliefs, patterns, friendships – to transmute into old gold, both before you go and while you travel. The gap between the ideal and reality provides much of our motivation. The disparity inspires us, inspires us to reach for our inner fire.

We contact our shimmering opalescence through our heart and our Higher Self. Our intuition is the best guide of all.

INTUITION

....

I closed my eyes and told God that it was up to Him to find me a new road to travel
Immaculée Ilibagiza

Intuition comes from the Latin word *tuitus* meaning 'look after' – which holds a sense of guardianship. Your intuition is your guardian. It is your little voice inside, your angel, your guiding light. Your intuition is your connection to something higher and better than yourself. Our intuition, our eternal accompaniment, is our most valuable resource.

Following your intuition launches you into a very different reality, as Captain Cook found way back in the eighteenth century, where he sailed 'farther than any man had gone before', without the help of any of the technical aids we take for granted today.

Captain Cook goes exploring...

Ike no i ka là o ka 'ike; mana no i ka là o ka mana
(Known in the day of knowing; mana in the day of mana)
Hawaiian proverb

James Cook, Britain's greatest explorer, had always had a strong intuition. Reports said he 'went his own way' even when out bird-nesting as a young boy. In later decades going his own way would result in him literally sailing through unknown waters all the way to Antarctica, and mapping them for the first time. Always his intuition kept them all safe – sailors said it was as if he had a sixth sense when to move the ship on before the iceberg broke up in its path, or the storm hit. He joined in amazing rituals in the islands of the Pacific, where he was honoured and treated as a god. As a result of trusting his intuition, much of the unknown world was named and mapped.

Some people experience intuition as Captain Cook did, as little nudges or promptings, to go in one direction rather than another. Others experience it as a feeling, a knowing that they just can't explain. All of us have those experiences, and the less you deny them, the stronger and more accurate they become. Dr Janez Drnovsek, the former Prime Minister and President of Slovenia, was the first – and still the only – President to speak about the importance of always following your inner voice, as the start on the road to your truth. That's how you will gain internal balance, a wonderful state which is not dependent on the outside world.

Following your intuition is an exercise in learning to trust, for we cannot understand it with our conscious mind (which is often the very one to contradict it, saying 'Oh I can't do that'). Our subconscious mind does not like intuitions, for it enjoys our familiar habits. So we need to push ourselves to leave our comfort zone. Yet every time you do, you become a little more alive. Every time you do, the decision becomes easier. Moving according to your intuition is 'being in the flow'. Your intuition is your road to your magic.

YOUR HIGHER SELF

> *Do you know magic? Can you utter the name of your soul and bring yourself back to light?*
> **The Egyptian Book of the Dead**

Your Higher Self is the home of magic. On the slate paving stone at the entrance to the maze at the house of popular children's writer Roald Dahl, there lies the inscription: 'Watch with glittering eyes the whole world around you because the greatest secrets are always hidden in the most unlikely places. Those who don't believe in magic will never find it.'

Most of us would believe in magic if only we could, but we can't. The key is simple. The key is to join our minds. For joining our minds leads to our Higher Self, or Mind of Light. Our Higher Self, like an overarching rainbow, is distinct from our other selves. The conscious mind looks at what is visible and rational. It takes others' opinions and judgements into account and works on received knowledge, it's like the sun. Our subconscious mind contains our emotions and resembles the moon. When we allow our other minds to illuminate our Higher Self, our sun and our moon unite. The different lights come together, glimmering through the rain, and we bring ourselves back to light.

Our Higher Self is incredibly important. Awakening it is the most important journey we'll ever make. Our Higher Self communicates with us in all sorts of ways. Intuition, dreams, signs. We shall see lots of examples throughout the book. Here's an example of someone who activated his old dream, and ended up with a new life.

Phil's long road west

May the road rise with you, and the wind be ever at your back
Irish blessing

After Phil lost his wife Jayne to cancer, he said 'Nothing made sense any more. Each day bled into the next.' One day in South London, lying down clutching her photo, he knew what she would say: 'There's no point lying there, make the most out of life.' He remembered his dream to walk the 3,000 miles across the USA, from New York to Los Angeles. Five months later he'd arranged an 18-month visa and rented out the house. He was ready.

In New York, Phil put a banner on his backpack which said 'Coast to Coast' and started walking. With every step he felt his cloud of grief begin to lift. He did not feel he had to go directly to the other coast, but went, and stopped, where it felt right. A few months later he reached New Orleans, and wanted to stay for a while to help repair the hurricane damage. He dropped a note on a popular website, asking if anyone wanted to go out to dinner with him (he was sick of saying 'Table for one' when he went into a restaurant). A woman called Pam responded. Phil said 'Without either of us expecting it, something clicked between us. Before I left, we shared a kiss.' Then he carried on with his trip, walking across America for the next six months. Pam joined him for the last 30 miles and together they stepped on to Venice beach, just west of Los Angeles. It would have been his and Jayne's eighteenth wedding anniversary, and he finally felt ready to begin a new life.

Phil's physical journey became the road to his Higher Self. He found his heart again along the way, and at the end of his journey, was able to claim it. The question is always 'how do you create your world to reflect the beauty that you truly are?' The answer is to nourish the spark of light within you, so that you create your desired reality. That is what Phil did, by bringing to life his old dream, to walk across America, at a time when he was full of leaden despair.

We all hold this dream deep within, this sparkle, this essence. We can neglect it so it flickers and dims or guard it so that it grows strong and true. That is why integrity – alignment of thought, word, feeling and action – is so important. It helps your light to grow, so you will merge with your Higher Self. Then you will always know wherever you go that you will be protected. For you are treading your right path and you can no longer turn in the wrong direction. Whether you go to the left or to the right, to this country or that country, you will always know. And in the going is the knowing. It is a fabulous feeling to know that you are consciously creating your country, your world.

And now we need to look at our final two concepts. The first is the journey of our soul and the second is vibration.

THE JOURNEY OF THE SOUL

> To know the universe itself as a road
> As many roads –
> As roads for travelling souls
> **Walt Whitman**

Many great poets and philosophers have said that we are here on earth so that our immortal soul can have new experiences. Our experiences are specific to each of us and every soul gathers them as it travels on its unique journey. Our body is only an envelope and the soul the letter inside. Our soul of light and fire is surrounded by an opalescent egg sparking pale fire. It's who we truly are.

Some say our journey 'into the magic' is only a metaphor for the journey of our 'travelling soul' from incarnation to incarnation. Only part of our soul is incarnate at any one time – the rest may be playing among the pattern of the stars or shared among those closest to us in essence. We travel in groups of souls, known as 'soul groups' and we meet those who share our essence as if by an appointment with destiny. Usually recognition is instant or almost instant and we experience a deep familiarity as well as a feeling of reconnection to our source. We may know them as our 'soulmates'. Sometimes the road to our soulmate can be a joyful experience, as Barbara found, when she followed a more literal dream that led to the luxuriant growth of her Higher Self . . .

When Barbara went to Hawaii

Dreams are illustrations from the book your soul is writing about you
Marsha Norman

Barbara dreamt that her true husband was in Hawaii. She booked a flight to the Big Island, picked up a hire car and drove out from the airport. As she went into the fragrant air she followed her intuitive voice which told her to go 'this way' past the luxuriant vegetation, then 'that way' to take the road to the right and so on. Then Barbara ended up at a bed and breakfast, which felt like the right place for her to stay and happened to have a room free. She really clicked with the owner on many different levels. They had lots of chats, and she ended up marrying him and living a life of sarongs, flip-flops and flowers in her hair, far from her home in England. Result.

Barbara found her destiny quickly and easily by following her dream and her intuition. Is it always like that? Not usually, no, but it can be. For the message of Barbara's Higher Self was in alignment with the journey of her soul. She was 'meant' to meet her soulmate – he just happened to grow up in a different culture. That will be the case for many of you, and perhaps it's the reason you long for a particular country, which we shall explore further in 'Where do you really, really want to go?' Barbara is also a spiritual teacher and so did not block her knowing, for example through her conscious mind saying 'this doesn't make sense' or 'I don't have enough money to go to Hawaii' or her subconscious mind not putting up obstacles such as 'I don't deserve happiness'. She was ready for her gift and her gift was given.

Perhaps our purpose for being on earth is to learn deep lessons.

They include letting go, being happy and the power of compassion. Most of all we are here to learn to love. Many spiritual teachers say that once we have learned our lessons thoroughly, we need never learn them again. The experiences we have gathered and the learning we have chosen to take from them have become part of our soul. So unlike everything else on earth, they travel with us when we die.

Even if we only see the journey of the soul as an interesting construct, discussed by various philosophers such as Pythagoras, it's worth reading about the fourth and last concept, vibration, about which many scientists talk. It helps explain how we attract experiences, magical or otherwise.

VIBRATION

....

> *Black holes used to be called 'frozen stars' in the old days because time literally stands still there, relative to us here*
> **Paul Davies**

We each have a particular 'vibe', the way birds have radar and whales sonar. Our tone is made up of our experiences and expectations.

Notice that some people make you feel better, others worse. You are responding to their vibration. For example, someone who is angry may make you feel angry, without knowing why. Likewise, you may find yourself feeling unhappy around someone who thinks and talks in a depressed fashion. You can 'pick up' someone else's resonance – but you still choose your own. For ultimately *you* are responsible for you.

Never forget your own power to change. Much like the string of a musical instrument is tuned to its particular pitch and creates sound when it is activated, our vibration attracts people to us. Physicists call this phenomenon attraction and so, indeed, do analysts of love and sex! It makes sense that we learn to attract with the highest and best part of ourselves, rather than with our other minds. Then we will have far more fulfilling experiences. So we need to raise our vibration.

A visit to a sacred place will help you raise your vibration. The power of the sacred is known, but not readily understood. The director of the National Trust for Scotland said 'The act of making pilgrimages to certain special or sacred places is probably the most popular of all world tourism motives, and the least understood.' The English Tourist

Board, for example, reported that an astonishing 72 per cent of tourists who come to Britain from abroad said a prime motivation for coming was to visit sacred places. There is more about how to do this in the chapters on visiting the sacred in Part 2. Let's see an example.

When Margaret went to Glastonbury

There at the place whence comes the power to grow, a road begins.
Blue Spotted Horse

After Margaret spent a week at a guesthouse in Glastonbury, England, she plucked up the courage to leave a husband who didn't love or appreciate her. She went for walks on the Tor, to the bookshops and cafes of the town, and slowly remembered what it was like not to be put down by anyone else, that she was enough as she was. She chatted with people in town and in the guesthouse and became more aware of things she had always been a little curious about, but had no time for in her old life. She also discovered healing and began training to be a healer. Today, ten years later, she is single and in a much happier place, where she is doing her soul purpose. Oh yes, and she is loved and acknowledged.

Margaret was blessed in that her week's stay away from home gave her the courage and the tools she needed to create a new and happier life for herself, but she also took advantage of her opportunities. She is really glad she did. Margaret also ended up caring about the planet more – recycling and eating locally produced food – because she had become sensitive to higher energies. So she freely chose not to perpetuate her old patterns, and to tread a new road. Our Higher Self lives along this road . . .

Margaret's experience shows us that we have many roads to go down, but that when we choose the silver road of growth, our opportunities come together like magic. Margaret is part of a grand tradition of women travelling during mid-life. Professor Bolen put it well in her book *Crossing to Avalon: A Woman's Mid-life Pilgrimage*: 'Every sacred place and every sacred person is indeed like a point of light in a great web whose strands grow brighter each time a pilgrim travels from one place or person to another'. How true.

Your vibration and you

I made my way through groves of avocado trees to the distant place of calm
Pico Iyer

When our contact with our Higher Self is magnified, then our vibration is raised. For nothing is constant, even things we might think of as constant are not. Time, as physicist Albert Einstein (1879–1955) showed us, is not. It changes according to what we perceive. In other words, it changes according to our level of awareness. That is why Margaret could not live the life now she was living ten years ago. She has changed and her vibration is faster.

Our rate of vibration accounts for a lot. Rebecca can live in a country for years, and learn little about it, and little about herself, whereas Julian can go there for a few weeks, and learn a huge amount. The difference? Julian is ready to learn, Rebecca is not. Time has little to do with it. So, if you have only two weeks, then should you still go on your dream holiday, even though you may be flashpacking rather than backpacking? In most cases, yes. When you travel this way you'll find many more things happening to you than at home. If you do your right thing you'll gain so many corresponding insights that two weeks away can be the equivalent of years at home. Travelling magically will take you from a denser, slower state (where things happen less quickly and perhaps you are a bit bored) to a life of 'high vibes' and tremendous excitement. Your vibrational energy has speeded up, and experiences on your journey and in your life will be more numerous and of a far deeper significance.

BRINGING THE ROADS TOGETHER

....

> *Heard melodies are sweet, but those unheard*
> *Are sweeter, there, ye soft pipes, play on*
> **John Keats**

When you marry the concepts of intuition, the Higher Self, the journey of the soul and vibration, you go on a tremendously exciting journey which never ends. You do face your challenges more quickly, even if they are not as extreme as Captain Cook's. By following your gleaming path you will reach an ever-higher point on the mountain. From here you will deal with them from a place of greater wisdom. Eagle Walking Turtle called it 'The Beauty Path' – the 'journey our spirit takes through the whole of all living things for the time of the eternity', which is also 'the path to sacred places'. For visiting the sacred helps us to raise our vibration. Raising our vibration is the reason we hear, and we heed, the invitation from all the spheres.

To travel along the high road of silver, we must follow the soft pipes of our intuition. That's how we access our true heart's desire and design. As you read this book you may find your own vibration changing and be drawn to one chapter rather than another. Follow it, for this book is to be used as and when you need it. And at the finish is the end of all our travels. Home is where the heart is, and you will know to leave your headland and then create your heartland, wherever you are. The route to your root is accessing your intuition.

CHAPTER 2

Accessing your intuition

Wake, butterfly –
It's late, we've miles
To go together
Basho

By making the decision to go away on your magical trip you are making it even easier for your intuition to speak to you. As Robert Hopcke said in his book *There are No Accidents: Synchronicities and the Story of Our Lives*, 'if you want a meaningful coincidence to change the story of your life, wander the world randomly and be willing to listen to whatever life presents'. For you are free of your old constraints – except those you bring with you. Let's look at how you can wake up your intuition so you can begin your outer journey, and transform it into an inner one.

If your intuition is still a snoozing caterpillar, how then do you call it forth? Here are three exercises to help. The first exercise involves you simply requesting that your intuition becomes clearer. The second exercise is another simple one, and involves you imagining that your being is becoming filled with colour that is growing ever brighter. That will help you access your intuition on a deeper level. The third exercise involves a simple method to check whether your insight is really your intuition or wishful thinking. Then we'll look at some results of accessing your intuition – a greater safety, a higher alignment and a deeper kind of travelling. So let's move on.

INITIAL CONTACT

Each choice creates a future. It brings into being one of many possible futures.
Gary Zukav

The first exercise involves you going to your favourite place. It may be a wood, a beach or a room you feel comfortable in. But it should be quiet and undisturbed, and you need to be there alone.

Inspiring exercise

1. Stand quietly and breathe deeply and slowly from the centre of your belly. Three times. One, two, three.
2. Ask for your intuition to be clearer.
3. Pause for about one minute.
4. Then ask for a sign that your request has been heard.

The sign may be as simple as the falling of a leaf, the blowing of the wind or a particular symbol that pops into your mind. Remember it, for it will come to you again. Meanwhile you will find yourself becoming more and more conscious of your intuition. Your growing intuition will help you both in your life, whether it's helping you to find a parking space or to know when the next bus is coming, and in your feelings about your future trip. Keep a written or oral record you can refer back to when you doubt yourself. Knowing that your intuition works will help you feel protected. For your intuition works wherever you are. For example, you will feel when it's a good idea for you to avoid this plane or that bus on your trip. Therefore you will feel safe and protected – because you are. You will know how to follow the signs. Why not choose to follow them even further?

DEEPER CONTACT

....

> *Another world is not only possible. It's on its way. On quiet days*
> *I can hear her breathing*
> **Arundhati Roy**

The next exercise helps you contact your intuition on a deeper level, by opening up a symbolic silver channel between the sky and your head. For this exercise it's also good to be alone.

Colour exercise

1. Sit quietly and think of your favourite colour, or any colour that feels right to you.
2. Visualise it hanging in a cloud above your head, whatever shade feels comfortable to you – it gradually becomes more and more vibrant.
3. Now imagine a hole in the bottom of the cloud and the light pouring through.
4. The light enters your head through your crown.
5. Slowly at first, and then more quickly, you become aware of all sorts of things you need to know, either now or later.

The Colour exercise takes about three minutes at first but less with practice. You will also be able to access your creative springs, so your work or your play will become infinitely quicker, easier and better. You will lead an expanded life.

IS IT REALLY YOUR INTUITION?

....

> *The world outside is a large place. The world within is even*
> *larger.*
> **Joseph Dispenza**

Accessing your intuition correctly involves getting yourself, your own likes and dislikes out of the way. When you don't do this properly, you get confused. For example, Cindy thought it was her intuition to go on holiday to the Bahamas. It wasn't, it was just that she wanted it to be true, so she persuaded herself. Let's do another quick exercise to see how you can tell. Have a question in mind before you start.

Hand exercise

1. Relax by breathing in and out and focusing your mind on darkness.
2. Allow your colour to come into your mind again through the top of your head.
3. Allow it to settle and become conscious of the colour all around you.
4. Ask your question.
5. Lift up the hand you don't write with (usually your left hand, but if not, replace the word 'left' with 'right' in the following steps).
6. Bring the fingers of your right hand closer until you are circling your left wrist with the thumb and third finger of your right hand, which should be just able to touch each other.
7. Hold your question in your mind and push against your left wrist with your circled fingers.
8. If your left hand moves down easily the answer yes is correct.
9. If it encounters resistance and feels heavy, the answer is not correct.

This is a great exercise to do for questions such as 'does he fancy me?', or 'is it safe to go in that direction?' It's surprising how many questions there are with a 'yes' or 'no' answer. Your intuition will be honed. The more you follow it, the more you will know it is worth following.

The great news about accessing your intuition is that the more you do it, the easier it gets. You become lighter and your vibration speeds up. Therefore do these exercises as much as possible, both before you start your trip and while you are on it. If you are new to these kind of exercises, treat them as a job and do them regularly when you wake up and before you go to sleep (even if you can't always be alone, such as on your trip, with practice you'll be able to manage). They should be done as many times as you like, in fact the more the better. For the more you do them, the faster your intuition will grow and communication with your Higher Self will no longer be in snippets. In fact, you can even try a technique now known as 'cosmic ordering', whereby you specify what you want – or something better now, to give your Higher Self the option of producing something even better – and a time frame for it to appear. There are some ideas in the Resources section.

RESULTS OF FOLLOWING YOUR INTUITION

What the caterpillar calls the end of the world, the master
calls a butterfly
Buddhist saying

Your butterfly spirit will flutter awake. Things that previously seemed impossible you will suddenly just know. You will *know* whether a book is good for you to read or not, and your reading will become very quick. You will know whether a person is good for you or not, and even if you need to go on holiday at a particular time or travel to a certain country. When you do go, you will find that your intuition not only leads you to the right places and people in the culture, your experiences will be far more intense. You will communicate on a deeper, more satisfying level and will not be just another friend, traveller or lover. You will also be far more connected to the world where you go, which will suddenly come alive with meaning. Like a butterfly you will always know where to fly. Your trip will be transformed.

As you travel the silver road you will be fitting into an accepted context. *Vagabonding* by Rolf Potts refers to the American word for wandering without a goal. Vagabonding is in synch with the first three principles of travelling magically – follow your intuition, be spontaneous and go local. It's a great book to pick up before you go, to help you gain confidence and ideas on how to cope with the different situations you'll come across. Many of the suggestions are worth copying into your travel diary. Rolf defined vagabonding as 'a pilgrimage without a specific destination or goal – not a quest for answers so much as a celebration of the questions, an embrace of the ambiguous and openness to anything that comes your way'. That openness is the place you get to by following your intuition – which is guaranteed to get you all sorts of interesting results.

The fourth and fifth principles of travelling magically go beyond even this. For they encourage you to have sacred experiences, and help you integrate the changes and fit them into your life back home, or wherever you choose to make it. The rewards of following your intuition are tangible. You can find answers to your questions, the answers that are right for you, the answers from your Higher Self. The ending of your old world will lead to a new and brighter one.

Let's now look at when to go.

CHAPTER 3

When do you go?

*Travellers it is late. Life's sun is going to set. During these
half days that you have strength, be quick and spare no
effort in your wings*
Rumi

When you actually take off depends on two factors: a good time for the
place you intend to visit and, most importantly, a good time for you. For
you don't need to follow the crowd. I'm also going to be throwing a
slight spanner in the works by suggesting that you might also want
to visit a place at the 'wrong' time of year, illustrated by an experience of Kashmir in the winter. It is often easier to find magic when
you remove yourself from others' experiences and expectations. Good
times for you may include answers to such questions as 'When are you
able to take leave from your job?' or 'When do you really want to get
away?' Follow what you feel.

GOOD TIME FOR THE PLACE

*Though we travel the world over to find the beautiful, we must
carry it with us or we find it not.*
Ralph Waldo Emerson

There are a number of resources from which to find out what's going
on in a particular country such as the Internet, books including guidebooks, travel bookshops and tourist offices of a country. Travel shows
also give you an idea of popular times to go to different countries. Be

aware that not all of them offer independent advice. I've found the best way to navigate my way through the plethora of resources is to use my intuition. I make my decision within the parameters of the available information, being prepared to change it, for example, when more information becomes available.

Every place has its particular associations, whether it's Paris in the springtime, Scandinavia in the summer, New England in the fall or Hawaii in the winter. There may be some activity you want to take part in, such as trekking among the blooming rhododendrons and the icy peaks of the Himalayas in March, or a festival you want to hit, such as one held on the slopes of a volcano just off Iceland in early August.

Festivals

Each person who follows his or her own light is a light on the web
Jean Shinoda Bolen

Here's a starting guide to festivals covering all year and most of the globe. I've chosen ones where the festival is part of an ongoing tradition and travellers are welcome to join in the revelry with the local community. Please look at the advice for how to act at festivals in Part 2, Chapter 9, 'Travelling ethically'. It's usual to camp and bring your own tent at the rural festivals. Festivals held in a city usually require that you book accommodation in advance (unless you stay up all night partying of course) and dress is generally a bit smarter or sexier. At almost all of them, plenty of delicious food is usually available for sale, and each have their own guidelines. See whether you get a 'zing' from looking at any of them. If you do, why not follow it?

Date	Name and Place	Description
13 Jan.	Alternative New Year, Foula, Shetlands, off Scotland	One of Britain's most remote inhabited islands, Foula is the only place in Europe to keep to the old Julian calendar, celebrating Yule (Christmas) on 6 January and Newerday (New Year's Day) on 13 January. Nordic traditions of language and myth on this island full of birds.

Date	Name and Place	Description
3rd week in Jan.	Film Festival Tromso, Norway	Coinciding with the yearly return of the sun over the horizon, quality films are shown in this magical city, just inside the Arctic Circle. Several are screened outdoors in snowy squares where the Northern Lights may illuminate the dark polar nights.
Last Tuesday Jan.	Up Helly Aa Shetland Islands, off Scotland	Europe's biggest fire festival in which a replica of a Viking longship is burned after locals, dressed as Vikings and virtually all descendants of them, parade through the streets. Then the Viking squads go to designated areas such as community halls and hotels in Lerwick where skits are performed, the audience joins in and partying carries on until morning in true Norse tradition.
First two weeks Feb.	Winter Carnival Quebec, Canada	Biggest winter festival in the world in this French-speaking Canadian city. Skating along the frozen river, winter fairs, night parades, sleigh rides, carnivals, spectacular illuminations. See www.carnaval.qc.ca
Late Feb./ early March	Carnival Rio De Janeiro, Brazil	The most famous carnival or 'carnaval' of all features a Samba parade, balls, beach parties and skits. Lasts for four days of amazing celebrations in the height of summer, starting on Saturday and ending with 'Mardi Gras' or 'Fat Tuesday'. Carnival Sunday falls 49 days before Easter. The city of Salvador, 800 km (500 miles) to the north-east, provides a less commercial alternative. See www.ipanema.com/carnival
First Sat. in March	Mardi Gras Sydney, Australia	Huge festival, the highlight of which is the Saturday in March, where the parade and party in the streets are attended by about half a million people. The partying starts three weeks before. Still largely gay, but everyone can join in the sultry nights of the southern summer, although the party at 10 pm is for lesbians, gays and bisexuals, and you need to be very broad minded. Focused in Sydney suburbs of Kings Cross and Paddo (Paddington). 'Recovery parties' carry on for days.

Date	Name and Place	Description
March/ April	Cherry blossom festival Japan	This month-long festival features *hanami* parties under cherry trees celebrating the light and frothy beauty of spring. Family groups, companies and sets of friends gather to drink, sing and be uncharacteristically exuberant. You can usually join in; look for the city parks, among which temples are scattered or the slopes of the mountains where the white mountain cherry trees have been planted to flower in procession. Best times are daily after 6 pm or 7 pm and all weekend.
March	Spanish festival Miami, USA	Over a million revellers converge on this 23-block-street festival in Little Havana for the day with entertainment, local cigars, Afro-Cuban jazz and tamales.
Easter	Rustlers Free State, South Africa	Held from Good Friday to Easter Monday on a spacious farm at the feet of the sand-stone Maluti mountains, this festival features music, sweat lodges, West African drummers, eco-warriors, healers and both live and dance music with havens such as the New Age Green-field with crystals and shamanic ceremonies, and the Futures field, Rustlers' bastion of alternative energy. See www.Rustlers.co.za
Third weekend May	Rocket festival Andalusia, Spain	Three-day celebration of life and alternative culture from Friday–Sunday in sun-drenched southern Spain. High-wire acts, acrobats, Cirque du Soleil, dance tent, tribal funk. See Rocketfestival.com
Mid June– mid July	Heiva i Tahiti Tahiti, Borabora	Month-long celebration, the biggest in Poly-nesia, featuring the sexiest dancing on the planet! Enjoy traditional dancing by groups of men and women, outrigger canoe racing over the Pacific, fire-eating and thrumming drumming in hot days and nights mellowed by sea breezes on these idyllic islands. See Thetahititraveler.com/general/arteheiva for programme.

Date	Name and Place	Description
End of June	Gnaoua music festival Essaouira, Morocco	Five-day celebration of North African devotional and world music in this Atlantic city of golden beaches. The Gnaoua, descendants of slaves from Africa, are divided into groups such as master musicians, metal castanet players, clairvoyants and mediums. They perform healing ceremonies as well as featuring devotional music. See www.festival-gnaoua.co.ma
4 July	World Rainbow Gathering Somewhere rural!	All those who believe in peace and love gather to celebrate for the week of 4 July in this huge, hippie festival. Everyone is encouraged to participate and not be a 'drainbow'. There are many smaller camps around the world. See www.welcomehere.org for place and details of the 'big one'.
First weekend Aug.	Westmann Islands Westmann Islands, off Iceland	From Friday to Sunday this mostly Icelandic celebration is held on a small, young volcanic island off Iceland. An active volcano smoking away, hot pools, immense bonfires, lava fields, perpetual northern daylight, DJs and fancy dress for a unique, northern experience.
Labor day	Burning Man Project Nevada, USA	Annual arts festival of radical self-expression and self-reliance caters for slightly older, more eclectic crowd. Covering the week before Labor Day and culminating that weekend, the first one in September, America's craziest meet in the desert features a temporary city in the Black Rock desert of Nevada. Optional nudity, bring your own water.
Early October	Navajo Fair Shiprock, New Mexico, USA	Week-long celebration of Navajo culture in the most important Navajo fair. Traditionally held after the first frost, the fair features the conclusion of the nine-day Night Way, the ancient Navajo healing ceremony, as well as pow-wows and pageants and so on.

Date	Name and Place	Description
Sep./Oct.	Eid al Fitr, End of Ramadan, Muslim countries and communities	Day-long celebration to mark the end of the month-long fast of Ramadan. Day dependent on sighting of crescent moon in local area by an authoritative source, so varies in different places. A time of forgiveness and family reconciliation, celebrations and feasting occur.
New moon Oct./ Nov.	Diwali India, Nepal and communities	Lamps are lit to celebrate the victory of brightness over darkness in this five-day 'Festival of Lights' marked by Hindus, Jains and Sikhs. In India people take to the streets in new clothes, with decorated bodies and animals. Schools are closed and jugglers, acrobats, astrologers and snake charmers join in the celebration. Sweets and other gifts are given. Ganesh the elephant god and Lakshmi the goddess of prosperity are worshipped. Now a popular festival outside India too.
5 Nov	Bonfire Night Lewes, England	Shops and schools close early on this special night, where the most famous 'bonfire night' celebrations in England take place. They commemorate the failed attempt of Guy Fawkes to blow up the Houses of Parliament in 1605. The real fun begins when it gets dark. Street processions and firework displays light up this normally quiet seaside town on the Sussex Downs from 6.30 pm. Revellers throng the medieval cobbled streets, followed by bonfires where effigies of Guy Fawkes and others are burnt. You need tickets for the most famous. Contact Lewes tourist office.
Christmas	Junkaroo The Bahamas	For those who want an alternative Christmas, the Bahamas' most important party floods the streets of Nassau in whirling, singing and dancing floats and groups. Floats go past without any Santa Claus as the Junkaroo the emancipation of the slaves in the Caribbean. Stilt dancers, clowns, goatskin drummers and cowbell players all celebrate. Best days are Boxing Day and New Year's Day.

Date	Name and Place	Description
31 Dec.	Hogmanay Stonehaven, Scotland	Heralded by a pipe band, a procession of local men and women swing fireballs around their bodies with dazzling dexterity after dark. They then drop the burning objects, about two feet in diameter, into the ocean. The fireballs take in the dross of the old year, and speed in the new, in this midnight festival with pagan roots.

Generally be aware when festivals are happening in a place you want to go to, even if you don't like them. Then you might want to avoid the area altogether, for it will be more crowded, expensive and many of the usual amenities are likely to be closed. So be smart, be aware and then make your decisions.

BAD TIME FOR THE PLACE

There is no season such delight can bring, as summer, autumn, winter and the spring
Anonymous proverb

Don't necessarily visit a country at the most popular time. There are lots of advantages to visiting a place at the 'wrong' time of year. You can get to know the local culture much more intimately, it's cheaper and you will stand out as not being just another tourist. In fact, many people who go to a place at the 'wrong' time much prefer it to the 'right' time. England gets more sun in September than August for example, and is much less crowded as it's not full of holidaying families.

Some examples can be more extreme. For example, Gretel Ehrlich spent time in Greenland because she really liked the ice and the opportunities for contemplation it offered. She wrote, 'for seven years I used the island as a looking glass: part window, part mirror'. Likewise, I found that going to the Arctic in winter was much more satisfying than in the lighter months, because there was a quality of magic in the slant of the light that was lacking when the sun was higher in the sky.

Indeed many travellers report that it's easier to find magic when you are away from the usual expectations – and going out of season, so you are not a typical tourist, is a great way to begin.

I find magic in Kashmir

While the stars that oversprinkle
All the heavens seem to twinkle
With a crystalline delight
Edgar Allan Poe

I visited Kashmir in the midst of winter. The 'Super Deluxe Video Bus' took three days, as both the bus and the heating broke down. The cold was terrifying, yet I felt a strange sense of peace creep up on me as the road from Delhi to Srinagar also went up and up. On one side was a sheer escarpment, on the other a precipice. Birds were wheeling in the blue air and range after range of the Himalayas, the mountain tops wreathed with soft cloud, came into view. On occasion you could see the shells of buses which had gone off the road far below. But I knew I was in my right place and felt safe.

After the bus finally arrived in Srinagar and I had spent the night on a chair in the local police station, being the only place that was open in the early hours of the morning, I organised a houseboat on Dal Lake. I was 18 and wasn't scared, but exhilarated. Srinagar was having its coldest winter for many years, with a 40 degree difference between night and day. Fair Kashmiri women dressed in their long, dull, blanket coats looked like they were pregnant, with their *kangri*, a small woven basket filled with glowing coals, bulging out from under them. The men, dressed the same way, looked like they were pregnant too. They travelled around in small wooden boats as the rim of mountains shone around the lake. The crystalline world of winter is an invisible, almost unimaginable world to the summer visitor who does not need to make holes to travel across the lake.

I travelled for three hours up the mountain to Gulmarg, where I wanted to go skiing. On occasion Kashmiri men would pass in the chair lift smoking hookahs, but generally they skied very little. Some days I would be the only person skiing in the whole resort. Sometimes, when I tumbled over, I would just lie in the snow of perfect powder and watch the highest mountains in the world cascade into the blue distance, and feel completely happy, for the first time. The nights were also wonderful. I would walk up the hill from my wooden chalet among the pine trees to where the stars glowed and the snow froze. The stars were brilliant crystalline atoms, just like the snow squeaking under my boots. The snow fields lay open and shining under the copper moon and I was exultant.

I needed a change. That's why I intuitively went to Kashmir out of season. The conditions there – bright blue skies and the brilliant white powder snow – helped me to be happy, even though 'I' didn't decide that's what I wanted and what I needed. So just because no one you know has been somewhere out of season, why should that stop you, if it feels right? You must always follow the clarion call of your heart.

WHAT ABOUT YOUR JOB, YOUR FAMILY, YOUR MONEY?

Security does not exist in nature
Helen Keller

Most of us do things to make us feel secure, but they can also be used as a reason not to do things. The tipping point is a delicate one. When you approach your boss and ask for some holiday, for example, you may be told 'your job or your trip'. In that case I wouldn't automatically beat a safe retreat into 'Sorry, I was just thinking about it' but seriously question the validity of keeping that job in the first place. Would you be happy, when you are 70, to look back and know your life has been dedicated to that job? If the answer is 'yes', great, go for it, carry on in that job. If the answer is 'no' then you need to re-evaluate your options, and decide just how much your need for security functions as a 'can't' in your life and is stopping you from reaching your greater good.

For example, your family situation should not necessarily stop you and there is advice on how to decide in Part 1, Chapter 14, 'What do you do about the kids?'. Nor should not having money. There are tips in Chapter 12, 'What about money?'. Evaluate your situation rationally. If, for example, it's better to wait until your twins are 18 and have finished their exams, which will be the case in two years, then wait. Travelling magically isn't about being stupid or selfish. But it does allow you to question what you've got – and this includes before you take off. And the questioning then acts as a springboard for your intuition. Now it's time to look at you.

More importantly, what about you?

> *If a man does not keep place with his companions, perhaps it is because he hears a different drummer. Let him step to the music which he hears.*
> **Henry David Thoreau**

Your intuition is the most important factor of all. You *know* when it's the best time for you to travel. When you are ready to take a leap away from the familiar you will know it. You will be feeling restless and dissatisfied; the things you used to enjoy such as drinking with your old friends seem wrong to you now – maybe you never really did enjoy them anyway. You are hearing a different drum. You are ready to question your old beliefs, attitudes and preconceptions and are ready to move away from your old friends and relationships. Your soul has its own timing, but it does not mean that you will never see your loved ones again, although you will do so from a new space and decide whether you want to renew your friendships or move on. Step to the music of time – your time.

For, as you change, so will the world around you. And if you feel you need to go to a country suddenly then follow that urge – like Barbara did in going to Hawaii. Maybe the universe is waiting for you to make a shift. Your greatest good doesn't wait for the 'should' factors to be in place, rather it arrives and then everything shifts to another, higher plane. Think of the way someone who wins the lottery doesn't need to worry about a boss at work any more. Because this person doesn't need the job, they have created a new reality. Allow yourself to do the same.

We've looked at many factors to take into account when you

decide when to go. They include both going to a country at the right time and the wrong time, and maybe timing your trip to include a festival you want to go to. The most important factor though is you. What's holding you back? What do you dream of? What could you gain by following your dreams? Allow the question of 'when' to draw you into your greater rhythm, one that resonates with the world around you.

And now we'll look at the question of how long you go for.

CHAPTER 4

Fortnight off, year off or life off?

Why go out on a limb?
That's where the fruit is
W.M. Rogers

So now you've decided to go, how long do you go for? You may have definite constraints that will serve to bring you back to your country. You can only take a week off from your job and you're not ready to give it up yet. You may have sub-let your place for a certain amount of time. You may have an airline ticket that is only valid for a year or a working visa valid for two years. You may be due to start a university course in nine months' time. Or, you may not have to fit your trip into a certain time frame, although of course we all have to fit our life into a certain time frame – no exceptions there. So why not fill your life with your dreams? To access them, you need to go out on a limb. The fruit is at the end of a tree's branch, not on its trunk.

In this chapter we shall look at several examples. The first is of people who have very little time to spare. It's still worth going and you can make the most of your trip with one simple tip. Then we come to people who want to take a year off, and at the importance of questioning your assumptions sooner rather than later. Then we come to some popular categories of people who take time off, such as student gappers, career breakers and travelling seniors. For it's never too late to travel, never. Then lastly we explore the concept that having 'time off' is really having 'time on' for it helps you decide what you really want to do with your life and then you can seamlessly integrate work with what you love. Let's start with those who don't have much time to spare.

VERY LITTLE TIME OFF

He pai rangi tangi
(The beauty of a single day)
Maori proverb

In the cash-rich, time-poor society of the West, people are often keen to head out to the rest of the world, even if they have very little time. Is it worth it? And as long as you are going for the right reasons, then 'yes it is'. You don't need time or money in order to get an answer to the important questions. You can always make the most of your annual leave as Maria and Bob did. They were only able to get three days off at the same time, so they travelled from the USA to Mexico for a long weekend. Americans, on average, have very few days of annual leave compared to other countries, so they need to treasure it. Value the unique beauty of a single day. Maria and Bob had a nice trip, but not a magical one, for they didn't follow the one simple tip we shall see below.

TIME OFF WHEN YOU'RE HAVING TIME OFF

Don't be afraid your life will end; be afraid it will never begin
Grace Hansen

However short your trip, don't completely control it. Be sure to leave some time free when you're away. Take time when you're in a new place, even if it's only for one evening in a weekend off, to ask a question of yourself. Take notice of what you see, or the signs that come to you. There's more about the process of following signs in Part 2, Chapter 4, 'Travelling spontaneously'.

Without this time you may see extra places, but will you really know how to see them? For we can all learn to see in a new way. We all need valuable time for reflection in a life otherwise mapped out and controlled. It may be time for you to think about such questions as 'Am I really on the right path?' If you don't ask important questions now then you will regret it. There might not be time to think about it in university or when you're in the first flush of starting a new job, or when you're married and raising a young family, but at some time these questions will come up. When they do, they could cause what is known as a mid-life crisis and could manifest themselves with you running off with your secretary. So why not save time, emotion, expense and trouble and do your questioning sooner rather than later? This one simple tip can transform your trip – and even more. Let's see some examples of how it works.

SOME EXAMPLES

Every dream is given to us with the power to make it come true
Richard Bach

Every dream indeed is given to us with the power to make it come true, but how about if you don't know what your dream is? For example, have you always fitted in with your family and done what they wanted, rather than what you wanted to?

Brian has a week off
The power of a single wish can change your life
Caroline Myss

Brian, a young student of 21, was wrestling with the question of whether he should be a lawyer like his mother. But he had only a week off his studies, and not very much money, so he decided to go camping near his home in Tennessee. He pitched his tent where it felt right and did whatever he felt like, when he felt like it, without coming into contact with another soul. The time for reflection that his free retreat afforded him made him decide not to go to law school, but to become an environmentalist.

Brian didn't need much time to work out what he really wanted. And nor did Rachel, who was a bit older, in her thirties when she decided to have a road trip around her home state in Australia with her friend

Jules, which she wrote about in her book *Are We There Yet?* On it, with lots of conversation and laughter, she became much clearer about her true dream.

Rach and Jules have a fortnight off
The best way to make your dreams come true is to wake up!
Muhammad Ali

A road trip around the blue valleys of New South Wales, sometimes staying in nice hotels, sometimes camping by a river, was enough time for Rach to decide she wanted to stay single. She decided that the pressures she felt to change her state came from other people rather than from her inner self. For example her parents were disappointed that she was 'a poet with aging eggs and not even the hint of a boyfriend'. But she had had enough of loathsome single parties, was 'happiest alone with her books' and loved her friends and her life in Sydney and one day would like to be known as a great poet.

Both Brian and Rachel didn't have much time, a week and a fortnight respectively, but it was enough to make a life-altering decision, one about a career, another about a relationship. Just because your time is a valuable commodity does not mean that you cannot find the answers to your innermost questions. Just give yourself a bit of time and space, and remember enlightenment takes only an instant. You only need to know what your dream is to give it the power to come true. Who knows, you might enjoy it so much that you may decide you want even more time off.

THE YEAR OFF

Twenty years from now you will be more disappointed by the things you didn't do than by the ones you did do. So throw off the bowlines. Sail away from the safe harbour. Catch the trade winds in your sails
Mark Twain

Many people are worried about having time off, thinking that they'll never get back to real life. But what is real life? Is it only defined by the society they are a part of? What more is there? Without taking time off you may never know. If you follow the suggestions contained in this book, you can have some of the best experiences of your life and be able to continue them wherever you decide to go and whatever you decide to do. This is the case whether you're a gapper (a young person taking a year off before or after studying) or a career-breaker (an older person who takes time off). Make sure you don't have regrets in 20 years' time.

QUESTIONING OUR ASSUMPTIONS

The difference between a flower and a weed is a judgement
William Blake

The automatic assumption that time off is not a good thing is well worth questioning. I was once hitch-hiking around a volcano in Hawaii, when I was asked 'Why are you hitching, why don't you have a car?' I replied that I was used to driving on the other side of the road and besides I enjoyed meeting people hitching. Then I was asked why I didn't have a job, to which I said 'I'm a student.' Then I was asked next how old I was and why didn't I have a family? My interrogator was a four-year-old American boy – social conditioning starts young.

People are too scared to question (and are too scared for you to question) because they don't want to lose control. A successful Western lifestyle is all about control. You control your time through parcelling it out, your money by spending it carefully, your body by going to the gym, your family by encouraging them to keep busy with school, sports, cooking and other worthwhile activities.

Travelling magically is not about control. Through it, you will either decide that you want to carry on along your existing path, or you will find a new one that is right for you – either way you will benefit. Your family may not, indeed almost certainly will not, see things that way. They're not going to be thinking about the meaning of your life, that's your job, just as it's your job to find your inner light. Your family may even think a mid-life crisis is the inevitable result of age. It's not, it's the result of an unquestioned life.

Now it's time to look at three categories that are known for taking longer periods of time off. They are student gappers, career breakers and older people (seniors).

Student gappers

If we don't go right now we'll be haunted by our unrealised dreams and know that we have sinned against ourselves gravely
Tim Cahill

Admissions tutors recognise your need to find out what you really want to do. The chief executive of the Universities and Colleges Admission Service in Britain said 'UCAS is often told by staff in higher education that they value the added maturity and experience that a year out can bring to the prospective student.' One tutor said 'think about what you want to do and why'. Your year off can bring motivation and the knowledge that you're doing the right course in the right place, and it gives you extra time to get in. That's how I got into Cambridge – by taking a year off and reapplying. It was well worth it.

When I was at Cambridge University, at least 50 per cent of the English students had had a year off. The ones who had, tended to be highly motivated; they'd seen a bit of the world first, had had time to do the things they really wanted to do and knew they wanted to be where they were. They were far more able to be themselves, and so had a far happier and more productive university experience. The ones who hadn't had a year off, by contrast, tended to be far wispier creatures, often working less hard because they were partying harder, they'd already worked hard to get into Cambridge – right? Paradoxically enough, they also appeared to be enjoying themselves less as they were so worried about what other people thought of them. They might be the ones who, by making so much effort to put their life on, end up having their life off. In other words, some students might look back at the end of their life and wish they had pushed the boundaries a bit more. Not everyone of course – some were quite happy with the way things were – but some students may have felt this.

It is now a tradition in English society that young people take a year off, for example after they've finished school and before they go to university, or just after they finish university. In Australia or New Zealand, by contrast, the year off (or two or three) tends to be in the middle of, or at the end of, a degree course. This is when people have their OE (or overseas experience), which is a valued part of the culture that provides jobs, friendships and a talking point for the rest of people's lives when they end up returning to the Antipodes. In the USA, however, having a year off is not yet acceptable in mainstream society. The people who do it are 'slackers' or 'generation X-ers' (the sixties generation who often refuse to fit into the status quo) and people say they are simply running away from having a proper job, raising a family, spending money and getting down to the serious business of what being an American is all about. Here too though, things are changing.

Many organisations exist to facilitate the process of taking a year off, whether you're a gap-year student, a generation X-er or an older career-breaker. Prince William volunteered in southern Chile with Raleigh International. You could count turtles in Central America or teach in Africa. Going with them is far better than doing nothing, but why not be far less organised and travel freely and magically, or at least spend some of your trip in free travel? You will be more open to wonderful energies and incredible places and people.

Career-breakers

The mass of men live lives of quiet desperation
Henry David Thoreau

Today in Britain, more and more people are planning to take a sabbatical from work and escape the rat race, according to a study by Direct Line insurance in 2007. Almost one in five employees plan to take a career break and one in four says their employer offers sabbaticals as a perk. It's the same story in Australia, where an upsurge in long-term international departures began in the 1990s. Since 62 per cent of Australians are now entitled to long-service leave following several years' employment within an organisation, a career break is a reality for many. Government departments encourage retention of staff by guaranteeing employees on sabbatical a job on their return. This certainly gives career-breakers a chance to do some magical travel and then see whether they want their old job back, or even leave the country altogether, as over 41 per cent of Australians now do. In the USA, a third of employers offer sabbatical programmes, which provide great opportunities for their employees to try something new and different – maybe in a country where they have never been. Of course, older people may have particular concerns but these are addressed in the appropriate parts of this book.

Generally though, having a career break is becoming more and more viable – both in terms of working regulations and society's consciousness. It is certainly likely to ensure that you are not one of the ones leading a life of 'quiet desperation'.

It's never too late

It is positively insulting how well the world functions without one
Nigel Barley

Some people use their age as a reason not to travel. This is a great shame, for whatever our limitations – and we all have them – they can always be overcome. Let's look at a few: feeling it's too late, worry about what will happen when we're gone and concern that we won't meet interesting people.

If you feel it's too late for you, don't beat yourself up. Society puts so many pressures on us: 'finish school, go to university or get a trade, get married, have children' – by the time we are empty nesters we are often OAPs. However, as they say, 'fifty is the new forty', 'sixty the new fifty', 'seventy the new sixty'. In other words, society is also encouraging us to 'act younger' even as those pressures are over. Don't be overcome by your limitations before you even try. This book features several stories of older people: American Rita Golden German started travelling at the age of 48, Canadian lady Jill Frayne first went out into the wilderness over the age of 50 and Anne Mustoe only started cycling the world when she retired.

The hitch-hiking grandmother
If I take the wings of the morning
Psalm 139:1–9

Grace Small, the highly respectable 'hitch-hiking grandmother', started hitch-hiking in her 'Third Age' to see her grandchildren. She would wear a good suit and a hat, and clutch her handbag and map. She loved it and she started to travel for the sake of travel. She went all over America, up to Alaska and through Europe – all on her own. Many newspaper articles were written about her. Grace carried on travelling this way until she was in her eighties, when enforced bed rest enabled her to look at her 83 albums every day. Then Grace serenely moved into her 'fourth life' to live with her daughter in Texas. 'However this trip to Austin is not my last trip, I have one more trip to take and it won't be by plane, and I won't have to indicate I need a ride by using this old curved thumb.'

Grace's example shows that it is never too late to grow your spirit serenely by travelling magically. Indeed a category called 'Grey Nomads' that refers to the older traveller has even been created – although Grace certainly does not fit smoothly into this one. But when we travel magically we do jump out of the categories – for we do what's right for us, according to our Higher Self, not what society tells us to do. Such actions are very freeing.

Let's get to the second point – worry about what will happen when we're gone stops many. But people's lives do just carry on without you there – none of us are indispensable. As anthropologist Nigel Barley wrote when he got back from a couple of years in Cameroon, the world does function very well without you. In fact anthropologists are authorities on this matter, as our work involves us being involved in another, local culture for years at a time, and then returning home to 'write it up', and make sense of it. Besides with technology today, keeping in touch can be very easy if you want it to be.

Sometimes we worry that if we take off alone, especially as an older person, we won't meet interesting people. Nothing could be further from the truth. For anyone travelling alone is usually alone for ooooooh, only the first 15 minutes or so. People enjoy talking to a person on their own, whatever their age, and in many cultures of the world you will get more respect. Societies such as Egypt and China and most of the developing world revere the old, unlike the West. There is more to be gained from chatting to an old person than cooing over a baby for example. So your wisdom, garnered from years of experience, may be exactly what someone needs to hear. You will find yourself having just as sociable a time as you want. Some people find aspects of their former careers to help people, such as a former accountant helping a business in Africa set up a business plan. If you ever feel lonely where you are, then take off – there are people out there waiting to meet you.

Thus we've seen three 'excuses' for not going demolished, and in the end, just like for any younger person, the challenges you face will certainly help you to grow. Isn't that what you want for your life now, before you die?

Let's move on to look at some more general concerns, which may also be your concerns.

LIFE OFF/LIFE ON

Und im See bespiegelt
Sich die reifende Frucht
(And in the water mirrored
The fruit is ripening)
Johann Wolfgang von Goethe

Why not allow yourself to be free? Many of the most successful people in the world don't need to plan, nor do they follow the plans that others make for them. You can learn not to care so much what other people think of you. For example, Richard Branson used to find his way home in Sussex at four years old, when his mother would make him get out of the car. He said it was a huge impetus for his future career in starting new businesses and making his millions, for he learned to trust himself and his judgement. Following your intuition gives you the ability to make quick decisions.

It might not be the right thing for you to be a businessman like Sir Richard. It might not be the right thing for you to meditate alone in a cave in the Himalayas for 12 years as Dianne from East London did

– she remains in India today, doing her spiritual work. It might not be the right thing for you to run away to an island in the South Pacific like Paul Gauguin – but my point is that it's possible. It's possible for you to do all of those things. Arguably though, what's best for the earth is that you should learn to integrate your 'work' and 'leisure' time so one flows seamlessly into the other and you are always in the flow.

Today, new technology makes it possible for many of us to live and work wherever we choose. That's great for the next in line, Generation Y, the techno-nomads, who are defined as wishing to find meaningful work, and being ready to change employers and countries in order to do so. They are not fitting their trip into a specific time frame, but allowing what happens to alter their life path. They are even finding creative, fulfilling work for only a few hours a week, just the way hunter–gatherers used to. The 40+ hour work week tends to be a product of developed societies, but by following your own rhythm you will be far more in tune with yourself and what you really want to do. For the fruit that is 'out on a limb' will ripen in your inner waters of freedom and fulfilment.

BOUNDING OUT OF THE CATEGORIES

Follow your bliss and doors will open where there were no doors before
Joseph Campbell

So we have seen many ways in which you can take time off. You can do it for a very short amount of time, such as an afternoon within a weekend trip. You can take more time off, such as a week, a fortnight or even a year. It doesn't matter how old you are, you can be a young student, a middle-aged career-breaker, a 'grey nomad' or any combination of the above. What is important is that you give yourself the freedom to ask the questions that are important to you – then you will get the answers. And finally, remember that even though many people allow categories to define them, you do not need to. For example, taking time off may mean that you are really having 'time on'. You will be ready to enjoy your life, for you know how to be spontaneous, follow your intuition and have great experiences.

It's time now to explore where to go.

CHAPTER 5

Assessing your risks

At the Gates of the Sun, Baghdad
James Elroy Flecker

Now we come to four chapters to help you decide where to go. They are divided into risk assessment, finding a culture that suits you, the role of ethics and finally the importance of following your intuition. As I've said previously, worldly factors need to be a springboard for your intuition. By first assesing yourself and your experience, and next taking factors like culture and language into account, before considering ethics, then you are building a firm platform for the final and most important question, going where you love. For you will not be going where you love blindly.

So let's begin our assessment. In order to establish the potential risks and problems you may face on your travels, and what to do about them, we need to look at a few factors. Take into account where 'you are coming from'. These include variables such as your gender, sexuality, your physical abilities, your level of travelling experience and your country's relationships with your chosen destination.

Gender

....

> *If adventures do not befall a young lady in her own village, she
> must seek them abroad*
> **Jane Austen**

In most countries it is acceptable for a man to travel on his own.
The same isn't true for women, so this section will focus on them. It's
usually safe for a woman to be on her own in Asia or Polynesia for
example, but in certain countries women are expected to either be
at home, or to travel with their husband or immediate family. So it is
essential that you are aware of the wider culture of the country you
wish to go to. For when you are smart then you are safe.

Kimbra's trip

> *My favourite thing is to go where I have never been*
> **Diane Arbus**

Kimbra from Australia really enjoyed her time in South Asia, which
she took off to alone when she was 18. Delhi worked for her, Kathmandu worked for her and Varanasi worked for her. She enjoyed her
first experience of a cold climate in winter and adored the cafes and
temples and the Himalayas. She soon got used to the overland travel
– it was cheap. She was easily able to deal with hassles from men and
she met lots of lovely travellers, and left many wonderful memories
behind her.

Kimbra was smart. She didn't go to a country such as Saudi Arabia
where she may have found it harder to be a young woman on her own,
and she was open and receptive to other people and cultures – no
wonder she had a great time.

However, you do need to bear in mind your level of attractiveness
according to that culture. If you are considered very attractive, for
example being a blonde in India, then you are going to be approached
more than if you go to Iceland, where blondes are common. Do you
want to be considered very attractive? Often it's much easier not to

43

be! Your physical type is also important. In some countries such as Africa large women are considered desirable, in others such as most of Europe, slender women. Some countries such as India prefer fair skin, other countries such as Hawaii darker skin. Be aware that as a woman, the older you are the better you will be treated – senior citizens will get respect in a lot of the world; for example, in a Muslim country you are likely to be treated well and not seen as a sexual target. So bear that in mind when choosing your destination.

SEXUALITY

Man is disturbed not by things, but by his opinions of things
Epicurus

If you are heterosexual then your sexuality usually isn't a problem. Almost every country and culture is accepting of heterosexuals (certain tribes of New Guinea are an exception). If you prefer making love to your own gender, then gay-friendly places like Barcelona, Brighton, New Guinea or Tahiti will make your life easier. In some more conservative countries, it may not be safe to speak out about your sexuality, let alone ask for a room with a double bed if you are two men or two women travelling together. In a couple of countries such as Dubai and the Maldives homosexuality is even illegal. Of course this advice isn't prescriptive, and it's important to follow your own intuition, while not offending local sensibilities.

YOUR PHYSICAL ABILITIES

Asiye na mengi, ana machache
(*Even he who has not many troubles has a few*)

Your physical abilities are another relevant issue. If you are differently abled, there are now an enormous amount of access groups and guides to help you; for example, most cities have special guides. Assess your needs. Most are basic: where do you sleep, eat, visit, how do you get around and (crucially) where do you go to the toilet? Bear in mind whether you are travelling with a companion or not. If you are not, you will need to be very resourceful.

Accommodation

> The seat of the soul is where the inner world and the outer world
> meet
> **Novalis**

As far as accommodation goes, then you need to be organised. For example, if you are restricted to a wheelchair, then you need wheelchair-friendly accommodation. Book in advance and always call to check at the time of booking, and just before you go, as you do not want a mistake to be made. If you are sometimes in a wheelchair but can walk, then you can afford to be a bit more flexible. You may still want a ground-floor room, but if it isn't available then it isn't a disaster. So then book in advance, but your checking can be less rigorous. For certain conditions, such as most viral syndromes, you do not necessarily need to plan ahead. You can adapt where you go according to your intuition and how your health is on the day. Autism may be more of a challenge, as many autistic people like to have everything planned – and travelling magically is the opposite of this. For conditions such as autism I would recommend choosing a suitable place, such as a quiet animal sanctuary, and staying there.

Getting around

> First winter rain –
> I plod on,
> Traveller my name
> **Basho**

Getting around is another important issue. Public transport isn't always viable for use by the disabled, although sometimes it is – most destinations have special guides which will tell you. Trains and most big boats are usually suitable modes of transport. Nicola Naylor went to India alone and studied aromatherapy and travelled by local transport, despite her blindness and wrote a book about her experience *Jasmine and Arnica*. Depending on the severity of your disability you may need to hire a car or alternatively, a local car with a driver, such as a taxi, and negotiate special daily rates or longer. Most aeroplanes do have disabled facilities although they are only as good as the people who operate them. I spent some time travelling when I was sick, and

I remember on one memorable trip, someone spoke over me and turned the 'wheelchairs' to face the wall in the airport at Heathrow. There was no thought that we were even people in wheelchairs. Book in advance and confirm the availability of the services.

Eating out

Familiarity blunts astonishment
Aldous Huxley

Eating out is harder than for an able-bodied person. Sometimes you may not be able to physically enter certain restaurants, or they may not be suitable for you (for example, if you are epileptic, a restaurant with flashing lights could trigger a fit). You may not like the type of food, or may feel uncomfortable in certain restaurants (a lot depends on the attitude of the manager, waiters and waitresses). Generally, it's a good idea to be prepared to prepare your own food, even it is only a matter of bringing a kettle to boil hot water to your hotel room for times when you are not up to going out.

Visiting

Blessed are they who see beautiful things in humble places where other people see nothing
Camille Pissarro

Finding places to visit can be more of a challenge. If you are differently abled and sometimes need a wheelchair, a trek on rocky mountain trails in the Andes may not be suitable for you, however an adapted narrowboat on a canal, where you don't need to walk very much but can still see new scenery or access a waterside pub, might be very suitable. If you get breathless from anaemia, avoid mountain heights and ocean depths where less oxygen is available. If, however, you suffer from a disease such as multiple sclerosis and are wheelchair bound, diving might be the very thing for you; there are some anecdotal accounts about paralysed people walking again, and certain doctors support it as therapy. Visitor attractions such as museums and art galleries in the developed world have facilities for the disabled, as they are needed for funding. Outside of the developed world, you may need to ask a local association for your disease (if there is one) or hire a local guide. Most importantly you need someone who is a nice caring person – this is usually not difficult to find as these qualities are valued in most societies.

With some conditions, the most insuperable problem can be the toilet. For example the 'hole in the ground' found in many parts of the world may be unusable by you if you cannot squat down – therefore you may need to restrict yourself to more expensive places with Western toilets if you go to these areas. Bear this in mind when visiting local attractions – in the worst case scenario you may not be able to eat or drink if you know you cannot use the facilities to relieve yourself. In some cases, it may be possible to use the waiting room of the local hospital – bathrooms there are usually adapted for the disabled and you may even find some new information about your condition.

Freeing your mind and spirit
Travel has a way of stretching the mind
Ralph Croshaw

If advance planning is required for your disability, you must work to make more effort to be free in your mind and spirit – but that is very possible to do. You have already overcome a lot, and have the courage to travel. Acknowledge yourself. Now allow in the unexpected. Take time off within your trip. Chat to people you meet. Find several places you can go, then throw a dice to decide which one. Allow yourself to be open to help – most people do want to help you, allowing them to is heart-warming. Also don't judge yourself. All of us are differently abled in one way or another – your condition may be obvious, someone else's may be hidden inside their mind, but they will still have some things they are better at than others, and others they are worse at, just like you.

By travelling magically you can also help others. James Holman travelled widely around the world in the nineteenth century and did not let his blindness stop him. Many have been inspired by his travels. There can be advantages to anything – even disability, if you go for things with a positive attitude. Chris Moon lost a leg and an arm and the next year was running marathons. You don't have to do this, but by doing something in a joyful way you will certainly help change people's thinking. By doing things even through your visibly different ability you will be a huge inspiration for others and that will give you a great deal of lasting satisfaction. For if you stretch your mind far enough you will free it.

So we've seen a number of factors that need to be taken into account. They are the basics: accommodation, eating, getting around, visiting and going to the bathroom. We've seen that you can still travel magically even if advance planning is required, and some examples of people who have inspired others. So your different abilities need not stop you taking off – and having a wonderful time while you are there. And now it's time to look at an arena where your mental abilities count for a lot – your level of travelling experience and know-how.

LEVEL OF TRAVELLING EXPERIENCE

All I ask: the heaven above
And the road below me
Robert Louis Stevenson

If you are a traveller who is not used to cities, don't go to one with a dangerous reputation like Johannesburg or Nairobi. Get streetwise in your own country first, where at least you know the customs and the language. Generally speaking, start off in easier countries, and build up to countries with a worse reputation when you have more experience and nous to fall back on.

In challenging countries mental factors are very important, and all of us have the chance to develop these. You will more likely need more resourcefulness travelling alone in Tibet than you will travelling alone in France, but if it feels right to you then do it. But you do need to be aware of where you're 'at' as well as where you want to be. If you are not street smart, then start off with an easier more 'developed' country and build up to places and people more off the beaten track in that country, then go to the harder countries. If, however, you have heaps of common sense and tend to do various extraordinary things without problems in your home country, then heading for a much more different experience – such as trekking into the rainforest and finding a native group to spend some time with – might give you just the challenge you need.

Your country's relationship with your destination

> *And where are they? And where art thou,*
> *My country?*
> **Percy Bysshe Shelley**

We all come from a country. If your country is at war with another country, it is not a smart idea to go to that country, or to the allies of that country. Your nationality could be dangerous for you, and it's wise to contact your own country's embassy and heed any warnings they may give. If you have two passports then take the one which is least controversial for that country – and make sure you say you're from the appropriate country. Not being stupid is the baseline for enjoying your trip.

Deciding

> *When you come to a fork in the road, take it*
> **Yogi Berra**

We've seen several factors that need to be looked at in your risk assessment. They include your gender, sexuality, physical abilities, level of travelling experience and your country's relationship with the destination. None of them are discrete and all are interwoven. For example, I had a difficult time travelling alone in Pakistan as I was very young, thin and blonde. Whenever I went outside, I was immediately surrounded by so many men they blocked the view, and they even tried, very hard, to get into my hotel room. My gender affected my experience in the country. I would love to go back, and if I were a man I'm sure I would have returned several times by now, as I found it a very unusual and beautiful land, filled with the most generous people I have ever met. But now I would only return with a man, therefore negating my risk factor. So bear in mind where you are coming from when choosing your destination.

Of course, remember too that external factors are important but they are only part of the picture. Your Higher Self needs to be the ultimate arbiter, and the need to discriminate between your Higher

Self and your other minds is important. Be sensible, yet also have sense – a sense of what you really want. If a place feels right to you, then move heaven and earth to go there. We have a chapter on deciding according to your Higher Self three chapters on, but now we need to put the picture you are building up of yourself together with an external one, the local culture within a country. So let's move on.

CHAPTER 6

Finding a culture to suit you

Asiyefunzwa na mamaye, hufunzwa na ulimwengu
(He who was not taught by his mother was taught by the world)
African proverb

Cultural factors are another thing that need to be taken into account. Culture is a complex phenomenon and there are many definitions of it, not one of which is agreed upon, even among anthropologists, whose job it is to study them. The one I prefer is about generally agreed patterns of behaviour. Even here, there is always differentiation, including within that society. Nothing is simple, for within almost any culture we have sub-cultures (located in urban areas) and local cultures (located in rural areas).

In choosing where to go you need to take practical factors into account, which we saw in the last chapter, such as how you fit into a culture. You should also go by ethical choices which we explore in the next chapter, as well as more intuitive factors, which we shall cover two chapters on. This chapter looks at culture and language, and how to make an informed choice about where to go through, for example, the books, music and language you like. It explains the importance of 'going local' in harmony with the third principle of travelling magically. For learning about other cultures will help you and the world.

In general we all have cultures we feel more or less drawn to. How do we identify them?

Culture

....

> *This country cannot afford to be materially rich and spiritually poor*
> **John F. Kennedy**

The place you go will be the piece of the world you learn from. The lessons are universal, part of the human condition, and do not depend on where you are in the world. However, the place you learn them in is the medium for your message. Some places will be more congenial to you than others.

But how do you choose a place? Often we travel to places or to a culture we like. There are so many sources of inspiration. There are some great travel magazines such as *Wanderlust,* which has many ideas and a useful website, and *National Geographic,* with delightful pictures and articles that have inspired many. Some cities, such as London, are lucky enough to have bookshops devoted to travel, as well as several travel shows a year. It's also worth going to the tourist office for each country and seeing what you want to do and don't want to do. Get ideas about tours but don't book them. Sometimes you find your inspiration within a film or the music of a culture strikes a chord within your being.

Different people love different cultures. I might love Polynesia, you might love Spain, your friend might love Germany and your daughter America. It is important to understand there is no right or wrong. For we all find a culture that fits us, and that might change at different times in our life. For example, the writer Elizabeth Gilbert was very drawn to the joy and good food of Italy following her difficult divorce. Certain cultures resound within us like a drumbeat.

Sometimes the culture we like is influenced by our nationality. For example, the British often travel to India; Americans to Central America; Australians to Britain, Ireland, Greece and Italy. Certain countries are so popular they have become part of our national psyche. It may be harder to meet locals and to be judged on your own merits by them when you do, as they are used to your compatriots, and you keep on bumping into people you know from home. So you can do things differently too. Todd, a North American guy, loves to spend time in Asia, and he really likes to listen to Tibetan music – in fact that was how he first decided to spend time there. Rob from Australia hangs out in Africa. Moana from New Zealand likes to travel only around her country. All of this makes sense. Both Asia and Africa are cheap for Todd and Rob, and they like the cultures. Moana really loves her country, New Zealand, and travelling around it means she spends time with her relatives and learns about her Maori culture – that's important to her.

There are so many wonderful books about travel now, they deserve a section to themselves. We'll divide them into two, guidebooks and books that concern a particular culture.

BOOKS

A book is a marvellous companion . . . It is inanimate, yet it talks . . . It will join you when you are alone, accompany you in exile, provide light for you in the dark . . .
Moses Ibn Ezra

Books have been inspiring intending travellers for the last several hundred years. For example, Pacific-art historian Bernard Smith wrote that the descriptions and paintings of Polynesia, which became so popular in late eighteenth-century Europe, had even more effect on Europe than Europe did on the islands. If you consider the effect of Europe on the islands was immeasurably huge, affecting most aspects of life, then that is quite some statement. Today, travel literature has become a much bigger industry. Let's look at one aspect of it, guidebooks; then we'll move on to look at books from an 'outsider perspective', and books written from an insider view.

Choosing a guidebook

I move around my page like I move around the world
Nicholas Bouvier

To help you decide where to go, I would recommend getting hold of a guidebook of the country you are interested in, especially if you are an inexperienced traveller. It will be very useful to you. If you live in Britain you can buy one cheaply through Green Metropolis, and donate money to a woodland charity at the same time, then sell it on through the same source, or give it away to a new traveller when you have finished your trip. Of course you can also borrow one from the library, but it might not be suitable for you to take a copy on your trip, depending on the length of your journey. There are many ranges of guidebooks, each one offering slightly different countries and perspectives. Some series are more suitable for your needs than others, and I give some recommendations in Resources, especially ones designed for budget travellers that often have a wider range of ideas for things to do, even if you're not on a budget. Remember though, the guidebook isn't your true guide – leave it behind once in a while and strike off on your own. But it's certainly useful to have it in the beginning.

Novels and non-fiction

A new world is only a new mind!
William Carlos Williams

Books about a culture can be divided into two categories. One is those books written by people from outside a culture, the other is those books written by people from within a culture. Often people ignore the last category, but that is a great shame, for they provide another perspective, which shows even though people might be 'different', they still care about the same things.

Choosing books written by 'outsiders'

The earth is a book and those who do not travel read only one page
St Augustine

Travel literature fits into the category of books written by people outside a culture. Classics include T.E. Lawrence, Paul Theroux and Jonathan Raban, and there are many exciting new writers discussed here.

Several companies specialise in publishing books about a culture written by travellers. These inspirational guides, may be based on themes such as women in Asia, or spiritual experiences of travel as in the *Travelers' Tales Guides.* Eye Books choose the authors for their travel section according to their ability to embrace life-changing experiences, congruent to travelling magically. The Summersdale travel section also represents adventurous authors.

Don't forget anthropological accounts. For not only have people been trained to understand a culture and compare it to others, they usually spend quite some time there. Often the quality of the writing is extremely high, classic accounts include Gregory Bateson on New Guinea and Clifford Geertz on Bali. Margaret Mead's account of sexuality in Samoa provided the first written account of sexual life there, and her comparisons with teenagers in the West helped to illuminate cultural understanding.

Other categories include fiction and historical accounts. For example, Robert van Gulik's detective stories provide a fascinating window into the court of Imperial China, and Isabella Bird's travels around Hawaii in the nineteenth century give a picture of a society less touched by change than today.

Of course there are disadvantages to reading books written by 'outsiders'. For we could be filling ourselves up too much with other people's representations and not seeing the other cultures as they truly are. Generally though it tends to be quite difficult to see other cultures as they are, not as we would like them to be, for we all grow up with blinkers and preconceptions and a little informed choice is generally a good thing, especially if the writer admits their own personal bias. Personally, for example, I am suspicious of writers who visit a culture for only a few days and then make dismissive generalisations. To a great extent, we find what we bring with us.

Choosing books written by 'insiders'

One can never read all the books in the world, never travel all its roads
Anonymous

Reading books written by people within a culture avoids many of these problems. The novels of Milan Kundera give a new view on a particular slice of Eastern Europe and their concerns which are just like ours, the magical realism of Gabriel Garcia Marquez illuminates Latino culture and Chinua Achebe Nigeria. For it's important not to forget local and sub-cultures too, and they deserve to be represented and read. Writers such as Keri Hulme and Witi Ihimeara provide a valuable perspective on the Maori experience in New Zealand for example. John Kennedy Toole's work will transform your visit to New Orleans by bringing the spirit of place alive. The more diverse your readings the more perspectives you are likely to be able to take on. This will mean that you are both more interested and interesting on your trips.

So we've looked at how valuable books can be. Of course they are not all of the same value, and you will find that some speak to you more loudly than others. Also reading a lot about a culture, unless a book has a very high vibration, can make you too 'heady'. It's important to realise that sometimes we need to just trust our own intuition. And of course if you do not like reading, then do something else instead. Why not go and meet people and learn from them directly? We need to take language into account.

LANGUAGE

The world we live in is in the words we use
Wittgenstein

If you adore a language, why not go to the culture? Whether it's the mellifluous vowels of Italian or Hawaiian, or the complex words of German or the poetry of Arabic, take note. For language is the bridge to a culture. By making the effort to speak the local language you will immediately stand out from being a tourist, you will get things more cheaply and you will find a culture opening up to you. The least you should know before visiting a culture are the greetings, and the numbers 1–50 and then multiples of ten up to 100 and the word for 1,000. English, French, German and Spanish tend to be the most useful European languages for communication in most of the world. This is for no good reason, except that historically those countries were the biggest colonisers.

Few people learn languages the traditional way any more, going to classes and receiving lists of vocabulary and grammar disassociated from active context, although of course you can if you want. More and more 'right brain' courses are springing up, which include games and contemporary items such as news broadcasts. New technology means they are more accessible than ever. Go for these if you can. You will learn more quickly and have much more fun.

The reward of learning a language will be a greater understanding. For a language provides a door into how other people really think. In

Russian for example, a request is couched in terms of the negative: 'nyelzya li . . .?', 'is it impossible . . .?' It shows an expectation perhaps for the request to be refused, which does not happen in some other languages. In Hawaiian, in contrast, a word out loud is traditionally believed to bring the quality contained in the word into being. Is the difference due to a happier and more fertile climate? Or is it a deeper cultural difference? Whatever you decide, language is the key to opening the door, as well as being a thing of beauty for its own sake and something that will 'switch on' previously dormant lights in your mind.

There might be an indigenous language or culture you feel really drawn to. For example, Keith really wanted to learn about the Mayans. He didn't know why, he just did. So he went to Guatemala, and learned Mayan in a language school there. These indigenous languages are usually easiest to learn within a country, when you know the area you wish to stay in, as there are usually particular dialectical forms. You do not need to sign up to a language school as Keith did, but can learn the traditional way – through helping people with their occupations, or maybe offering exchanges for your native language. If you visit a country unexpectedly, then you will generally find it possible to learn the native language while you are there. Learning another language expands our world view, and this is particularly the case with languages with very different structures from the ones we grew up with. So even if it seems a bit odd that you're drawn to a certain language and culture that doesn't really fit into the people around it, follow your knowing, for it is your knowing – and who knows what value will arise?

And now we'll look at the importance of the third principle, going local, in choosing where to go.

GO LOCAL

Non sum uni angulo natus; patria mea totus hic est mundus (I am not born for one corner; the whole world is my native land)
Seneca

I would certainly recommend choosing to visit a country where there are still active local cultures – which luckily is most countries. That usually means going outside the cities. If you stick to towns, you are more likely to find sub-cultures, whether they are the Creole of New Orleans or the Garifuna of Punto Gorda in Belize. That's all good. The most important thing is that you put yourself among people who think in a different way from you.

By learning to think in a different way you will help yourself. For example, you may learn practical knowledge such as the use of herbs to treat certain diseases, or the value of preparing and eating fresh food. You will also help yourself in other ways. It is far easier for you to have magical experiences in societies where they are commonplace. It may mean hanging out with shamans or helping your hosts learn what they need to know. It is amazing how you find your right host, like iron filings attracted to a magnet, when you let go of control. We may find ourselves inhaling new ideas of time, love and money from indigenous concepts, which will then feed into every area of our lives. As many tribes are disappearing very fast, we need to learn before it's too late.

Your learning will help restore the world. For the economic and cultural systems of the West have impacted brutally upon the systems of most other countries. Money has been introduced almost everywhere, the Trobriand Islands of New Guinea no longer trade primarily in shells and the Aztecs of Mexico in flowers. In fact the famous Aztec economy has disappeared and only traces of the culture remain. The same sad story is repeated in much of the rest of the world where the tentacles of the West have spread, monotyping and destroying. It's now time to respect and support the indigenous cultures, for we in the West need to be taught by the world. You can support the remaining indigenous cultures through your presence and money by travelling into the hinterlands – and no, you do not need a tour group to do so, in fact it's better to go without one. In most places, you will be perfectly safe going on your own, as long as a few common-sense rules are followed, which I shall discuss in Part 2, Chapter 6, 'Meeting people'. So, as long as you have a basic level of common sense and the ability to say 'no', which I talk more about in the chapter after that, do consider travelling to local communities. For 'going local' will help you leave the majority mindset behind.

THE POWER OF LANGUAGE AND CULTURE

....

And spirituality requires even more effort than culture. No one else can pray your way to it other than you
Rabbi Lionel Blue

How true this maxim is. Yet finding out about a new culture is a great first step. A maxim of anthropology is that you need to spend at least 18 months in a place to understand it. In fact this is not the case when you travel magically, for your learnings will be faster as your vibration is raised. Just like the power of asking questions we saw in the previous chapter, spending time in a smaller-scale society will help you work out what's truly important to you. By leaving your own culture and spending time in a new one, you will question your beliefs and maybe even change them. For the way you think and feel and believe *is* important. So, by shedding society's layers, you will become more 'you'. You will attract magical experiences, which will make you question your assumptions even further. So you may even, to your surprise or desire, find that spirituality becomes an important part of your life.

Where to go – well, in the end, it must be an individual decision. Here's where ethical factors come into play.

CHAPTER 7

Planning an ethical path

There's a time when silence becomes betrayal. That time is now
Martin Luther King

It's important to plan an ethical path. For ethical concerns are a keystone of this book. Indeed, we have another chapter just on them in Part 2, Chapter 9, 'Travelling ethically', and they occur as a keynote for many of the chapters.

First though we have to look at what ethical travel entails. Ethical travel is often known as responsible travel or green travel, and involves taking various things into account. Various organisations have been set up to monitor concerns, and recommend places to go and stay, some of which are mentioned in the Resources. Typical concerns include green transport, the type of hotel accommodation, waste treatment and avoiding countries with a record of human rights brutality. However, I was surprised to find almost every organisation recommends going on tours. Most tours (exceptions may be those that provide access to places you could not otherwise get to due to your level of experience) are not in harmony with travelling magically, which is actually travelling far more ethically.

For by arranging things yourself your money will be going directly to the people who need it most, the local population, and you will interact in a more genuine way and have the freedom to do what's right for you. And by finding places to stay on your own initiative, you are likely to end up in greener places than if you go on a tour. A treehouse in a forest with no bathroom may not meet quality control standards, but may still be a place where you would feel happy and free. Or it may not – but by sorting things out yourself you have the opportunity to decide.

There are two main factors to take into account in deciding where to go ethically. One is what you believe in and the other what you don't want. Let's see how they work.

WHAT DO YOU BELIEVE IN?

To say . . . to the big advertisers and mind-controllers: you will not think and feel on my behalf, you will not define my life on my behalf, you will not dominate the globe with your version of morality
Anita Roddick

If a country has values you believe in, why not go there?

If you really believe in the importance of psycho-analysis and love huge expanses of nature and eating lots of meat doesn't bother you, then go to Argentina. If you're a Christian and want to find out more about the esoteric traditions, and are ready for some new challenges, try Ethiopia. If you're a strong Mormon, then go to Utah, the home of your faith. If you have always been interested in Native American beliefs, go to an area where the natives are common, make some friends, and you'll maybe end up staying with them on a reservation and being shown their sacred places – if they like you. If you want to turn vegetarian or vegan, then try countries such as India or Bhutan, where killing anything is strictly prohibited in whole cities, even valleys.

If you're not sure what you want, then go where you are led. For example a visit to the Holy City of Jerusalem will take you to the sacred shrines of three major religions, Christianity, Judaism and Islam, and seeing them close together may help you realise how much they have in common. Even if you are still a wee bit confused, somewhere within you will be less confused, I promise you.

WHAT DON'T YOU WANT?

To do nothing is in everyone's power
Samuel Johnson

It's also important to look at what you don't want. Each of us has our own values where we draw the line and territory beyond which we would not venture. See 'Assessing your risks' two chapters back for how to look at specific factors such as your gender and level of travelling experience; this chapter encourages you to clarify your moral line.

For example, Kylie, an Australian, has never been to the USA. She does not like the values there, such as the emphasis on individual freedom at the expense of caring for the community – for example the right to carry a gun – and would rather travel to countries like Scandinavia where she prefers the social system.

Some organisations advocate avoiding countries with a strong record of human rights abuse. See if this fits with your beliefs. Charles has always been fascinated by Buddhist culture but would never visit Tibet while it is under Chinese occupation. So instead he goes to Ladakh in the High Himalayas where the Buddhist culture is still practised freely. He has taken ethical factors into consideration in coming to a decision that works for him and the local Ladakhi community.

Many people take the way a country treats its animals into account. If you love cats, avoid Cambodia where they are eaten. If you love dogs, you will probably find Korea difficult for the same reason. If you're fond of pigs, you may find the islands of Melanesia, where they are revered, an illuminating place to visit.

Don't do nothing. Act by going to a country with values you believe in. Choose your country wisely and you will become all the wiser.

CHOOSING WHAT TO BELIEVE

Lying is done with words and also with silence
Adrienne Rich

So we've seen two ways in which you can look at a country and see where it 'fits' in terms of your personal values – both in terms of what you want to find, and also don't want to find. Each factor has the weight you give it. Ethical travel always involves the process of choice. Remember you are the one doing the selecting, for you are the only one who knows what you believe in. By making your choice you will not be lying to yourself, the most important person of all.

Meanwhile remember your decision involves checking where a country is 'at' and comparing it to where you're 'at', to see if there's a fit. Where there is a fit, for example, on a certain issue that's important to you, you will benefit by choosing that country to visit. For as Martin Luther King said, now is not the time to stay silent, and we have to vote with our feet as well as our mouth.

The final point is to hear your true voice, the one deep within. That's from the silvery spring of your intuition. How then do we best choose where to go?

CHAPTER 8

Where do you really, really want to go?

Grace illuminates your path by moving through your intuition
Caroline Myss

In this chapter, the final one on deciding where to go, we shall look at the importance of your intuition in deciding where to go. For we've already seen the sensible things, we've looked at risk assessment, language and culture and ethical factors. On this basis, you've probably got a shortlist of places. Now it's time for you. Where would you really, really like to go? Don't discount the other factors. Yet your intuition should make your decision. Remember the first principle of travelling magically is to follow it.

First we shall look at the importance of going where you love. Then we look at what happens when you seek new lands – and how following your intuition can lead to a quality you need. Next we see what happens when we *don't* follow our intuition through three examples. Then in the final section of the chapter, we see how we can help grace illuminate our path.

GO WHERE YOU LOVE

Kennst du das Land wo die Zitronen blühn?
(Do you know the land where the lemon trees bloom?)
Johann Wolfgang von Goethe

Going where you love is the road to wonder and delight. For just as we are all unique, so we don't long for the same island, or the same man or woman.

If you are a mountain person, go to the mountains to hear the song of the earth. If you are a sea person, visit the ocean in your quest for the mermaid air. If you long for the skyscrapers of Chicago or New York City, ride your dream and aim high. If you have the feeling to go somewhere else, whether it's a park bench, a grove of lemon trees, a supermarket or the cave on your right, go there. Just as you prefer some areas of your city or country to others, so you will be irresistibly attracted to certain places on your journey and repelled by others. If the dry horizons of the desert call you, hop along there; don't go to the place of waterfalls instead. Sounds basic, but other travel books don't actually tell you to go to the land you like. For there's something there for you.

You will respond like magic to your right place, which may be for a moment or a lifetime or more, and every part of your life will improve. For the ultimate factor that decides where you go must be where you love.

SEEKING NEW LANDS

When I went to Venice – my dream became my address
Marcel Proust

Have you ever tried to relocate a sleeping cat? All creatures know where they want to be, except perhaps humans. We all have a place we've always longed for, somewhere that represents the pinnacle of our hope and dreams. If only we could get to that country, we say to ourselves like the sisters in Chekhov's play *Tri Sestrii* (The Three Sisters), things will get better. We may know our land through posters, films or books or we simply like the name – the country which inhabits our dreams.

Whatever the reason, we simply want to go there and that desire does not leave us.

Trust the call is there for a reason. For example, a quality you need may be found in a quality of the land you long for. Here are a couple of examples:

Jenny finds purity

Colour is the nature of eternal powers that permeate reality
Victor Turner

An established author, Jenny Diski was comfortable with boundaries, her home on Cambridge being 'an island on an island'. She loved the colour white and her bedroom was a shrine to whiteness. Then one day she experienced an uncontrollable urge:

> *That thought was there. Antarctica. And along with it a desire*
> *as commanding as any sexual compulsion that Antarctica was*
> *what I wanted and that therefore I had to have it . . . The Arctic*
> *would have been easier, but I had no desire to head north.*
> *I wanted white and ice for as far as the eye could see, and I*
> *wanted it in the one place in the world that was uninhabited . . .*
> *That was Antarctica, and only Antarctica.*

Jenny followed the call and in that place without boundaries she contacted her sense of freedom. It had always been inside her, but the surrounding skins needed to be unwrapped in the land her intuition told her to go to. She experienced the pale silver light, the clouds and the icebergs, divided yet united. On one of them a sentinel penguin was standing, looking heroic as he floated by the window of her ship. The freedom she felt in the sublime and unmarked landscape helped her put her past, in which she had been abused by her mother, in perspective.

The power of slowness

West of these, out to seas colder than the Hebrides, I must go
Where the fleet of stars is anchored and the young star-captains
glow
James Elroy Flecker

Some years ago I spent some time in Hawaii. I had to be there, the call was very strong and from my Higher Self and I wrote about my experiences in my first two books. A few years ago, I was drawn to spend the summer in north-west Scotland. After my time on the magical isle of Raasay, where I swam in the dolphin-dotted pewter sea and visited windy beaches scattered with crystals, the peace seeped into my bones. The shining seascape infused a space within me that I didn't even know existed.

I ended up buying a cottage on the nearby Isle of Skye in the Hebrides, with magical sea views. In summer, the sea gleams for hours at sunset, silver and pink, spread out under the midnight sun. Basking sharks glide and eagles soar through the streams of quiet air. In winter, as the mist rolls in from the sea and I build the fire, knowing there is nowhere I need to go, I am glad. I learned to slow down. Yet all I knew was a longing for islands in a silver sea.

Bonnie doesn't go to Alice

Those who lose dreaming are lost
Aborigine proverb

A vivid childhood dream about Alice Springs, a town in the 'red centre' of Australia, drew Bonnie to Australia. When she was offered a cheap deal to Melbourne, thousands of miles away, she went there, because she thought 'well, it's still Australia'. She had a nice trip, but that was it. Melbourne didn't feel right for her. Her magic didn't happen.

Bonnie still hasn't made it to Alice, which is as different from Melbourne as man is from woman. What was there for her? Perhaps a reconnection to ancient knowledge a visit to Ayers Rock would have given her, perhaps a significant encounter that might have changed her life. She still doesn't know. Bonnie still hasn't been to Alice.

Don't go expecting a country to offer you a similar experience wherever you travel in it – it won't. If you've always dreamt of a particular place, there's a reason. Somewhere else, even somewhere in the same country, simply won't pull you along your path to your magic. So if you do have a longing for a special place you need to take notice of it. When you inhabit the silver plain, the Mag Argnatal, the place of wisdom, vision and enchantment, your reality perfectly collides with your place. In the collision is no collusion, for you have followed the call and you are creating the land of your dreams.

So do not deny the land you dream of . . . but what happens if you do?

DENYING YOUR INTUITION

You only feel bad because the Universe is trying to help you
Gill Edwards

In this section, we shall look at three examples of denying your intuition. In the first, the person passed away restless and unfulfilled. In the second, someone didn't have as good a time in a country as they could have done. And in the third example, the person didn't learn what they were meant to learn. Let's see how denying your intuition has an effect.

When Tania didn't follow her dream
One of these days is none of these days
M. Tupper

Tania had always longed to go to the mountains of South America. She was talked out of it, first of all by her family who said it wasn't safe for her to travel there alone, then by her boyfriend who didn't want to go with her. She did love her boyfriend and she ended up marrying him, having a couple of kids and then tragically dying in her forties of cancer. There were books about South America by her hospital bed when she passed away.

South America was a dream Tania never gave herself the chance to fulfil. She'd put sensible factors first and had never taken her true wishes and passions into account. Don't be like Tania and never follow the drumbeat of your soul. Magical travel involves filling in the gaps between your reality and your dream. Generally, if the longing for that place has been there as long as you remember, then that is a very significant signal. The call is there for a reason. If you hear it, you need to heed it.

Paul, following the call of the past
Unfortunately when you travel, you take yourself with you
Lucy Edge

When Paul, from Ireland, went to Brazil he got robbed and didn't enjoy himself much at all. It all seemed quite hot and crowded, and he wished that he was there with someone else. He didn't meet any nice women, although he did gather some stories – such as the robbery – to tell in the pub back home. But overall – although he wouldn't say it to anyone – the whole trip just wasn't worth it. He didn't know why he bothered.

Paul was hearing the call of the past, not the present. For his ex-girlfriend loved Brazil and he later guessed he wanted to prove something to her. Paul would have been better off going to a country that was right for him, not her, and it would have helped him get over her more quickly.

David, listening to the wrong self
When the heart is right
'For' and 'against' are forgotten
Thomas Merton

David from Scotland loved to travel, for he really enjoyed politics and meeting people, but he also longed for the right relationship. He spent a lot of time and money on dating, but it only felt right a couple of times. When his relationship with Rachel was breaking up, David went around Australia. Likewise, when his relationship with Ruth ran into problems, he fled to Argentina.

David followed his subconscious self, which just wanted to run away. He got as far away as possible, but it didn't work. He genuinely wanted to go to both Australia and South America, unfortunately the call was from his 'wrong self'. As a result he made the journey, but his life didn't change as a result and he returned to the 'same old, same old', although with a facility in Spanish. Had he followed his Higher Self, which in this case happened to speak to him in the voices of two different women, and delayed his journeys, it is likely his life would have been far more fulfilled.

All of us have conflicting things going on, so it is hard to know which part of ourselves the voice is from. Paul and David didn't know about the Hand Exercise I gave you in Chapter 2, 'Accessing your intuition', and even if they had they probably wouldn't have done it, for each of them valued their independence of mind. They did not realise that going into your Higher Self offers true freedom, and that going to places pointed to by your Higher Self is a great way to access it. The more you practise the intuitive exercises the more aligned you will become.

THE IMPORTANCE OF YOUR INTUITION

Throw your dreams into space like a kite, and you do not know what it will bring back, a new life, a new friend, a new love, a new country
Anaïs Nin

In this chapter, we've seen some examples of what happens when you follow your intuition and some examples of what happens when you don't. When you do follow it, you reach a new level of peace, even though you are initially shaken up. You may even be drawn to the land where you meet your soulmate. But when you don't follow it, and travel anyway, your problems will still be there when you return – and you will be older in years and poorer in money. Or if you don't follow it, and don't travel, then you will live your life without fulfilling your dream.

So what does it all show? Your intuition is important, for it is the home of your dreams. The place you go to is also important, for it will allow you to infuse a particular quality, somehow associated with it, as if through the spirit of place. We shall explore the spirit of place more in Part 2, Chapter 15, 'When to visit the sacred'. Eventually that quality will be integrated into your life, in the fifth principle of travelling magically, for your benefit and the benefit of those close to you, a process we explore more in the final section. For remember that your journey is unique to you. Your soul added to your experience and expectations makes up your vibration. Your vibration is your unique calling card. So that's why just because your friend had a great time in one place doesn't mean that you will. For your vibration is yours alone. Make sure you follow your intuition – the piper at the gate of your dreams. And go where you really, really want to go.

Now let's view your options for that actual letting go. How do you leave your country?

CHAPTER 9

When do you fly?

Higher and higher
From the earth thou springest
Percy Bysshe Shelley

This is the first of two chapters on how to travel between countries. Of course your magical trip may be within your own country – in this case you can skip to Part 2, Chapter 3, 'How do you get around?'. There are as many ways to go as there are to know. One of them is particularly in the news at the time of writing – flying. It is so popular and controversial it deserves a chapter to itself.

I shall begin by looking at when to fly, as well as when not to fly. Then I move on to the type of ticket that's best for shorter and longer trips, as well as discussing the process of booking, and then carbon offsetting. Then, linking in with the first principle of travelling magically, following your intuition, I show a couple of examples of what happens when you do – and how your increased awareness actually helps the planet, so flying can be a good thing. But then I show an example of when not to fly, when someone joined in a stag weekend with his friends. The purpose of the chapter is to help stimulate questions within your mind, so you can decide yourself about this controversial topic.

WHEN TO FLY

Away! Away! For I will fly to thee
John Keats

Flying can be the wonderful aerial gate to the realms of travelling magically, and the fact that it causes pollution does not mean you should never do it. It does mean, however, that you should be conscious of it. Let's look at when it's acceptable to fly, when to look at alternatives and at how you decide.

Flying works when you don't have enough time to go to a place or you simply can't get there any other way. You may have to take a 'flying' visit somewhere and air travel provides your only opportunity. Also there are still places in the world that can only be reached by flying.

So fly when you really get the call to go to a place and:

✧ You have the money but no time.
✧ You can't reach the place you really, really want to go to any other way in the time you have available.

Don't fly when:

✧ Alternative less-polluting methods are available, and you have the time to enjoy them.
✧ You shouldn't be doing the trip at all.

We shall see two examples of good times to fly in a later section of this chapter, as well as one example of a time not to fly.

If you do get the green light to fly, let's look at the process of booking.

TYPES OF TICKET

When flying it's best to book your ticket in advance, and necessary when going to certain countries such as America. Some people go to private airfields and manage to air-hitch, a process that is easiest for pilots, or you can even join the empty leg of a private jet or be a courier (see Resources). This chapter will focus on the process of flying by commercial airliners.

You can purchase different types of tickets:

Type of ticket	Advantages	Disadvantages
Return	Cheaper	Usually pay extra for flexible return date, lots of stopovers, may want to return from somewhere else
Open jaw	Return from elsewhere	Inflexible
Round-the-world	Go to lots of places	Inflexible, must follow prescribed route. Much more expensive than return ticket
Inclusive tour	Includes car, hotel etc.	May be less motivation to travel magically. Shorter amount of time
One-way	Flexible	May cause visa/entry problems

TIPS FOR A SHORTER TRIP

When going on a short trip, such as a weekend, a week or a fortnight you will probably just want a return ticket.

Remember, the cheapest ticket may not necessarily be the cheapest when other factors are taken into account. Are you being charged for baggage and meals? Is it viable for you to get to the airport by public transport or do you need a taxi? For example, if your flight leaves at 6 am then you will either need to get to the airport the night before or pay for a not-very-green taxi. Look at when you arrive too. Flights arriving after dark aren't ideal when you are in a strange country, and in that case, you may want to book a night's accommodation in advance, as it is much harder to find quality accommodation for yourself when you can't see easily. You could purchase the IT 'Inclusive tour' if you go on a shorter journey. They are often very cheap and include extras like car hire or a hotel. For magical travel, use the extras for a day or two – then take off.

TIPS FOR A LONGER TRIP

Those going on a very long trip may want a one-way ticket, which gives you great flexibility, although it can cause visa problems. If you're going for a year or less, it will be cheaper to get a return ticket; and try to find one that does not have large penalties if you need to change the date of travel, for you simply do not know who you're going to meet and encounter. Travel agents will often advise you to get a round-the-world ticket as they get more commission. These tickets enable you to mix and match airlines, but I'd only choose one of these if the trip wouldn't work by the airline of a single country, so check first.

You need to be a bit creative. For example, a direct return ticket is usually cheaper than a round-the-world trip, and if you choose your airline carefully then you can often find stop-overs in countries you want to go to. Choose one – and sometimes you are able to choose many more – on the way there, and another one to four on the way back. Say if you want to go to New Zealand from Britain, and would also like to go to Mexico, Air New Zealand offers some wonderful stop-overs such as Tahiti where you would also like to go, but not Mexico. Why not take advantage of the Los Angeles stop-over, do a little shopping in Hollywood and then make your own way overland to neighbouring Mexico? You can then also stop in the magical isles of Tahiti on your way to New Zealand. Then on the way back maybe stop in the Cook Islands and again in Los Angeles and head further into California for a little skiing, instead of doing your skiing on a separate trip. The more creative you are in thinking about your booking the easier it will be.

TIPS FOR BOOKING

Most people don't book by a travel agent any more, but do it themselves on the Internet. Using a credit card to pay should mean you are covered on your card's insurance if anything goes wrong.

If you have special needs or want a special meal make it known at the time of booking. For example, I, like many others, book a vegetarian meal. Cath Urquhart, the travel editor of *The Times*, said 'it's long been axiomatic that vegetarian meals on airlines are better than the usual beef or chicken option – and are often served first'. You also have far less chance of getting food poisoning – an important consideration if your airline has originated in the tropics on that flight, or is going back that way, as new food is usually loaded then. As special requests often get lost, check with the airline 24 hours in advance because when you check in it's usually too late to deal with it then.

Of course you need to make yourself au fait with other rules, from baggage to visas, before you travel.

Throughout this book I talk about the spiritual principle of giving back when you receive. One way we are now very aware of it is negating your 'carbon footprint' when you fly. Let's see how.

YOUR CARBON FOOTPRINT

And yonder all before us lie
Deserts of vast eternity
Andrew Marvell

To avoid the dismal prospect of an eternal desert in our future we need to do something now. Your 'carbon footprint' is the amount of the planet's land you are using. Many people use its increase as a reason not to fly. There is plenty of evidence to back this point of view. According to the Earthday calculator, the average environmental footprint of a UK citizen is 5.8 hectares (14 acres). Flying for 25 hours a year adds 1.5 hectares (4 acres) to your footprint. We know now that flying causes a great deal of pollution that contributes to global warming and is not sustainable in the long term. Friends of the Earth stated, 'Those in the west who can afford to fly will be the last to feel the consequences of global warming. But let's be clear, it's going to affect us all in the end.'

Yet stopping flying doesn't provide an answer to the problems of our earth. For at this point in our earth's evolution, there are still three good reasons to fly:

◇ Carbon offsetting schemes. Do check each one before you invest. For example, if they plant trees, confirm the trees are native and that local people have not been moved off the land.
◇ On a longer trip travelling magically you are likely to use far less carbon than if you'd stayed at home. You will be living like a local.
◇ Your consciousness heightening as a result of your trip. This is the best reason of all; with your new consciousness, you will be able to improve the earth far more than if you'd never flown at all and 'stayed the same'.

The third factor is an unusual one to take into account at the present time, but yet is vitally important.

CONSCIOUSNESS

> *Annihilating all that's made*
> *To a green Thought in a green Shade*
> **Andrew Marvell**

Consciousness is a wonderful concept, of great importance to the world. The *Oxford Dictionary of English* states consciousness is 'awareness of', and if we see it this way, then it relates very well to other themes within the book. In Chapter 1, 'Travelling with intuition', we looked at the concept of vibration, and saw how it can be raised by a visit to a place that is right for you. This section on flying to a place that feels right to you continues the theme from another angle. For that's how you raise your vibration and become more conscious. And that is better for the world than if you had never travelled at all. Raising your consciousness is a very worthwhile goal in itself.

Now we'll see two examples in which the women concerned wouldn't have gone on their trips if they hadn't been able to fly, as they both have full-time jobs. Then, by way of contrast, we'll look at another example, where it wasn't worth flying. So hopefully then we'll have enough information to choose appropriately.

Nicky's story

> *Kila ndege huruka kwa bawa lake*
> *(Every bird flies with its own wings)*
> **African proverb**

An executive from London, Nicky, had never been to the developing world before. But she had always been interested in her African heritage, and really wanted to visit West Africa where she had some relatives. Nicky spent two weeks there, as a fortnight was the only time she could get off work. She became more aware of issues of poverty and the East–West divide from chatting to the locals she met there, and of the West's role in creating it. She also grew to love eating the locals' food of beans and rice, even though her relatives laughed and told her she was eating 'poor people's food'. She also gained a stronger sense of her own identity.

That trip worked for Nicky, because her growing awareness was definitely worth the fossil fuels used in flying to another country for a short time. The changes you make to your life as a result of your magical journey into higher consciousness *will* help the earth. For example, Nicky went on to negate the carbon impact of her trip by changing her lifestyle by becoming a vegan, thus reducing her carbon footprint to only 0.5 hectares (1.2 acres). And that's without the effortless change that your new consciousness will bring to the people and land around you, which Miranda's journey illustrates.

Miranda's journey

Miranda had a mystical experience in a Cambodian temple (see Part 2, Chapter 16, 'Opening to the mystical') and found a creative way to offset some of her carbon footprint. She said a short prayer and planted a cherry tree in some wasteland near her home in Seattle in memory of the wonderful 'flying visit'. She enjoys seeing the tree as she walks to work every day.

Today the cherry tree is flourishing in what was previously stony earth – a frothy tribute to the burgeoning of Miranda's consciousness. Maybe other people have their vibration raised too, simply by seeing it.

Both Nicky and Miranda show what can happen when you fly in a conscious way. Now it's time for a contrary example.

Niall's trip

*The definition of insanity is doing the same thing over and over
again expecting different results*
Oscar Wilde

Niall loves to travel. His trip from New York to Amsterdam for a stag
weekend was part of a greater pattern in which he flies a great deal,
both for his work and holidays. Travelling so much way gives him
a sense of being successful and 'keeping in touch' with his group of
international friends, as well as going to lots of exciting places that he
can then tell people about.

Yet what did he learn from this trip? Nothing. For unlike the girls, he
didn't go from any promptings of his Higher Self. So he didn't gain
anything except some momentary sensation from his interaction with
the stripper, and he got quite drunk which may affect his health long
term. Niall is part of a band of young men and women who travel
for sensation rather than for growth. Just because flying is available
cheaply and easily does not mean you should always take advantage of
it, just like you shouldn't take advantage of a person who is available
easily and cheaply.

Yet stopping travelling this way is a decision everyone must make
for themselves. It takes courage to do so. It may mean staying at home
and feeling the things you are trying to escape from, which I talk about
in Part 2, Chapter 19, 'Going within'. Yet when you do, then you'll be
comfortable not rushing around the world, and be able to concentrate
on other things.

To fly away?

....

> *Once you have flown, you will walk the earth with your eyes turned skyward, for there you have been, there you long to return*
> **Leonardo da Vinci**

In this chapter we've seen times to fly, and times not to fly. It's always your choice. Just be aware of the part of yourself that you are making it from, and know that you are far more likely to have a worthwhile experience if you go from your Higher Self. If you're not sure which part of yourself the desire to fly away is coming from then use the Hand Exercise to check.

When you get it right, then the results of your magical journey can help the earth, as we saw in a couple of examples. For your consciousness will grow, keener and greener, and then you can help regreen the earth – both literally through carbon offsetting and vibrationally, through growing your consciousness you know how to make new choices and help the Earth to flower.

Now it's time to move on and look at other, greener, ways of travelling.

CHAPTER 10

How else can you travel?

A thousand mile journey begins with one step
Lao Tsu

In this chapter we will look at methods other than flying to travel between countries. It complements Part 2, Chapter 3, 'How do you get around?', which looks at modes of transport within a country, at internal flights, driving, ridesharing, hitch-hiking, taking the bus, swimming, kayaking, rowing and walking. Forms of transport I explore here include driving, hitch-hiking, railway, boat, motorcycling, cycling and walking. We consider travelling with an animal in Part 1, Chapter 15. These particular chapters are not discrete, and it's worth looking at them in congruence with each other, depending on the form of transport you are seeking.

The first section looks at travelling with a vehicle, whether this is choosing and driving your own vehicle or hitch-hiking. It's an interesting point that the most expensive and self-contained thing to do – driving – is the least green. The more you 'downshift' from that, to ride-sharing for example, the greener you become. When you hitch you are not responsible for any pollution – and indeed a good hitcher will always be able to show a driver an alternative 'way to go' by example. So let's go.

INTERNATIONAL DRIVING

> *My campervan has allowed me to experience the vastness of our*
> *continent*
> **Jackie Hartnell**

Drive if you've always had a dream to drive. For example, if you've always wanted to travel across Africa. It is best if you are already an experienced driver, and you know how to do things like basic repairs on your vehicle.

Start off by driving around your own country, as Jackie Hartnell did. Having emigrated to Australia, she and her husband intended to drive around the continent in a campervan after they retired. But sadly he died, and she wrote an article about her regret about the delay, called 'Carpe Diem, Seize the Day'. Then she chose her own campervan and travelled around the continent alone. She wrote about her experience in her book called *No Fixed Address*.

Then work up to driving abroad, if you'd really like to, but make sure your driving licence is valid, or you get an international one, are properly insured and up to date with the driving regulations of the countries you are passing through.

There are many advantages to driving. For example driving is convenient, and if you are travelling with children or animals, it's often easier. More and more people are leaving cars behind and travelling in more self-contained units, such as campervans or RV's (recreational vehicles) or caravans. Campervans – or their more expensive counterpart, mobile homes – have the 'home' part of the van in the same unit as the engine. Caravans though are separate and detachable, and usually need to be pulled along by a vehicle tow bar. Both of them can be a 'complete home on wheels', with extras such as toilets, showers, curtains, solar panels, cookers, beds and even desks. You can use the extra space to bring along things you care about and share them with people, such as leaflets about a cause close to your heart or gifts. You can ship or drive it abroad and usually sell it on again.

There are also disadvantages to driving. You are 'tied down', you may need spare parts, and you will need insurance. A big disadvantage is that it is not green. But if you decide to drive you can go greener. Buy a second-hand vehicle. Get local food and cook it along the way, rather than bringing pre-packaged supplies with you. Park in wild places. If you have a diesel engine, you can run it on different types of fuel such as vegetable oil, thus helping to save the planet. If your engine is not diesel, it can also run on LPG liquid petroleum gas although you should check its availability in your destination countries. Check out rideshares, so someone else doesn't need to drive their own vehicle. And lastly, as long as the individual feels right to you, do pick up hitch-hikers. By picking up a hitch-hiker, you are helping regreen the planet. As Gabriel Morris pointed out, hitch-hiking is 'a reasonable, efficient use of energy and resources. Hitch-hiking is the transportation equivalent of recycling.'

HITCH-HIKING

In the light of flowers
I travel
Just for the sake of travelling
Nagakawa Soen-Roshi

People have been hitch-hiking since transport was invented; for example, by getting a lift on a wagon to save walking along the track. In the 1960s, hitch-hiking in motor vehicles was at the height of its popularity, with people in Europe hitch-hiking to different continents in cars, lorries and everything in between. Indeed, most of the older generation remember hitch-hiking themselves. As Simon and Tom Sykes pointed out when they researched their book *No Such Thing as a Free Ride? A Collection of Hitch-Hiking Tales*, they found evidence of 'hitching's continuing popularity and relevance around the world'. And many people still hitch today.

For example, many networks, clubs, communities and websites exist to celebrate the art of hitch-hiking, which even includes an International Hitch-hiking Conference in Vilnius each year. Today, however, it is vilified by the media, as a dangerous way to travel. This is a great shame as, in fact, a woman in the West is statistically more likely to be raped and murdered by staying in at night with her husband or boyfriend – 70 per cent of murders and rapes occur by people we know. The unfamiliar may actually be safer than the familiar – and it can be a lot more fun.

Of course there are some common-sense rules to be followed. Let's look at hitching from the point of view of the driver and hitcher.

Tips for the driver

If you want to avoid George Monbiot's definition of hell, 'millions of lost souls whom our diabolically stupid transport policies condemn to travel alone', pick up a hitch-hiker. Who knows, they could be on the road to greatness! For example, the film director Mike Leigh called hitch-hiking 'a gas' and preferred it to taking the bus. Sir Ranulph Fiennes had most success in France when he wore a kilt. Take a chance, and help save the planet. Your growing consciousness will metaphorically help to regreen the earth. Your consciousness that is willing to allow a lonely and predictable car journey to be transformed. Not only do you get decent conversation, you also have a wonderful opportunity to influence someone. You might help your passenger by something you say, as well as on a practical level of course. Your passenger might tell you exactly what you need to know. For when you help others it always comes back to you.

Laurie's ride

I wondered how one small sentence uttered from a stranger could somehow make a difference to your soul
Laurie Gough

Laurie, an inveterate traveller, was 21 when she was given a ride by a businessman in Oregon, on a day when she was feeling frustrated and aimless. He thought her journey, travelling around alone without a plan, was wonderful; she reminded him of a time when he was younger and freer. She immediately felt much better about what she was doing. He also suggested that one day she should write a book about her thoughts on the differences between the USA and Canada and now she has, *Kiss the Sunset Pig*, a book loved by many. In addition, meeting her made him consider quitting his job to pursue something which made him happier.

So do open yourself to the spontaneous, the second principle of travelling magically, by picking up a hitch-hiker if it feels right to you.

The hitch-hiker

I thanked my lucky stars
Lembit Opik

From the point of view of the hitch-hiker of course, drivers make it possible, a piece of the universe in motion coming along just when you need it. That's the case even with the ones you don't much like who pick you up when dressed in a top hat and tails, which happened to Liberal Democrat MP Lembit Opik when he hitch-hiked to Germany and back to Britain when he was a student. Drivers help you without expecting anything in return, except some good conversation. They provide continual opportunities for you to learn to trust. And trust. And trust.

Tips for the hitch-hiker

If you follow certain guidelines, you are likely to stay safe. The following strict set of guidelines are for a woman travelling alone. If you are a man they need to be followed less strictly and, likewise, if there's more than one of you hitching, although the rules should still be taken into consideration. They are:

✧ Dress modestly.
✧ Find a suitable hitching spot, where drivers can see you clearly from at least 50 yards away.
✧ If you have a bag make sure it's visible, so that the driver can tell you're not a vagrant.
✧ Smile when a car comes close.
✧ Have a destination in mind when you ask the driver where he or she is going. If you don't trust him or her, say you're going some-where else.
✧ Be very careful of your body language when you're in the vehicle.
✧ Don't talk about anything inappropriate, or make sexual innuendos.
✧ Do chat and ask questions.
✧ Don't hitch after dark (drivers may assume you're 'asking for it').

And, of course, the most important rule of all, the first principle of travelling magically is to follow your intuition. By having the courage to 'let go' you are now in a wonderful position to learn what can be learned. By practising common sense and the dress codes of the country I'm in, and being very careful of my voice and my body language, I have rarely even had a proposition. And the power of the trust you develop is immense. For, the fact is, most people you meet can be trusted, and your intuition will help you discern the ones who can't be. Kinga Freespirit, who wrote *Led by Destiny*, hitch-hiked the world with her boyfriend, taking several years and meeting wonderful people and having amazing experiences. She wrote, 'It feels like our Protective Spirit is working overtime. Everything is working out better than we ever could have wished for.'

Another way of seeing the world is by public transport.

INTERNATIONAL PUBLIC TRANSPORT BY LAND

Going overland is the only serious way of travelling
Paul Theroux

Encouraging public transport is as green as green can be. Public transport exists almost everywhere where there are people, and if you have the time and the inclination then it provides a wonderful way for you to see the world, and to meet people. You can get everywhere by public transport, including almost all the way across the world, from England or Australia, for example. Any shortfalls aren't usually to do with the lack of transport, but other issues, such as visas.

Of course public transport has a great advantage: it does not usually have to be booked in advance. So it's perfect for travelling magically, because you are free to follow the energy. Turn up, and if the bus you want is full – then why not try going somewhere else instead. Be experimental, be spontaneous, you won't regret it – or if you do, it will only be for a moment or a day, and in later years you will be glad of the experience, I promise. Bill loved his trip through the countries of Central America, and one reason was that he 'felt free' to spend as long as he wanted in each place. When the energy changed he met less exciting people or felt drawn to somewhere else and so he moved on. But he didn't move on for the sake of it, on a prearranged date. He always followed the flow, and what a wonderful time he had, and how many people loved meeting him. For when you're really in the flow then you inspire others too.

Public transport includes trains, buses and boats. We'll look at buses and very small boats in Part 2, Chapter 3 and here will explore trains and boats.

TRAVEL BY RAIL

....

There isn't a train I wouldn't take
No matter where it's going
Edna St Vincent Millay

There are many wonderful rail journeys in the world. You can travel around Asia, the Americas, across Australia and New Zealand by rail; in fact, rail is a very viable way of travelling around most of the globe. It's all eco-friendly and relatively easy, and it's quite possible to book directly with the company themselves, and thus take advantage of any discounts on offer.

You might try the night train between London and the Highlands of Scotland. There you may book a cabin and set off from the centre of London in the evening. There is a comfortable lounge bar on board, and when you fall asleep to the trundling of the train you can look forward to waking up, pulling up the blind above your washbasin, and suddenly seeing the Scottish wilderness – all effortless on your own part. *The Orient Express* through Europe, *The Ghan* across Australia, and *The Canadian* across Canada are some other classic train journeys. But of course your journey does not need to be a classic one for it to be enjoyable. There is much pleasure to be gained simply by hopping on a train and going somewhere – because you can and because it's there.

Christopher Portway did just that – and has spent decades travelling around the continents of the world by train. He has a fine eye for observation, and experienced many adventures, from proposing to his future wife on a railway platform in (the former) Czechoslovakia to driving a train in Korea, as well as having had much time for contemplation. As he wrote in *World Commuter: Great Journeys by Train*, 'for a willing traveller, a voyage by rail, wherever in the world, in this modern age can be a journey inward and backward; an invitation to unwind, ruminate and enjoy'.

Discounts may be in the form of cards, such as young person cards or promotions the train company offers, although this doesn't happen if you book with a tour. Also you can usually book at the last minute, especially if you are flexible about timing. For example when you are in Moscow, wanting to go on the Trans-Siberian to Vladivostok in the far east, and experience the vastness of 'All the Russias', from the golden cupolas of the walled cities to the steppes of Siberia, the chances are the train won't be full if you avoid the peak season. If it is full, as a magical traveller you have the time to wait for the next one and meanwhile you can have an adventure in or around Moscow. Maybe there is someone you are meant to meet or a monument or a museum you are meant to see.

When you go by train you have an opportunity to get off at the various stops, thus you can travel spontaneously, in keeping with the second principle of travelling magically. It's also a far better way than driving to meet people. For example, Peggy took the train from Germany to Switzerland, and met a wonderful lady on it, who became a teacher to her. That train trip changed her life.

Now it's time to look at the second form of transport, travelling by boat. Here public transport will segue into individual transport, and we'll come to the final individual examples, motorcycling, cycling and walking.

TRAVELLING BY BOAT

> *Protect me God because my boat is so small and Your ocean so vast*
> **French proverb**

In this section we shall explore five ways of travelling by boat. The first is passenger ferries, the second cargo boats and the third cruise ships. Then we shall look at two ways of travelling by individual boat – either sailing your own yacht or crewing someone else's. Each method has its advantages and disadvantages but, generally, travelling by sea leads to a feeling of freedom.

Ferries

> *Pray to God sailor, but pull to the shore*
> **English proverb**

Ferries are a convenient and green way to travel between countries, or parts of a country, and for some communities they represent their lifeblood. For example communities on the Alaskan panhandle go to basketball games by ferry. Be aware though, that they are usually far more frequent in peak season, and out of it run infrequently if at all. On most ferries you can take cars, although often they need booking in advance, others are passenger ferries only. Ferries provide a greener way of travelling than flying, and also give many opportunities to interact with others. They can also provide some very special memories. For example, you can travel by passenger ferry between Seattle, on the west coast of the USA, to Canada and Alaska. On the way you will see glaciers shine, call into remote Native American settlements, be haunted by swooping eagles and the glint of the light on the sea. You may well see whales breaching and dolphins leaping. And who would really want to fly between the Greek islands, when you could go by boat and cruise Homer's 'wine-dark seas'? So if it's a choice between a ferry and an overland mode of transport, then for me a ferry often wins.

Cargo boats

There are secrets on my distant shore
Anonymous

A more unusual way of going between countries is to be a passenger on a cargo boat. They have the advantage of being relatively cheap, as well as charging no single supplement. Most boats take only four or five passengers, and the quality of the accommodation tends to be very good, as they were often designed for the owner of the vessel. There may not be the amenities of a passenger ship, but you will have a far more genuine experience. You need to be pretty flexible, most boats don't know when they're going to move until fairly close to the time, but you will get a scheduled route, and you will have chances to get off the boat.

You do need to be reasonably streetwise to find your way around the harbour, and be sure to leave plenty of time to get back to the boat. Of course if you are the only woman among a male crew the attentions may grow irksome, so be sure you can cope with that kind of situation. So for the experienced, sociable traveller, who isn't in a rush, cargo boats provide a wonderful way to travel.

CRUISE SHIPS

....

> *All are nothing but flowers*
> *In a flowering universe*
> **Nagakawa Soen-Roshi**

Cruise ships can be a good option to get to your destination where you begin travelling magically. One of the ways of taking them cheaply is to work on them. They offer a great range of jobs, from accountancy to croupier or beauty therapist. You'll get to see different ports, and perhaps at some point you can disembark and have your adventure. You may want to work on them for a few years while learning more about other cultures and the world, then at least you have that option, while practising your skill. It's best to get your qualification or experience first and then apply for a job, although many ships offer a very favourable policy towards employing young people. Otherwise cruise ships are a wee bit too comfortable and controlled to travel magically on!

YOUR OWN BOAT

....

> *I thought how crazy it was that this river, this bank, this had*
> *been here forever and this was the first time we'd seen it. In fact*
> *this was the first time we had dared look for it; and yet, in a*
> *strange way, it was just like drifting home*
> **Dorian Amos**

Sailing away in your own yacht is a dream option to many. It is easier to do than you may think. Kevin was a disillusioned young Canadian doctor, who wanted something different, but didn't know what.

A doctor goes to sea

The sea is calm tonight
The tide is full, the moon lies fair
Matthew Arnold

Kevin could not sail, yet he bought a yacht, the *Sea Mouse*, on impulse. Then he met a man, Don, who *did* know how to sail. Both upset after failed relationships, and wanting to forget their women, they set off for Tahiti. On the way, Don found happiness on an unexpected island, Penrhyn in the Cook Islands. Kevin ended up sailing from Hawaii back to Canada alone. He thought, in surprise, 'A week out I was eating supper – curried noodles and tea – and thought, "This is it, I'm out here completely alone. Nothing awful has happened." I was surprised. The ocean was orange and pink.' He tried hard to remember what he had been looking for, for he had found it. He went on to say: 'Memories of my old girlfriend seemed remote now . . . barely remembered, true but unimportant.'

He was ready to complete his journey. Kevin still keeps himself afloat by working as a doctor, with plenty of time on his boat.

Perhaps so many people dream of sailing their own boat for a reason. French yachtsman Bernard Moitiessier put it beautifully, 'the sun, the sea, the wind, the Southern Cross so high in the sky, and the albatrosses that see all things alike, the song of the great luminous silence where I had been sailing my soul for so long . . .' So inspired was he, that he gave up his dream of being the fastest single-handed yachtsman around the world, which he was on track for, and carried on sailing, going where the winds and his soul directed.

This could be you. You could buy a yacht, learn to sail and set off. Or you could just get the yacht and do what Kevin did, learning to sail on the way. Another way of going to sea is as a passenger on someone else's boat, following Don's example.

Someone else's boat

Give me the life that I love
Robert Louis Stevenson

Crewing and sailing are viable options that enable you to go off the beaten track into paradisal coves, down remote rivers and out onto the phosphorescence-filled open ocean. There are organisations you can join to be a passenger on a boat, even with no crewing experience. Many people go to boat-yards and 'hang out' and see who they get on with, in terms of asking for a passage. There are even books about how to boat hitch! Unlike having your own boat you won't be making the decisions, but at least you have the freedom to leave the boat in port and have your own adventure; nor are you responsible for the repairs and maintenance and mooring fees when you are in dock. So if you do want to travel by boat, then you can choose between those five ways. Enjoy the journey.

Now it's time to get to some more individual methods of travel such as motorbiking, cycling and walking.

Motorcycling

Movement never lies
Martha Graham

Motorcycling around the world has become more and more popular since Ted Simon made a tremendous trip in the 1970s, and wrote two great books about it. In fact he enjoyed his trip so much that he motorcycled back to the same place 25 years later, when he was in his seventies. There are now many more books, but Ted's is still a classic of the genre.

Men do it on their own, women do it on their own and you gain qualities such as self-reliance and independence. You feel part of the world around you as Robbie Ray wrote, she feels like she's 'part of the weather or a piece of the landscape'. She rides so fast her wheels lift off the ground, she forgets all her worries and passes from town to town as though on a magic carpet.

Of course motorcycling is not so green, but if it's a choice between that, for example, and staying in a corporate job – well, you may contribute more to carbon damage through the policies of that company. It's also harder for you to raise your consciousness if you stay somewhere where you are not happy. So be prepared to think 'outside the box', and if it feels right to you then go for it. Give yourself permission.

Or would you prefer to travel a quieter way?

Cycling

Life shrinks or expands in proportion to one's courage
Anaïs Nin

Cycling is an even greener way to travel around the world. There are some great books by people who have gone around the world this way on their own – surprisingly often written by British women, such as Anne Mustoe, Bettina Selby and Josie Dew.

Anne cycles around the world – several times
Be not afraid of growing slowly, be afraid of standing still
Chinese proverb

Anne was a retired headmistress when she set off alone on the first of what was to become several trips around the world. She travelled slowly along ancient trails, staying in local accommodation on the way. 'I discovered that cycling was the perfect way to travel. It was faster than walking, but slow enough to appreciate all the signs and scents of the countryside. With no possessions to speak of, no complicated mechanisms to go wrong and no timetables, my days were wonderfully carefree and my only duty in life was to get myself safely from one shelter to the next before nightfall. Everything I needed was to hand, in two small bags on the back of the world's greenest and most energy-efficient machine. My life was simplicity itself. After years of responsibility, I just couldn't believe my luck.' In fact Anne enjoyed cycling around the world so much she did it again, the other way.

Anne had a far better – and cheaper – time than she would have done had she stayed in London, and has since written a number of thoughtful and interesting books. Exactly the same is true for Bettina Selby, who took off when her children grew up, and Josie Dew, who started to travel when she was very young. They all still love to cycle, whatever the distance.

Now we come to our final, and in many ways easiest method of exploration: walking.

WALKING THE WORLD

....

Walking is man's best medicine
Hippocrates

There is much to learn by walking. The very act of putting one foot in front of another repeatedly, if carried on, will eventually take you around the world. It is not right for all of us to go that far, but you are left vulnerable and open and humble by your very choice of transport. You are connected to the earth and unlike cycling, you have the energy to talk to others as you go. The act of walking itself will always bring you closer to where you want to go. Perhaps that's why the Hindu *saddhu* at the end of his life renounces everything by leaving his family behind, for the time of householding is behind him, and takes his bowl – and walks. He walks and walks until he finds inner peace.

Routes over sacred ground are known as pilgrimage. Many of the world's religions advocate walking to your destination. One famous pilgrimage is to Santiago de Compostela, the seven-week trek across the Pyrenees from the Basque country in the east to the Atlantic city of Santiago in the west. Perhaps the most famous destination is the Qabah, in Mecca, Saudi Arabia. It contains the holy black stone and is the most sacred building in Islam; it must be walked around seven times, ideally every year, but hopefully at least once in a lifetime. It is the reason all Muslims pray in the direction of Mecca. According to cultural historian Rebecca Solnit, every walker is a sentinel guarding an ancient way of being out in the open world.

You can set off like a turtle with your home on your back and just – go. You need very little else apart from maps and your own supplies, depending on how remote the area you go to is and the availability of food and water. Some people, such as Ffyona Campbell, walk with sponsorship and support vans. She described her experience in her searingly honest autobiography *The Whole Story*. Or you can go without a van, as Ffyona did when she returned to America to walk across it – pushing a pram instead. Diane also walked across Australia with a pram, a convenient way of taking her luggage. Going alone and unsupported is closest to the experience of travelling magically, for that way you learn to trust that you will get what you need on the way. But there are some places and countries it may be best to avoid – such as Rwanda during civil war. But even then Immaculée Ilibagiza's story in Part 2, Chapter 8, 'Three qualities for true expansion', shows what is possible when she walked safely through a murderous group of guerillas. You benefit from every step you take in alignment.

Green travel

May your life be like a wild flower growing freely in the beauty and freedom of each day
Native American proverb

In the last two chapters we have looked at some of the possible ways of going around the world, from flying to driving to hitch-hiking, and going by train, boat, motorbike, cycle and finally, walking. Which method resounds with you? So many ways of going and only one life to do it. It's a big decision, but perhaps the most important thing is that you make a decision and just take off. The act of moving itself will lead to growth.

Green travel has been the theme of the last two chapters, which funnily enough chimes with the 'green movement'. But green travel is important in a greater sense. Miranda's tree planting in the last chapter is a wonderful metaphor for the ability to make growth happen where there was none before, the wasteland in her story representing the unused portions of our mind. Magical travel needs to help us connect up parts of our mind that were previously disconnected. For green is the colour of consciousness. And the qualities of openness, humility, interconnection and intuition fostered by magical travel serve to aid our growth.

CHAPTER 11

Who do you go with?

The man who goes alone can start today; but he who
travels with another must wait until that other is ready
Henry David Thoreau

Now you've got some ideas about where to go, possible ways of getting
there and how to choose between them. The next question is who do
you go with? The wrong choice of travelling companion *will* ruin your
trip. It will leave you feeling resentful and angry and wary of trying
again. It may even be an excuse for you to give up on the possibility
of change and growth. On the other hand the right travel companion
will help every aspect of your growth. You will learn infinitely more
from this person than you will alone. But just how do you meet him
or her, or recognise your right person when you do? There are three
golden rules to choosing your right travel companion.

1. TRAVEL WITH SOMEONE YOU WANT TO BECOME LIKE

To the extent that you can experience the suffering of another as
your own, you can also experience the joy and power and gifts of
another as your own
Joanna Macy

Aisha followed this rule and was very glad she did.

96

Aisha and Jane go to Europe

I don't know the key to success but the key to failure is trying to please everybody
Bill Cosby

During her summer break from university, 22-year-old Aisha wanted to go round Europe by train, but who with? She knew she wanted to go with only one person, as she didn't want the delays in making decisions that come from travelling with a group. But how could she choose from among her group of friends? She knew she could not please everybody. In the end she decided to go with Jane, whom she didn't know that well but really liked and admired. They had a great trip together and Aisha ended up with one of the firmest friendships of her life.

Aisha stuck to the first rule of travel, only go with someone you respect and admire and want to become like. For whether or not you want to, you will inevitably absorb their energy. So make sure before you go that this is really what you want. Aisha was glad that she didn't go with her close friend Sheila, whom she really liked, but found quite fearful and wary of trying new things.

Many times during your trip, you will be confronted with your own power of choice. You may hold back this choice, so that you will keep your companion happy. The German philosopher Schopenhauer (1788–1860) wrote, 'We forfeit three-fourths of ourselves in order to be like other people.' If you choose to travel with your safe companion you will never know how much you miss, maybe only intuit it in vague, half-formed regrets. You will have chosen your comfort over your bliss and will be even less motivated to change your safe life back at home.

Aisha simply wouldn't have had the adventures with Sheila that she had had with Jane, such as travelling on a gondola in Venice at midnight or finding that unexpected flamenco dancing and singing in Madrid that connected up her cells with a rod of light. When Aisha and Jane returned home they carried on trying new things, learning belly dancing for example, and their life became brighter in every way.

2. FOLLOW YOUR INTUITION

....

> *Surrender is an openness and a willingness to receive*
> *Surrender is giving up control but not losing power*
> **Sondra Ray**

The second golden rule is no surprise. Follow your intuition. Follow your intuition. Follow your intuition. Go into your Higher Self (see Part 1, Chapter 1) and ask for guidance about whom to go with. But a word of warning, this means *your* intuition, rather than what other people say to you.

Most of us come from families and communities who would usually prefer you travel with someone they know. One example is the way groups of Australians huddle together. People say you'll be safer that way, and they'll worry less. Perhaps what they really mean is that *they* will feel better.

That other people will worry less may be true, but in the end they are not responsible for your growth, you are. And you cannot let other people hold you back if your intuition tells you to seek freedom in another place. Sure, travelling with others is cheaper and safer, but are those the values you really want to rule your life? Going with a companion, particularly someone of your culture, acts as an insulating barrier between you and the worlds you desire to discover. You will be less open to experience and so will inevitably experience less.

One of the unacknowledged goals of your family and community is for you to return and fit comfortably back into your old life, their life. Travelling with someone else makes you much more likely to do that, which is perhaps one reason why society puts so much pressure on you to do so. But that doesn't mean it's the right thing to do, as the following example shows.

Saul and Carol

People change and forget to tell each other
Lillian Hellman

Saul and Carol were together 24/7 on a very long trip without a break, causing great stress to their marriage. Before their big trip they spent about only four waking hours a day together, after they arrived home after their jobs. Because they had established a comfortable routine with drinks, dinner, housework and going out, they always thought they got on together very well. But travelling revealed all sorts of differences between them, like the way Saul thrived on pressure and new experiences, whereas Carol preferred things always to be the same. Their marriage didn't survive their journey; and, funnily enough, they both felt that it wouldn't before they set off. What a waste of a journey they could have enjoyed separately as a rite of passage.

From one perspective travel speeded up what would have happened anyway and made it possible for them both to move on rather than spending decades stuck in a marriage where they couldn't grow. Even if you get on well now, travelling this way forces you to change. You may well change in different ways, and almost certainly change at different paces. So that's why you must follow your intuition which knows better than you do who it's good for you to be around. And you must accept it may not be the person you expect.

3. TRAVEL WITH YOUR SOULMATE

All who joy would win
Must share it – Happiness was born a twin
George Gordon Byron

The third golden rule of travel is to go with your soulmate if you are blessed enough to have found yours. First of all you must recognise your soulmate, as the world is full of people who will say they are, when actually they are not. There are three certain guides to recognising your soulmate.

First of all, from somewhere within soulmates just *know* each other and feel they always have done. There is a deep familiarity which distinguishes the relationship from any other partnership. You have many things in common and have been led along similar paths, even before you meet, which was destined to happen. This is because your souls have agreed on a union in spirit before you were even born – hence a deep feeling of coming together, as if it were your essences meeting, not your personalities.

This is reflected in the second guide – and a fun one this – which is when a stunningly good physical relationship becomes better and better with time. You don't become bored or jaded, your souls are so close you continually spark off each other and *always* find each other attractive. Of course, this is if you are soulmates who are involved in a physical relationship, which isn't always possible or appropriate, but it's fabulous if it is.

The third guide is a mutual respect for each other and being eternally able to see each other's best qualities, even if you cannot always see your own. Hence you will have a desire to work out your issues and would sooner cut off your arm than refuse an honest conversation with your soulmate, for the huge motivating force is being with this incredible person.

When you are soulmates you need to cherish this union beyond all else, for it is truly more precious than gold, diamonds or rubies. Being together provides a quality of soft blissfulness that was missing from any other union you might have had or could have and there is nothing more you need or desire in this world. You will learn far more together as you continually help each other expand beyond your personal limitations to your combined greater good.

Soulmates go camping

What does the man who transient joy prefers?
What but prefers the bubbles to the stream?
Edward Young

Soulamates Antera and Omaran went camping on Mount Shasta, in California, where they read, swam and meditated. Everything came up, including a huge amount of anger from Omaran due to the unre-solved grief of his past. But their closeness to the mountain and the earth and their sense of connection to each other and beyond helped them let the emotions go. In so doing, they travelled beyond the bubbles into the stream.

Treasure your soulmate and travel with them if it feels right to do so. And stay with them, even when it is not easy. For the journey into your Higher Self is not pain-free, although you can make it far easier by choosing to let go; but the gift is the goldening of your centre and the rich reward of meaning. If you feel you need to step into a new dance in your ever-evolving relationship together, then travel with your soulmate.

Goldening yourself

Essentially man is not a slave either of himself or of the world;
but he is a lover. His freedom and fulfilment is in love, which is
another name for perfect comprehension
Rabindranath Tagore

We have looked at three golden rules of choosing your travelling companion before you set off on your trip. The first is to choose someone you want to become like, otherwise you will become like someone you do not wish to become like. Simple, eh! The second rule is to follow your intuition in making your choice, rather than relying on the advice of people around you. The third golden rule is to go with your soulmate if you are blessed enough to be with him or her. By following any of these rules you will become a true lover who will find far greater realms of freedom and fulfilment through your travelling companion. You will alchemise yourself and become true to your core of silver and gold.

Your travel companion must fit into one of these categories. If not, there is another way to find your travelling companion, to choose your own wonderful Higher Self. This is by no means second best – how could you be?

TRAVELLING WITH YOURSELF

....

> *Solitude is fine, but you need someone to tell you that solitude is fine*
> **Honoré de Balzac**

Travelling with yourself is something we all do – all the time. Every day in every way – think about it. Wherever you go you never leave yourself behind. It is time to reclaim your power and say you *choose* to travel with yourself, in much the same way some women choose to wear a ring on the fourth finger of their right hand to celebrate their ongoing commitment to their own growth. Travelling solo, you will be more vulnerable, a great precursor to opening yourself up to peak experiences.

Advantages of travelling alone

> *No one is free who is not alone*
> **Isabelle Eberhardt**

Setting off alone requires a lot of courage. Simply by doing it, you will be preparing yourself for the many changes you are about to allow in. The greatest advantage of travelling with yourself is that you are free to follow your *own* intuition, so following the first principle of travelling magically. It need not matter to you that your ideas sound crazy to others. You will be more likely to find yourself in odd places and situations, but are also far more open to them. You can experience more of the energy of the different places you are in, whether it is the Turkish towers of Crete at sunset, or sitting on rocks in the middle of a stream in the Australian bush.

You will meet far more people, interact with them on a far deeper level (one reason is you will be so isolated you will need to) and be far more likely to be taken to heart – with all that that means. You will make more and deeper connections than you otherwise would have made. You will create some fabulous moments for yourself and feel glad you're you, you're here, you're now. You will also learn the great lesson of self-responsibility as you realise, again and again, that you are the only one accountable for your actions.

You will learn anew that you are a creator. If you need a certain quality, and you have no one else to rely on but yourself, you will find it in yourself. You will draw it out of yourself simply because you have to – there is no alternative. Qualities such as independence, self-reliance and common sense will be of great service in your life, whatever you choose to do. Your goals will be far clearer too, I guarantee it. You have put yourself in the wonderful position of using your physical journey as a metaphor for your internal journey.

Disadvantages of travelling alone

It is easier to sail many thousands of miles through cold and storm and cannibals . . . than it is to explore the private sea, the Atlantic and Pacific Ocean of one's being alone
Henry David Thoreau

You need to be strong to avoid social censure. You may have a lot of negative reactions both before you go and when you're there, and this is often the case if you're a woman. People seem to find it hard to believe that you're travelling alone because you choose to. They think you may require company at all costs – particularly their company. They'll ask you why you're not married and, if you are married, why you are alone. You will need to learn to deflect those inquiries with patience and good humour.

One of the greatest disadvantages of travelling alone is that it can be lonely. It is also more expensive. You often pay the same for a hotel room whether it is a single or a double. Most countries are not as enlightened as New Zealand, where the hostels tend to charge by the person, not the room. Expenses such as taxi fares are usually the same, but there's no one to share the cost. Food is more expensive if you self-cater and you're alone. If you don't, you have the awkwardness of eating by yourself in restaurants, and in many countries it's still difficult for a woman on her own to do that. If you do, make sure you convey a sense that you have the right to choose to do so – it will help change the social stigma.

Nevertheless, in almost every country, the benefits in travelling alone outweigh the problems. The biggest advantage is that you will be open to making the greatest discovery of all. Yourself. What you will find is guaranteed to surprise, delight and amaze you.

INTO THE MAGIC

....

A fire and silver lifetime
Sabrina Dearborn

In this chapter we've seen the three golden rules about making a decision about who to travel with. Travel with someone you want to become like, follow your intuition and travel with your soulmate. Never forget to acknowledge your eternal travel companion, yourself. For remember, the first principle of travelling magically is being prepared to travel solo with your intuition as your travel guide. There are some excellent reasons for that, for you will be bestowing the gift of freedom upon yourself, the freedom to grow and expand into your Higher Self. The freedom to reconnect to your true source, your bright and beautiful soul.

One way in which you will be able to explore just how endlessly resourceful you are is to see how you could – if you had to – manage without money.

CHAPTER 12

What about money?

Do the thing and you will have the Power
Ralph Waldo Emerson

What to do about money is a question that remains with us for much of our life, and I chose the above quotation because we often use 'I don't have the money' as an excuse not to do things. I say 'Don't let it stop you.' For money is energy and our attitude to it determines what happens to our life and growth.

In this chapter we explore how it's possible to travel without money if you need to or want to, and how it can even be an advantage, on both practical and spiritual levels. Then we see how you can effortlessly save money before your trip by choosing the cheapest options for things you are paying for already. Another way of saving money is one that requires a little more effort – giving up your particular indulgence. But you are likely to need to do that anyway when you travel magically, so why not speed up the process a little? Then I give some tips for travelling with money, by looking at how you manage credit and debit cards, for example. Then we finish by looking at the advantages of budgeting, and at how it can give you more access to the local culture, the third principle of travelling magically. So money is transformed from an emotive and loaded subject to a pain-free opportunity.

TRAVELLING WITHOUT MONEY

....

Let go and let God
Catherine Ponder

You don't need money to do magic. Andrew, now a successful veter-narian, hitch-hiked across Australia with only A$2 of Australian money. If you don't hitch to your destination you will need money for the outward ticket and money for emergencies (although in emer-gencies it is even possible to do without money). By following your intuition, you will be in your right place, doing your right thing, and life has a way of taking care of the rest.

Practical advantages

Prosperity is a way of living and thinking, and not just money or things. Poverty is a way of living and not just a lack of money and things.
Eric Butterworth

There are many advantages to being without money. For example, you will not be seen as rich, even if you hail from a country which is considered rich. So you are not likely to be a victim of crime, and the local population is unlikely to feel resentful towards you. You will also meet people on a more genuine level. You will not be that rich tourist walking around in a bubble, herded from here to there, with no opportunity to interact with the locals. By travelling magically you will be on the ground and there will be no barriers between you and your environment. This will aid your magical trip, for you will have the time and the space to interact in a much more genuine way. According to certain research, travelling in the local manner makes you safer. Bruce Newsome, former lecturer on terrorism and security at Reading University, found that taking mainstream package holidays, staying in large hotels and travelling on Western-style tour buses is not so smart these days. By travelling magically and staying in local places, you are unlikely to be a target.

One of the main problems in travelling to many places now is the way you are perceived. For travelling is such a big industry, that people in the major tourist destinations are used to meeting people from other countries. They may be bored and just see you in terms of your money and what you can give them, rather than who you are. By arriving without money you are confounding their expectations. You are also ensuring you meet a wider range of locals. Many temples or ashrams will put you up for free, as will certain organisations; more about this in Part 2, Chapter 12, 'When do you accept hospitality?'. You can find out about alternative barter schemes such as LETS, as well of course as creating your own fine meetings and your own fine lessons through the power of your energy. Sometimes this is known as having spiritual power. Let's read on.

Spiritual advantages to being without money

> How much better is it to get wisdom than gold!
> Solomon

Being without money can be a huge positive, if you make it one. For there's always a lesson to be learned from your situation. It may be the one of trust, the one of true value, the one of letting go or any one of many others. Your vulnerability in being without money, as advocated by spiritual traditions all over the world, means your lesson can be learned much more quickly and thoroughly. In Hawaii I learned to be vulnerable, and in return I received the gift of sacred knowledge.

The rocky path to the sacred

> When you travel on your own you grow at such an accelerated rate it's alarming
> Laurie Gough

When I first went to the islands I was quite resentful about not having money. I'd received a scholarship that exactly covered the plane fare, but nothing else. I didn't even have a spare US$50 for emergencies, nor money for a tent, and so sometimes slept on the beaches without one. I found the islands very expensive and couldn't afford to hire a car to get around them – the method most people use, for on the outer islands there is very little public transport.

I was faced with two alternatives. I could either not follow my intuition, which was calling me to go in search of the ancient temples and the people with the mysteries, or I could hitch. I hitched. With each ride, I met someone with a lesson to teach me and the Hawaiian drivers led me to some amazing sacred discoveries I never could have made on my own with a hire car. My vulnerability, being alone on the road with a backpack and no place to stay, helped me to be perceived differently from other, richer folk and helped me to be entrusted with some sacred information.

So by following my intuition and making the most out of some rather difficult circumstances I received an extremely valuable gift, one I always endeavour to use appropriately. By 'chance' I had put myself in the position advocated by holy people the world over, moving around alone and impoverished and vulnerable. So not having money meant I was far more open to magical experiences, and of course, to learning valuable lessons.

However, if you would rather take things a bit more easily – who could blame you? – and travel with money, but don't have very much, then how you can save it?

SAVING MONEY BEFORE YOU GO

What are we worth when motionless is the question
Antoine de Saint-Exupery

Anyone with expenses can save money quite painlessly. In fact the tips in this section will help you at all times of your life, which makes this book worth it for that alone.

You need to look at how much you are paying out, and how you can lessen the amount. If you are on mains electricity, get a gadget which measures how much electricity each appliance uses – it will be a great motivation to use less. Then save on bills by switching to the cheapest and greenest provider of your service. Look at everything you spend money on and see how you can get it more cheaply and ethically. For example, buy your vegetables at the local market or join an organic box scheme, rather than going to a supermarket. Go to an optician for your sight test, then get your spectacles or contact lenses by mail order. Look for some 'vintage' clothes in second-hand shops instead of buying new ones. Put some effort into researching how to get things cheaply and you can save several thousand pounds a year. Remortgaging can save you many hundreds of pounds, as can questioning your bank charges and being prepared to switch your savings, maybe to a more ethical bank. There are books and websites to help you save money (see Resources).

The above tips are for the things you are spending money on already. But now is a great chance to choose again what to buy. Let your little luxuries go. You're going to have to give them up on your trip anyway, so why not do it before you go? You will be amazed at how fast you can save money if you are able to give up the coffees, the book-buying, the gadgets or whatever your particular indulgence is. Put the money towards your trip instead.

If you can't bear to give up your little indulgences yet, then explore ways of getting them more cheaply. If it's coffee, bring a thermos to work and save plastic cups as well as money. If it's books, borrow them from a library or buy a full-price book from a living author so they can receive the royalties. Look at ways of giving and getting all sorts of things for free on local websites such as freecycle.org. Divided into local communities, these sites list both what people no longer want and what they would like. Then people make arrangements independently of the website. No money changes hands. Freecycling saves resources, for example you are no longer buying a printer with all its associated manufacturing pollution, but getting one from someone who no longer needs it. Win, win. Then, when your needs outgrow it, you in turn pass it on for free. You can also recycle your unwanted items in your local communities. These kind of smart choices are not only good for you and the people concerned, they lead to a greener planet.

So you can, relatively easily, save enough money for you to last for quite a long time in many parts of the world. What happens now?

GOING WITH MONEY

....

> *Money is the intelligence of the universe*
> *A New Zealander*

How do you carry your money? Here are some suggestions:

✧ Bring two credit cards of different types.
✧ Bring a debit card too.
✧ If you spend a long time in one country, try a pre-payment card.
✧ Bring some cash in US$ and some in Euros for emergencies. Travellers' cheques can be a useful back-up.

TIPS FOR USING CREDIT AND DEBIT CARDS

....

✧ Get as high a credit limit as you can before you go.
✧ Get a Visa card and MasterCard (many countries favour one over the other, and you will have some insurance if one of them stops working).
✧ Make sure you know any PIN numbers.
✧ Copy down any telephone numbers you need to call in case of loss or theft.

WHEN DO YOU USE CREDIT OR DEBIT CARDS?

....

✧ If avoidable, don't use a credit card in a bank to get cash. There's usually a 2.75 per cent currency fee, a charge of 2 per cent for the amount withdrawn, interest charged from the time of withdrawal, and a higher rate of interest on cash withdrawals.
✧ If you use a debit card to withdraw cash you will pay a cash conversion fee of 2.75 per cent and a cash transaction charge of 1.5 per cent – cheaper than a credit card.
✧ If you use a debit card for day-to-day transactions be aware there is a retail conversion fee of 2.75 per cent and a retail transaction charge.
✧ If you use a British-based credit card to pay for a transaction in a shop you have automatic payment protection if the item you purchase is over £100 and under £30,000.

Therefore, it's smarter to use a credit card to pay for a transaction and to withdraw cash using a debit card or travellers' cheques.

PRE-PAYMENT CARD

An additional tip is to use a pre-payment card. These are linked to the Visa or MasterCard network, but can be loaded with cash at a time to suit you, or when the exchange rate is good. You access it using a chip and PIN number. You can check the balance online or by text and only spend what is on the card, and you can also lock the card online and unlock when you're ready to spend. I would recommend choosing one without monthly maintenance charges. There are usually limited transaction fees and exchange fees if you use it outside the currency zone it is programmed for.

BUDGETING

I could throw myself over that edge into what, what is out there, what is it that I am so afraid beyond this last safe step where I am now standing? It is only my own life I now realise.
Jamie Zeppa

There are many things in life we cannot control, but the amount of money we spend is one we can. The less money you spend each day, the longer you can stay away. If your budget is US$1,000 for example, and you spend US$200 a day you can stay for five days. If you spend US$10 a day you can stay for 100 days. You will be in a position to know where the work is and should have made some genuine contacts among the locals.

Spending less money can be a blessing in disguise, as you can really get to know the local culture. You will be staying in cheaper accommodation and travelling by local transport. Of course be careful not to exploit people, or take advantage of their good nature. There are rules about this in Part 2, Chapter 12, 'When do you accept hospitality?' and Chapter 22, 'When do you make love?' And you don't need money to have a good time – many of the best things in life are cheap or free. You can easily turn your perceived disadvantage – not having money – into an advantage.

Summing up

There is only one success: to be able to spend your life in your own way
Christopher Morley

In this chapter we've explored the advantages of being without money. It can help you to be safe, meet people on a more genuine level and also, by following your intuition (the first principle of travelling magically), learn your spiritual lessons more deeply and more quickly. But if you *do* choose to make your trip with money then we've seen easy ways of saving it, as well as smart ways of using it on your trip. We've also taken a quick look at the importance of budgeting and its advantage in helping you to live like the locals, thus following the third principle of travelling magically.

So whether you have the money or whether you don't, if it feels right – take off anyway. Do what you desire and you will have the power.

CHAPTER 13

What about your place?

Mind over matter
English proverb

Owning property, even renting property, may be an excuse given by many people not to travel. After all, how do you know it's going to be all right when you're away? You don't, that's just the point. What you are doing is making space for things to happen to you. You are not letting the things you own thwart your desire for experience. However, you can definitely follow some smart tips to make sure your property almost certainly is okay.

If you neither own nor rent then things are likely to be easier. If you're still living with your parents then you can just leave, and most housing cooperatives and similar associations have provisions that allow you to be away for six months or a year. Otherwise, the question will depend on whether you own or rent.

In this chapter I make suggestions for each category. Owning property is a bit more complicated and options include getting a friend or house-sitter to look after it, or renting it out when you are away. I give some practical tips for that. Owning property is a complex business, but putting some time into getting it organised for tenants now will mean you have far more freedom to do the things you really want to in the future.

IF YOU RENT

You could give up your place completely if you rent. After all, you may decide when you come back it's time for a change. Meanwhile you can put your possessions in storage and ask the Post Office to redirect your mail. Alternatively, if you want to keep your place and have been a good tenant, the landlord may allow you to sublet. In that case you will also be interested in the tenant-finding process further on.

IF YOU OWN

If you don't need the money or it's for a shorter trip you could leave your place empty, and ask your friends or family to keep an eye on it, or have a friend to stay. Sometimes people with money pay someone to look after their place for them when they're gone, in which case you need to check your house-sitter's references. Some people want to let their place even for a short trip, so they can have some money while they're away. In many parts of the world, having tenants will allow you to pay your mortgage and even give you money to live on. Make sure you inform your mortgage company first, and if they're not appreciative then switch mortgages – you may be able to get a better rate anyway (see the previous chapter).

Now I'll talk about ways to get good tenants. Finding one is not like picking a rare jewel on a mountaintop, although to hear people talk, you might think it is. It is more akin to a goldpanner finding gold in a river bed; tenants are there in quantity, if you know where to look and have the right equipment to find them. Of course you can ask a managing agent and pay them a percentage; alternatively, you can do it yourself, which is very viable as long as you follow some common-sense rules.

You need to begin by advertising in the right places, and then select the right tenant.

Advertising

> *Technology may make it easier to reach beauty but it has not*
> *simplified the process of possessing or appreciating it*
> **Alain de Botton**

When you advertise, try the Internet (don't worry if you're not comfortable with the Internet – places were rented out for a long time before it!), your local newsagent's windows and asking around. On the advertisement, include the following details:

✧ Describe your place as it is while highlighting its best features, such as that it is quiet or has a good view.
✧ If it's small some people won't mind. But say it and you won't waste time, theirs and yours.
✧ Make it clear whether rent includes utility costs or not, and other costs such as council tax.

If you're going on a long trip, it's best to include utility costs as you won't be around to pay the bill or to sort out any squabbles. Make the rent a reasonable one, remember you are looking for someone to tide you over (although that rent can ensure you live very nicely in certain countries, thank you, if your mortgage is not too high) and someone you can trust when you're away. Making a fortune out of your place should not be your priority.

Selecting (interviewing and your intuition)

> *Take your attention off the forms*
> *And focus on what's inside*
> **Rumi**

Interviewing is important in the process of selection, and I would suggest a preliminary interview by telephone. Ask people lots of questions, even intimate ones, to weed them out before they come to look at your place. An important one is 'Do you have a lover?' If so, 'How much time will the lover be spending there?' Will you, in effect, be renting it to more people than you think? If you don't agree on the terms, it's best to find out now.

When you meet your potential tenant or tenants, follow your instincts about whether they're trustworthy. After all they'll be living in your house among your possessions and talking to your neighbours.

If you don't trust them, don't rent to them, however suitable they may seem. Someone who wants the property too much may be suspicious, especially if they know you are going away. I would recommend not telling them you are going away yet, as it makes it less likely you'll get a tenant who is out to take advantage of you.

Of course your intuition may not be perfect at first, but make a record of what you thought and felt at different points in the interview and what happened later on, and learn from it in the future. Your intuition will soon become more refined and accurate. As with all things, it is a matter of learning from your mistakes. And you will be following a grand retinue of people who have rented out their property and travelled magically, some of whom are featured in this book.

TOP TIPS

- ✧ Make sure your place is prepared for renting, gas safety certificate completed, mortgage company informed and valuables put away.
- ✧ Get all rent in advance for a shorter trip (up to a couple of weeks).
- ✧ Confirm the tenant's identity by looking at documents, such as their passport, if they have one, birth certificate if they don't, and make a copy.
- ✧ Get photocopies of the last three months' bank statements, otherwise they could be on benefit without telling you.
- ✧ Tenants from certain countries will be unable to go on benefit. If they don't belong to a bank in your country, they may offer all the money in advance.
- ✧ Always get cash in advance for a deposit, and the first fortnight's rent in advance.
- ✧ Check all the utility meters, such as gas and electricity. Write the details down on a form, then sign and date it – and keep a copy for your records.
- ✧ Make sure you can check payments are being made from wherever you are.
- ✧ Put everything in writing, even if you are friends. You may wish to seek legal advice and have a properly drawn up tenancy agreement. Alternatively, you can download one from the Internet.
- ✧ Make it clear that the only people allowed to stay are the ones on the tenancy agreement, and that it will be checked.

✧ Don't automatically ban pets – a tenant with a well looked-after pet shows that they are capable of being caring and responsible, and that's the kind of person you want in your place.
✧ Be clear about potential points of disagreement such as smoking or overnight guests.

When you find the right tenant or tenants, ask a trusted friend or neighbour to keep an eye on things while you're away and, as an additional precaution, make sure they know how to contact you in case of emergency.

BEFORE YOU GO

The next stage of our evolution is to be free of our visible things. Then we shall become sublime forces in the universe
Ben Okri

✧ Leave your tenant(s) a folder with a list of people to contact if necessary, from a plumber to neighbours. You won't be there, so foresee every emergency.
✧ Lock your valuables away.
✧ Leave your financial details with someone you can trust.
✧ Cancel bank statements, and so on, that are sent through the post as they may be used for identity theft purposes.

Having followed these precautions, you should have someone in your place you can trust and who is not in a position to do too much damage. This will provide the dual purpose of someone looking after your place while you're away, and a steady income for your trip that you can access en route. Renting or owning property should certainly not be seen as a reason not to embark on your great adventure.

So we've seen ways in which you can give up your property, whether it is completely or to someone else. By moving on you're not only freeing your energy, you're helping someone else find their place in space. Remember your magical trip does need a certain amount of preparation, and the more things you've got the more preparation it needs. But it is so worth it. For by becoming free of your visible things you are giving yourself a priceless gift, the gift of freedom. That's how we become sublime forces in the universe.

CHAPTER 14

What do you do about the kids?

We must teach our children to dream with their eyes open
Harry Edwards

Having children can be used as a reason not to live your dream. That is a great shame, for your fulfilment helps them. If it feels right for you to travel, do consider taking them with you. Studies show that the best parent is one who is a healthy person. If you keep in touch with the generation of your soul as well as your offspring, you will be a healthier parent. You will show your children how it's possible to live your dream, and so you will encourage them to do the same in the best way possible, by example. You will be teaching them to dream with their eyes open.

Travelling with children is usually easier than people believe – but there are some common-sense rules to be followed. Of course if you have a difficult relationship with your children, don't expect it to become better just by the act of travelling. You may want to see a counsellor and work on issues, such as boundaries, first. Travelling magically intensifies what is already there, it does not provide a magic panacea, especially if you are not willing to do the inner work to change.

There are all sorts of myths about travelling with children. In this chapter we'll look at when to do so, whether to travel as a single parent or a family, and the importance of taking your own space when you do. We'll look at where to go and include issues such as education and language, as well as, crucially, when not to travel with your children – or your family. There might be times when it's best for you all to stay home, for example, and better to sort that out now than when on the road.

ADVANTAGES OF TRAVELLING WITH CHILDREN

....

Come, children dear, let us away! This way, this way!
Matthew Arnold

There are three big advantages to travelling with children. One is their ease at picking up a new language and culture, another is you can still go to many of the same places you would have gone to on your own. The third is that it might just inspire you to grab the future you really want, for you love them so much you want to show them the power of a different life.

Language and culture

Language is not simply how people speak, it is who they are
Craig Storti

There are many advantages to your child spending time in a different culture, such as exposure to a different language. This may be best learned at the toddler stage, when the child is already speaking their first language; but the child won't have too many problems at any time up until the age of eight or so. It's much easier than learning a language – with effort – as an adult.

Useful languages include Spanish and Indonesian, spoken by hundreds of millions of people, as well as Hindi – knowledge of this South Asian language gives much easier access to a range of related South Indian languages. Harder, but very useful languages include Mandarin Chinese, Japanese and Arabic. Or you may decide to expose your child to a smaller and endangered language you would love to help keep alive. In that case, if and when you leave the society, make sure you continue to speak it. You may receive visitors from the culture, or play games or sing in that language. Only about three hours a week is necessary to maintain fluency once it has been established – and it is well worth it, for the greater opportunities, as well as the flexibility it will offer your child. We live in a multi-cultural world, and such experiences are usually of great benefit for the young.

Don't worry about harming your child's first language skills.

Research shows that bilingual children do better at both languages, not just one. On the Isle of Skye in Britain, children have the chance to go to Gaelic schools or English schools. Although the two languages are very different, and family factors cannot be discounted, studies show children educated in Gaelic-medium do consistently better. They may have the chance to go to Britain's first Gaelic university, as well as access to a wider range of jobs, and access into the world of Gaelic poetry, literature, myth and song. Another language is a gift – why not give it to your child at an age when it is easily accepted?

Where do you go with children?

A man has no business to travel in foreign countries who cannot make up his mind to conform to their customs
John Murray

Your palette here is very wide – the globe. You can travel magically with your child just as you can on your own. If the idea of a 'family resort' in the Mediterranean or a child-friendly cottage in Cornwall leaves you cold – then don't do it. You shouldn't expect to suddenly change because you have children, you are still you. If you love mountaineering for example, that is too dangerous for your baby, then maybe you could go hiking in the mountains at a lower altitude with your baby along in a sling. You will be happy, and most babies are far more resilient than we give them credit for. But of course do take your child's needs into account too, and there is more about this in the latter part of the chapter, which concerns when *not* to travel with your children.

Go where you are inspired to go. I wouldn't hesitate to take a healthy baby to most undeveloped countries, for example. Most societies love children, and they will love you the more for having your child with you. Most people will still welcome you into their restaurants and homes, and most parts of the world are more child-friendly than the developed West. Children will also be exposed to new people, new languages and new ways of doing things that will stand them in good stead for the rest of their lives. Of course practise certain precautions to minimise risk of illness, and if you are going well off the beaten track then take a first-aid course – that's useful anyway. Go where you are happy and it is likely your child will be too, for your child does pick up your feelings, so make sure they are good ones.

Then your child will learn not to feel responsible for your unhappiness in your later years, and you will never need to make comments like 'you gave up your life when you had the kids'. Isn't taking off with the kids worth it for the gift of freedom it bestows on both you and your offspring?

Now we'll look at when to travel with your child.

WHEN TO TRAVEL WITH CHILDREN

I can retrace the first steps I took as a child and be stunned by the beauty of the islands. The trembling blue plane of the Pacific. The moss-covered cliffs and the cool rush of Manoa Falls with its ginger blossoms and high canopies filled with the sound of invisible birds.
Barack Obama

There are all sorts of times to travel with your loved ones, and you can create some fabulous memories for them. Usually it's easiest when the child is very young. As the child grows older, other factors such as the language and culture you are exposing him or her to come into play as well as what your child may be missing out on at home. This is particularly important for teenagers, who often need this time to grow away from their parents, rather than the enforced contact travelling creates. Thus, with the exception of the toddler stage, generally the younger the child, the easier the journey. But ultimately of course, the best time depends on what's right for you and your child.

The baby

Life is either an adventure or it is nothing
Helen Keller

It's possible to travel well, even with very young children. Babies are relatively easy, as they can be breastfeed, and need be less concerned about hygiene. Most airlines allow infants under two to travel at 10 per cent of the full price, and you may get priority seating. It's not usually worth bringing a buggy. If you use a sling, you won't have a cumbersome piece of luggage to worry about. You can also keep a closer eye on your offspring, and with a front sling they can look out on a whole new world. When they become overwhelmed, then you can turn it round and they can snuggle back into you.

You do need to avoid climatic extremes – babies are far happier being neither too hot nor too cold, although closeness to you, the parent, is always the most important thing. Remember too, they do have babies in other countries so you don't need to bring everything but the kitchen sink. Learn how to say your child's age in months in the language of the country you are going to, and you will find it easier to find a nappy that fits, or the correct size high chair in a restaurant, for example.

The toddler

> *The art of travel and perhaps of life is to know when to give way and when not to*
> *Freya Stark*

When a child reaches the toddler stage, then things become much more of a challenge. Your child is now beginning to develop his or her own autonomy, whilst still needing your constant care and attention. In addition, they are usually too big by this stage to carry in a sling. You need to keep a close eye on your little one, and provide child-friendly activities while still doing things that you enjoy – quite a balancing act. You also need to make sure your child isn't upsetting other people or animals. It is not acceptable to allow your child to bite or attack anything else, and if your child is having a tantrum, as toddlers so often do, then you will need to get your child away from the general public. As such, 'quiet places' such as museums and concerts may not be suitable for a toddler.

Obviously you should never leave your child alone when you are abroad, just as home. As a result, your own movement may be restricted for a few years, if you cannot find a trustworthy babysitter. But realise that your child will benefit from the prolonged contact with you (most children simply do not have the chance to spend 24 hours a day with their parent these days), and in most places it is quite easy to find trustworthy people to look after your child. In addition, you may be giving your child some other gifts, such as a new language or 'brothers' and 'sisters' from a different culture.

The young child

*There didn't seem to be any kind of future in front of me that I
wanted and could have*
Paul Scott

If you don't want to march into a predictable future then do consider
travel with your child. Once the toddler stage is over, it becomes
relatively easy. Up until the age of ten or so, they're usually delighted
to be in new surroundings, and relatively flexible. They are keen
to make new friends, and your young child may be a positive asset
– ensuring you meet many more people and have an even better
trip than you would otherwise. Do bring along a small bag of your
child's favourite toys and books, including ones about the area or
culture you are travelling to. Younger children can carry their own
daypack at least. Encourage them to carry their amusements in it
and to be responsible for packing their bigger bag. They may like to
fill it with exciting stories about other cultures and there are some
ideas in the Resources.

Remember reliable and experienced babysitters are in every nook
and cranny of the world, for bringing up children is a universal activity.
It can be a great opportunity to set up unofficial cultural exchanges,
for example, if you each have children of the same age. Your child and
the native child can learn about each other's language and culture, and
your child may gain access to local resources such as football in the
jungle or swimming in a waterhole.

The older child

*Reality can destroy the dream, why shouldn't the dream destroy
reality?*
George Moore

Older children are likely to have their own ideas and want their own
friends around them. From the age of 11 onwards I generally do not
recommend travelling with your child – they need this time to be able
to strike out away from you, not be forced to remain falsely dependent
on you in a new culture. And schooling becomes far more important
at that age, although there are alternatives such as home schooling
that I discuss later in the chapter.

Now, if you do want to take your child away, it's time to look at who he or she should travel with. There are two main choices here, travelling as a single parent (even if you are not one) or travelling as a family.

TRAVELLING AS A SINGLE PARENT

If a child is to keep alive his inborn sense of wonder without any such gifts from the fairies, he needs the companionship of at least one adult who can share it
Rachel Carson

People often travel as a single parent either when they have no choice, or with the agreement of a partner back home, who is maybe unable to get away but recognises the positive changes travelling is likely to bring to the family dynamic.

When do you go? Of course you should get on with your child or children. And, as with any venture, travelling is harder when there is more than one child involved; then you should make sure everyone fundamentally likes each other, and have strategies to cope with fights and so on. If not, counselling first to devise ways of coping might be a good idea. If your ex-partner is anxious, go to a less adventurous destination first for a shorter time, making sure your child keeps in touch exactly when you say they will. With phonecalls, emails and stories and gifts, then your partner is more likely to allow you to travel again with your offspring. Again, you may need to modify your trip to suit your ex, but you can still have some amazing experiences – and remember you can travel magically in just a weekend.

We shall see two examples of people who travelled alone with their children.

Dervla and Rachel

Reach high for stars lie hidden in your soul. Dream deep, for every dream precedes the goal
Pamela Vaull Starr

Dervla Murphy, a popular travel writer from Ireland, did not let the birth of her daughter Rachel curtail her adventures. For example, when Rachel was six they spent the winter in Baltistan in north-west Pakistan, which she wrote about in her book. Rachel coped very well; even if she could not climb all the mountains, she stated her needs and her mother adjusted their activities accordingly. They spent a memorable winter among the glittering peaks and friendly people of a different culture.

Daniel, an American travel writer, went with his children Kolya and Zoe on a five-month trip around the world. The trip marked a turning point for them all, after their mother had left.

Daniel, Zoe and Kolya

Nothing happens unless first a dream
Carl Sandburg

Kolya and Zoe, aged 13 and 9, went with their father Daniel on a five-month trip around the world from their home in the USA. Some people say it is harder travelling with more than one child, as you must weigh up competing sets of needs. Yet being together helped them bond and develop shared jokes, as well as giving the children new experiences, such as following orang-utans in Borneo and exploring lost temples in Cambodia. Daniel was at a difficult time in his life, being a new single parent and coping with the loss of his brother, and this trip marked a new closeness.

Alternatively, travelling as a family might be the right thing to do.

TRAVELLING AS A FAMILY

....

You white people are so strange. We think it is very primitive for
a child to have only two parents
Aboriginal elder

When everyone gets on, travelling as a family has many benefits. It provides lots of uninterrupted time together and you can try out new things. Geoff and Maureen Wheeler, the founders of the Lonely Planet travel series, have travelled extensively with their children. You build up a fund of memories, cooking dinner around the campfire or visiting museums around the world. Or you can be even more adventurous.

The Ridgways

What had we done to deserve those months in paradise? Now
I could understand the allure of cutting ties with home and
leading this gypsy life
Marie-Christine Ridgway

The Ridgway family left their adventure centre in north-west Scotland to travel around the world on their yacht. John, his wife Marie-Christine, their grown daughter Rebecca and younger adopted daughter Isso, aged 14, went all the way to Peru, the South Pacific and Antarctica over a period of 18 months. They had a wonderful time and their family unity was strengthened by the adventure. For their unity was already there.

A later trip found John and Marie-Christine raising money to save the albatross in a campaign that reached around the world. Their travels had made them very aware of their plight due to pollution and the use of long-haul fishing lines, which the albatross often mistakes for food, leading to an agonising death. So for this brave family, not only was travelling as a family the right thing to do, it inspired them to help others.

The next example is also a very positive one.

The Boutenkos

What if we had never hiked the Pacific Crest trail?
Victoria Boutenko

The Boutenkos, Victoria and Igor and their children emigrated to America from Russia, where they lived materially successful but unskilled lives. One day they walked from San Diego to Canada along the Pacific Crest Trail in the United States. It was a journey that changed their lives. They travelled simply, wearing Teva sandals, using garbage bags as raingear and eating raw food they found along the way. Then snowfall meant they were stuck in Ashland, Oregon for six weeks. They asked if anyone in town had work in return for a place to camp and were offered a job in a raw-food restaurant. Funnily enough, the owner had prayed for a raw-food chef the day before. The Boutenkos ended up settling there, 'We now live in the town of our dreams', and lead a much more satisfying life than their previous one in Denver. Likewise their family bond has only bene-fited from their trip. They followed their feelings and left their old life and are so glad they did.

The two previous examples show how wonderful travelling as a family can be, and how going away as a supportive unit can lead to everyone finding their greater good. Nothing would be worse than a fighting family stuck on a boat or on a long trail, so if you are one of these types of families please don't put your kids some-where where there are not the usual escape outlets, such as sport or friends. But let's assume that you all get on and are travelling together. It's still good to spend some time alone, good for you and good for those around you – for you are stronger when your spirit is replenished.

TAKE YOUR OWN SPACE

....

> *The surest and most reliable way to know whether you are*
> *following your intuition, is that whenever you do so, you feel*
> *more alive!*
> **Shakti Gawain**

However well you get on, it's important you get a bit of space from each other. If you take it in turns looking after the kids for example, then the other person can go off and explore. Maybe one of you will go away for a couple of days. This will balance getting in touch with yourself and your responsibility to your partner and children. Otherwise you will get your own space somehow, and if it is not offered you will unconsciously take it. For example, you may detach yourself when you are together. Jamie and Sue, one couple I met in Crete, were proud to say they spent all their time together, yet they appeared detached from each other, as well as their son, Karly. Taking your own space occasionally is preferable to this image of perfection. You don't need that, you need to be real. Spending time on your own without guilt helps. Check it's okay with your partner to look after the children and the amount of time you'll be away for, and go off and do your thing. Of course you'll also need to help in return.

So there are many times to go away with your children, when they are very young, when they are still young and when they are older. When you are a single parent or a family who gets on together. And of course, by keeping in touch with your dream, you are making it easier for those close to you to fulfil their dreams in the future without feeling guilty about you. For being a parent is expressing the ultimate love, letting go. Travelling magically helps you let go. And now it's time to look at when it's not a good idea to travel with your children.

WHEN NOT TO TRAVEL WITH YOUR CHILDREN

....

Circles, though small, are yet complete
On a monument to two children

There are a few times when it's best not to travel with your children. For example, if you need to bring your partner and you don't get on, your children have a medical condition or they will miss important schooling, or if the place you're going to is simply unsuitable. Don't worry about it and don't blame your kids – you brought them into the world after all. Know that the country you want to travel to won't run away and concentrate on being the best person you can be, until your children are grown and you can get away then.

When you don't get on

Teach us to create in sacredness
Noble thoughts of thy children
Wrought in thy image
Swami Yogananda

Don't travel with your partner and children when you don't get on. Travelling magically will magnify irreconcilable differences, not reduce them. Therapists say it is worse for children to be with two unhappy parents than with one, well-adjusted one. It is also not a good idea if you are in the throes of a messy divorce and separation. Running off and leaving a court case or custody battle behind, tempting as it may be, is not recommended. And of course don't abduct your child and run away with him or her – that is not travelling magically, and your child has a right to know both parents, not just you. After you've separated, if your partner agrees, you can use that trip as a bonding time for you and your children and a chance to know that you can get by without your partner.

Schooling

Als de maan vol is, schijnt zij overall
(When the moon is full, it shines everywhere)
Dutch proverb

It is inappropriate to travel with a child or children in certain circumstances, such as when they may have a medical condition that requires specialist treatment or when it is likely that their education will be adversely affected. So it's not wise to disrupt teenagers' secondary education by taking them to live on a desert island. It's far better for them to remain within the comfort zone of their own school and friends. They have enough adjustments to make to their changing body and thoughts without running around the world with their parents at a time when they need to forge their own way without their parents.

Of course with the availability of new technology, this situation is changing fast and there are popular alternatives such as home-schooling; some families manage successfully on yachts or in vans for example, which give a reasonable amount of stability for their children to learn (family environment allowing).

Unsuitable places

You are the bows from which your children, as living arrows, are sent forth
Kahlil Gibran

Unsuitable places for dependents include countries at war, or where there is not enough food and drink available. Generally it is your responsibility as parents to protect your children, while also exposing them to new things and experiences – a tricky balance. A child who hates deserts, for example, shouldn't be taken to one. Sure it's great to face your fears, but let your child do that in his or her own time, don't force it on them. Listen to what they say, because children also deserve to be valued for their intuition; just because they may only be a child in years does not mean they do not have knowledge. For example, a child who is empathic with animals shouldn't stay on a farm where he or she might pick up the animals' feelings about being killed. On the other hand they are likely to appreciate staying on a well-run animal sanctuary. You do have to take the characters of your children into account.

CONCLUSION

....

> *So the journey is over and I am back again where I started,*
> *richer by much experience and poorer by many exploded*
> *convictions*
> **Aldous Huxley**

Remember that children can be delightful and curious travelling companions, and as their carers your place is usually with them, not leaving them behind. Remember that they are beautiful beings, complete in themselves, and don't need to be 'changed', but, like all of us, can usually benefit from some exposure to other ways of doing things. It will almost certainly mean new friendships for them, and may even mean a new language or career. Make your decision to travel or not to travel with their best interests in mind, although do take your own into account too, both in choosing when to take off and where to go.

Don't make your decisions out of fear, and an automatic 'Oh, I couldn't possibly do that because of the children.' What sort of an example are you setting anyway?

CHAPTER 15

Travelling with your animal

'And an elephant, sir?' I enquired with diffidence
Mark Shand

Travelling with your animal means that you will see the world anew. There are two ways: bring your animal with you, or find your animal while you are away. Travelling with an animal, just like going with a child, opens you up to a smorgasbord of delights and a huge range of feeling.

In this chapter we shall look at options for travelling with your animal, at how to travel – including a secret tip for travelling through America – and at when to leave your animal behind. A beloved animal stops many people travelling, so we shall also explore options for care, as well as seeing how an animal can act as your guide. But first of all we need to hear from the animal – would she or he like to travel with you?

WOULD YOUR ANIMAL LIKE TO TRAVEL WITH YOU?

For love will not be drawne, but must be ledde
Edmund Spenser

How do you know whether it's a good idea to travel with your animal? How bonded are you? Does your animal make you feel better? Do you make your animal feel better? Does your animal come towards you or try to get away from you? If you are not sure whether your animal would enjoy travelling with you, try relaxing and asking him or her. When you sit quietly together, an answer or an image will float into your mind. You may need to practise for some days, but you will get answers from the source, and if you want any extra advice animal communication is becoming quite big these days (see Resources).

Receiving a 'no' in the animal communication exercise can happen in all sorts of ways. You might hear that word or another phrase in your head when you are sitting quietly with your animal. Alternatively, you may ask your animal to walk in one direction if he or she wants to travel with you – and the creature walks in the other. Or you may receive a 'feeling' that the animal would rather stay where he or she is. Trust that and move on to the end of the chapter.

How to travel with your animal

I need to live with the land and the elements. I want to hear the rain close by and see the birds when they sing
Spud Talbot-Ponsonby

If the answer is positive, there are an enormous amount of resources for travelling with your animal. However, they almost always refer to dogs. Paris is a city which is almost as friendly to dogs as to children. In Britain, Australia and New Zealand 'helper animals' only refer to dogs. This is a shame, for as wonderful as dogs are there are many other wonderful animals who make good travellers – and grand helpers. I give a couple of examples here of travelling with cats but the possibilities are limitless. Gerbils, parrots, horses – just like travelling with children, your animal will ensure you come into contact with a wide range of people, and you will have an immediate talking point. In general it is easier to travel with a child than with an animal – but that's simply due to the anthropomorphic (human-centred) nature of developed human societies. The further off the beaten track you go the easier it is to travel with an animal.

In travelling with a cat or dog there are only a few necessities to remember. You'll need some sort of a carry case for a cat or a dog. Even if you are driving, it is useful for getting in and out of the car – and provides a refuge for a nervous animal on a long car trip. You need bowls for food and water. You can get collapsible bowls for dogs, otherwise light is best, such as plastic – unless your animal will knock it over, then you need a heavier metal one. Keep the water bowl refilled with some of the water for your own use, and make sure you remember to bring food along – dried food is usually best, as it smells less, and can be repacked. A favourite treat or toy can be a good idea too, or a piece of clothing with your smell on it for reassurance. Bring some old newspaper for spillages, and you will want some litter if they don't have access to outside to do their business – and a scooper if they do.

Of course you do have to take notice of the wider society too. Geographer Yi Fu Tuan asked, why do we revere cats and dogs, yet kill pigs and sheep? It's all in the categories and they are *cultural*, not natural. We talk more about that in Part 2, Chapter 1, 'Culture shock'. In many parts of the world pigs are considered dirty and unclean, and opportunities for travelling with them are limited – I have a theory, though, that they would make excellent travelling companions, being intelligent, loyal and responsive, rather like dogs. Rory MacLean wrote a widely acclaimed travel book about his travels through Eastern Europe with his aunt – and her pig. As the categories are cultural, they are not hard to change – you just need to change your conscious and your subconscious minds.

If you do decide to widen your choice of animal companion abroad, you need to let go of your should nots, such as 'dogs like to travel, but cat's don't' in order to live your dream with your animal. Dr Jeffrey Masson, for example, wrote about how his cats love walking with him along the beach and through the rainforest, and how much he loves to walk with them. My cats enjoy travelling too; it gives a different feeling from going on my own, for going at their pace gives a new experience – whether it is noticing the cave in the woods they dash into or watching them as they scramble up a tree.

Of course, just like travelling with a child, you sometimes need to change what you are doing to take other needs into account. Also, your expression is important. If you are anxious then so will your animal be. Speak calmly in a reassuring voice and always choose a quiet environment if possible. If you are in a crowd of hysterical people, then your animal is likely to get upset. You will need to spend time with your animal – your animal may not want to be away from you, so make sure you stock up on food and drink that you will need before you travel – you may not be able to access a restaurant. You may end up spending more time outdoors than you otherwise would – for example, eating outside. No harm in that. If travelling with more than one animal, make sure they get on – a cat fight would be too much for you to cope with, on top of all the decisions you need to make about travel, and it would be hard to keep them separated while on the move. Sometimes homeopathic remedies help both you and your animal – there are specific ones for travel, and their use is covered in many insurance policies.

WAYS OF TRAVELLING WITH YOUR ANIMAL

What's essential for a road trip? A cat? I have one. Some Gucci slingbacks? I have some
Clare de Vries

There are as many ways to travel with your animal as there are to travel without. In this section we'll look at a few of them: flying, trains, wheels and walking, as well as looking at a secret tip for travelling anywhere with your animal in America, providing you fall into a certain category.

Flying

It is illegal to fly with your animal accompanying you in the aircraft cabin in or out of Britain, Australia and New Zealand. Your animal is classified as living cargo and put in the hold with your baggage. This is not as safe as is commonly thought. Conditions are such that airlines refuse to accept liability for death or injury. Even though the hold is temperature controlled, the loading and unloading areas are not; in addition your animal will be affected by flight delays and you will be unable to reach him or her. There have been many stories about people waiting for their animal at the other end of the flight – only for the animal to come out dead. For these reasons I do not recommend flying with animals unless they're in the cabin with you.

This is possible in many countries, such as on most American airlines and some others, and also between France and America. But you need to check with your airline, and book your flight in advance as the number of animals is restricted on each flight. The carrier should fit under your seat. Additionally, sometimes it's possible to go with your animal on a military flight, especially if you have military contacts – or you could hire a private jet, funds permitting.

But if you feel it's easier for the animal to go in the hold than to travel with you another way, then there are a few guidelines to follow. Book yourself on the same flight and make sure it's direct. Avoid going in very hot or very cold weather, as conditions will be worse for your pet. Make sure there is plenty of water available – if it starts off in ice form you will avoid spilling. Buy two of the recommended carriers, one in a larger size. Put your animal inside the smaller one and then put this inside the larger carrier. It will cost more, as you'll have to pay for the amount of space the larger carrier takes up, but it's worth it, as it should ensure that when your animal is thrown around by the baggage handlers, the door will not spring open and your animal escape. It also means your animal is less likely to be crushed by larger, heavier baggage.

Train

Trains are usually fairly good ways of travelling with companion animals. In Britain they no longer have to go in the guard's van, and can go next to you. This is good news for a dog who can move around at will. Again, be sensitive to other passengers and if they obviously don't like animals don't sit near them – they certainly won't sit near you and your animal. But, equally, other people will be drawn to you and it provides a great talking point.

Generally, when booking it's worth enquiring if there are private facilities or carriages on a train where you can be with your animal. Journeys of more than a few hours are not suitable for a cat in a carrier – they cannot walk around or defecate and many refuse to eat or drink. For that reason, if it's a long journey by train, I would recommend taking a sleeper, where you have your own cubicle and can let the cat out. Some carriers do make it harder, for example, on the night train between London and Scotland, you and your animal are not allowed in a second-class sleeper and must go in first class and then pay a substantial amount of extra money for cleaning, so travelling with your animal results in a tripling of the usual cost. And it will usually be necessary to take a taxi at either end, rather than subject your already stressed animal to the vagaries of public transport.

Wheels

Going by wheels has many advantages when travelling with animals and children. You are in your own self-contained capsule, which means the animal is in a familiar environment, even though an ever-changing world passes outside. If possible, bigger vehicles often work better than smaller ones – for example, if you have cooking and sleeping facilities in them, then you won't have the problem of finding food and accommodation with your animal. If you are concerned about the environmental aspect, then many big vehicles can be converted to bio-diesel fuel. Your vehicle should have air-conditioning and curtains or screens or you'll need to avoid hot environments and areas – most animals such as cats or dogs don't sweat the way we do and, effectively, temperatures are several degrees higher for them. Be sure to leave a window very slightly open so that air can blow in, but not so far that the animal could possibly get out. And many animals can get out of smaller spaces than you could dream of.

Clare's road trip with her cat

Whatever I am, woman, cat or lotus, the same god breathes in every body. You and I together are a single creation
The Egyptian Book of the Dead

Claudius, London socialite Clare's beloved 19-year-old Burmese cat, accompanied her on a road trip around the USA, which she wrote about in her book *I & Claudius*. They flew to New York from Paris, where the elegant grey Claudius strolled around the cabin of the plane, and then Clare bought a car over there. Claudius sat on the front seat next to her as she travelled from New York to Los Angeles, stayed in her motel room, visited restaurants, hot springs and the beach, where he settled down on a sand dune next to her, sitting quietly and coming when called. In fact the elderly Claudius even hiked the Grand Canyon with her. It is likely that Clare's tender perception of her cat as part of her led to this amazing bond, and a journey she will always remember.

If it's a long journey you may wish to let a well-behaved animal out in the vehicle (mine usually find a spot and quickly settle down), but have a carrier or lead ready for emergencies. For example, if stuck in a traffic jam and you are with a companion, one of you might want to take your animal and go for a walk – to help both of you de-stress. If the animal becomes obviously distressed, defecating, vomiting or howling, you will need to stop for a bit – not having a tight schedule in travelling magically is to your advantage here. If possible go outside with your animal and let them reground themselves on the earth – this will help a lot. Don't leave your animal in the vehicle alone, but if you are travelling with a companion take it in turns to get out. If not, bring your animal with you, or if this is not allowed, why not practise things like eating and going to the toilet outside?

Most carriers don't allow travel by bus, so I will leave that out here, and you are likely to have more problems if you hitch with an animal, so I wouldn't necessarily recommend this until more people's attitudes change. In general, going by wheels, providing a few common-sense guidelines are followed, can be a great way of getting places with your animal.

The last method we'll look at is the simplest – walking.

Walking

Most animals love to walk, and if you love to walk too, then why not join forces? Spud strode across Scotland with her dog, horse and young son – and that after a diagnosis of cancer. They camped in fields, and got permission from local farmers to keep the horse with them overnight. Previously she had walked around the coast of Britain with her dog. There are no limits except those which you perceive. So if you love your animal why not bring him or her with you? It will help you get in touch with nature – and your own soul.

Going with your companion

So there are many ways of treading the silver path with your animal. In fact, I discovered a little known American law while researching this book. The definition of a companion animal is not restricted to dogs, nor does the animal have to be trained in a recognised facility. Rather it is unlawful for any State in the Union to ban your animal from travelling with you by any means – whether train, aeroplane or walking – if your animal is a 'helper' animal and you have some kind of disability which can be physical or mental. Therefore a quadriplegic can have his helper monkey with him on the aeroplane, or your autistic son can bring his beloved rabbit who helps him socialise into the restaurant on the train. You – or a companion – need to have the ability to express why the animal is helping you, but the animal cannot, by law, be asked to travel away from you. The definition of helper animal should be changed in Britain, Australia and New Zealand too, and that would open the way for many more vulnerable people to be able to travel with their animal, which would in turn widen their world.

WHERE TO STAY WITH YOUR ANIMAL

If people can learn to live with bears, there's a good possibility that we can learn to live with other people, in short to live with ourselves
Jill Fredston

Often it's best to stay in self-contained accommodation, with facilities for your animal, such as a fenced garden. Easy access to it is ideal, such as a cat-flap for a cat or small dog, and it's good if the accommodation owner doesn't mind you leaving the animal inside if you go out without him or her. In very rural areas you may even be able to leave the door open so that a big dog has free access between inside and the fenced outside. Some places encourage animals, and there are many directories – but generally it's still hard to get a hotel or motel room where a cat can go outside. Clare travelled round America with her cat staying in motels and not letting the owners know. But this isn't ideal, for not only are you not being honest, but it means your animal has no independent access to outside – the advantage of many self-catering cottages. Even though fences tend to keep in dogs rather than cats, my experience has shown me, contrary to old wives' tales, that a well cared for cat will come home – even if they may be really excited at first by the new environment.

Alternatively you could bring your own vehicle with you, as we saw in the last section, or try a boat – in which case give your animal a trial run first and see how they get on. With a bigger animal such as a horse or donkey you could try asking a local farmer for a field overnight or contact a local animal charity in advance in the area you're going to. Even if they don't deal with your particular animal they are likely to be animal-friendly, and know other people in the area who might help you. If more people do this, doubtless suitable facilities will spring up. Most campsites and many self-catering cottages allow dogs, few at this point allow other animals. Hopefully this will all change with education. Of course don't forget 'wild camping', an animal is usually very tuned into this and will help you to be too – just check the nearby environment for predators.

WHEN NOT TO TRAVEL WITH YOUR ANIMAL

Care for animals as you care for your good friends
A peace message

Don't travel with your animal when you receive a 'no' answer in the animal communication exercise, if you are not very fond of him or her, if your animal is not well, if you can't arrange suitable care or when bureaucracy makes things too hard.

Let's look at bureaucracy. With quarantine restrictions, residents of many countries may not find it worth taking their animal abroad. For example, you cannot legally get your animals in and out of Britain, Australia or New Zealand without a period of quarantine or the pet passport. The whole process is such a palaver maybe you should just travel with your animal in your country. In addition, the 'pet passport' requires microchipping your animal, and the rabies vaccine has been associated with the shortening of life. So it's your choice, but be aware. If you are an American or a Canadian things are different – then it is much easier to take your animal in and out of your country. But if you are from the Commonwealth and wish to travel abroad with your animal, then it's not easy.

Not everyone is bonded to their animals, and you shouldn't travel with your animal to make your journey 'new' or 'exciting' or have something to talk about, or use it as a way to meet girls or guys. Travelling with an animal is a lot of extra work, from arranging access to water and food, to finding a safe and suitable place to stay the night. Your animal's needs must be taken into account, and if you are too selfish to do that, and would rather go out partying when you are abroad or eat in nice restaurants, then leave your animal behind. Naturally, you must be very careful about travelling with a 'dangerous' and hostile animal anywhere – what exactly are you trying to express anyway?

If your animal is not well, many animals feel better in the familiarity of the home environment. However, if you get a positive answer to the travelling question from your animal, you may be led to the very trip which would make a difference.

HOME CARE

There's no place like home
English proverb

Arranging suitable care while you are away can be a challenge. Usually the animal's own home is better than a boarding facility, unless your animal is extrovert and you know the facility is a good one. There are several things to take into account if you leave your animal in your home. You should not leave your animal with someone who doesn't like you, even if they're a family member, because they may take their dislike of you out on the animal. So leave your animal with a trusted carer or find a petsitter. In this case check references and make sure you meet the person first and have a written contract, including what to do in an emergency and who shall be contactable. But good references are not enough, a lot depends on the empathy of the person for animals, including your own.

On a longer trip, you may wish to go away for a weekend first on a 'trial run' and see how the sitter gets on with your animal. Check your animal's reactions to the sitter carefully when you get home and have a 'de-briefing' session. If the animal doesn't appear to like the sitter, there is a reason. Some people leave a hidden webcam on the trial run, and some sitters with problems that they take out on the animal have been caught this way. Alternatively, you may wish a friend or someone who loves animals to stay in your home for free. Arrangements can be negotiated between the two of you. Again, follow your own intuition – and always get written references and check them. Ask how the referee knows the sitter and check that, so you can know they're not just a friend.

PET INSURANCE

....

Take care of the sense and the sounds will take care of themselves
Lewis Carroll

Pet insurance is a good idea whether you bring your animal with you or whether you don't. Unlike human insurance in many countries, it is almost certainly worth it, because of the high cost of treating your animal. Even older or unvaccinated animals can be insured, as can 'exotic' or agricultural animals. It's usually cheaper to insure crossbreeds than pedigrees, for they tend to be stronger. Pet insurance means that your pet is more likely to survive an accident or illness; vets normally give a wider range of options to those with insurance, and the small monthly premium will provide peace of mind for you and the person who looks after your animals. There would be no hard decisions to make, for example, if an accident happens that requires expensive surgery. In addition, many providers cover complementary medicine.

You can choose from many different policies, but unlike other things, it's best to stick with the same one for the life of your pet – because if you switch or stop and start then pre-existing conditions will not be covered. Compare policies carefully and try and pay a straight excess, rather than a calculation on a percentage basis, as veterinary bills soon add up. A policy with a yearly limit per condition is better than a policy with a financial limit per condition – for that may mean a long-standing illness is no longer viable to treat. Some policies will even pay for you to come home if your pet has an accident, or for a petsitter while you are in hospital. If you have many animals check out farmers' insurance – it may work out cheaper. As for any deal, it is usually possible to negotiate a discount.

FINDING AN ANIMAL ABROAD

....

Heb je geen paard gebruik dan een ezel
(If you don't have a horse, go by donkey)
Dutch proverb

Finding an animal when you have reached your destination provides another option. Christopher Rush travelled with a donkey around the

Pyrenees on a journey in memory of his late wife, treading a journey Robert Louis Stevenson had done before him. Mark Shand travelled with an elephant, Tara, across India, and began to love her and all elephants – and later set up a foundation. So you never know where your journey with a companion animal will take you.

Pack animals are best bought within a country. If you hire an animal, make sure it is well treated. If it is not, you will be contributing to the problem. An exception is if you spend a long period of time together and are in a position to make a difference, for example if you go hiking with your animal for several weeks. Most countries don't have ethical policies for treating their animals, although there are organisations you can report abuses to (see Resources). If an animal is being badly treated, don't give money to the owner to improve conditions, try and find another home instead. If you become fond of your animal, of course, an option is buying him or her, but you may need to find a good home. In my experience this is not difficult to do. The act of kindness itself opens up new roads, and you will gain the help you need.

Ffyona's dog

The shortest answer is doing
English proverb

Ffyona Campbell is famous, often unjustly, for many things, not least of which is walking across the world as a young woman. In the book *The Whole Story* she described the way she rescued Boy from the pound on the day he was due to die and took him with her on her walk. She touchingly describes his exuberance on first reaching the outdoors after his incarceration, 'there's nothing quite so wonderful as watching a dog pelting around on the grass in the sunshine after nine days locked in a cage'. It was good for Ffyona to have the protection of a companion and good for Boy to be alive and outside and loved. When Ffyona needed to find a home for him she easily found a good one from a truck driver she hitch-hiked with.

So please don't let your worries about passing an animal on stop you from taking care of him or her. Remember you *will* be helped, especially when you ask for it (see Part 2, Chapter 8, 'Three qualities for true expansion').

Unless you go to Antarctica, where all foreign animals are banned, and there are no native mammals except seals, you will meet animals everywhere you go. Then you can try to forge a connection. If you do so, then your animal may remember you when you return, even years later. If you decide to leave your animal behind and you are missing him or her, try volunteering at a local animal shelter or feeding animals when you are abroad. It is often possible to find animals to look after abroad, whether this is feeding stray animals or visiting a centre for the type of animal you like. By taking care of the animals, you are taking care of your own Higher Self, for we are all connected.

YOUR ANIMAL, YOUR GUIDE

I often thought I'd been looking all over for a guide and yet here was one right beside me and he was more loyal and more brave than any human I'd ever met
Ffyona Campbell

This is a little-discussed benefit of travelling with your animal. If you allow yourself to be guided by your animal, rather than control him or her too tightly, you will open yourself up to all sorts of adventures. In addition, you will be close to the 'First Nations' of the world, all of whom see animals as guides. Yes, all of them. A new concept for the developed West – but actually not really new, for the Druids and other peoples also saw animals as spirit guides. As they do in New Guinea, in Latin America, in the Arctic, in the islands of the South Seas, in Native America – in fact everywhere. Interesting, eh? Many peoples do perceive animals as a kind of overlighting guide, containing the qualities of the creature in its highest development, an aspect of our Higher Self.

Perhaps that's one reason why my anthropological studies have led me to conclude that indigenous people tend to treat animals in ways that are more aligned to spirit than we do in the West. For example, animals usually have names, and their spirit is honoured. Philip Pullman's 'His Dark Materials' trilogy, in which Lyra knows that her daemon Pantalaimon is an integral part of her, provides a fictional example. In Hawaii animal spirit guides are said to live in the higher, brighter realms around us, the realms that we reach through opening to our Higher Self – which we can do through the animal if we choose.

Your animal may be your guide along the road of silver in more ways than one. You may notice animals and follow one down a mysterious trail, the way I did in Tikal – see Part 2, Chapter 16, 'Opening to the mystical'. You may simply open your heart and perceive them differently. Many Hawaiians say that your animal acts as your '*aumakua*, your guide to your Higher Self. Even if you cannot be with your animal this trip, you can call on him or her for help.

Your animal and you

Come my friends,
'Tis not too late to seek a new world
Alfred Tennyson

So we've seen some examples of travelling with your animal, and thought about when not to as well. We have also widened our definition of animals to encompass animals as guides. Of course children can be our guides too, for example when children come in with the knowledge their parents need. The parents then have to get past their categories such as 'he or she is only a child' to accept it. It's exactly the same with animals. Allow the possibility that animals are your amazing friends who will show you a new world – and you will find one.

Now it's time to view some more practical guidance – what to prepare for a safe trip.

CHAPTER 16

Preparing for a safe trip

Wanfu xinfang
(May endless blessings embrace your affairs)
Chinese blessing

Some things need to be discussed to help you prepare for a safe trip, as hassle-free as possible. Your passport, visas, vaccinations and other medicine and insurance all need to be considered, as do other issues of safety, such as how you'll keep your valuables safe and even a secret resource. Then, in the following chapter we'll look at what else you take.

Your passport and any relevant visas are essential items when you travel abroad. Embassies can tell you visa requirements and who needs them and who doesn't, and many embassies also have checklists of things to consider before you depart (see Resources). Meanwhile, check your passport.

PASSPORTS
....

Over the last few years, passport regulations have changed enormously. Check yours has at least a year left before expiry, and is suitable for the country you're going to, as certain countries now require biometric passports. Make sure you leave enough time to get one – it can take months now in Britain.

If you have dual nationality, make sure you travel to a country on the appropriate passport. For example, if you hold dual Australian and Indonesian nationality and get into trouble in East Timor, the

Australian embassy can't help you unless you travelled to the country on that passport.

VISAS

⬦ Make sure you know before you go which countries you need a visa for.

⬦ Don't rely on what people tell you, check with a country's embassy.

⬦ Do you need to get a visa in advance (before you go to a country) or can you get it at the border? Again, check with the embassy.

⬦ If you want to go to a restricted area of a country and you can only get the permit abroad, then make sure you do so first.

⬦ Don't pay an agency to get the visas for you, unless you're cash-rich, time-poor.

⬦ Take spare passport photographs with you in case you need them for extra visas, permits and so on when you're away.

MEDICAL NOTES

Before you travel, medical decisions can broadly be divided into two types. The first concerns vaccinations and anti-malarial medications that need to be started before you arrive in a place to be effective. The second concerns medicines such as antibiotics or homeopathic remedies you may wish to bring with you.

Vaccinations

When you go to a tropical area you will often be recommended to get vaccinated against diseases prevalent there, and if so, you should start planning in advance.

Find out which vaccinations you need by contacting a specialised service. Don't expect your local doctor to know, it's not part of his or her training. Check with your country's specialist hospitals, as these are usually cheaper and more reliable than agencies. Then get your vaccinations from your neighbourhood doctor, in which case you must order them in advance as they will not be normally kept in the surgery. If you order them to be delivered to your GP's surgery, make sure you write the instructions down exactly. Before you are given them, double check the dosage and timing with the doctor or nurse on site and compare it to your written instructions. Don't be afraid to speak up if it differs, and insist it's checked. If you are time-poor, a specialised service will usually vaccinate you on the spot, although some vaccinations require a wait between each dose.

Alternatively, you may read up on vaccinations (see Resources) and decide they are not worth the risk to your health. You decide.

Anti-malarial medications

Courses need to be started a week before you arrive in a malarial area. Confirm with a specialised service that you are getting the right type for the area that you are visiting. Strains of malaria vary according to area, as does the type of medicine used against them, so you do need to check. Anti-malarial medications can also usually be ordered more cheaply through your GP, and remember to allow plenty of time for them to arrive.

Alternatively, you may decide to make sure all exposed areas of your body are covered when the mosquitoes are active, and guard against malaria by not giving them the chance to bite you. Additionally if you avoid low-lying watery areas on still nights, and go to places where the wind is strong, such as out on a boat, or up a mountain, you are very unlikely to encounter mosquitoes.

Preventative medicine

It may be worth getting these medicines in advance if you know you are going to areas where there is no doctor. Your GP is only likely to prescribe them to you if he or she is convinced you will use them responsibly. You may want to consider the following medicines:

Co-amoxiclav is a good general antibiotic. It's effective against most soft tissue infections (boils, wounds) and respiratory infections, but avoid if you are allergic to penicillin.
Clarithromycin is an antibiotic for chest infections, particularly for bacterial chest infections contracted in non-Western societies.
Ciprofloxacin Quinolone is an antibiotic for gastro-intestinal infections. It won't treat amoebic dysentery.

Over-the-counter medicines

Loperamide is an over-the-counter anti-diarrhoea medication which blocks the immediate symptoms – useful if you're about to go on a long bus journey.

Rescue remedy For magical travel I would recommend the liquid form of the Bach flower medicines called Rescue Remedy. It is great for emergencies – and for sudden shock, whether from sunburn or the culture. It really works, even if you don't believe in it.

Multi-vitamin Your daily multi-vitamin should include 500mg of Vitamin C as you lose it through exposure to unfamiliar toxins, as happens when you reach a new environment. Menstruating women should make sure they choose one with at least 24mg of iron in it too.

Be sure you know about the symptoms the medicines are designed to treat before you go, so you can recognise an attack. Don't carry them in your hand luggage, and make sure they are easily accessible in case you need them. Be aware that if you take them out of their original containers (for reasons of space and lightness) there may be situations where you need to prove what they are, so it's often worth keeping your prescription or your receipt among your valuables. Also be aware that if you are going to areas where there are local doctors, it may be an advantage going to them if you get sick as they will know the local diseases.

Many travellers choose to travel without any preventative medicines at all, and rely on their body's own ability to recuperate.

The next thing to become familiar with is insurance.

INSURANCE

Fire is winter's fruit
Arabic proverb

Today there's a choice of many insurance companies. Several of them even specialise in student and 'gap year' travel. Insurance is harder to get if you are a senior or suffer from a pre-existing medical condition. A list of some organisations that will help can be found in the Resources section. You do need to declare any pre-existing medical conditions or your policy will be invalid.

Some things to bear in mind when looking for insurance are:

- ✧ Get the right type for your trip. If you're going away on several short journeys, get an annual multi-trip insurance. If you're departing on a longer trip make sure it covers you for the amount of time you're planning to be away for, and that you can extend it if you need to.
- ✧ Are there any extras you may need, such as winter-sports coverage?
- ✧ It's worth getting a policy that repatriates you to your homeland in case of medical emergency.
- ✧ Become familiar with terms and conditions. For example, if you need a police report to claim baggage loss, make sure you get one.
- ✧ Check that you're covered for countries you're going to (your coverage may be withdrawn if your government issues a warning that travel to that country is unsafe).
- ✧ Most insurance policies don't cover items of additional value such as laptops and mobile phones.

It's also worth checking whether you need insurance. For example, if you are a European citizen travelling around most of Europe, then your medical care is included (apart from a small excess), providing you get the EHIC card before you go. Therefore you only need baggage insurance, which may be provided by another policy (such as your household insurance), or your baggage might not be valuable enough to justify it. Of course, insurance does cover you against other things such as transport delays, but generally such incidents aren't too serious for the flexible magical traveller; they may even be learning opportunities.

Some people decide they don't need insurance as they have learned to trust their intuition, for example, whether it's safe to leave their luggage in a particular hotel room, or drink water from a river. Of course, your sensibility plays a huge part in whether you get robbed, as does whether you follow some basic safety tips, such as those below.

Safety tips

- ✧ Find creative ways to hide your possessions. For example, you can put some money in an elastic bandage around your knee (you can buy it from a chemist) or a hidden pocket in your trousers.
- ✧ Keep track of bigger valuables, such as when your bag is on a bus or a train, by putting a padlock with a long chain around them and attaching it to an immovable object.
- ✧ If you spend time in the water, get a waterproof pouch on a string for your valuables (for example, from a dive shop) so you can keep them with you.
- ✧ Don't advertise where you're from. Put as little information on your luggage tag as you can – your last name, initial and country is sufficient. Do not include your address, so no one will try to burgle your place while you are away.
- ✧ Don't bring a weapon. You are likely to have problems crossing borders and it can easily be used against you.
- ✧ Don't drink alcohol (increasingly insurance policies don't cover you if you're drunk).
- ✧ Remember, ultimately, your best safety is in your mental attitude. Indeed it's your 'secret weapon'. Your attitude needs to be positive and uncompromising. If it isn't yet, well travelling magically will give you plenty of situations to develop it.

The value of resourcefulness

Things going wrong gives you the chance to show self-reliance, and isn't the assertion of self-reliance one of the chief objectives of independent travel?
Philip Glazebrook

I once met a self-defence teacher on a ferry in Greece, who told me, as we disembarked on the low brown island the boat was docking at, that attitude was more important than physical skills. For example, a weapon is less important than the ability to think on your feet. Let's see an example:

'Crazy Simone'

We must travel in the direction of our fear
Sir John Berryman

Simone lives in New York and loves to travel by metro, even late at night. She doesn't want her freedom to be restricted by worrying about 'crazy people'. She has a great method for dealing with them when she gets approached – she pretends to be crazy and shouts and hollers and swears. She has memorised bits of the Bible and some-times quotes them. Simone even quite enjoys it – and any potential aggressor quickly backs off.

Simone, despite her pretend craziness, was working on the level of an underlying spiritual truth. Changing the mind is usually easier than changing the action. Therefore, she felt quite safe having the ability to change someone's mind – even without a weapon.

CONCLUSION

There is only one journey. Going inside yourself
Rainer Maria Rilke

Safety issues are important, and doing your preparation in advance means you have less reason to worry on your trip. You will have organised your passport and visa situation by going to the most repu-table sources and likewise you have found excellent sources for your medical situation. Additionally, you are covered by the appropriate insurance for your trip – or have taken a responsible decision that you don't need it. You have also experimented with safety issues and know that your inner resourcefulness will help you reach the true source of knowledge – yourself.

Now it's time to move on to the next chapter – what else to bring.

CHAPTER 17

What do you take?

Angels fly because they take themselves lightly
Anonymous

Travel is the world's biggest industry, and if you visit a travel shop or website, the amount of goods on offer is overwhelming. But most of them aren't necessary. The fact is we travelled successfully for many, many centuries before these articles were invented. Some things such as a heavy metal travel thermos are actually *less* practical than the common plastic one. Magical travellers tread with a light footstep across the world.

In this chapter we look at what you do need to bring. Obviously this depends on the sort of trip you're going to make, as well as how long you're going for, while leaving room for some flexibility. We'll start off by looking at the type of bag you select, then at clothing and some other essential items. We explore the need for bringing gifts, and I make a few suggestions. Some things are better bought at your destination, and others you can do without altogether.

We also look at what you *don't* need to bring. For example, technology, as sometimes we use it to fill up our time, even when we're away. On a magical trip we need to give ourselves the time and space to grow. Thus by exploring what is essential we'll see how our magical journey can act as a vehicle to help us leave our old baggage behind. Then we can truly learn to travel light.

YOUR BAGGAGE

....

> On a long journey even a straw weighs heavily
> **Spanish proverb**

When travelling magically you'll need to be able to manage your baggage yourself (now there's a metaphor), so take just one big bag and make it as light as possible. Choose between a wheelie bag and a backpack as suitcases are too impractical for magical travel.

Wheelie bags

A wheelie bag works well on most surfaces, except steps or cobbles or mountain paths. A wheelie bag is a good idea for the urban environment, the more settled traveller or if you don't want to carry the weight of your own luggage. It looks smarter than a backpack and it's easier to find your stored things. For example, you can put your nice items of clothing on a light clothes hanger, then hang it up immediately when you get to your room. To keep it smart you can even wrap it in an old dry-cleaning bag when you travel. With practice you'll soon pick up many tips and tricks.

Backpacks

For more off-road travel and camping, you will need a backpack. Make sure your pack is very comfortable. I've had a wonderful green backpack for the last 15 years. It's now coming to the end of its life, but we share a lot of memories. On one trip I walked the West Coast Trail in Canada, carrying gear almost as heavy as me. It was a hard 70 miles, as it was over pretty rough terrain, yet, exhausted and injured though I was, I still liked it at the end of the week – that's what a pack should be like. Go to a shop selling a number of different packs and try each one on filled with weights. Also, practise standing up from a crouching position (something you'll frequently have to do), taking it on and off and walking around. You'll soon discover which is the most comfortable. Buy this one, even if it's the most expensive. The extra price is well worth it.

Many people advocate rolling things up, or packing them in separate bags, which I've never found a particularly useful practice, although you might. As ever with packing though, make sure heavy items go at the bottom and lighter ones at the top. Utilise the pockets and try and know what goes where – for example, keep your vitamins in a particular pocket so you can access them if necessary. Many travellers swear by a liner either within the backpack or on top of it, to stop your things getting wet or stolen. If you're stuck, a large plastic rubbish bag will also do the job.

Now we'll look at what to put in your bag. We'll start with your clothes.

CLOTHING

Adornment is never anything except a reflection of the heart
Coco Chanel

Select your clothing carefully. Remember, you don't need to buy clothing especially for travel, in most cases your normal clothes are fine. In general go for comfort a lot more than you would back home, for you'll be spending far longer in the clothes and shoes you choose. Avoid clothes which need ironing as you may be away from electricity, although if you have access to a bathroom and a hot shower you can hang up a set to 'steam clean' effortlessly. Take care of what you choose.

Of course you can also express yourself through your clothes, but even younger people are better off with classic rather than trendy styles. Your clothes are probably trendy only in your home country and may look ridiculous when you wear them in another. Also, it's probably better to avoid slogans (they may cause offence) and patterns, which can appear loud and garish – keep things classic. Many travel writers recommend coordinating only two or three colours in your clothing. You'll look smarter if you get clothes in toning colours (if you're not sure what goes together and suits you, go to an image consultant). Of course don't forget your favourite colour. Make sure you take some items of clothing in it on your trip, it will effortlessly raise your vibration.

Finally, remember magical travel is about who you are, as Coco Chanel so beautifully put it, *not* what you have. You don't need your society's style to be beautiful, whether it is blonde hair and fake tan in the West or body paint in New Guinea. You are beautiful simply because you are. By leaving your usual accoutrements behind and taking off into your dream you'll be proving that to yourself. For nothing is more attractive than the bright eyes and glowing countenance of someone who knows who they truly are.

Clothing for men and women

✧ Swimming costume (if you like swimming)
✧ Underwear
✧ Baggy T-shirts, which are comfortable in a hot climate and can be used as underwear and nightwear
✧ Light, not tight, trousers
✧ Long-sleeved cotton top for modesty and to keep insects off you
✧ Loose fleece or sweatshirt
✧ Baggy tracksuit pants
✧ Outdoor jacket – its type and material will depend on the climate you're going to
✧ Comfortable shoes or trainers (you will be walking a lot)
✧ Socks (cotton for a hot climate, wool for a cold climate or hiking)
✧ Nice pair of dress shoes, lighter than leather (see Resources)
✧ Shirt – one which doesn't need ironing is useful for social occasions
✧ Lightweight suit in a dark colour which doesn't need ironing (men only)
✧ Light shoes such as crocs, which you can wear in the water and when walking in the rain, and which also work as slippers
✧ Hat – choose a folding cotton one for hot or rainy climates, a woollen or fleece one for cold climates
✧ Cashmere jumper, which is light, smart and doesn't need ironing
✧ Sarong, which can be used as an item of clothing, a towel, table-cloth or blanket
✧ Make sure you have one or two items of clothing in which you'll look very good in photos, so you can be reminded of your great times.

The above items are useful for many situations, such as walking around town or country, going to the beach or even out dancing. Your one smart outfit can be worn on occasions such as crossing borders, going out to dinner or on unexpected occasions. And because your clothes match each other you can look reasonably smart with very little effort on your part, which local people often appreciate – the 'hippy look' still hasn't hit many out-of-the-way places. It will be obvious you don't have many clothes with you – but that's an advantage for it will help you fit in better.

As for women, well, we need a whole list to ourselves, as there are many times when it's appropriate to wear feminine attire, such as a long dress, in local cultures, which will almost certainly be more traditional. It's also more important for women to dress modestly, due to the way people may perceive us if we don't. Enjoy the feeling of lightness you gain by not having many clothes with you.

Clothing for women

- ✧ Long floaty skirt. This is fabulous for modesty, as well as being cool and useful for visiting certain sacred places.
- ✧ Scarf. This works for covering your head, again useful for visiting sacred places, keeping insects away and also acts as a shawl.
- ✧ Dress. Choose one that is slightly form-fitting, below the knee and feminine (flowers are good on summer dresses) and doesn't need ironing.
- ✧ Tights are very light and useful for warmth.
- ✧ A ring that looks like a wedding ring, even if you're not married. It will save you hassle in certain situations.
- ✧ Bras. If you are travelling in hot conditions, bring cotton rather than nylon. Generally avoid lace, as it is less practical, and underwiring, which makes it harder for energy to move around your body.
- ✧ Leggings. These keep you warm and you can wear them under a long skirt or trousers.
- ✧ Nice light silk tops. These are great because you can wear them under your outer clothes for warmth, they weigh almost nothing and are smart enough to be used as outerwear when going out.

It's getting easier to buy items made from fairly traded goods and organic cotton and it is definitely worth you doing that if possible. It's a win-win situation, for example cruelty-free vegan dress shoes are lighter than leather, easier to keep clean and nowadays appear in some great styles and colours. You will be helping to raise your vibration, as well as helping the planet.

Now we'll glance at what else you are likely to need. This is a basic list, which will alter depending on the climate and your activity. Most of the items below do more than one job. For example, your daypack can also be your hand luggage on an aeroplane. Solid shampoo can do the same job as soap, and your sleeping bag can provide a handy underblanket to lie on top of, or bagged, a cushion to sit on as you wait for public transport, as well as sheathing you in its warmth while you are sleeping. Magical travel is all about being creative with what you've got.

MORE ESSENTIAL ITEMS

> *Simplicity is making the journey of this life with just baggage enough*
> **Charles Dudley Warner**

Essentials for your trip:

- ✧ Water bottle (with string to hang around your neck or attachment for your waist)
- ✧ Lightweight thermos flask for hot drinks
- ✧ Daypack for excursions
- ✧ Sponge bag – one with a hook to hang it up with is good for many bathrooms
- ✧ Neck pouch (for keeping valuables on you)
- ✧ Folding bag for extra items
- ✧ Earplugs, as many countries are very noisy
- ✧ Light journal and a few cheap pens for recording your experiences
- ✧ Toothbrush, toothpaste – buy travel sizes for a shorter trip
- ✧ Shampoo – buy a solid block, as it's lighter
- ✧ Soap for washing yourself and your clothes
- ✧ Nail clippers
- ✧ Comb
- ✧ Padlock and chain for locking your bag to a rail in public transport or providing security for your hotel room

✧ Torch
✧ Plastic bags for your washing, dividing your items, shopping and so on
✧ Light alarm clock
✧ Small plastic document folder
✧ Sleeping bag, which is useful for dirty ho(s)tel beds and covering yourself against biting insects, as well as being nice to snuggle into
✧ Silk inner bag which adds enormous warmth for very little weight, and can be used as a 'sleeping sheet' in hot climates
✧ Plant-based wipes
✧ Liquid form of Rescue Remedy
✧ Spare glasses or contact lenses (if you wear them)
✧ Guidebook to your destination
✧ Dictionary
✧ Sanitary protection for women. Disposable towels are handy for emergencies, but both washable towels and Mooncups are better for the planet – as well as being much less for you to carry. I do not recommend tampons for magical travel, as they 'plug up' your energy – which is the last thing you need.

Do bring along at least one treat for yourself. It may be a favourite book or crystal, a hot water bottle, a totem or a collection of favourite photographs. Bring something to help you recentre when times get tough. Finally, bring objects from home to give to people you meet on your trip. For many locals will prefer things from your country, rather than their own.

Gifts

As we prepare for the journey, do not forget the gift
Joseph Dispenza

Do take gifts. Many cultures, whether it is the Kwakiutl of Canada, the Trobrianders of New Guinea or the Polynesians of the Marquesas work on the principle of gift-giving. Gift-giving is also important in Western cultures, not just at Christmas, or when it's someone's birthday. For example, we bring a gift when we go to someone's house for dinner or when we go to stay with someone. You will get these invitations abroad too, and it would be great if you brought something from your home country. Things you can take that are easy to carry and unbreakable include:

✧ Toy mascots of your country, such as a kiwi from New Zealand or a kangaroo from Australia
✧ Photographs (a picture is worth a thousand words) of you and your family, and the place you live
✧ A packaged foodstuff that represents your country, such as Earl Grey tea if you're English
✧ Collectable items, such as your country's stamps.

So we've come to the end of the list of what we need. KISS – Keep It Simple Stupid. Remember that you can do without most items or find them when you are there. Sometimes people get put off by the amount of items they are told they need to travel, and don't set off at all. That is a great shame, for probably none of these items are indispensable. If you don't have something then take off anyway. You'll be allowing in new energies, and who knows, you might find that very item.

THE IMPORTANCE OF FLEXIBILITY

> *Ka pu te ruha, ka hao te rangatahi*
> *(When the old net is worn out and cast aside, the new net is put into use)*
> **Maori proverb**

The best rule for travelling magically is to bring as little as possible, trusting that you'll find whatever you need along the way. For example, I was making a salad one balmy evening in my favourite youth hostel in the Pacific, the one near the university in Honolulu run by the Akau family. I was in the kitchen near the open-air tables with their sentinel palm trees and overhanging bougainvillea blossoms. I thought some olive oil would be nice, but didn't have any. At that moment, a tall Italian lady called Katarina came up and called out 'Does anyone want any olive oil? I have some.' I took it and we became friends.

In other circumstances, you might be surprised to find something that works just as well, or better, than the thing you thought you needed. For example, it's best to wait until you arrive to buy items like moisturiser, and you might find a wonderful local one such as the aromatic Monoi oil of Tahiti, which traditionally consists of coconut oil and the fragrant tiare (gardenia) flowers. Or you can even make your own from fresh food. Buy insect repellent, if you use it, at your destination for it will be suitable for the local conditions. And don't forget the local clothes. For example, in Muslim countries women should wear local outfits, such as a *shalwar kameez* (the Punjabi tunic, trousers and scarf which cover the body) or even a *burkha* (the long black cloak which completely covers your body and face). Well, it will save you from some attention from men. Be aware of the provenance of the clothing you buy. I talk more about the ethics of shopping for clothes in Part 2, Chapter 10, 'Spending your money'. Through your personal choices you can easily help to create a new reality for yourself and the world.

And now it's time to look at the things we need to leave behind.

WHAT NOT TO BRING

> *A fine woman can do without fine clothes*
> **Steele**

Letting go and being spontaneous, following the second principle of magical travel, is the route to your greater good. You will be surprised at how much you can do without. What does this say about what we think we need? Well, basically we need to question our conditioning, that says 'this must be that way' or 'that should be that way.' None of it's true.

Things you think you need but don't:

- ✧ Laptop computer (unless you are a professional writer)
- ✧ Expensive photography gear (unless you are a professional photographer)
- ✧ Personal music system
- ✧ Mobile phone
- ✧ Toilet paper (do what the locals do)
- ✧ Sexy clothes (you are enough)
- ✧ Hair-dryer (so is your hair)

- ❖ Shorts, unless you are on a beach holiday. They give offence in many countries
- ❖ Jeans, which are heavy to carry, awkward to dry and mark you out as a Westerner
- ❖ Expensive jewellery (except a wedding ring if you're married)
- ❖ Watch – your alarm clock will do the job if you need the time
- ❖ Unpackaged foodstuffs or seeds across borders, which may be confiscated when you travel across borders
- ❖ Baseball cap or anything habitually associated with your country of origin.

Several items in the list above are technological ones. Let's look at the importance of not bringing them with you.

Unhook yourself from technology

Leave now while you can. Be free of this impossible place,
this rigorous land . . . where the journey towards perfection is
continued without any hope of ever arriving. Find joy! Live your
life! Make your mistakes!
Ben Okri

The twenty-first century is full of distraction. New technology offers constant contact, but has created a culture of shallowness. People are no longer encouraged to discover their inner core and find out what really motivates them. Indeed they don't have much time and space for it in the race for ever-better. But you are leaving that race now, at least for a while, and so make sure you leave it properly. Don't spoil it by bringing any twenty-first-century addictions with you in the form of new technology.

Travelling magically enables you to tune into a higher frequency. To do that you must lose your familiar one. Leave behind your laptop; there was life without it for most of humanity's evolution and you can manage just fine now. Leave behind your personal music player. There will be music almost everywhere you go and bringing your familiar noise provides an insulating cocoon which is likely to disturb your neighbours. An expensive camera is usually a liability. Unless you are a serious photographer, the quality of photos from disposable cameras is so good now, you might want to bring one instead or use a cheap digital.

You will be less paranoid about losing it, and using such a camera will not mark you out as a potential victim of a crime. 'Forget' your mobile phone. It's great to be without your familiar ringtones and callers.

It is no coincidence that depression is found for the first time in cultures when films are introduced, because suddenly a gap between the ideal (on screen) and the reality (the watcher's daily life) appears. Whenever you bring technology with you (with the sole exception of a camera which is more representational) you recreate that gap. For example, at a backpackers' hostel in Los Angeles many travellers spent time checking their email from home on their wireless connections instead of connecting with the other travellers right there, right now.

Jettison the familiar and create depth by going within. To do that you must leave the sea of the majority and plunge forth – without your headphones. Remember you chose to be away to have some wonderful experiences. So really be away. Don't let another virtual world bring you down from your cloud. Create a new world. Be brave and unhook yourself.

But what if you really can't bear to be without your technology?

> *You are living in a new path*
> **Sitting Bull, Sioux**

If you can't bear a holiday without access to the Internet, then bring your laptop along rather than miss out on your magical trip altogether. If you do bring it, there are some excellent solar chargers, which save you messing around with cords and plugs. Some of them work as backpacks, so you can effortlessly recharge your computer while leaving it inside.

Be sure to spend some time away from your laptop, even if only for a few days, and set time aside every day to interact with people, rather than your computer, to help your familiar shell be penetrated. And of course do choose websites and resources on your computer that pull you towards your greater good, rather than away from it, such as computer simulations of violence or horror DVDs. I write more about that process in Part 2, Chapter 20, 'Keeping in touch'. Everything you do, even the websites you surf *is* significant and does have an effect. So make every choice you make count.

LEAVING YOUR BAGGAGE BEHIND

....

*It is not what you carry in your case, but what you carry in your
mind that spoils a holiday*
Rabbi Lionel Blue's mother

By leaving many of your usual things behind, you are helping yourself
fly. For it's much easier to travel into the airy realms of the Higher
Self if you are not weighed down by your old baggage. It's one reason
why people feel better on holiday – they are away from many of the
familiar objects and memories. Taking off with the minimum amount
of things, as I advocate here, is wonderful preparation for following
your heart. Wonderful preparation for going, and growing, into the
magic.

But, of course, there's one more aspect we need to view: Rabbi Lionel
Blue's mother's statement that it's what you carry in your mind that
spoils a holiday. How true. The sunny judgements of our conscious
mind, and the mooning emotions of our subconscious mind, will
ruin any experience if we let them. But luckily we always have the
choice. For just as we choose carefully which items we bring with us,
so we can also choose what remains in our mind.

We explore the process of integrating our mind throughout this
book. There are many methods, such as walking your talk, dealing
with change, taking rest or going to sacred places. You are likely to get
the opportunity to use several of them in your magical travels. What
a gift. For our journey into the light is the most important one of all.
By rising up into the rainbow radiance of our Higher Self, we create a
world where *everything* is magic, not just our travels. For the magic is
in our mind. And when you know how to bring yourself back to light,
then you will effortlessly create a magical life.

In the meantime, travelling light means we are starting off our trip
on the right foot.

CHAPTER 18

Clean up your life before you go

You can run but you can't hide
Sara Scott Simonsen

Cleaning up your life is the most important part of the preparation for travelling, yet I've not seen it talked about in a travel book before. The rationale is straightforward: what we do in one part of our lives affects every other part. If you leave unfinished business behind, it *will* affect your trip. Travelling magically is not an escape, and can never be an escape. Quite the opposite, travelling magically brings you face-to-face with many uninvited and unwelcome parts of yourself that you will have to acknowledge. Your problems will always catch up with you, whether you go hundreds or thousands of miles away. You can run, but you can't hide.

This chapter explores the importance of letting go, and how to do it. We have already seen examples of losing your baggage in previous chapters on organising your money, renting your house and what to bring. Now we'll look more deeply at the things we bring. For we create with all of our minds and the more baggage we remove from our subconscious mind, the more aligned we will be to our Higher Self. We look at this on two levels – removing objects in a process called de-cluttering, and moving on from people who no longer resonate with our highest good. It will then be much easier to follow our guiding star. Thus we complete our most essential preparation and are ready to take off into the magic.

THE IMPORTANCE OF LETTING GO

....

Out beyond the land we know
Lie the seeds of earth's rich flow
Rima Morrell

Your subconscious mind doesn't want to change. It really enjoys the familiar habits and emotions. Therefore you need to help it along. You've already made a brilliant and brave decision to go on your journey. This chapter shows how you can make your journey much, much better.

We need to let go on a number of levels, including the material and emotional. For they are inextricably bound, and doing one helps the other. When you're feeling stuck, clear out a cupboard – you will feel better. When you're feeling really stuck you may want to have a quick session from a professional who deals with these kinds of issues, whether they specialise in the material such as de-cluttering, or emotional such as helping you let go of somebody. Some even help you rearrange your space on a physical and psychic level – for example, through principles of feng shui, the Chinese science of space-clearing. Whatever method you choose, I'd caution against having a series of sessions at this stage; go on your trip first to get your energy moving, you will need fewer sessions when you return. If you don't feel able to get rid of anything don't worry – you may well have a 'second wind' when you get home. Many people respond to a period of travel by feeling motivated to jettison some material possessions.

To let go on the material level examine your things and decide if you really want them. If you don't, pass them on to someone who does. You can do this for money, selling your goods and chattels through eBay or a garage sale, or give them to charity or your local community. You will have fewer possessions to worry about when you're away, avoid high storage charges, and the vacuum you create will leave you more open to new experiences.

If it's right for you to let go of material objects, it will help you emotionally. Objects hold the energy of people who gave them to you, so if you want to let go of the person, then let the object go. On your trip you will bring in new things which also need to be carefully selected, as we see in Section 2, Chapter 10, 'Spending your money'. Whether you are intending to leave for a weekend or a lifetime, you will get far more out of your trip by dealing with this stuff before you go.

FAMILY AND RELATIONSHIP ISSUES

We are all in the gutter but some of us are looking at the stars
Oscar Wilde

We all have family and relationship issues. Therapists tell us that problems with one often spring out of the other. Try and talk about things that have been bothering you. If talking about a problem is not encouraged where you are, at least write about it to yourself. The important thing is that you do something – anything – to clarify it. Try and work out your role now rather than on your trip.

Consider who you don't want to keep in touch with, then you are free to consider the most important thing of all – your own growth. Don't keep in contact with people you do not like. If someone gives you a feeling of heaviness, create lightness. By freeing yourself you are freeing him or her. Everyone benefits.

Don't keep in touch with your exes, unless you have some sort of ongoing commitment to each other, such as custody of children or animals. Truly growing means encouraging others not to feel needless pain. If you are allowing someone to send you lots of devoted emails talking about how much he or she is missing you and you are smugly going about your trip thinking you're doing the right thing, beware. Some soft words of letting go, so that your guy or girl can move on and find someone else, are needed here. For it will help you, in turn, create from your Higher Self, not from your ego. That will give a much better result.

Don't, for goodness sake, travel with a lover you know is wrong for you, and don't take up the offer to meet somewhere along the way 'just for a quick holiday'. He or she may mean a lot more than that and try to use that opportunity to manipulate you into coming back unchanged. That happened to Scott when his girlfriend, Annie, met him in Indonesia. He didn't want to hurt Annie's feelings by saying no. But Annie's feelings were hurt a lot more when they broke up a while later. And who is to say what amazing girls Scott missed meeting along the way? And what he missed learning? It is infinitely healthier to use this opportunity to be alone. Doing so seeds your future reality. You will learn that there is not only one right person for you in the whole wide world, and you *can* be happy again.

Often our emotions stop us growing into the magic of who we really are. The following example shows how we must vanquish them to grow into our essential self. We must let go, even when it's painful, even when we don't know why. I had to break off a relationship before my first trip to New Zealand. Had I not done so, I would not have been open to reaching a magical world and could not be writing this now. Doing so opened me up to a range of experiences I would never have believed possible. But I did not know that, as far as I was concerned the magic was with my guy. Have you ever felt this way?

My own experience – leaving love behind

There was the Door to which I found no Key
There was the Veil through which I might not see
Some talk awhile of Me and Thee
There seem'd – and then no more of Thee and Me
The Rubaiyat of Omar Khayyam

The timing of my break-up was atrocious, but intuition takes little notice of what we think we want. I was very sick with a tropical disease and had to give up everything, including my Anthropology course at Cambridge. I had a boyfriend there for eighteen months, a scientist called Andrew, who looked after me and whom I loved very much. So why did I break up with him? Only because of a feeling. Leaving was incredibly hard. I knew that I would experience utter despair on the other side of the world without him. And I did. Lying in our bed hugging him, in his brown pyjamas, for the last time was exquisite pain. Yet I left England and I left him.

When I arrived in Australia nothing quite worked out, not even the weather – 'Sunny Sydney' did not live up to its name that summer. I remember sitting in Bondi one afternoon, drinking jasmine tea and missing Andrew desperately. Then, on my flight to New Zealand I glimpsed a pink and shining land below and felt a deep sense of peace I had never known. All I knew was that I felt it and was glad. The beauty and calm of the land seemed to cloak me and keep me safe. Then, my intuition told me I had to lose touch with Andrew completely for the next six months. Reluctantly I told him by letter, knowing it would irrevocably change our relationship.

Then the deep magic began. I had heard about a healer. When I met him my body sparkled with light. If you'd told me that before I would have sniffed and snuffed, but it felt so right. By following the simple exercises he gave me, similar to the ones I share in this book, I became much healthier and realised that I was the creator of my reality. I met several guys called Andrew (funny how those names follow us) and fell in love with one. Although he didn't have some of the qualities of the first Andrew, he had other ones. We spent time together in Wanaka on the South Island, where he showed me how to appreciate a world of resounding beauty. He'd suddenly say 'I'll bake some scones and we'll go and eat them by the lake.' We'd savour fresh scones at a glacial lake circled by white-topped mountains where the air rang like crystal and the sunset turned the water blood-red. The light was part of us.

Getting healthier, 'wholer', meant a relationship where I didn't have the old problems, meant memories so bright they always shine in the back of my mind, and I can access them whenever I need to. Most remarkably of all, I realised that magic was not in another person, it was in everything. So my happiness would never again be dependent on someone else. By letting go and feeling my way through the most agonising experience of my life, I gained everything – a world of meaning, a world of wonder.

Again, I had no idea that any of this would happen, or even could happen. But the decision to finish with Andrew in England before I left, rather than knowing I should but delaying it, opened me up to every one of those new experiences. Not only that, he moved on to new relationships and a brilliant career in academia and business. The other Andrew and I learned to 'feel' our feelings – even when it was difficult – and we moved through them and the world became even more beautiful. Fifteen years later he was to call our time in New Zealand 'a tremendous life-changing journey' and together with his subsequent marriage and kids, 'the best experiences of his life so far'. Your Higher Self will not only show you the right thing to do for you – it will also be right for the other person as well as anyone you are subsequently drawn to. That is the power and glory of your Higher Self.

Following guidance

··

Who can contain the soul? Every star of the sky calls him
Rabindranath Tagore

My experience is not so unusual for we all have the little voice deep inside or a shining angel above, or an animal on our shoulder (however you want to conceptualise it), to guide us. Your guidance tells you when to go, when to stop and what to do – all you have to do is respond. By following your shiny Higher Self you will know when you have to finish a relationship, change your job or do whatever you need to do.

All the stars in the sky emit light, but you particularly respond to your guiding star. The courage to follow it is all you will ever need. For once you know how to set sail towards the star that you are, your life will magically open. It is as though your star is suspended above a hidden island, often invisible among the glowing clouds or glimmering mists. By following the signs, you will reach your hidden island of paradise. Then you can create a bright new land, with a beach of pink sand, as if you were in a painting by Gauguin. Then you can learn how to link it to the land you have left behind. That is the secret to true homecoming, the source of all our joy, which we shall explore in the final part, 'Coming home again'.

And in the meantime, the lesson is, 'clean up your act' before you go. You will be making room for experiences beyond your very dreamings, at the other end of the sunrise. And now – be gone.

PART 2

When you're there

The world is so full of wonderful things. We should all be as happy as kings
Robert Louis Stevenson

CHAPTER 1

Culture shock

*Every man takes the limits of his own field of vision for
the limits of the world*
Schopenhauer

Congratulations! You've made it. You have been longing for, praying
for, saving for, this trip. Now you are finally here. Everything is new
and everything is great and you just can't get enough of it. You have
never seen elephants in the street before, or people eating their food
from leaves, or women with rings round their necks or men wearing
skirts. Wherever you go, you are assailed by new experiences.

Travelling magically outside your country means you learn about
other cultures and civilisations. In this time of global change, we all
need to become citizens of our earth, not just of our race, religion and
country. In the process your mind will expand, and you will embrace
new things, new ways of thought. You will be giving our troubled
world what she really needs: tolerance, respect and the willingness to
let go of outmoded concepts, whether they are general such as 'the
world is a dangerous place' or particular, for example, 'I don't deserve
to have time to enjoy myself'. Never underestimate your own importance. A wider, brighter world is a wonderful thing, but the process of
opening your consciousness does not usually occur without a hitch.
That hitch can be called culture shock.

In this chapter we will look at how different the world can be. I am
reminded of the saying, 'the past is a foreign country. They do things
differently there'. Then we will see how adjustment begins as soon
as you arrive in a country, and at some examples of culture shock.

To adjust successfully you need to let in elements of a foreign belief system. This is of great benefit, for you and the planet. For culture shock is good for you – it shakes you out of your normal ways of doing things – new situations demand new reactions. Making these adjustments helps you to become a healthier being, one who has the courage to embrace a new way of life. But that does not mean everything will be easy from now on as your 'field of vision' is about to be challenged and changed, as are the limits of your world.

One thing you will have had to cope with to get to your country, is crossing a border. Here is some guidance.

BORDER CROSSINGS

> *Then felt I like some watcher of the skies*
> *When a new planet swims into his ken*
> **John Keats**

The rise of both surveillance and terrorism has meant that people are more suspicious than they used to be, particularly ones who work in these areas. Make sure you dress in the smart set of clothes you have brought with you, and are clean, well-groomed and conservative-looking. Take out any piercings, don't wear your usual hairstyle if it is not conservative. Remember hippies and extreme casualness are associated with drugs in many parts of the world, and even though you don't do drugs border guards do not know that. They are likely to judge you by your appearance.

Answer any questions politely and with respect, and remember always the image you are projecting – a desirable visitor to a country, which after all doesn't have to accept you. Crossing borders is one time *not* to travel magically. If you are asked where you are going, try not to say 'I don't know', but mention confidently a part of the country you would like to visit and the length of time you would like to spend there. And no, you would never dream of doing drugs if they ask you. These border guys appreciate certainty. If you need to book your accommodation in advance, make sure you have reserved a night, and likewise book travel out of the country in advance if you are required to. You may be able to change it when you are there.

I get quite bad culture shock
It is hard to relate this land to the rest of the world
Dervla Murphy

I had just bumped into travel writer John Pilkington, the only other Westerner in our small hamlet in Gilgit, and then, for some reason I can't remember now, I decided to travel alone, further up the Indus Valley in Pakistan. The jeep went careering up the Karakoram, a land stripped bare like the bleached bones of creation. We went past singing cataracts of rock, on which radiant clouds were impaled, glowing as if they were lit from within. The air was thin and washed clean, here at the quiet limit of the world.

When I reached a certain hidden valley, there were houses made of stone with flat roofs where apricots were dried. Women were suddenly visible again, working in the fields with their yaks. People were friendly, but spoke no English at all, and there were no vegetables, milk or tea. The only food and drink available was apricots. Three months of the year the villagers live on fresh apricots, the rest of the time on dried apricots. I unwittingly caused a riot when I went to the local polo ground in my scarf and *shalwar kameez* (Pakistani dress), when a couple of hundred men surrounded me, but I was then rescued by some policemen with rifles. I was invited up to the Raja's palace on the mountaintop, where I found out the Raja and his family were the only people in the valley who were literate. But there were a few cultural misunderstandings when the Raja told me he was the proud possessor of 'three children and one daughter!'.

Just as I was feeling adventurous, and planning to carry along on the Silk Route to China, like my old colleague William Dalrymple, my tummy had other plans. All my food suddenly needed to come out. I was writhing in agony with stomach cramps, while the Pakistanis wrongly told me 'baby, no husband'. A hellish jeep ride took me to the hospital in the mountains, where many seasoned travellers will be sympathetic to the dilemma posed between wanting to explode and giving samples. But at this trying time there was an interesting conversation with the young Pakistani medical student:

Me: 'Urine – you have something?' (to put it in).
Gormless but English-speaking medical student: 'No Sahib.'
[After some time a bloody syringe was reluctantly produced]
Me: 'Stool' (wanting to give sample).
Student: 'Impossible – you have matchbox?'
Me: 'I no have matchbox – no smoke.'
Student (interested): 'Why no smoke?"
Me: 'No important. You give me something?'
[Student reluctantly produces pill-box]
Me (sense of relief): 'Where is toilet?'
Student: 'No toilet.'
Me: 'Come on, you must have toilet. Where do you go?'
Student: 'No go.'
[After a considerable pause]
'Toilet, no door. Many Pakistani man.'

This little dialogue, which came at a crucial time during my illness, was rich with constructs. The medical student was struggling as he didn't have proper sample pots available, and needed to save face by trying to pretend he didn't go to the toilet, as the only toilet available was unsuitable. He was also very interested in why I didn't smoke, but unfortunately by that time I was too weak to discuss it. Sometimes adjustment does mean a big shock to your system.

ADJUSTING TO A COUNTRY

It is not the eyes that see but the mind
Craig Storti

The process of adjustment begins as soon as you arrive in a country. When in Rome do as the Romans do. It is not always possible to act appropriately (for example, in some countries women are not allowed to venture outside alone at all) and if you visit a certain New Guinea tribe you are expected to kiss the headman's penis – but it is usually good to try. If you don't feel you can ethically obey the rules, then go somewhere else instead. Don't expect to act the way you would back home. If you want to, stay home. And do respect the culture you are in (even if you don't initially, act as if you are trying to). Any good guidebook will describe the unspoken rules of that culture. They may be very different to what you know:

✧ On the island of Yap women go bare breasted, but they cover their breasts if they leave the island. If they did not they would receive a lot of inappropriate attention.
✧ In Japan the penis may be wrapped before it is offered in a process called *kokigami*.
✧ In Australia it's fine to wear shorts on most occasions.
✧ In Indonesia it's rude to wear shorts, but that does not stop many travellers from doing so. (They will never know how much more respect they would have got had they followed protocol.)

Culture shock is the process of opening your mind. You are in a foreign country and that means, simple as it may sound, that people do things differently there, such as:

Custom	Country
Laying your unwashed body in standing water and calling it getting clean	England
Taking off your shoes before you enter a house	Asia
Avoiding a temple when you're menstruating	Israel, India
Greeting: kissing the headman's penis when visiting	New Guinea
Kissing: pressing noses	The Arctic
Seduction: wrapping the penis like a present	Japan
Eating: good to slurp your food	China
Friendship: calling everyone 'mate'	Australia
Toilet habits: using your left hand and water	India
Gift-giving: cementing of ties	All cultures

There are no 'quick fixes' like there are back home. You'll soon find that complaining won't get you very far. The locals will resent you, and if you can afford to talk to people back home, they'll probably say 'Well, why don't you go home then, if you don't like it?' They may not understand the reasons why you're there, so it's probably easiest to deal with culture shock alone.

Oh, it might not seem that way at first – when you have someone to talk to and to share your reactions with – but all you are doing is delaying the inevitable, the process of change. And people change at different rates and in different ways, for we do indeed boil at different degrees. The last thing you want to be doing is to continue to wear a mask and to be the person, the other person you want you to be, whether this is hero or homemaker. You need to have the freedom to express yourself authentically, and to work out what's really important to you. Culture shock is the 'smoking mirror' that holds you up against – yourself. It is the most brilliant chance to question your assumptions and beliefs.

ADJUSTING YOURSELF

> *If you want your world to change, change your world*
> **Neale Donald Walsch**

There are two main ways of dealing with culture shock, focusing on blessings and questioning your beliefs. Remember that you chose to go somewhere different because you want to *be* different. And to accomplish that you must allow change in. When times are hard, remember the *adjustment*, not the shock, is the cause of your pain. And keep remembering it.

Focusing on blessings

Put your focus on blessings. In a Muslim country, for example, notice the generosity of the people, their incredible hospitality and the way old people are looked after in their family, not in a home. There are always things to appreciate. Other people will appreciate you appreciating them too, and feel better, even if they do not consciously know why. Your alteration will ripple out and have an effect on the world.

Questioning your beliefs

Be prepared to adjust your belief system so you can let in elements of another one. We all know the results of not doing that with Islam. Adjustment means you have to question your old concepts and decide what you want to keep and what you want to let go. It's a continuation of your process of 'removing baggage', something you have been doing before you even started off on your magical trip.

Chris gets culture shock – and India

I am a barbarian here, because I am not understood by anyone
Ovid

Chris found India quite hard to handle at first. He hated the way everything was on view, whether it was going to the toilet in the street in the city of Delhi, or killing a chicken for the pot; he'd rather have just eaten the chicken without thinking about it as a living creature who didn't want to be strangled. He also didn't like being harassed and followed all the time. As he was quite a shy guy, he was used to blending in. That was impossible in India, where his white face made him stand out. He didn't know what to do, but started travelling around as that was what he had planned.

In the state of Rajasthan Chris suddenly 'got' India. He stopped minding when the buses didn't go on time, and enjoyed responding to the inevitable questions people would ask him. He even stopped minding the Indian toilets. He left his toilet paper behind and started using his left hand and water. When he returned home, he became far more outgoing. The Indian curries he ate every Friday night meant something to him now and he'd chat away to the staff in the take-away. He also learned that his own way of doing things wasn't the only right way.

Chris 'getting' India influenced more people than himself. The statues of Ganesh in his home were objects of enquiry, not derision, to his friends in the north of England. They became more open minded and began really talking to the Indian family who ran the local curry house too. The power of even one person's belief system is immense.

Changing yourself means reality changes, as Chris's example shows. Our belief system creates our reality. Our society influences our belief system. For example, many Americans prefer to earn money rather than enjoy free time, whereas many Hawaiians value free time above money. Yet our society is not the whole answer for it does not take perception into account. Otherwise, two sisters would have the same talents, as the influences upon each of them have been the same. We know that's not true.

Yet our belief system isn't everything. There's something even more powerful, even more resounding. There always is – our soul. And its influence may be so great, we don't even develop culture shock when we arrive in a society, for it's like we'd somehow known it before.

Soul power

You cannot see things until you know roughly what they are
C.S. Lewis

The concept of the soul gathering experiences as if on a giant journey through many lifetimes was addressed in Part 1, Chapter 2, 'Accessing your intuition', and some examples are shown throughout this book – for example in meeting your soulmate or learning spiritual lessons. Our rolling soul is gathering experiences so we can learn to integrate them through the power of our three minds and through the power of our heart. That's how we eventually return home to our soul-land.

Our soul journey helps explain why you feel more familiar with some societies than others. Some say it is because you have spent 'past lives' there. In other words, you may have known that place before, when your soul was inhabiting another body, in another time. This can be the case even if you don't believe, or know about, the journey of the soul – for example if you are a young child. Your soul simply longs for the land where you once were happy.

Callum returns to Barra

The soul has many mansions
Edgar Cayce

A television documentary described the lure of the Hebridean island of Barra to five-year-old Callum, a Glaswegian boy. He would often talk about it to his mother, to his friends and neighbours, and when he went there for the first time with a television crew, he knew who had lived in which house in the 1970s, a long time before he was even born. He remembered the Robertson family and the house they lived in by the airstrip and the beach and described it to the crew before they had travelled there. It was as young Callum recalled.

Some, including those who value rationality above other qualities, think this scenario is due to present-life influences. Yet Callum's mother denied that he'd ever heard the name Barra. She knew everyone he knew and no one had ever had any connection to the sandy island. If, however, you believe in past lives, then a past-life connection would seem likely, and, interestingly, many travellers feel 'they've known this place before'. Could that be why? Because you actually have?

It could also explain why you may get 'reverse culture shock'. That is getting culture shock not when you arrive in a country, but when you arrive back in your country, a phenomenon we'll explore in the final part of the book. That is because you have reconnected your soul in a place you once knew and it breaks you apart to leave. You are no longer the same. The way through is always integration. But first we need to adjust.

THE RESULT OF ADJUSTMENT

*Of course I was not looking for islands, I was looking for a way
to live my life*
Margaret Fay Shaw

In this chapter we've looked at the phenomenon of culture shock and at the necessity to adjust to let in a greater belief system. We've seen a couple of ways of doing that. For culture shock requires that you change, but that change can certainly be for the better, even if it doesn't seem like it at first.

Your adjustment may only be obvious when you return to your own society. Hence you must be prepared to discover that you don't 'fit in' any longer. It will inevitably be painful, nothing dies without a little sadness, even when it is time for it to go. We'll look at how best to adjust in the final section, which brings the first and fifth principles of travelling magically together, following your intuition and integrating your change.

For now, remember that the process of adjustment is a very healthy one, for you are leaving your familiar 'seen' or 'scene' and allowing the magic in. You are becoming a conduit for new light, new life. You are expanding the limits of your vision and so are able to see a new horizon, a new world. Allow the process to continue. You will never be the same again, so choose to expand, not to contract. You won't regret it. In years to come, you will be grateful for the shock. Your system will regain equilibrium and live at a higher potential than before.

CHAPTER 2

Where to stay

Life is God's novel. Let God write it
A rabbi

The question of where you stay is an enduring one on spontaneous trips, unless you learn to have faith that the perfect place will turn up. In that case you need never worry; you are well on the way to being a *saddhu*, a Hindu monk, who travels the highways and byways armed only with his begging bowl and his blanket. He trusts in his ability to create the perfect respite without money or intent, armed only with his spiritual force and a basic trust in the goodness of others. He trusts in God. And you too need to trust in God. Travelling spontaneously without booking accommodation in advance is a great way of doing that. You are open to who you meet and the suggestions that feel right in a way you simply are not if you are constrained.

This chapter looks at what you can do for your first night, the advantages of staying in local places and ways you can find them, and what to look for when you find your room – and when to ask for cheaper rates. It also looks at staying in dorms in backpackers' or youth hostels, and gives some guidelines that will make your stay there much more pleasant, as well as at other places you can stay such as college dorms and flats or apartments. Then we take a brief look at the place of stories which can help us deepen our knowledge. The chapter ends with camping and some advice on not to be afraid to do something different. For by opening yourself to the unexpected you are giving God the chance to write the book of your life. And believe you me, God can do better than us all.

Booking in advance?

I think it's good for people to just roam around. Stay where your car breaks down. Get on the damn bus, get off when you have to pee, then move there. That's good
Gretel Ehrlich

In general, you do not need to book in advance. Even if your travel agent in your country tells you to, or tries to sell you an expensive hotel or tour – you don't. They're just trying to make money out of your naivety. Booking in advance normally 'blocks' the energy and the magic of the place you are going to. Don't dam the energy by trying to control it.

There are only six exceptions: when you are arriving somewhere with a big event going on; when you are arriving late (after dark) in a place you are not confident about; when you are differently abled and need to check your room has certain facilities you need; when you are required to, for example on entering certain countries; when you are on a romantic break; or when you are tired and you just need to relax and rest a little before you set off into that country. For those reasons I mention in the Resources suggestions for booking in advance. Alternatively, Part 2, Chapter 12, 'When do you accept hospitality?', may be useful too.

Your first night

A tourist never knows where he's been, a traveller where he's going
John Ridgway

On your first night you will be tired from the journey and most likely be experiencing culture shock to some degree. You've already taken a huge leap in letting go of your world at home and going to a new place where you will undoubtedly be challenged. If it makes it easier for you to book ahead for the first night, then do so. It's usually a good idea to telephone to check that your reservation has been received, particularly if you have special needs, as well as to confirm that your transport is being met, if that's included.

Another reason to book in advance is that it often takes at least a night's sleep to adjust to the resonance of a place, and you will certainly create more effectively once you have 'allowed it in'. Some people of course won't feel the need to book in advance. They will be happy pitching their tent on the beach down the road a few miles from the airport, or confident of their ability to distinguish between the different touts and find decent accommodation when they arrive – great. No one way is right – all that is important is what's right for you.

HOSTELS AND BACKPACKERS

A hammer shatters glass but forges steel
Russian proverb

Hostels now exist in many towns of the world and are excellent if you want to meet other travellers. Another advantage is they usually have kitchens for you to cook in, and it's often possible to get unbiased advice from people who have just been to the places you want to go to. They are usually a mixture of private rooms and dormitories, with or without bathrooms. They are always cheap.

Private rooms are great if you want to have your own space and have a place to unpack your stuff. If only a double or twin is available and you are travelling on your own, then don't worry. In my experience, no one has ever breached the 'code' of not coming onto someone in a hostel arrangement – I have ended up feeling perfectly safe even sleeping with a strange guy in a hostel room. But as ever, follow your feelings.

Even if you hate the thought of sleeping in a room full of strangers, don't dismiss the 'dorm' out of hand. The reason is that among the press of humanity, you are likely to meet at least one person you get on with very well – and may even decide to travel with them. Dorms usually consist of bunk beds, and a wide age range of travellers, from grannies to young students. By no means everyone is poor – your bedmates may be doctors or businesspeople – some like the opportunity of meeting people and would rather spend their cash on other things.

The dorm 'code'

There is a dorm 'code' to follow:

✧ Keep your bed tidy and make sure there are signs that you are occupying it

✧ Keep your luggage tidily in a bag or two by your bed

✧ Bunks furthest away from the door and bathroom are usually quietest

✧ Use your earplugs to help you sleep

✧ Keep the bunk to yourself. DO NOT have sex in the dorm under any circumstances. If you want to do that go outside – or get a room

✧ Be considerate of other travellers. If you are having a night out prepare your bed in advance, so you will not need to switch the light on and disturb others

✧ If you are leaving early, then also prepare in advance leaving only a few last-minute things to pack. DO NOT rustle plastic bags and disturb your fellow travellers. Where possible bring your luggage outside and pack there, or leave it until after your bath and breakfast when more people are likely to be awake

✧ Keep the bathroom clean and don't spend too long in it

✧ Offer a share of your food and drink (usually outside the dorm) to people you would like to be friends with

✧ Put your food in its allocated place in the kitchen and label your things in the fridge.

When these common-sense guidelines are followed then your time in the dorm is likely to be a very good one. They provide a cheap, sociable base for you to see a new area and a reservoir of people like yourself, with curiosity and time on their hands, to do it with.

You may want to consider some official organisations too, such as the Youth Hostel Association. Now hostels are found all over the world, membership entitles you to a guaranteed bed for the night – which can be invaluable. They are usually clean and the cooking facilities have the little extras that are so useful – such as spices. In addition they are often found in wild and beautiful areas, and the manager will often let you camp outside or be flexible about your use of the facilities (maybe offering a 'day fee' so you can get warm and dry and cook, while you are sleeping elsewhere). I've had some lovely times in hostels, met some great people – and even found them good places to write my books in. Sadly, in Britain more and more hostels are now being sold off for housing development, so support them while you can.

University dorms are great places to stay. If you are travelling to an area with a university out of term time enquire about this in advance – they usually need to be booked in advance. They usually offer single rooms with study facilities and shared communal space. They certainly provide one of the cheapest ways of seeing the Edinburgh festival for example, and, in addition, you may be able to use the library on site and meet graduate students and professors as well as attend out-of-term lectures.

RENTING FLATS AND HOUSES

Oh, bed! Oh, bed! Delicious bed!
That heaven up on earth to the weary head!
John Hood

Renting is usually best done when you are in a place – so you know the area of town you feel comfortable in, for example. There are two main kinds of lets – short-term and long-term. For travelling magically I would recommend short-term, so you won't feel stuck. You can usually choose to share a flat or be on your own.

Sharing a flat usually has advantages in terms of price, but it can be difficult to meet people on the same vibration as you; additionally your flatmates will probably not be at a transitional point in their lives, unlike you, so for that reason I would not recommend them for magical travellers – unless of course it does feel right to you.

Getting your own place means that you will not meet people as effortlessly as you would if you were in a hostel; but, on the other hand, if you are really going through a lot then you might really appreciate your own space to retreat to, after you have bravely ventured forth to explore a new place. Liz Gilbert, for example, found renting flats or houses on her magical trip around the world gave her space for her diary writing, and to make the connections she needed – which enabled her to join up the previously disconnected bits of herself. How valuable is that? And if you get a place with more than one bedroom then you can choose who joins you, if you ever feel you want to be a bit more sociable. Generally, you don't need to use an agency, but ask a local or the people you meet – you will be amazed at how often someone has just been told a friend is ready to rent their place for a while. Allow the vibrations to align.

For tips on staying in a local home, see Part 2, Chapter 12 'When do you accept hospitality?'. The last thing I will recommend as far as getting a roof over your head for the night goes is a small and discreet local hotel.

GOING LOCAL

> *I can see only what I have now, this view and the dark, bright land below*
> **Jamie Zeppa**

Going local is the third principle of travelling magically and we see it again and again throughout this book, for example, in the importance of taking other belief systems into account as well as where you go, your diet and the things you buy. For that way you ensure the money you spend goes back into the community. Let's now see the third principle in the context of places to stay.

When we are living local then we are in tune with our environment. What a gift. We want nothing more than to be where we are. Right here, right now. This day. To get there all we need is faith. When we live in faith, like the penniless *saddhu* who wanders India naked, then we know we will always be provided for. Your situation may be easier as you probably have some money to spend. Do avoid the multinationals and the tour-group hotels and make sure you spend it wisely for the good of all – we are talking local.

Advantages to going local

To awaken quite alone in a strange town is one of the pleasantest sensations in the world
Freya Stark

You can usually tell a true traveller for they will eschew the multinationals in favour of the local. They will relish the chance to eat the local cuisine, learn a bit of the language and meet the people. For them, staying in an international hotel would be pointless – it would be like being at home. For what is the point in being in a sanitised environment, where you eat the same kind of food you get at home, wear the same kind of clothes and meet the same kind of people? Your masks are able to stay in place, whereas a true traveller is always seeking to drop them.

Local hotels are staffed and run by local people – and money is not siphoned off to some faceless conglomerate overseas. They often do not include a kitchen, but are usually situated near local cafes, markets and hang-outs, where you can get cheap and delicious food. Standards may not be quite what you are used to, but on the other hand you have an unrivalled view into local culture. They are also likely to attract interesting people. In addition many of these places have a very valuable quality – soul. Now we'll look at how to find one.

Finding your local hotel

I prayed that the hotel would be full but it wasn't
Eric Newby

Your right place may not be in the city or port you arrived in, it may be elsewhere. You may want to be in the mountains or by the sea, or somewhere different. After a few days you are well rested, armed with some of the local currency and are ready to go out and about. Now is the time to consider the transition to a new place, one that is more reflective of who you are, who you are becoming and what you hope to gain from your trip.

Local hotels are best found on the ground, not from guidebooks or the Internet. First of all, situations change, and what was good once may not be good now. For example, the recommended ho(s)tel may have gone into new ownership and not be as good, or the area might have gone down. Next, you don't need to rely on others' recommendations, you are quite capable of finding the best place yourself. This has two huge advantages: one is that you will be finding the best place for your resonance; and two, you will be growing into your own power by making your own decisions according to your intuition.

Of course if a hotel from the guidebook jumps out at you, great, go for that. 'Pilgrim hotels' are often a good bet. These are places where pilgrims stay, are usually safe and often have a spiritual atmosphere. It is no coincidence that they are simple and local as the values of a pilgrimage, which include putting the development of your soul above materialism and giving yourself the peace necessary to do that, are the same as the values of travelling magically.

Questions to ask in your prospective hotel
Every moment the universe is whispering to you
Denise Linn

✧ Is there a lock to your door? Does it work? If not, then can you use your padlock and chain?
✧ What floor is your room on? If it's on the ground floor there may be security issues. If it's on a higher floor you may want to know where the nearest fire escape is.
✧ Where is the nearest bar or restaurant? Might the noise bother you?
✧ If you are in a dangerous country, are there armed guards patrolling or iron bars on the windows?
✧ Is there electricity? Is it constant, or only available sometimes? If so, when?
✧ How much is a room?
✧ Is there a better room that's free, for the same price?
✧ Do the rooms have their own bathroom or a shared one? Can you see it?
✧ Are there cooking facilities?

Decide for yourself if a great view is important to you, or if you want a quiet room. Do you want the use of a washing machine, or is there a library of books to swap? What sort of memories do you desire? Some people will fall in love with a room in the Himalayas with its own fireplace and roaring fire, in a hotel built in the time of the Raj and now run by locals. Someone else will enjoy the quirky hotel on Livingston Island, Guatemala, which doesn't have a sea view, but has rustic art and a lovely courtyard with a wooden booth that sells fresh smoothies every morning. Now is not the time to negotiate a long-stay discount, however; firstly you may not want to stay a long time and secondly you are likely to get a better rate when you have been there a while and are better known. Generally though, if you just turn up and a room is free, then you will get it for less than its advertised price.

Advantages of a local hotel

One realm we have never conquered – the pure present
D.H. Lawrence

- ✧ You can find out directly about the country and the prevailing situation; for example if certain areas are 'no go'.
- ✧ They are usually smaller.
- ✧ They are always cheaper than international hotels.
- ✧ They are more personal.
- ✧ They are closer to local communities.
- ✧ These hotels are simpler and often made from materials from the local environment and so use fewer resources.
- ✧ You can meet local people, as they also stay there (if it's popular with locals it's likely to be okay).
- ✧ There are few, if any, advertisements about tour trips, but there is advice on visiting local attractions, using public transport or hiring a guide, which is recommended in situations that may be dangerous. If you are a woman alone, be sure you dress modestly, and be sure you trust your guide.
- ✧ You are usually without the familiar temptations, such as television and the Internet. You have plenty of 'spare time' to enjoy your 'pure present'.

I could write paragraphs about each one, but let's stick to three: the advantages of being without familiar temptations and being able to forge closer relationships, as well as being closer to your environment.

In a local hotel, familiar temptations will be thin on the ground and your room probably won't have a television, telephone or Internet access, and nor will you be kept awake by the noise of the television of the people next door. You will also get to know the locals in a deeper way.

Alexandra finds a job
I measure travel inward
Henry David Thoreau

While staying in a local hotel in Egypt, Alexandra ended up teaching English to the hotel owner's child. She received free food and accommodation in return for her English lessons. She loved to hang out in the courtyard garden and chat to the family and drink mint tea. She will always remember the call of the *muezzins* from the local mosque, the scent of the desert air, and she really got to know the family and their town. Alexandra is always welcome back there as a guest of the family.

Alexandra gave a service, and got a great deal back in return. Her small hotel was also far closer to the natural environment, which is important as then we have a chance to connect with the 'soul of things'.

CLOSER TO NATURE

> *Nature has created us with the capacity to know God, to experience God*
> **Alice Walker**

In a local hotel you will be much closer to the local animals and wildlife, away from the sanitised, air-conditioned environment of the multinationals. This is something to embrace, as spending time watching a group of kittens play, or a beautiful sunset with a flock of birds flying in front of it from your verandah is really very productive. For these sights nourish your soul and teach you to appreciate the value of 'being here'. You might even learn to enjoy the sight of a spider spinning its web in a corner of the room, or the lizard lazily extending his tongue, and realise that insects and reptiles, for example, aren't scary and 'other' as we have been taught, but contain whole worlds. You will learn how to experience God in the moment. There is great virtue in simplicity. Being in a simple, natural environment with human warmth and creatures running around – isn't that the place that humanity came from? And isn't it the place to which we will return? For there is great value in local knowledge.

In our stories are our soul

When the tide is out, the table is set
Tlingit proverb

Jimmy George from Angoon Island, Alaska, would tell a story about a man who found a dead salmon in bits and pieces along a stream. He tried to restore the fish to life so it could be food for his people. Each time he removed a bit more of the sand and leaves and branches attached to the fish, until the life was finally breathed in. The bits and pieces of the salmon represent the bits and pieces of the Tlingit culture. The contamination was the materialism that pervades modern life. The culture could only be restored to life through a return to the spiritual beliefs of the ancestors.

I did not know whether to use that example, then I realised that my only visit to the island of Angoon coincided with Jimmy George's funeral potlatch to which I was invited. So I put it in. We all have something to learn from others. For stories like the one above have a lasting value, and help return you to your original values. For the local knowledge must become universal if the world is to survive.

GOING LOCO

You were once wild here. Don't let them tame you!
Isadora Duncan

It's no coincidence that the Spanish word for 'mad', *loco*, has the same prefix as the word for local. For if you go 'local' too much then you may well go a bit 'loco', at least by the standards of the culture you came from. You may become an American who no longer believes that the system of health care there is the best there is. You may become an Australian who no longer thinks that 'Strailyer's the best country in the world, mate.' You may become a Scot who agrees with the slogan

'Scotland is the best small country in the world', well, apart from the weather in New Zealand, or the social cohesion in Bhutan, and so on. For you will have developed your own standard of comparison and you will no longer accept what you are told. This is no bad thing, for we all need to stretch ourselves.

There is no doubt that you will change as a result of your trip. But even though it's harder for you to fit in with those from your society, you will be correspondingly truer to yourself. Additionally, you will find resonance with those from other countries, other cultures and the whole of nature. And you help the change along by following the third principle of travelling magically, 'going local'.

Sometimes when we go too local we are called a little *loco*, a little mad. All I can say is it's a fun place to be. I will always remember my old crony Grant in New Zealand (the 'Hank' immortalised in Laurie Gough's wonderful tales of her travels in *Kite Strings of the Southern Cross*), who dressed up in my miniskirt and top and stood in the road, his moustache blowing in the wind, in utter confidence he'd get a ride. He did.

We do not need to tame and control our outer and inner wildness. For there is nothing to be scared of in setting ourselves free, and a new world to be won. You will 'fit in' everywhere and nowhere, yet be oddly true to yourself. Let yourself become wild.

CHAPTER 3

How do you get around?

There is no way to happiness, happiness is the way
Buddha

The following chapter looks at getting around within a country. We look again at methods such as driving and hitching, as well as including a section on ridesharing. Public transport is explored, except going by train which is covered in Part 1, Chapter 10, 'How else can you travel?'. We also explore individual methods of travel, such as by pedal or pedi (foot) power, a little further. You can even go by water, such as by rowing, kayaking and swimming. Be open to every possibility.

By expanding your comfort zone every part of your life will benefit. The new energy you draw in will lead to a surge of creativity to help you attract the experiences you need to grow. And in the end, of course, we need to remember that where we are is the perfect place, so choose to be happy now, not when you get 'there'. And enjoy the journey. For at the end of our life we don't die wishing we'd worked harder.

This chapter relates to the two previous ones on how to travel, for, like them, it uses green imagery, which represents growth. Now though it also relates to the process of learning spiritual lessons – another theme of the book. For isn't that one of the purposes of growth? The journey is important, for the most important place we ever go to is inside ourselves, the journey within. Let's see how the type of journey we take within a country can be a metaphor for that inner journey through the process of learning spiritual lessons.

FLYING WITHIN A COUNTRY

....

The air traveller is not free
Jean Baudrillard

Flying within a country isn't normally recommended. The reasons are myriad. Safety standards are not as high on a country's internal airlines as they are when flying internationally, so more crashes occur. And of course there is the environmental aspect too, which we have already discussed. Surely the point of being in a country is to experience it – and one great way of doing that is to travel by surface within it. Going by bus for a week across Iran will show you the sharp, broken mountains and allow them to fill a space within you in a way that flying over them could not. Flying is great for the overview, and can help you get to a country quickly. But it does not, and cannot, give you the experience of a country. Explore other methods of internal travel.

DRIVING

....

The great thing about man is that he is a bridge and not a goal
Nietzsche

Driving within a country is often easier than doing it internationally. For example, you don't have to worry about taking your vehicle across borders, and if you are going to be in a country for some time, then you can even choose your vehicle according to the ease of getting spare parts within that country. Why not choose the national car of that country, such as a jeep in America or a Volkswagen in Germany. Getting hold of them is usually quite easy, as is selling them again.

You need to make sure your driving licence is valid and try driving in smaller, quieter areas until you are confident enough to venture on to the bigger roads. Remember also that each country has different rules for driving (see Resources), which may be explicit – for example you need to carry certain items in your car or drive on a certain side of the road – or hidden. Even driving around London varies according to suburb – the smarter suburbs usually boast more careful drivers than the rougher ones.

In some countries, such as America, driving is the essence of the country's culture, and doing a 'road trip' is a classic way to explore it. I still haven't done one, but hope to one day.

Road trip across America

The long, brown path before me leading wherever I choose
Henceforth I ask not good-fortune, I myself am good-fortune
Walt Whitman

Road trips across America are immortalised in celluloid and in print, and are part of the essence of freedom the Beat Generation represents. You can do what you want, go where you want, stop in a cafe in the South for fried green tomatoes or choose to motor north up to the badlands of Dakota, and then head west – again. You can go to the sandstone deserts of Arizona, or run in the piney Cascade Mountains of Washington State. You can see for yourself how different each State and the people are, and it provides a fascinating look at the country's local cultures. The further west you go the 'wilder' the country and the people tend to get. Say you want to have an adventure, in the east you may be asked 'how do you get time off work?' and in the west 'when are you going?' America is a fascinating country, and a road trip a wonderful way to learn tolerance, or confidence or joy or whatever quality you need.

And now it's time to push out the envelope even further. What about ridesharing?

Ridesharing

The open road is the essence of freedom
Isabelle Eberhardt

Like hitching, ridesharing has advantages for both parties. If you are a driver you get to meet someone new, if you are a passenger then you get to pay a share of the petrol and settle back until you get to your destination on a pre-arranged ride. People do rideshare within cities, usually on regular journeys and between places, usually one-offs. Some websites even allow you to provide references for the driver.

If you are always a driver and never a passenger then maybe you need to give up control for a while and experience lying back and taking it easy. Why not go along to your nearest university and check the bulletin boards there, or go to your local website and experiment with being a passenger, just for a change? If you are always a passenger, then why not learn to drive and experiment with being in control for a change? Change is good. It helps you grow.

In Part 1, Chapter 10, 'How else can you travel?', we looked at how picking up a hitch-hiker can help both the driver and hitch-hiker to grow, for example through a well-placed sentence that can touch someone's soul. For, sometimes, one sentence is all you need to change your life. In this section, we'll look at the lessons hitch-hiking can teach you, such as trust and tolerance.

Hitch-hiking

Every mysterious event in our lives is a message
James Redfield

It's much easier to hitch-hike within a country than it is internationally. You have no borders to worry about and often only one national language to learn to speak a little of. You can be as eccentric as you like. Will hitched north in Japan following the cherry blossoms as they ripened, meeting the wide variety of Japanese people who picked him up; whereas Tony Hawks famously hitched round Ireland with a fridge. Hitching demands quite a lot from the passenger, but that's good. It provides continual opportunities to let go of control, and a place to go and say 'yes' or 'no' to the offer of a ride. You need to become in tune with your driver and chat away when appropriate, which raises your vibration. The effort has magical benefits.

Hitch-hiking teaches spiritual lessons
Whenever I hiked something happened to remind me of God's faithfulness
Grace Small

I have hitch-hiked thousands of miles in many countries and have to say that out of all the ways I've travelled hitching was always my favourite. Hitching helped me develop my intuition and, as a young woman, I often hitched alone. The first time I ever hitched was in

Ibiza, when I was 17. I had a really bad feeling about one car that passed. It went over the next hill and burst into flames. That little incident showed me I could trust my feelings.

Trusting my intuition opened me up to a great range of experiences and I am still here and much the richer for it. I have gone from pow-wow to pow-wow one shining summer in North America and been invited to native feasting and dances with masks, where I was the only white person. I met some tremendous people, and there's always something to learn. Then it's time to get a new ride to start the process again. The process of being vulnerable and learning to trust encapsulates the spiritual experience.

For when you have to learn a lesson then you learn it. For example, there is nothing like being in the space with a driver of opposing political views, knowing there are hours of journeying ahead and the other person is in control, for teaching you tolerance. You have to get on – you have no choice. On a similar note, I have heard it said that if you put two people of different faiths on a small boat together for a week and leave them alone, they will pull together and learn to bridge their differences. Be assured that those alliances on a microcosmic level are reflected on the macrocosmic and, as a result, help the whole earth. That's one reason why your lessons are so important.

Now it's time to check out some of the lessons that can be learned in travelling by local transport.

LOCAL TRAVEL WITHIN A COUNTRY

Subira ni unfonguo wa faraja
(Patience is the key to tranquillity)
African proverb

Local transport is one of the best ways of regreening our earth. In most countries there are many kinds of public transport, whether it consists of elephant rides, trains or rickshaws. If it feels right, do it. You will store up new experiences, and open yourself up to the culture of a country. That's the way to learn. For example when Tom from Ohio visited Russia in the days when it was Communist he was vastly impressed with the underground system in Moscow. The stations were decorated with works of art, sometimes on loan from a major art gallery, and vandalism was unknown. It made him realise that there is another way of doing things. Humans *are* capable of acting in a different way. You learn that by travelling in a different way.

We looked at travelling by train in Part 1, Chapter 10, 'How else can you travel?', and now we'll look at how to travel 'local-style' on the coaches and buses.

Going by bus teaches spiritual lessons too

The memories that do not fit at all well into the patterns of our day are the richest sources of insight
Kevin Patterson

Going by bus may be physically uncomfortable, but it can certainly be mind-expanding – it's up to you. For in its essence it means that you are dependent on someone else to take you to your destination. Wonderful, especially for those ever-ready 'Type A' driver-type personalities. Your bus may not arrive at the destination on time or may be driven in a way that makes you feel scared. You may share your journey with chickens or screaming babies. Great! Let go of control, and the idea that you know best. If that's the lesson you need, then that's the lesson the universe will give you through the medium of the bus ride.

As the communication theorist Marshall McLuhan famously said, the medium is the message. The world consists of much more than we can ever know – and thank goodness for that. In the next chapter we'll look at the importance of following signs, in this chapter we'll see how you can slow down. Local transport travels slowly, but by travelling slowly you can also learn to slow down. For you have more time to chat, contemplate, make connections. Rolf Potts wrote: 'Slow down . . . just to underscore the importance of this concept, I'll state it again: SLOW . . . DOWN.' Notice the details. Appreciate the gift of time. Your time.

Slow means you have time for what's really important. You have plenty of time to check out the scenery along the way, and see how it compares to your own seen-ery, or your own treasured beliefs. Are you prepared to let any of them go, and replace them by new ones? Keep a record of what you see and what you learn. Go back to it in the future. Notice the changes. Your changes. For the real richness in learning about the world lies in what you learn about yourself.

For example, one lesson going by bus can teach you is patience. You'll almost certainly need to learn this one. Other lessons may include openness, connection, even faith – it will depend on what comes up for you. Be assured though that each lesson is immensely valuable. Your internal journey can become so exciting that you will choose low-impact transport for the right reasons. Not because 'you know it's good, but you don't really want to' but because you *do* really want to. Our meaning is in our memories, so create magical ones that will glow forever. Try a new way of travel.

Be adventurous, for example, and create your own transport. Even if it's difficult to reach your destination that way, it may be a very suitable mode of travelling around when you get there. How about cycling, walking, rowing, kayaking or swimming? They are all quiet and environmentally friendly, as well as being potentially great vehicles for your growth.

Cycling within a country

The most potent weapon in the mind of the oppressor is the mind of the oppressed
Steve Biko

Generating your own power from your two-wheel bicycle is a wonderful way to get around. You are not dependent on anyone else. You get to keep fit and have more chance to interact with the environment. You can feel the breeze on your face, or feel truly part of a country by getting thoroughly drenched. Great. Some countries such as the Netherlands have brilliant cycle networks where you don't need to share many roads with cars, thus reducing the pollution you experience, as well as the risk of injury. This is something I would love to see more countries prioritise.

You can generally go with your bicycle by public transport to a particular destination then start cycling from there. As far as equipment goes, you won't be able to take much in your saddlebags and you should choose a bicycle that you can lock easily and quickly. You also need to make sure you know how to do the basic repairs before you set off. You don't need the latest model of bicycle and, indeed, it's more likely to be a target for crime. Another possibility is that you hire or rent a bicycle when you're within a country. Some cities, such as Ljubljana, the capital of Slovenia, even provide them for free – you pick them up at one destination and drop them off at another.

Walking within a country
Above all do not lose your desire to walk
Kierkegaard

Walking is one of the best ways of experiencing places. Take some 'time out' wherever you are and just walk around a new place. It's a wonderful way of soaking up the atmosphere, as well as interacting with other people on a casual basis. It's also one of the best ways of aligning your vibration with a place and a great way of realigning your own vibration, especially if you use poles which help shift the energy around your body. Walk.

Many countries have long-distance trails. Americans call walking a long distance 'hiking' and New Zealanders 'tramping', but whatever you call it it's a great way to rebalance. You are moving, your body is moving, your consciousness is moving. Perfect. An added bonus is the wonderful things you can see within a country. You can walk or ski the trails in Finland, depending on the time of year. The huts which break the silence of the Arctic may be saunas – you can walk in, take off your clothes, enjoy your sauna and then plunge back outside into the elements. I am particularly fond of the trails within New Zealand which are well maintained and feature cheap huts to stay in. That is because of the memories I associate with them – I experienced a closeness to nature that enabled the beauty of the white mountains of the Southern Alps to zing through every atom in my body. Like every lesson truly learned, the joy has stayed with me.

Another way of immersing yourself in a country is more literal – swimming.

Swimming

The part of you that is wettest is full of life
Henry David Thoreau

You can go on holidays where you swim round Greece, or Spain or even the Caribbean. Or you can do it on your own (often quite dangerous), or with a guide, preferably one in an unmotorised boat.

Swimming a couple of kilometres down the Cayo river in Belize, behind a native canoe, gave me the best experience of my journey to Central America. Why? It was the wetness coupled with the toucans in the trees and the gentle rhythmic movement of the canoe gliding down and down the green river. That's why I travel. For the feeling of oneness.

Of course that feeling is always there, whatever you do, we simply don't always allow ourselves to feel it. It's easier to access it in certain situations. That's why, if you like the water, water-based activities are so enjoyable.

Let's move on to look at the section on very small boats we didn't cover in our section on larger boats in Part 1, Chapter 10. Small boats have many advantages over big ones.

Very small boats

Every man paddle his own canoe
Frederick Marryat

Travelling by small boat can be a fabulous way to get around. When in the tropics for example, you avoid the heat, hills and insects by being out on the ocean. Or, if you're really adventurous you can even paddle through an Arctic summer. Jill Fredston and Doug Fesler rent out their home in Anchorage, Alaska every summer and 'disappear' for several months. They have travelled over 25,000 miles in total – she by rowing boat and he by canoe. One year they had a particularly wonderful journey:

Jill and Doug experience Spitsbergen fully
You're not in charge. Breathe, find a rhythm, stay loose, balance the boat, keep pulling
Jill Fredston

Jill and Doug were the first people to row and kayak around Spitsbergen island. They had a number of extraordinary experiences. One day, Jill looked up and to her surprise saw a whale in the sky. It was held in a glacier in the emerging sun. She surmised that it had died hundreds of years ago. They were the first people to record it. They later found a small beach to camp on, past the beach of the sleeping polar bear and the beach of the standing polar bear. There, young guillemot birds were leaving their nests on the cliffs half a mile from the ocean and learning to fly. Not all of them made it. Jill and Doug were the only people in the world to see that particular sight.

The beauty, and the precariousness, of life had their impact: 'Doug and I made special love that night, a keening for the murres that didn't make it to the water, a celebration of the bears, a wonderment at the whale, a precious understanding of the ephemerality of the being called "us". We were joyous and sad, afraid and free, humble and bold, vulnerable and strong. We were the ribbon of foam along a wave-pounded beach, a fragile connection between land and sea, here and there, now and another splinter of time.'

Such is the deep reward of having the courage to leave your familiar shore. You open yourself to experiencing the ever-flowing miracle we call life.

So how do you travel?

....

In your own Bosom you bear your Heaven
And Earth: & all you behold, tho' it appears without, it is Within
William Blake

We have seen many choices about forms of transport when you reach your destination. You can of course fly, although it is not usually advisable. You can drive, rideshare or hitch. Or you can take another kind of local transport. Alternatively, you can try getting around under your own steam, whether by bicycle, small boat or on foot.

As ever, the only arbiter is you. The key to magical travel is to be open to new ways of looking to the world. Finding new ways of travelling through it helps. At the same time, be responsible and responsive. Follow the first principle of magical travel, your intuition, and you won't go wrong. For there is no way to happiness, happiness is the way.

You can travel even further, for you are now in a position to learn tremendous spiritual lessons. Hitch-hiking showed me the power of following my intuition. Travelling in Russia showed Tom that the way he was used to wasn't necessarily the best one. Going to Spitsbergen enabled Jill and Doug to feel more deeply. Learning spiritual lessons means your outer journey is transformed into an inner one. Enjoy the ride. And follow the signs. Read on.

CHAPTER 4

Travelling spontaneously

Peculiar travel suggestions are dancing lessons from God
Kurt Vonnegut

Travelling spontaneously is the second principle of magical travel and one of the most fun. By 'spontaneous' I essentially mean letting go of control. Don't plan. Have ideas, but don't always carry them out, come what may – death or disaster, earthquake or destruction. Sometimes problems are in our way to illustrate other options.

The idea behind following those 'dancing lessons' is that we are part of a greater pattern, whether you call that pattern God, the universe or something else. We are not necessarily the best people to control our life. We must step out of the way to allow the signs to direct our course. Many books, from the Bible to *The Celestine Prophecy*, show us the importance of following signs. I wish I'd known this lesson when I started travelling, but I had to work it out as I went along. Coincidence after coincidence, so many that even dismissive me couldn't ignore the possibility, then the probability, then the certainty, of being part of a greater pattern.

In this chapter we shall see how signs appear to us. They do so in a myriad of different guises, some, such as shooting stars, are significant to many people, others only to you. Some can be easily understood, and you give a wry smile as soon as you notice them, others need interpreting. All of them are beckoning to you, showing you a path to follow. When we follow our signs then we are growing into our Higher Self, and we may need to change our belief system to incorporate that concept. We then receive more and more signs and our universe lights up. Sometimes enjoyable signs appear in the guise of another person, someone we are very attracted to. Following the signs is just like falling in love. For ultimately signs show us the way home, the home of our golden soul.

Sometimes our signs are unmistakable. Let's see what happened when Dymphna went to Delphi.

The healing waters of Apollo

μηδὲν ἄγαν
(Nothing in Excess)
Saying attributed to the oracle at Delphi

Dymphna was visiting Greece with her husband. One day she suggested that they return to Delphi, to the white temple complex on the mountainside sacred to the god Apollo. She had always loved her visits there where she had experienced an extraordinary electricity that seemed to transport her into a different dimension. Her mind would tell her that was a fanciful concept – at least until the day of the unmistakable sign.

Dymphna had been suffering from cystitis, a painful urinary condition. After walking on the slopes of Mt Parnassus to find wild cyclamen in the crevices of the rocks, they climbed up to a ledge above the Castillian spring, the fount of Apollo's healing powers. She felt a great sense of freedom as she turned to look at the marvellous space of the cliffs hanging over the valley far below, as though she could fly into the blue space. It was from this place of freedom that she looked up to where the water came out of the mountainside and found herself saying 'Please Apollo, help me. Take this pain away.' She drank a little of the clear and sparkling water as it ran over the ledge. Then they climbed down from the mountainside, and drove on.

As they drove towards Thessalonika on that blue day, the sign appeared. On it were the words: 'Thermopylae. Hot sulphur healing springs – beneficial for many complaints, particularly urinary'. The next day the pain was completely gone.

Dymphna had no doubt Apollo had answered her plea and the next day she was healed. There is a lovely coincidence in the waters of Thermopylae specialising in healing urinary complaints. More and more people are getting gorgeously literal signs like that one.

Sometimes though, we need to help ourselves find significance. Let's move on and see how.

SEEING SIGNS

Teach me, my God and King
In all things thee to see
George Herbert

Seeing significance can be taught. All things only have the significance you give them, so why not play with adding meanings you would normally ignore? The more signs you follow, the more you will find. Worlds of significance await.

If you've never experienced significant signs and would like to, then simply sit quietly, take a deep breath and ask for signs to appear to you in whatever form is most appropriate. If you'd like to experience more signs, do the same simple exercise and ask for more. When Gina did this exercise, she saw, through her third eye, a silvery female angel standing at her shoulder, which she understood was her 'angel of the signs' – her angel sent to bring meaning into her life. James didn't experience anything at all when he did the exercise, and wouldn't have wanted to – which is perhaps why he didn't. But soon after- wards logical James followed his inner nudgings and was guided into a certain shop – there he met the woman who became his girlfriend. So he found his sign.

Some people find meaning in everything – they live in what is known as a magical world, a world of significance. You might not want to inhabit that world, then all you need do is deny significance to the wonders and coincidences that are coming at you. They will largely cease. It all depends on how you interpret your signs. And that is always your choice.

INTERPRETING SIGNS

Polishing our mirrors so that they reflect back to us a clear idea of God as He is to be found working through His universe, is the first of many steps now to be taken
Max Freedom Long

There are always signs. Signs from the unlikeliest, as well as the likeliest of sources. Signs can appear to be random or looked for, personal or collective. They are ambiguous, we can assign many meanings. Take illness, an accident or the weather, for example. To you your illness might be random, to your neighbour it might mean something. The same goes for accidents or the weather, also believed to hold meaning in shamanic societies. Sometimes the bigger the event the easier it is to find meaning – more people are likely to find significance in a hurricane than a breath of wind. But really the meaning you find is up to you.

Some signs are personal, such as a snippet of overheard conversation that means something to you. You may hear a particular song or piece of music again and again. You may bump into people with the same name as someone you know or with the same birthday. You may meet a person who reminds you of someone in the life you left behind. Take note, there's a message for you. You may notice a creature crossing your path as you're thinking a certain thought or you may be the only one to look up to see a peculiarly shaped cloud – there's a message here too. What or who does it remind you of? What were you thinking at the time? Leanne notices colour a lot, and sometimes literally follows the path where the colour appears brighter. My personal signs include place names which often give me information I need. William practises stichomancy – asking a question, opening a book at random and seeing how the sentence his eyes alight on answers it.

Other signs are widely shared, such as language and money. Here meanings shared by many are ascribed to certain words or objects – they are called sign systems. Systems of shared signs include astrology and numerology, the I Ching, even the 'language of flowers' – most of us would give one meaning to a red rose another to a white. But even within these shared systems of signs we each have our own interpretation, which changes as we change. For example, we may start off disliking money and feeling we don't deserve it, and then change our mind, and see it as something we can do a lot of good with. The system of money is the same, yet we interpret it differently.

Ultimately the point of signs is to learn. What do we need to learn? Our spiritual lessons. First though, we often need to change our belief system. That's another lesson I learned the hard way. But something seemed determined that I should learn it.

My first sign

Twinkle, twinkle little star
Indian guide on lighting a candle in the hall of mirrors
in Amber, Rajasthan

My first sign was on the first day of my first trip around the world alone when I was 18. I was walking along a street in Janpath, New Delhi, doubtless looking like many other backpackers with a long, slightly scruffy skirt and a bag hanging off my shoulders. A Sikh called out to me and offered to tell me my mother's first name. I didn't believe he could, but then he did. This surprised me greatly, because no one in India knew her; I had told no one I'd met and I wasn't carrying anything which had her name on it. Antoinette is an unusual name, unfamiliar in every Indian dialect, and it was almost impossible an Indian would guess it. He told me some other things about my next few years that I thought couldn't possibly be true, but they did happen. I didn't know it then, but my belief system was in the first stages of being replaced by one that allowed in a greater sensing.

That encounter with a bearded, turbaned Sikh on a city street next to the Imperial Hotel showed me that there was a lot more going on in the universe than I realised. It was there, in India, that I first lit the lamp of surrender and in so doing created my first light. The light that would lead me to leave behind my previous belief system because its isolation and cynicism took no account of the experiences I knew I had had, even if I was not always believed. The light that would eventually, through my writing, be reflected in a hall of mirrors. I still remember the shudder of awareness I received when I discovered that there was far more 'going on' in the universe than I had realised with my logical mind. I had begun to access the magic of my Higher Self.

YOUR HIGHER SELF AND MAGIC

Soul-shine, all light and fire
Kristin Zambucka

Your inner light is always beckoning to you. All of us create much more effectively when we are in our right place, doing our right thing, because then magic happens – our inner magic. That's why we need to follow the call of our soul. You access your soul through your Higher Self.

But it isn't just 'your' Higher Self, and therein lies its strength. You find yourself doing and knowing far more than 'you' could ever have done on your own. You are allowing in help from all sorts of sources. Your job is to follow the signs – your Higher Self's way of communicating with you. That means clearing your conscious mind – what you think you want, what other people tell you you want – out of the way. It also means *feeling*, rather than denying, your subconscious mind, the home of your emotions and your murky past. The more you can do these things, the greater the magic you will create. Feeling is the road home to your soul.

FOLLOW YOUR FEELINGS

> *Will you, won't you, will you, won't you, will you join the dance?*
> *Will you, won't you, will you, won't you, won't you join the*
> *dance?*
> **Lewis Carroll**

When you arrive in a place, then, with the right attitude you'll find the true things going on in a country (the ones that aren't mentioned in any tourist office or book). For example, at the *Hula piko* festival in Hawaii which happens in Moloka'i every year, the true dedication to Laka, the goddess of the Hula, occurs in the early hours of the morning, hours before the official festival, full of unsuspecting tourists and travellers, begins. So keep your ears and heart open and you won't be disappointed.

Follow your feelings in every single decision you make, and you will have extraordinary experiences. The exercises on honing your intuition contained throughout this book will make it much easier for your 'guardian angel' to tell you to avoid this plane or that bus, if necessary. Your only role is to listen and take the appropriate action. Don't go to places if they feel wrong. However unimportant it may seem, if you really get the feeling to go to this house rather than that one, this village rather than that one, do it. You never know who or what may be waiting for you there. The more you follow your feelings the stronger your little voice will become.

Remember, the feeling you get when you notice the sign is important. Even if you are not used to receiving good feelings, nourish each one you receive. As your vibrational energy becomes higher and higher you will become aware of more and more signs. Resisting the radiance is no longer an option you want to take and you will inhabit a world of wonder. When we allow our good feelings to lead us into our Higher Self, then we dance our dance.

Sometimes falling in love is our motivation. In this next section we shall see how signs bring us to our true home – our soul.

Raven opens the box of daylight

Swift, swift you dragons of the night, that dawning
May bare the raven's eye
William Shakespeare

I arrived in California expecting to find a lot of things. But when I got there, it just didn't resonate with me, like a good-looking date you're not actually attracted to (it's changed since, but I was meant to be going further north then). A bus was going to Seattle in Washington State and I hopped on. We called it a magic bus, which was friendly and where everyone pitched in to cook a delicious meal, among pine forests or by hot springs or wherever the bus happened to be at the time. There was a tall guy sitting at the front left-hand corner of the bus. I approached him and a small voice said to me 'If you speak to him you'll never be the same again.' I looked into his pale blue eyes, spoke and wasn't.

Dan also loved India, Native American myths and the thirteenth-century Persian poet Rumi. He invited me to come and stay with him in Seattle. There I experienced a perfect quality of silence, like water. Yet I was in deep transformation, symbolised by my address book that year on which I had drawn a picture of a raven's eye, and the postcard of a blonde girl and a raven I had stuck on to my diary. I wanted desperately to be 'normal', be with the guy and let the signs go. But it was not to be. Meanwhile, there were many signs: the black raven, the green tortoise and the green turtle, the spotted owl, the brown bear. They were to help me on what was to become a very deep and healing journey. They were the only thing that did.

Dan and I went camping by a rushing river in the Cascade Mountains and on the beach at night, where I remember wishing I knew the secret of a seagull knowing his place in space on top of a post at the edge of the sea. Although we never made love, we shared a deep bond, but Dan and I had no home together. He told me angrily that everything I said 'triggered him off'. When soulmates meet 'triggering off' is actually a fast track to the Higher Self, but only if you choose to perceive correctly and to open the box of daylight.

Accessing the soul
Unbarred the gates of light
John Milton

After some time in Seattle, I had to leave for Hawaii, a purpose to which I was already committed. I promised Dan I'd return. He said that if I left, he wouldn't be there when I did come back. When I returned, as I had promised, Dan indeed wasn't there. In body yes, in spirit he had withdrawn. So he was right. He had made himself right.

I was feeling rather despairing at a bus stop in the U-district one day, but noticed some inlaid footprints which made up a dance step. I marvelled at what a great idea it was to have that in a place where people wait, and tried to learn the step. When I looked up I saw Richard, an anthropologist friend from Cambridge. He was working in Seattle as a labourer and doing a dissertation on hitch-hiking. I enjoyed Dan receiving another less stereotypical view of Cambridge people, as we hung out together, quite platonically, as often happens with the English. Richard provided me with a sense of the dance carrying on.

After some time of Dan not responding to me, I said I had to leave. I thanked him for what I had learned. He sat like a stone and twisted his Thunderbird egg in his hand and told me he had learned nothing. He also said he was secretly in love with me. It was too little, too late and I had to move on. I truly hope Dan is happy. I could never regret following the voice of the angel, for even though I didn't get the guy, I got the meaning. I became more me. I opened to an even greater flow of feeling. I now have the ability to write and access of the 'gates of light'!

Correct interpretation of signs leads you to your true home, your effulgent soul, where it is always day.

THE SIGNIFICANCE OF SIGNS

There are only two ways of spreading light – to be the candle or the mirror that reflects it
Edith Wharton

We have seen that signs are incredibly important, for they hold the power to sing your soul back home. Simply by letting go and stepping into the magic as Gill Edwards said in her book of the same title, you will put yourself in a position to receive them. The more signs you follow, the more signs you will receive. Then you will move to being the candle or the mirror. Either way you will be on the side of light.

Following the signs enables us to bring our inner and outer worlds together. We think a thought. It happens. A person pops into our mind. They immediately call. We notice a place on the map. Its name triggers off a memory. We arrive in a country. The sun shines for the first time in months. It's the right place for us. That blending of the inner and outer leads us into an exalted state of significance, one where we are able to express our true selves. Then we are truly guided home.

Synchronicity leads to synchrony, a happy state where we are all dancing, if not to the same tune, then at least to the same rhythm. Let's see how we can seize synchrony in the next chapter on peculiar coincidences and their underlying pattern – or the importance of timing.

CHAPTER 5

It's all in the timing

Time is the music of our being. It is to us what water is to fish
Jessica Julian

By now you'll be aware of all the synchronicities that cross your path, and of some of the many wonderful opportunities and possibilities out there. How do you know which part of the river of time to navigate? It's time to peruse the second principle of travelling magically, travelling spontaneously, further.

First of all we'll notice that signs change, and when they change they affect us. When we are not in the flow then it may be time to move on, which I illustrate by an Australian example. We need to learn to *carpe diem*, or 'seize the moment' by following our intuition when we receive it, such as when I went to Norway. Then I show an incident of a shift in awareness, and how you can turn the right place at the wrong time into the right place at the right time – through changing yourself. I end by exploring the power of those lessons of the spirit. So we'll travel along the silver route to our bliss.

Synchrony

....

The hills are shadows, and they flow
From form to form and nothing stands
They melt like mists the solid lands . . .
Alfred Tennyson

Remember the importance of signs. Now you have left behind your world of structure, your world will be full of change. You will be challenged and you will also be changed, on all sorts of levels. This means your signs change more quickly because *you* are changing more quickly. Just because the signs beckoned to you last month or last year does not mean they are right now. You must follow the signs that are appropriate for you now, not the ones that you want to see.

Sir Ranulph learns a useful lesson

The best magic words are those which come to one when one is alone out among the mountains
Inuit shaman

The British explorer Sir Ranulph Fiennes deeply regretted not listening to the local Inuit when he was on his way to Resolute Bay during the Arctic leg of his trans-polar navigation. His Inuit guides refused to carry on because a bad storm was coming. Ranulph could see no sign of danger, so forged ahead. He later said that it was 'only luck' that saved him from a watery end. The episode features prominently in his autobiography, and he said that he was 'suffering from the delusion that I knew better than the Inuit. There was no apparent danger, so why waste precious time?'

The Inuit people had been in the area for far longer than him, and are used to 'reading the signs', in this case the weather, which of course changes rapidly causing the 'solid land' of snow and ice under his feet to melt unexpectedly.

But at least Sir Ranulph was able to learn from his mistake and record it for others to learn from too. Knowing the signs may not always be a matter of life and death, although that will depend on how we define

217

life and death. For example, Mexico may no longer be the best country for you, even though you felt really drawn to it in the past. It's just like falling in love: the person who was right for you in the past may no longer be right for you now. The more you follow your intuition, the more alive you will feel. You will never again experience a boring life where you feel 'dead'. As you change, so does your world.

RIGHT PLACE, WRONG TIME

Stranger in a strange country
Sophocles

The right place at the right time – magic. The right place at the wrong time is not worth it. There might be some particular place you've always wanted to go, and you are now in the area. If you don't go then you may never go, but it still doesn't feel quite right. So then, do you go? No. If it doesn't feel 'right' then don't do it, even if it was what you have longed for in the past and it is what other people are expecting you to do. You are probably 'meant' to stay where you are, or to be somewhere else.

When you are not in the right place doing the right thing, there will be all sorts of signs to show it. Nothing will quite work and you won't meet interesting people. It seems as though 'coincidences' have forgotten you, and you no longer believe that there is a meaning to your experience. The right place at the wrong time is not worth it. If the timing is not right, the universe will not crack open to you.

When the Great Barrier Reef wasn't magic

Every time you don't follow your inner guidance, you feel a loss of energy, a loss of power, a sense of spiritual deadness
Shakti Gawain

I took a bus up to the Great Barrier Reef a month before I was due to leave Australia. I wanted to stay in Sydney, where I'd met some lovely people, however that was what I'd told myself (and others) I'd do so that's exactly what I did. Nothing quite worked, but in a very non-specific way, so I was never even quite sure things weren't working. I was in one of the most beautiful places in the world, yet felt oddly discontented. One day I remember I left my hostel in the jungle and went slowly down to the glistering sands where the translucent sea smoothed them, leaving unexpected corrugations against my feet. Under the sea were the creatures of the coral canyons, leading out to the darker place, where the denizens of that slow, unfocused world perceive through vibrations, not vision. I wandered along a nearby road by the mangrove forest, past scudding clouds and tree-clad mountains, the distinctive form of Mt Sorrow wreathed in flowering clouds, thinking 'But I don't want to be here.'

Now I don't even like to look at my (beautiful) photographs of that time, and I have never wanted to return to the Great Barrier Reef since, which certainly lived up to its name for me. Unfortunately the place itself lost its magic, simply because I went there at the wrong time. Of course it is still magic – just not magic to me. And who knows what wonderful things and encounters I missed in Sydney by not following my intuition and staying there? But, alas, I'd exerted my own will and control, listened to my old wants and desires, rather than the newer, brighter ones, and didn't step aside and allow the magic to happen.

Whatever you do don't stay in a place because you think you should be there, if it simply doesn't feel right. The solution is simple, either learn your spiritual lesson which we look at later in the chapter or move on somewhere else.

GOING WITH THE FLOW

> *Πάντα ῥεῖ*
> *(Everything flows)*
> **Heraclitus**

Going with the flow is a way of letting go and finding out who you really are and what you really want. Let go to move towards your higher purpose. You have followed the first and second principles of travelling magically and found yourself in the right place, at the right time. Everything resonates. Your days are full of sunshine, whatever the weather is like. Replete with wonder, you know you will always remember the Northern music by the sweep of the rocks on the beach or the beat of the gong in the Eastern temple as the river flows by and a monk offers you butter tea with a beatific smile. Your nights are full of splendour, whether the light is from the moon on the sea at night or the powerful conversations you have with the people you meet. If you need a lift someone is going where you want to go. If you want to dance the music starts up – and reaches your heart. You create powerful synchronicities that resound in your life and other people's. Everything is effortless.

There is no better feeling than being in the right place at the right time.

RIGHT TIMING IS VITAL

Le vierge, le vivace, et le bel aujourd'hui
(That virgin, vital day, today)
Stéphane Mallarmé

At home we may be used to putting things off. It may not really matter whether we go away for the weekend now, or a month later. In your shifting, shining world though, it really does make a difference. There may be someone you're meant to meet who will only be in that place at that time. You don't need to know why, you just need to follow your intuition.

When the music of your being is struck, then the power of the universe opens. The magic gushes in, like a trail of silver pouring through a chink in a cloud. The coincidences sweep you off your feet, and you feel a sense of homecoming. Whenever I feel stuck, I have a solution – travel. I book at the last minute, because my feeling at the time tells me where to go to get the experiences I need.

Tying up a circle

Creatures of land, we take a turn
Tie land, untie, carry on, learn
And always we have on earth the view
Of wild beauty luring us through
Rima Morrell

One year, I was feeling a bit depressed at the onset of winter. I had commitments which meant that I needed to be in England, but I really didn't want to be there. My solution was to go away. I was feeling so miserable I decided to invoke a drastic solution – go to a country I had never been to before to help shift my energy. I went to Norway, and, as I could only spare a weekend, a weekend it was.

I flew to Oslo, and quite enjoyed that, but felt some displacement. I then decided to go to Finse, the highest resort in Norway, which for eight months of the year can only be reached by train, and really embrace the coming of winter. The wooden station and the lodge stood out from the icy flatness. I felt better as the white rocks and dark water of the landscape reflected my frozen soul. But this place, so remote that the icy planet in *The Empire Strikes Back* was filmed there, still didn't feel like the right place for me to make a shift, the purpose of my trip. I'd spent quite a bit of money and for what? I didn't know.

My flight from Oslo wasn't until late on the Sunday evening, and so I decided to leave Finse early. When I got to Oslo, I had a bit of spare time and decided to go to the Kon-Tiki Museum, founded by Thor Heyerdahl, as it reflects my passion for Polynesian culture. I totally lost myself there, and as I was walking out I heard a voice saying 'Rima'. I thought 'No, impossible, it's not a Norwegian name' and carried on walking. Then the voice said 'Rima' again (it seemed to have an Australian accent), and I turned around to see some very special friends from Australia with whom I'd stayed for months during my big trip when I was younger. We were able to have dinner together and catch up on the intervening years before I had to get my plane.

So that trip – finally, and in a way I could never even have imagined – provided me with a wonderful affirmation that the universe was still working for me. It was my first and only trip to Norway, as it was for Glenn and Janice, and we were all there just for the weekend. None of us had the slightest idea that we would be anywhere near the area; indeed, I thought they were still in Australia. But Glenn Murcutt had gone to Finland to receive an architectural award and they were spending a couple of days in Norway afterwards. If any of us had gone on any other weekend we would have missed each other. If we had gone to the museum an hour earlier or later on that particular day we would have missed each other.

Follow the signs, and you will see that your path makes a circle, which becomes a trajectory that ripples out and affects other lives. Indeed in years to come, I was to write the first draft of this book in Glenn Murcutt and Janice's home in Mosman, New South Wales, Australia. I didn't plan it, I just knew that in half an hour I had a chapter summary and the book 'wrote itself'. I was later to speak in a conference on Polynesia with Thor Heyerdahl in far-away Arizona, and discuss many things with him. Even more years after that *Travelling Magically* was set free into the world. The circle is tied and a new path begins.

RIGHT TIMING MEANS SPIRITUAL LESSONS

We are obliged to repeat what we cannot remember. This world is repetition – compulsion, is karma
Norman Brown

Our spiritual lessons are usually simple. Words like 'love', 'faith', 'trust', 'compassion', 'letting go' sum them up. You may fall in love and learn about the quality of love. You may need to learn how to let go, wanting only the best for the other person. These kinds of lessons are much deeper than the ones we learn in school, for they are of lasting value. The *only* exception to being in the right place at the wrong time, is when there's a lesson for you to learn. That's why you are there. When you have learned the lesson, then you can change the energy. Like Richie did.

Richie enters the temple – finally

Before you enter the temple forgive
Jesus Christ

Richie had looked forward to visiting the Orkney Islands for years, particularly the famous St Magnus Cathedral in the capital, Kirkwall. But when he stood outside in the wind looking at it, it just didn't feel right for him to go in. He couldn't tell you why not, but he followed that feeling and sat on a bench by the sea instead and fed the gulls. He had a lovely time, and thinking of one friend back home, realised he should have given more of himself. And he needed to forgive himself for the ways he didn't open. It took the feathery softness of the gulls on an island far away for him to realise it.

On another trip to the Orkneys a couple of years later, Richie returned to St Magnus Cathedral. Now it was the right time for him to go in and he said the most powerful prayer of his life. He felt good, after all he had made up with his friend (the one he had thought about years before), and was ready to experience the sacred atmosphere, now there was nothing blocking him. The cathedral will always be a special place to him now, not just because of when he did visit it, but because of when he *didn't*. Richie was swept up into the higher harmonies of his being, dancing there by the ocean of time.

Of course, had Richie missed his lesson, it doesn't mean the chance to have his insight would have gone forever, it just means his guardian angel (if you believe in guardian angels) would have had to work harder on his behalf. If you miss your lesson, don't worry. It will come again – it is your karma. Once you've learned it, it will never need to return. You have broken the cycle.

223

THE POWER OF SPIRITUAL LESSONS

There is a good deal of untapped country within us
George Eliot

When you find a new quality in you, and you allow yourself to live it, then it will ripple out and affect every part of your life. You will have integrated it and will be living the fifth principle of travelling magically. For example, once you know the quality of compassion you will feel far more connected. That sense of connection is of great value for you and our earth. Likewise, once you've learned how to let go of a lover and experienced that it is for the higher good of you both, it won't stop you from needing to let go again, but the process will be far less painful.

If you miss your lesson, don't worry, it's in the nature of things that you'll never know what exactly you've missed, but you will experience a vague feeling of discontent, just like I did at the Great Barrier Reef. And know that you'll get another chance. Record your lessons in your travel diary and make a note of their effects. Acknowledge yourself for having the courage to know your lessons of the spirit, which meant that your trip isn't 'running away', but 'running to'. And where are you running? Towards your 'untapped country', forging a new silver path to your core of light.

Right timing is about manifesting the possible. Initiate, then step out of the way and let the magic happen. Right timing speeds up the rate at which you learn the lessons to help you be happier. Your vibration is faster and higher. When your vibration is raised, then your lessons will happen thick and fast. Isn't it wonderful that you have created the chance through magical travel to learn your spiritual lessons more quickly? What a blessing.

And, of course, there is one fail-safe way of learning our lessons – meeting people.

CHAPTER 6

Meeting people

A human being is a part of a whole, called by us universe
Albert Einstein

This chapter explores the first three qualities of travelling magically: following your intuition, travelling spontaneously and going local, and brings them up to a whole new level. They are understood in terms of accessing your Higher Self through meeting people. The people you meet will probably provide the most vivid memories of your trip. They could provide you with many other things as well. They may become your lover, your best friend, your guide, your teacher, your student, your inspiration, your nemesis. The people you meet can change your life.

You could potentially meet everyone on our great planet. But you will actually meet only a tiny, tiny portion of the whole, depending on where you go and who you know. Some you will look at and recognise, others you will decide you don't want to know, yet others you will look at and feel indifference. They will do the same to you. We are all part of a huge cauldron and the elements react in unpredictable ways to each other. The resulting mix has the power to transform every human in it – including you. When you feel a pull to someone else take note. There may be love to make, an insight to be given or a spiritual lesson to be learned. Maybe it's a good idea to travel with someone that you feel drawn to, for that person can provide the key to a quality you need. Sometimes our higher wisdom lives in other people.

Broadly speaking there are two categories of people you are likely to meet, locals and other travellers. Now I shall look at some tips for meeting locals, which include how to meet them without a tour group, and some general advice about how to act. The rest of the chapter is devoted to meeting other travellers. It includes guidance on why we're drawn to other people, when to travel with them, on the power of surrender and dealing with difficulties as well as a quick exploration of the higher wisdom it is possible to gain. For as you climb the silver road of magic you will soon attract the experiences necessary to transform into your higher light.

MEETING LOCALS

It is right to chide man for being blind to such coincidences in his daily life. For he thereby deprives his life of a dimension of beauty
Milan Kundera

Remember you do not need to go on a tour or book in advance to meet locals. Indeed such actions are likely to stop you meeting them – for you are only meeting the more Westernised ones, usually men and the 'spokesman' for their village or tribe. Don't you want to encounter others too? It's fairly straightforward to take off and stop where it feels right – whether it's a village or a grouping of huts in a desert. Remember we are all one, and spending time with those from a different culture helps you live that knowledge. What can be more valuable?

Tips for meeting locals

✧ Follow local customs, as set out in the guidebook or by observing those around you
✧ Give compliments, don't criticise. Focus on the good
✧ Keep a sense of humour
✧ Don't initiate, although it's fine to ask about places and people of interest
✧ Don't accept things without giving something back
✧ Don't talk too much
✧ Make an effort with the local language

✧ Don't assume your way of doing things is right
✧ Offer to help
✧ If in doubt, don't take photographs – and always ask first
✧ Dress modestly and act modestly too
✧ It's generally easier to talk to people of your own sex
✧ Be careful where you look
✧ Don't make promises that you don't follow through

Generally speaking, you will meet more genuine locals if you go to places where other travellers don't go; these are fairly easy to identify. If you avoid well-known attractions and points of interest, and the places mentioned in popular guidebooks of the area, it will be easier for you to immerse yourself in local culture. This is the case even for countries on popular backpackers' trails such as Thailand and Australia. Generally you only have to move to different districts in a town, for example, to get to see somewhere local and so follow the third principle of travelling magically.

MEETING TRAVELLERS

Sweet to ride forth at evening from the wells
When shadows pass gigantic on the sand
James Elroy Flecker

There will be times when you just want to 'hang out' with people at a similar stage to you, that is, those who've taken off, left their country behind and are ready to discover another culture, and themselves.

If you choose to go on a typical 'traveller's trail' – where other independent travellers are going – it is easy to bond with people in your hostel or local cafe, where the usual barriers are broken down. And indeed you may meet some fine people this way – including fine in the sense of successful for any worried parents out there. For example, I met a future Australian diplomat out in the desert, an intending ophthalmologist in a Delhi hostel and the daughter of a famous physicist, Paul Davies, with whom I had some interesting chats about the universe on another continent, in an Indian cafe. Not to mention the various Cambridge University students I bumped into. To me, they were simply people I got on with. By letting go of your judgement about what you 'should' do and whom you 'should' know and following your feelings, you may find yourself meeting an interesting bunch of people you genuinely get on with on a deeper level, many of whom will continue to know back in your own society. Thus 'time off' is truly 'time on'.

Meeting other travellers is usually very easy indeed. If they're around, they'll mostly be happy to meet you. Some well-known places draw groups of travellers together. Sometimes the energy of this group can be just perfect – you 'gel' and spark off each other. It may be for a night or some of you may decide to travel together. Eventually, the group energy, however good, will separate itself out. You are drawn to certain people and they are drawn to you for certain reasons. The reasons may not be for you to know right now, but following your call will spark off a series of transformational events in your life. At other times you may feel you need to get away and watch the stars, or travel alone. Whichever way, follow the energy. It provides the spark to set your inner being on fire.

LIGHTING THE LAMP THAT TRANSFORMS

I shall light that lamp with scented oil
Rabindranath Tagore

It was New Year's Eve in that famous traveller's hangout, Ringo's, in New Delhi. I was sitting around the cheap plastic table with Mike the Canadian, Andrew the Scot and lots of other backpackers. I felt more 'at home' than I had ever felt in the society I grew up in. Darkness fell and it was time to go out. We went to nearby Connaught Place where the Indians were celebrating with fireworks, hugs, hats and cries of 'Happy F— New Year to You!'. Andrew brought me a blanket and wrapped it around me, bought me a whistle and a hat made out of rose petals and we let off fireworks together. We later crashed the banquet room of the Imperial Hotel and danced.

It was lovely energy with the potential for more. One of the things I love about travel is the way the different vapour trails we follow in life are suddenly visible. Then one in particular will stand out as the trail of silver. It was the first time I'd come into contact with that path. The new energy meant a lot to me, and it invoked the spheres of light.

Having gone from not being considered attractive at school I was suddenly attractive, and more than attractive – in some parts of India I was even a goddess. All of my energy rose in turn.

The people you meet can change your life, for the lamp burns more brightly than the match that lights it. In fact it burns so brightly that you can overcome the usual limitations of space and time through the strength of your inner light. To get there you must surrender.

THE POWER OF SURRENDER

Surrender is an openness and a willingness to receive. Surrender is giving up control but not losing power
Sondra Ray

Don't you think it's strange that most people's travel plans don't depend on who they meet along the way? They decide they're going on a set track at a set time. They might be going to Tbilisi and then Samarkand at the end of March, or London, then Paris on 15 July, and absolutely nothing will change it. It doesn't matter who they meet, it doesn't matter how well they get along, they still want to stick to their original itinerary. They'll never even think about the possibility of change. That is a way of keeping control.

Someone you meet may hold the key to your wonder. But how will you ever know if you don't give them the chance, even as your heart sings with remembered joy? Even if you only have a weekend, you can still spend time with the person you're so drawn to. Don't think to yourself, 'Oh, I'd like to, but I've already made other plans. I don't want to let anyone down.' Let your timetable go. The development of your soul is the most important thing of all, and what is right for you will always be right for the other people in your life.

If the person you are drawn to supports the growth of your soul, there will be many signs. For example, you keep bumping into that person. Usually that means you are meant to know them. In certain cases, you may be meant to meet someone that person knows, or he or she may hold a piece of knowledge that's important for you. It is usually a good idea for you to spend time together and find out. And by giving up control, you will gain true power – internal power, sovereignty over yourself.

But you do need to employ common sense and choose your travelling companion wisely, and there's more about that in the following chapter, 'The power of saying no'.

Choose your companion carefully

···

> *Meeting is not in space and time. Space and time are in meeting*
> **Martin Buber**

When you travel magically you have a lot of energy around you, but you need to be selective about the kind of energy you allow to get close to you. Often when people travel magically they create a very chaotic energy that they don't know how to balance. This is holey, not holy, energy and its incompleteness leads to illnesses, accidents and arrests, in fact stoppages in any form. Our subconscious mind can be very powerful.

It's as if we each have a moon circling within us and we capture that moon in our relationship with others. Remember the moon represents our subconscious mind, and that mind does not usually know what's best for us. To go beyond the restraints of our subconscious mind, use the rules for travelling with someone that I mentioned previously, in Part 1, Chapter 11, 'Who do you go with?'. If your companion has aspects you really, really like, but he or she takes a lot of drugs or is a bit unbalanced, or if you are attracted to each other but he or she doesn't have the same values you do, then pause. Decide for yourself whether the other person will take energy away from you or if the flow between you both is more balanced. How do feel after being with them? Drained or exhilarated? If the answer is drained – beware. And be aware.

You could maybe play a little game to determine which part of your mind the characters you meet represent. For example, is the guy lurking in the shadows of the bus stop a manifestation of your Higher Self, conscious mind or subconscious mind? As he doesn't help you feel more connected he is not from your Higher Self. As he is not speaking in a lucid fashion he is not part of your conscious mind. As he gives you kind of an uneasy feeling, he is likely to be part of your subconscious mind. How about the woman who demands to know whether you are a Christian? She is speaking in a torrent, and you feel judged, so she is part of your conscious mind. How about the dog begging for a scrap of your food? Animals are usually part of our Higher Self, and if you help those who are more vulnerable than you, you will become more of your Higher light. That will benefit you and the planet.

But when you meet your travel companion from your Higher Self, then your world will open. For meeting is not in space and time, space and time are in meeting.

TRAVELLING WITH SOMEONE YOU MEET

I met a traveller from an antique land
Percy Bysshe Shelley

If you do decide to travel with someone you've just met, you'll find at least two advantages over travelling with someone who originally came with you. Firstly, your energy is the same; remember your level of vibration has altered since you left home. Secondly, you retain your essential freedom. You may find yourself travelling with someone for a day, a week or a month. You didn't start the trip with them so there are no implicit promises that 'they are only there because of you'. They decided to be there quite independently, and that gives you a remarkable freedom. If it's no longer 'right' for you to travel together or you meet someone else you like better, you can say goodbye without any guilty feelings, and each move on to your greater good.

I find going with the people I feel drawn to is a wonderful way of allowing the universe to work through me and for me. However, it's not necessary to carry it to quite the extremes that I do; on occasions when I was hitch-hiking and felt that I trusted the driver, when they say, 'Where are you going?' I reply, ' Wherever you are.' But I would only do this with someone I trust. Nonetheless, when you meet a person you really like and they're going to Macchu Picchu in Peru and you're going to Brazil, why not go with them instead? Trust your feelings and allow the other person to be an instrument of your good. The stronger the attraction, the stronger the lesson. Don't think 'I can always go to visit this person at another time and be with them then.' Timing is vital, for things change, and when you see that person elsewhere one or both of your energies may be different. Trust that you are here, together, right here, right now, for a reason. Don't delay the lesson or you might not learn it at all.

DEALING WITH DIFFICULTIES

*The key to understanding is simplicity. To see love in each other
and forgive one another for transgressions imagined or true
and then shall your heart play its part and show you the true
universal you*
Ken Dryden

Remember there will be times when you and your travel partner will experience difficulties with each other. He or she may say the very thing you don't want, or bring up an emotion that makes you uncomfortable. Just stay with it. Travelling with a companion you feel drawn to does not mean everything is easy. But it *does* mean matters of your emotion and ego will come up in order to be cleared. Don't use that as a reason to move on so you feel more comfortable. You need to move through those uncomfortable feelings – there are several chapters on that later in this section – so you can grow into your Higher Self. It's the most important thing for you to do.

Of course it may not be right for the same person to stay with you throughout the whole process; indeed, if they were to stay with you they would block the process. This person is not your soulmate. Even so, you do need to make this decision from your Higher Self, and there is more about it in Part 2, Chapter 23, 'Coping with goodbyes'. Put briefly, if you feel a sense of 'I am right' in making the decision to move on, your ego is involved. Don't make it from this place, or you will be blocking the unfolding of your true magic. Make it from your proper place. It's so important for you (for no one else is going to do it for you) to make your growth a priority. Don't get stuck on one person and one level. Follow the signs and move on. Move on in faith and trust. Move on knowing there is an abundance of wonderful people in the universe. Wonderful people waiting to meet you too.

If the other person wants to delay the lesson, then respect that. Don't try to force your good – move on. Move on in the expectancy that you'll meet someone else who is ready for you. The only thing you are responsible for is your own growth, not someone else's. Just make sure you are not the one who blocks the energy flow. If you can do that you are well on the way to inhabiting a magical world.

A HIGHER WISDOM

We are the pilgrims Master; we shall go
Always a little further
James Elroy Flecker

Thus, in this chapter we have looked at ways in which you can meet locals and at the benefits to be gained thereby. We've also looked at meeting other travellers, and as long as you follow your intuition and are careful about who you travel with, there is a great deal to be learned. For example, by following someone else's plans rather than your own you invoke the power of surrender. In dealing with difficulties, you discover that, as Rolf Potts suggested, 'perfect harmony on the road is a pipe dream'. But that doesn't mean the dream is not worth it. The rewards of your efforts are considerable. Every journey ultimately becomes an inner journey, a journey into your soul.

What can we learn from meeting others? Almost everything. Other people can, and will, illuminate you. There are so many lessons to be learned, such as surrender, acceptance and joy. Ultimately travelling teaches you humility, and humility is one of our most important lessons. For you are in a new environment, with new ways of doing things and it's only natural you question your old ways, as well as realising you don't know everything. By accepting the help you need from others, you fill in the gaps in your own psyche, which helps you in turn to become a fuller, sparkier, sparklier, more magical person.

Higher wisdom often speaks to you through other people. Ultimately, of course, you need to realise that the people you meet are only facets of your light-filled Higher Self, your true Master, and you are the pilgrim making progress.

In the next chapter we see the power of saying no to what you don't want. For the ability to say no is an essential part of the ability to say yes.

CHAPTER 7

The power of saying no

Virtue consists, not in abstaining from vice, but in not desiring it
George Bernard Shaw

Staying safe is usually quite simple. It involves the power to say 'no'. No to illegal activities, no to temptation, and even no to one or two substances.

Let's see some guidelines. By following them, we can avoid some common mistakes, as well as free ourselves to travel further along the path to our magic. Remember the desire to indulge our senses comes from our subconscious mind, rather than our Higher Self. Remember you need to integrate your subconscious and conscious minds in order to reach your Higher Self. This is done choice by choice, a process we'll look at more closely soon. When you resist the familiar for long enough, you will find all desire to act from your subconscious fall away, and you will effortlessly fulfil Shaw's definition of virtue.

First of all, let me remind you that it's your responsibility to know the law, even if you're in an unfamiliar country.

THE LAW

....

Yet it's very difficult to draw a line
Margaret Mead

One very important point to remember is: do not break the law of the country you're in. It may sound obvious, but it isn't. The laws are not the same as at home, and it is your responsibility to make sure that what you're doing, or even saying, isn't breaking the law. It's very difficult to draw the line, because the line abroad in a different place from where you are used to.

One British guy was put in prison in Spain for desecrating the Spanish flag. He had no intention of doing that, and had no idea that the games he was playing could possibly be perceived that way – yet they were. If this 'slippage of perception' happens to you, watch out. You will be tried under a different system, probably in a language you don't understand and could be imprisoned for months or years in a different country, in often appalling conditions, with quite possibly no right of appeal. It is not worth it, be careful.

SEX

....

It is so very HOT I do not know how to write it large enough
Emily Eden

Backpackers are often responsible for the spread of sexually transmitted diseases, including AIDS, so make sure you're not one of them.

AIDS is far more prevalent in some areas of the world. For example, the incidence is greater in Tahiti than in the neighbouring Cook Islands, where the government has put a lot of money into education on the topic. Always be safe and use a condom if you do indulge in sexual contact. Bring a supply with you (they will not always be reliable, or available where you go) if there is a possibility you may have sexual intercourse. Even if condoms are available locally, the sizing may be different; many of the ones available in Hawaii, for example, are smaller than usual in the West. You also don't know how old they are, or what safety checks they have been through. A defective condom is not a mistake you want to make; it is safer to bring your own.

Remember also that condoms can, and do, break. So don't have sex with anyone you think might be likely to have a disease, such as a prostitute. This isn't smart anywhere, and doing it abroad does not make it any better. And supporting the sex trade, is not, I repeat not, an appropriate way of putting money into the local economy. You are supporting the selling of sex, which often starts with selling children. The sex trade is a vile trade where control tends to be concentrated in the hands of gangsters and pimps, who often also deal in illegal drugs. Don't put your energy into those dark places.

Of course not having sex in return for money goes for women too. Unlike male sex tourism, female sex tourism is unlikely to be part of organised prostitution, yet still contributes to inequitable relationships between the developed and developing world. If you want to have sex, then find someone to have sex with who wants you for *you*, not your money. It's not difficult once your atoms start vibrating from your magical trip.

DRUGS

Be not afraid of life. Believe that life is worth living and your belief will help create the fact
William James

Drugs is drugs, whether they are known as 'soft' or 'hard'.

Do not smoke marijuana (hashish, pot, *pakololo*, to give it some other names). It is illegal in most countries, and just because everyone else seems to be doing it and haven't got caught, it does not mean the same will happen to you. Sometimes when you raise your level of vibration other people won't get caught and you will. It's as though you are putting yourself in line for spiritual tests, so you have more opportunities to learn and to grow.

While travelling in Asia, I met a lot of people who smoked soft drugs, but I've never taken drugs and I made the choice not to follow their example. It meant that I was open to a lot of new experiences. For even soft drugs deaden your senses. If you don't want to give up your 'smokes', think about the reasons why you smoke. What does it give you? What does it stop you doing? How would your life change if you let go of it? If you follow the advice in this book, yet still take drugs, you will not be following the advice in this book. You will be making yourself miss out – big time. Don't take anything 'harder' either. For it will make someone 'harder' and less light – you.

Hopefully some parents will love me, for I have included some harrowing personal accounts in the Resources, 'hard luck' stories of people who have been caught with drugs. Do not take marijuana or harder drugs across international borders or carry anything for anyone (that cute blonde over there in sunglasses and miniskirt could be a drug smuggler). The consequences of being caught are not worth it. Even if you have unknowingly taken the drugs for someone else, you will get the blame. Your intentions do not matter in a court of law, what *does* matter is that they were in your possession. Daisy, a British girl, met a guy through a friend of hers and ended up in a prison in India on a drugs charge. She did not know about the drugs in her bag which her companion may have placed there, and which were found as they attempted to leave the country. Daisy was in prison for over four years before she was cleared, as she refused to plead guilty to something she knew nothing about.

In some countries such as Malaysia, things are even worse. Taking a certain amount of drugs across the border sentences you to death by hanging. And yes, they do carry out the sentence. Your family and friends may not have the know-how and facilities to defend you and your government may not choose to. Londoner Derrick Gregory was pressured into being a drug carrier, caught and sentenced to death. He wrote a very moving letter to my family that stated he couldn't quite believe the sentence really would be carried out. Yet he was weighed for the rope, measured for his coffin and, tragically, there was no stay of execution. So be smart and be safe. Don't give in to pressure from others. Don't.

ALCOHOL

....

Alcohol lowers your frequency making spiritual connections more difficult
Diana Cooper

Another drug worth saying no to is alcohol. If you find yourself in a beautiful bar on the ocean's edge, with dancers swaying and the ukulele playing and a waiter comes up to you and offers you an alcoholic drink, why not try saying no? For surely you have all the ingredients to be happy without that drink. Why spoil perfection? Travelling magically is, after all, a chance to change your habits, and alcohol does stop you from feeling connected to your spirit. Let yourself feel and allow whatever comes up, to come up. You will also be far safer if you don't drink alcohol, as your judgement will not be affected. Otherwise, if you do drink you can make unwise decisions, such as going home with someone you would not normally look at. In addition you will find your local companions respect you more, as you will immediately and effortlessly be set apart from your compatriots who get drunk and act stupidly. You will be full of 'sense' and all the more radiant and attractive for that.

Rock 'n' roll

. . . .

> *Love – love – love*
> **A peace message**

We mentioned various festivals around the world in Section 1, Chapter 3, 'When do you go?'. Festivals are like the Internet, they're places where most things are permissible, and so it's important to make smart choices. Just as it's very easy to reach your Higher Self in the joy and the bliss of the music, dancing and delicious food, so it's also easy to get 'off your head' and enjoy it for all the wrong reasons. The ability to say no to drugs, alcohol and rock 'n' roll will stand you in great stead in your life, as well as your travels. For we all need to live in balance. Keep out the qualities you don't want, and allow in the ones you do want. You will fizz with celebratory energy. Let's look at some guidelines:

How to act at a festival

- ✧ Dress as you like – as long as it isn't smart. Wacky works – face paint, body jewellery, and so on. Wellies are usually good footwear for an outdoor festival.
- ✧ Bring your tent, sleeping bag and so on.
- ✧ Do join in, and get into the spirit of things.
- ✧ Dance, play the bongo drums, try something different.

✧ Groups will form and reform, often within minutes, and it's fine to move on when you feel like it.

✧ Don't take alcohol or drugs – you don't need them. Besides you need all of your senses.

✧ Be happy.

Festivals are great places to practise the principles of travelling magically. They are worlds within worlds – worlds where fairies mix with elves and angels and ballerinas, depending on which ones you go to of course. Alternatively, they are planets where windmills shake in with techno raves, surrounded by tables of leaflets on NGOs – and the odd waving pixie. But most of all they are places where the inherent vibe mean it's easier to groove up into your Higher Self. Keep your integrity and you will stay safe.

THE POWER OF SAYING YES

The appropriate use of the words Yes and No make more room for love
Sark

The appropriate use of the words yes and no does indeed make more room for love. For 'no' is an essential part of 'yes' and feeling fine about saying no is an essential part of travelling magically. Remember boundaries are not walls, but stakes to enable you to grow appropriately, like a plant, towards the light. You do not need to be spontaneous and free-flowing all the time (even if there are people around who want you to be for their own reasons). The power to say 'no' makes your 'yes' far more special. And when you do say 'yes', my goodness. Read Danny Wallace's book, *Yes Man*, for a true story of what happened when he decided to say 'yes' more; he went from being on the road to nowhere to a life full of strange experiences. He went to Holland due to an email spam (one of those which asks you for your bank details), then to a small island off Asia, he said 'yes' to drinks to his friends, he said 'yes' to offers of new work, even to a girl he met in a London pub who lived in Australia. Danny ends up with his life transformed in every way.

Now it's time to move on to three qualities we need for true expansion.

CHAPTER 8

Three qualities for true expansion

Love is the pursuit of the whole
Plato

There are three powers that accompany us along our road of silver. The first power is the power of asking for help, which leads to a place of trust. The second power is the power of belief, which leads to knowledge. The third power is the power of faith, which leads to feeling. When you develop one you'll find it much easier to develop the rest, for they each segue into the other. Every one of them lies within you. Every one of them will give you exactly what you need to expand into your Higher Self, to carry you to the destination of the road of silver. For every one of them leads to the place of love.

THE POWER OF ASKING FOR HELP

I want to be a sign along the way that points towards Heaven
Bethany Hamilton

The power of asking for help is the power to call on when you need an immediate result. Whatever difficulty you are facing you can deal with it. All you need to remember is the first power, the power of asking for help. By simply making the request you will receive help. You don't need to worry about from where, or how your request will be heard, or even when. That's not your problem. All you need to do is ask. That's yet another lesson I learned in North America.

Hitching around Seattle

It is not all pleasure this exploration
Dr Livingstone

When I was a little girl I vowed to myself I would never hitch-hike around Seattle. I remember being scared by the stories of the Green River murderer, who often picked up women in the area. Anyway, when I was a big girl, guess what I ended up doing?

I had been visiting Bainbridge Island, just off Seattle, with some friends. One sunny afternoon I got a ride around the pine-scented island in a rather large truck, with a rather large bearded driver, who could scarcely fit behind the wheel. The ride started off just fine. But then he leaned towards me, and I felt in imminent danger of being attacked. I felt that he suddenly decided I was 'asking for it' as I had hitched a ride in his truck. I couldn't jump out, as the truck was going too fast, and there was no way I could overpower him. I had no idea what to say to defuse the situation. So I asked for help. Some words dropped into my mind like pieces of precious stone. I said, 'You know I really love this country of yours, and I've found every American I've met so kind and welcoming. I'm really glad I've never had a bad experience here and will tell everyone back in England how wonderful this country is.' His attitude immediately changed, and he became very proud and fatherly and protective of me. He ended up dropping me at the ferry terminal, no problem at all.

Whether you believe in angels, or whether you don't, something definitely helped me then. I believe that by appealing to his patriotic instincts, I did the only thing I could have done to defuse the situation. The words were true. I do love America. But it wasn't 'me' who thought of saying them then.

When you have access to your Higher Self, you will always be shown what to do, even in a seemingly impossible situation. There is a higher purpose to everything that happens in your life; just because you cannot see it does not mean it is not there. And I mean everything. Trust that the universe is arranging events for your highest good. The power of asking for help will lead you to that place of trust. The next power, the power of belief, leads to the morning halls of knowledge.

THE POWER OF BELIEF

....

> *When men say they believe only this or that they put blinkers on themselves*
> **Pali Lee and Koko Willis**

Belief is the second power to aid us on our journey along the road of silver. For a powerful belief is like a sword to help us fight our battles.

We all have the power to choose our beliefs, so let's not choose ones from our conscious or subconscious minds, such as 'this nationality is better than that nationality' or, on visiting a new country, having a visceral reaction to a strange habit, 'oh my god, things are terrible here, I really don't like it', when all we really mean is that things are unfamiliar. We are bigger than each of those minds. So much bigger. Let's not allow them to rule us any more. For in judgements, wars begin. In wanting things to be the same as we've always known, we delay our greater good.

The key is to enter our Higher Self. And the way to enter our Higher Self is to allow a greater reality into us. Once we are in the place of our higher light, then it is easy to choose new beliefs, true beliefs, ones that are on the side of love.

The wonder is it takes only an instant. Let's see another example.

Realisation was revelation
> *In its purest state, the soul has infinite knowledge, perception, bliss and energy*
> **K.V. Mardia**

Paul was on his first trip alone to India, where he had long wanted to go, hoping for a reprieve from a rather tumultuous life. He found his meaning, unexpectedly, one afternoon. He was sunbathing on a golden beach in Goa, feeling very good as the sun lulled his pulse to match the rhythm of the waves. He was not noticing very much at all, when suddenly his attention became caught by a gentle cow ambling along the sand near the bright sea. Paul suddenly felt happy knowing that she was protected and cared for in the land where cows are sacred. In that moment, the true value of animals shone out at him, a key to life and happiness. He thought if we all revered animals then paradise would be everywhere, not just on a beach at the edge of India, one warm afternoon.

Paul changed his beliefs about eating meat and years later explained, 'I believed that peace could be brought about by regarding what we eat.' The desire to eat meat had been extinguished as though it had never existed. When a belief is from the Higher Self, the shining sword stretches upwards into a silver ribbon, which merges into a river of light. The belief becomes a knowing.

Now it's time to call on the third power to accompany us along the road of silver. We know it as faith.

THE POWER OF FAITH

To have perfect faith is to have wings
J.M. Barrie

Faith is a deep and powerful feeling. With it you can do and be all things. There are many powers to accompany you to the place of faith, but any one of these high and climbing roads leads to the same still and glistening point, the point of deep feeling vibrating within every cell of your being. You just *know* everything is going to be okay, one day, some way. All religions, and all traditions, know it as the place of faith.

The following story illustrates the power of faith reached through prayer.

Through civil war in Africa

Tei te ta'una pure
Te reo muatangaana
(The woman of prayer
Has the voice of the beginning)
Kauraka Kauraka

Most people know about the civil war that destroyed Rwanda in the 1990s. What they maybe don't know though, is the remarkable story that puts a human face on the suffering. Immaculée Ilibagiza, a 22-year-old former college student, walked alone and unarmed through crowds of men waving machetes and threatening to kill her. Why? She was from the Tutsi tribe, they were from the Hutu. They had already killed most of her family, and at the end of the war, the Tutsi were decimated.

Why was she not harmed? Immaculée said it was because of the power of her faith. Previously she had been imprisoned in a tiny room for months and months, where she constantly prayed. Perhaps she had called in a greater force that was protecting her. Whatever the reason, the guerillas waved their machetes, yet did not attack. Something stopped them, and the marauding murderers parted to make way for her.

Immaculée is a wonderful illustration of the power of faith. She later used it to help her create the life of her dreams, a job for the United Nations, a husband and children.

The development of these shining qualities along the trail of silver means we go straight to the feeling. The feeling of the high and the deep. The power of faith bows down to only one power, the one that resides at the top of the white mountain and sings all the way through it. The power of Love.

THE POWER OF LOVE

....

You can be anything you want to be . . . if only you love enough
Richard Bach

When we bring the three powers together, the power of asking for
help, the power of belief and the power of faith, then we have the
reason. The power of Love. Love is the answer. Love is always the
answer to our questions, asked and unasked. Love is the way. Love is
always the way. Pause. Feel the power. Allow it to run through your
being.

Love is a much abused word in the English language, and the
statement 'Love is the answer' doesn't mean returning to the person
who doesn't treat you well. It doesn't mean that you have to lead an
unacknowledged, unappreciated life. What the statement *does* mean
is that a higher kind of Love is the answer, a Love reached through the
three powers, the power of asking for help, the power of belief and the
power of faith. The higher Love does not deny any other emotion but
incorporates them into its greater golden being. Just as the sun shines
on all of our earth, the earthshadow is an integral part of the whole,
yet the world is still glowing and glorious.

Knowing that our spiritual lessons lead us to this other, greater
love is surely the reason why we keep going. To reach not the country,
but the state. The state way back when, where we once were, when
we were just a sparkle in our mother's eye. It's Love. And Love. And
Love. All Love. And when we reach this place maybe we'll turn around
and descend again, descend to a place that helps us remember our
wonderful school of learning: earth. Luckily for us the qualities we
have contacted will always remain with us, wherever we go. The next
chapter will look at how we can use them to create a shining world.

CHAPTER 9

Travelling ethically

Lead masks the potential radiance of pure gold
Marco Pallis

Throughout this book we look at the importance of making ethical decisions. Now we'll look at some of the results. You will be walking with your best possible companion, your Higher Self.

When your minds are in alignment, you will always have the ability to create a shining country wherever you tread your path of silver. For your path to remain in lightness, you need to take responsibility for the events you create. Transform into your Higher Self, and you will automatically choose to act ethically. You will be in communion. With yourself. We finish with a glimpse of the world it is possible to inhabit.

In Part 1, Chapter 17, 'What do you take?' we saw the importance of leaving your old baggage behind, metaphorically as well as literally. And now we'll see what happened when I didn't. I created a day from my subconscious mind. Then the next day I created another day. This time from my Higher Self.

A Pushkar vignette
All exists within
The Upanishads

All does indeed exist within. For example, I could walk down the same street two days in a row in Pushkar, and each time it would be like a different street. Why? One day the shopkeepers would yell at me as I walked past, and I would feel really hassled, and as though everyone wanted a piece of me. The next, the same people would be the epitome of decorum and politeness, and a little boy with a most beatific smile would gift me with rose petals, weave a ribbon for my long fair hair out of them and refuse to accept money.

Sacred Pushkar is a microcosm of the macrocosm and the instant feedback merely a result of Pushkar's high vibratory energy. Pushkar is widely recognised as being one of the most holy settlements in India, and a place with a very special feeling. It may manifest in the languorous monkeys preening themselves in the sacred temple, or in the Brahmins performing ablutions with their decorated camels in the sacred lake. My energy preceded, or pre-seeded, what I got in return. When I walked among the same people, in the same place, but with a higher energy, I created new experiences, such as my hair being woven with roses. The difference was not in the place, it was the same. The difference was not in the people, they were the same. The difference was in me.

You are the one who makes the difference, even if it's not always obvious. A place changes as you change. Check it out for yourself by going to the same place in two different moods. Write down what happens. Noticing difference, and your role in it, is the beginning of self-responsibility. Then you can make sure that your creation is from the brightness of your Higher Self.

YOU CREATE YOUR OWN COLOUR

Gold is the focal symbol of alchemy
Cherry Gilchrist

We are each our own alchemist creating the colour we experience. For colour ultimately lives in our Higher Self, we just need to 'bring it out' by accessing it. Everything seemed brighter when I returned from my first trip travelling magically, and the wonderful thing is that it still does.

We allow in a greater quality of light by accepting new experiences, abundant when you travel magically. For example, in Nepal I went with a curly haired British guy, Graeme, on his motorcycle, to Bhaktapur to see the temples. It was dusk when we rode back along the road to Kathmandu. Low, puffy clouds overhung the Himalayas. There was a crack in one of them through which poured a trail of silver light. The radiance extended, curving softly beyond the soft white edges and peeling back the cloud, like the wrapper of a chocolate bar. We rushed towards that mercurial flash, the cloud's silver lining. The cloud was a symbol for our trail of silver. I consciously forgot that sight, yet years later wrote in a poem:

> *Suddenly a chink in the soft lands unveils*
> *Bright, glinting light pouring forth in trails*
> *The soft lands catch the hard lands and tilt*
> *The axis of earth, old gold out of gilt*

The verse seems to be referring to the alchemy possible when you travel forth into the pure, metallic light of your Higher Self, which is always shining. All struggle will be left behind, as we saw in the example of Paul and his new belief in the last chapter, and you will want to do the right thing – simply because you do. You will be acting ethically. And guess what, you will still have fun. Maybe even more fun.

At the John Lennon festival

Every perfect traveller always creates the country where he travels
Nikos Kazantzakis

At the inaugural John Lennon Northern Lights festival in Durness, the most northerly and remote mainland settlement in Scotland, I didn't know what to expect. The weekend lay spread out before me, a break from writing this book, a gift waiting to be unwrapped.

I pitched my red tent above John Lennon's favourite beach, the golden belt below the green hill, a line of dark rocks running out to the Arctic Sea. Walking up and down the cliff by the beach between the venues, guided by synchrony, I met the people I needed to meet. The same woman, Iris, sold me sweets in the village shop who used to sell them to John 50 years before I 'happened' to be there for her delighted reunion with John's cousin, Davey, who used to buy sweets with him. I had no need of drink or drugs to enjoy the dancing or the *craic*, talk, whether it was with the Queen's composer, Sir Peter Maxwell Davies, or John's cousin Stanley. I danced to the Quarry Men, who played with John, Paul and George before they were famous, in a cave by the sea, and chatted to them for hours in front of the fire in the youth hostel while they drank wine and I had a nice cup of tea. I found out more about the human side of John Lennon, one of my childhood heroes, from them; barriers were overcome, and even the security people in their orange jackets were dancing to Donnie Munro's heart-piercing Gaelic music.

I was even lucky enough to get a ride with Donnie and his sound technician Chris all the way back to Skye. His memories of the island were so potent in his music that I can hardly bear to listen to it when I am away from the island.

It was a beautiful time, there on that northern beach, in the country of the Higher Self, one I will always remember, aided by the black labradorite crystal I picked up in a shop by the sea. It was the only good weather the town had had all year apparently, and it was perfect, even the organiser said John must have been watching over us. By day the golden sun shone and by night the full moon skimmed the skin of the ocean in silver, a sheen so smooth and complete it seemed like the insubstantial sea was rising into the night air. The molten, metallic qualities of the day and of the night chimed with the alchemy I write about here. Ultimately, we always have the power to create the perfect country of our Higher Self. And we do that by making sure we are in alignment. Our alignment is demonstrated through our actions.

ACTING ETHICALLY

....

Our path is leading to a golden age. And this age will come . . .
we should rejoice that its wind is already blowing around us,
making our hearts beat faster
Konstantin Pautovsky

Choosing to act ethically will help you to reach your Higher Self, from where you'll be happier and make much more empowering decisions. To reach it there are no short cuts, we must be in integrity. Every decision we make from this place helps, as does every thought we have and every emotion we allow ourselves to feel. The more we do it the easier it becomes. Until, finally, it is no longer a 'choice' but something we simply do. For acting ethically means we are in integrity.

Integrity means say what you mean and mean what you say. Do what you say you're going to do, and don't offer to do things that you won't do. By achieving this congruity between thought, word and deed you will be learning about one of the most valuable qualities of all. I once asked a young and smiley Tibetan monk, Thubten Jinpa, very close to the fourteenth Dalai Lama, what made His Holiness so special. He thought for a while and then said 'He is integrated.' Integrity is one of the most valuable spiritual lessons we can learn.

When you are integrated, you will be your own alchemist, recognising the essence that links the substances to be found at the beginning and end of the alchemical process, lead and gold. The essence, the sparkle is always there, as the essence is in you. You know that the gleaming connections between everyone and everything are within your mind. That means that even as you choose to make ethical choices from your higher mind, there is no need to judge those who don't. By acting from your Higher Self you are allowing yourself to be led. By allowing yourself to be led, your lead is alchemised into radiant gold.

Purifying your soul will help to propel the earth towards the age of gold. This is the age when things are simpler, purer and more honest. This is the age when the minds and emotion are in alignment. This is the age of intuition and integrity. Your role, O one of high vibration, is incredibly important.

Now we've come to the end of the three chapters designed to propel

us into integrity, the first on the power of 'no', the next on three qualities of expansion and this one on the importance of integrity. The
next two chapters will look at the ways we show where we are on
our journey – how we spend our money and how we make our food
choices. Read on.

CHAPTER 10

Spending your money

We bear the responsibility but we also hold the key
Ken Finn

It's important to spend your money on the right things, in the right way. After your trip you'll avoid having too much stuff, while still enjoying your precious objects and memories. Follow your intuition about what to buy and when to buy it, and you'll find the right object for you will turn up at the right price – it's amazing how it works. You'll also have more money, as you won't have been spending it on a lot of useless things, not to mention more space in your luggage.

In this chapter we'll look at what you buy. There are three main factors to take into account. The first is the power of certain objects, and what they can add to your life. We'll see which ones to choose and how they make you feel. The second factor is whether it's locally and ethically produced – the only factor green groups take into account. We'll see what happens when an object *isn't* locally and ethically produced, by seeing the way a young Briton followed a tree from the Spirit Forests of Cambodia to a garden centre near London. The third factor is how you buy, and examines the power of relationship and bargaining. Then finally we shall see how buying correctly means that you are following a spiritual law.

WHAT DO YOU BUY?

....

Come, come dance with me. I'm shimmering.
Uma from Fiji

There are no hard-and-fast rules for what and when to buy. It depends on your interests, your budget and how much you want to carry or send. Travelling tends to make people less materialistic. It strips you and reduces you to your essence, and so you care less about what other people think about what you have or haven't got. Rather you will tend to buy things that call out and speak to you – just to you.

Every object will either attract you or repel you. Sometimes one may stand out from the others, like it has a shimmer around it. You need to listen to the energy, just like you do with people. No one spends their whole trip looking for things to buy to take home, but it is a shame that some minimalist travellers do not buy anything at all. You wouldn't want the feeling when you go home of looking around your room and wishing you had bought that bowl in Hawaii, for example. The unique energy of a few objects will really make you sing; having them in your possession will be a tangible reminder of your trip and give you enduring pleasure. They will help raise your vibration so you feel more joy.

Antoinette goes to Egypt

Wise rising gives joy
Ancient Egyptian proverb

When she went to Egypt, Antoinette bought a statue of the goddess Bastet. She enjoys the sapphire gleam on her bookshelf at home, and on a subconscious level it reminds her of her huge link to Egypt and the deep melody she tuned into while she was there. Even though she doesn't believe in past lives, or the spiritual power of objects, it still makes her feel better. And other people admire the statuette too.

CHOOSE CAREFULLY

....

> *A tie occurring through things is one between souls, because the*
> *thing itself possesses a soul, is of the soul*
> **Marcel Mauss**

Of course if you buy everything, whether it resonates with you or not, then you create clutter. It's best only to get things you really like. In general, I avoid loading myself up with too much stuff – it has to be right. Sometimes I go away and think about it but then it might be too late. I still dream of a hand-woven Native American blanket I missed at a pow-wow years ago that was only US$50. But if I am in doubt I tend to err on the side of caution and don't buy things, because I do not want to spend money unnecessarily and have to carry the extra weight. Having the wrong objects about me is also a weight in an energetic sense. I like the feeling of lightness in a room full of things that mean something to me.

Traditional peoples around the world share the same view – everything has a soul. When I studied non-Western economics, to my surprise, I found it fascinating, for it includes concepts such as this. An old friend once said to me, 'I hate the way everything's symbolic to you, Rima. Everything means something.' I replied, 'That's right, it does,' and didn't mind at all. My place has jewel-like cushion covers from India, a gold-leaf painting from Nepal, a fertility statue carved for me in the Cook Islands, a jade statue from New Zealand, to mention but a few items. The small collection is a recognition not only of my physical journeying, but the journeying of my soul. A New Zealand Maori told anthropologist Marcel Mauss that everything is animated by the *ha* or breath. I find each object holds the energy of a certain place and helps ground me. And of course as energy is left behind in the object, we need to look at where and how it is made. It's time to take ethical factors into account.

ETHICAL SHOPPING

All objects, however solid and outwardly separate they may seem, are aspects or views of a flow
Paul Davies

Ethical shopping is now rightly at the top of the green agenda. For as we have seen, an object does not exist in isolation. How it is produced does affect our energy. It also affects the world.

There are certain products to avoid. For example, most animal products as recommended by the World Trade Organisation, as many of them will be made from endangered creatures, such as souvenirs made from ivory and tortoiseshell. You need to ask questions such as, 'are the materials sustainable?' Anything made from coral, for example, isn't, as coral is a very slow-growing substance which can't be replaced. In many cases the question will be more complicated, such as with items made from wood. Ken Finn thoughtfully described what happens when something isn't sustainably made in his book, *My Journey with a Remarkable Tree.*

The story of a tree
The spirits of the forest headed for a store near you
Ken Finn

Ken's arboreal journey began when he went to New Zealand and had a strange encounter with a two-thousand-year-old kauri tree in a forest. He wrote that he was 'taken to the point of understanding or recognition. The clarity blew me away . . . I enjoyed the freshness of the forest, its intense colours and a physical lightness. It was more than just a hedonistic rush; something deep inside me had taken a jolt.'

On the way back to London, he decided to stop off in Cambodia to learn about the Spirit Forests while his girlfriend studied yoga in India. In Cambodia, Ken participated in a ceremony to a tremendous tree towering above the other green trees. He learned more about the destruction of the Spirit Forests. He then visited a factory in Vietnam where he gave a touching description of the former gods being turned into furniture, their resin running like tears.

His investigation did not end there. He followed the tree to the 'end of the line', the docks at Felixstowe, and finally to a garden centre, where the majestic beings are now flat-packed garden furniture, maybe the kind of furniture in a garden near you.

I certainly won't be buying flat-pack garden furniture again after reading that. Ken's message is simple, exercise your choice not to buy, because by buying furniture not made to the Forestry Stewardship Council specifications, you are contributing to the deaths of trees, animals and people and the destruction of the environment. That is what Ken meant by you having the responsibility and also holding the key.

Buy local

E akatikatika
I te mataara o te ngakau
Kia ta'e mai te vai muna
(Straighten
The path of the soul
So the secret waters may flow)
Kauraka Kauraka

Today various organisations exist to monitor the provenance of your goods, such as the Fairtrade Foundation, which guarantees certain conditions of work and pay. But you must also ask questions. If a piece of clothing has a label, for example, then check it. 'Made in China' usually means made in a sweatshop. Do you really want to draw in that energy? Those latest low-cost fashions come at a price, and by this time next year they'll just be a parade of ghostly styles. Even if you think you're getting them for a cheap price now, you're not, because you are 'buying into' the energy of the little girl who was sewing on the sequins in a factory late at night – that night and every night, and who'll never go to school. Why not buy a blanket made in the village instead? That third principle, go local, isn't just pretty words.

On the economic level you need to be aware of where your money is going. Is it going into the local economy or to a multinational company? Your pound or dollar is likely to do far more good benefiting the local people. Your choice will beckon towards sustainability or leap away from it. 'Sustainability' is not just a buzz word, it is about restoring balance. Allow your money, as far as possible, to go to the people who made the object, avoiding these dilemmas altogether, as well as missing out the middlemen. Save energy. Buy in villages or markets, or even from the maker who may approach you in the street. Buy local and ethically produced goods when you can. Create good lives and vibrations for yourself and others. Help your soul to straighten.

THE POWER OF RELATIONSHIP

> *He who seeks to find the inward in the outward, is in better case*
> *than he who only finds the inward in the inward*
> **Henry Suso**

People leave their energy behind in an object. One of the founding fathers of anthropology, Bronislaw Malinowski, described the *kula*, the system of exchanging seashells in the Trobriand Islands of New Guinea. 'The enchantment of the seashell' describes the way an object holds the emotions of the giver, even long after it has been received. Many traditional people say the spirit of the object is the reason why you should give presents back if you no longer wish to keep in contact with the person who gave them to you. Otherwise you will continue to 'pick up' their energy. This fits in with the concept of 'de-cluttering' we explored in Part 1, Chapter 18, 'Clean up your life before you go'. Perhaps that is why giving is part of an ongoing relationship. The importance of gift giving in other societies and at other times cannot be underestimated – indeed it has a section to itself in the Cambridge University Archaeology and Anthropology syllabus. When we enter another society we are entering part of their world. Sometimes all we have to give is money. Even then, we are still in relationship with someone.

That being the case, take notice of whether you get on with the people trying to sell you the goods. Let the way the seller treats you be an indication as to whether you should buy from them. One day, I was looking at a small Native American statue at a market stall in Seattle. The seller, a stocky Native American guy in jeans and T-shirt, smiled and said to me, 'My friend made that and he's real sick with AIDS. He'll be happy it went to someone like you.' That small statue means a lot to me because of the special energy that went into it, from a carver knowing he was near the end of his life, but determined to create anyway. Even though I never met the native carver, whenever I look at the painted and feathered object which 'possesses the soul, is of the soul', I remember him, wherever he is now.

And now we'll look at how you buy – or bargaining.

THE POINT OF BARGAINING

If I speak in the tongues of men and of angels, but have not love,
I am only a resounding gong or a clanging cymbal
1 Corinthians 13:1

Bargaining sets up a relationship between the purchaser and the seller that helps you both. Many people feel guilty about bargaining and always pay the asking price, because 'it's so much cheaper than it is at home'. This is not a good idea. The seller won't respect you and the object will mean less, because you will not have set up any sort of energy.

We're not taught how to bargain in the West, because you usually walk into a shop and the price is fixed (although of course there are still plenty of opportunities to bargain here too). In most of the world price changes according to how you ask, and what the person selling it thinks of you. In other words the price is not impersonal, it is dependent upon *relationship*.

Bargaining does require a little homework. For example, you need to have a pretty good idea of the object's true worth (easily done by comparing it to other, similar objects, and possibly asking someone local who doesn't want to sell it to you), a knowledge of the numbers in the language of barter and a readiness to walk away. Most importantly you need that universal currency, a quick smile and a ready sense of humour. Start lower than you mean to pay and never divulge the highest price that you are prepared to pay; that is for you to know and the seller to find out. A game then ensues, in which you may pretend not to be interested, even at times walking away.

Like any game, you need to turn your disadvantages into advantages. For example, if you are a woman on your own, mention how expensive life is without a man to look after you; if you are a man on your own you can joke about how dear life is without a woman to cook for you. If you are thin you can even joke about it, remembering that thinness in most cultures indicates that you don't have enough to eat. However, like any game, don't push things too far. You want to pay a fair price, but you don't want to make it so that the person you are buying from has no margin of profit. The game should end with both of you smiling and happy, having exchanged a considerable amount of good energy in what is, after all, not merely a monetary transaction.

By bargaining successfully you'll end up with more confidence, a whole new set of skills (and they'll work well at many places in the West too), memorable encounters and some meaningful objects. And now we need to get to the final point, which is that by buying correctly you will be following a spiritual law.

FOLLOWING SPIRITUAL LAWS

Sith do d'anam, is clach air do charn!
(Peace to thy soul, and a stone on thy cairn!)
Gaelic proverb

We have seen how you need to choose an object carefully, and make sure it comes from a sustainable source – and the painfully catastrophic consequences if it doesn't. There are many advantages to buying locally, such as setting up a relationship and practising your bargaining skills. The thing you buy will be all the more valuable to you. In fact, by selecting and buying things appropriately, you are following a spiritual law.

Your actions help you and help the world. They help you because by avoiding things you don't need or love and only buying what you love and from people you like and value, you will avoid waste and energy dispersal. Everyone's vibration will be raised and yours will be maintained by the joy brought by the things around you. You may be able to sense the *ha*, the breath, and have a sensation your objects are almost animated – for example, you might get the feeling one would rather be in that patch of sunlight, another next to that statue.

You will not be contributing to unethical practices or the over-industrialisation of the world. You will be helping local and ethical industries. You will be part of the solution to the energy crisis in the world – which must be solved, in the end, by raising consciousness. Let the object you select help you to raise yours, by being another well-chosen and well-blessed stone in your cairn, bringing peace to your soul. I wish you all blessings in what you decide to buy.

CHAPTER 11

Your food choices

Our task must be to free ourselves ... by widening our circle of compassion to embrace all living creatures and the whole of nature in its beauty
Albert Einstein

Choosing our food and drink carefully is a wonderful way to grow into our Higher Self. It's also a great way to help the earth. Through every choice and every meal you are part of the problem of the pollution of our earth, or part of the solution. Which will it be? By reconnecting to your core through your intuition you will make the very best choice you can in the circumstances.

First I shall look at the power of going local, the third principle of travelling magically, and explore going to a local cafe and eating food grown locally, as well as gathering your own. I even include a couple of recipes. Then we will look at some advantages of going veggie or vegan when you travel, which will raise your vibration according to some of the world's major religions, and more practically, almost certainly, enable you to avoid food poisoning. Then we'll see how you can raise your vibration even further through your food choices. I finish by showing one example of a Swiss man who gave up eating and drinking a few years ago, yet still has a normal job and life, but simply feels happier. The power of growing into our Higher Self is immense.

But, like every great result, it starts with a small decision. In this case, what do you eat for your next meal?

Eating locally

Growth for its own sake is the ideology of a cancer cell
Anita Roddick

Every time you decide to eat a locally grown meal you will help the local economy and the world. When you have a meal at a multinational corporation, by contrast, you will be taking money out of the local economy, and giving it to something you may not believe in.

Eating small

A little golden girl of seven offered me a coconut. 'You shall be blessed,' she murmured
Arthur Grimble

Local food is everywhere because it *is* local, and one of the great advantages of choosing it lies in your interaction with the local population. It's generally easy to find cafes serving local produce in most countries. Then, by giving them your custom, your money goes to the people who matter, using methods that are likely to be organic even if they are not classified as such. You will also get a chance to enjoy a wide variety of beautiful food. Try *gado gado*, a vegetable salad with a spicy peanut sauce, when you're in Indonesia or a bowl of fresh cloudberries in the Arctic. Be open to learning new things – there is even a cafe in Belize, run by a Rastafarian, where he teaches you how to make tofu from the beans.

There's so much wonderful food in the world and so many gorgeous places to eat it. Tortillas simply taste better in a cafe outside a Mayan temple in Mexico, and whenever you eat them again you will remember that sparkling afternoon by the Caribbean. Fresh coconut will remind you of the beach in the Pacific where you ate it and were happy, and then plunged into the ocean. Your unique surroundings are another advantage of going local.

You can find out from the local people which foods are good to eat. Follow the third principle of travelling magically, 'go local' in your diet; you will learn about new foods and the greater variety in your diet will be good news. Gradually your tastes will change and you will come across some great food choices to make when you are back home. Eating local also helps you, because the choice of meals is usually healthier. You cannot lose by eating healthy, local meals.

EATING BIG

....

It is not enough to be compassionate - you must act
Tenzin Gyatso, the Fourteenth Dalai Lama

The movie *Supersize Me* illustrates beautifully what happens when we live on a diet of fast food – we get big. I'll look at only one aspect of what happens when you 'eat big', the destruction of the environment.

Multinational fast food corporations often participate in a system of animal foods that is responsible for the permanent destruction of the rainforest. Our most famous vegetarian, Sir Paul McCartney, said, 'Livestock farming is one of the biggest destroyers of the planet. When you see the Amazon being cut down for hamburger cattle, that's pretty obvious.' This destruction is proceeding at a scary pace, in South America alone about 122 million hectares (301 million acres) are lost per year. The loss is priceless. We have named less than 10 per cent of our rainforest species, the source of most of our medicines, for example. And the vertical world is alive with life, from the fish swimming in the slow river, to the Jesus lizards walking over water, the toucans calling among the trees and the iguanas high up in the emerald green incandescence. Most of the time you probably don't want it destroyed further so you can eat your burger and chips, do you? If you do, okay, your choice, at least you've thought about the issue. But it *is* important to think. Read on.

The United Nations 'Livestock's Long Shadow' report of 2006 recommended switching to vegetarian food. It was based on scientific data. For example, the World Resources Institute said that the expansion of agricultural land accounts for deforestation; most of it is used for maintaining livestock. Feeding an animal takes ten times more resources than growing a crop. Demand for crop production for concentrated animal feed means that billions of litres of pesticides are used every year. They affect wildlife populations and many are detrimental to human health. Meat comes from living animals that require

263

land, and the world simply does not have enough. Our system of producing animals for meat is simply unsustainable. Albert Einstein said, 'nothing will increase our chances of survival on earth as significantly as will switching to vegetarian food'.

Everything is linked, even seemingly unrelated issues. The European Union imports 70 per cent of the high quality protein used in animal feed in intensive farming, mostly from countries where there is widespread human poverty. As a result, these countries cannot use their land to feed themselves, and presently half the world's children go to bed hungry. George Monbiot wrote, 'As a meat-eater I've long found it convenient to categorise veganism as a response to animal suffering or a health fad. But, faced with these figures, it now seems plain that it's the only ethical response to what is arguably the world's most urgent social justice issue. We stuff ourselves and the poor get stuffed.'

Your meal choices are important. Every hamburger you eat contributes to malnourishment in the developing world, global warming, pollution, deforestation, land degradation, water scarcity and species extinction. Eat small, not big, if it feels right to you. And if it doesn't feel right don't worry – enjoy your burger anyway. One thing's for sure in life, everything changes. Let's help the changes along in the way that feels right for us at the moment.

And what better way to get in touch with the natural world than foraging?

FORAGING

Your ultimate local meal comes from foraging. There are so many choices: you can pick fresh flowers and put them in your salad, brew up tea from the local plants or eat berries like a bear. You can bake lily roots like potatoes or make your own flour from grass seeds. Christina Dodwell discusses some excellent bush techniques in her book, *An Explorer's Handbook: Travel, Survival and Bush Cookery*. The popularity of other books, such as *Food For Free* by Richard Mabey, means that foraging is on the increase, and courses on it are springing up all over the world. But you do not need a course to do it, just a bit of common sense and a willingness to ask the locals for advice. In addition you will discover some great recipes, such as the two below.

NUT BUTTER

Put fresh nuts which have been soaked in water for six hours into a container. Add some water and pound the nuts to make a smooth paste.

You can use this delicious fresh spread on bread like peanut butter, when you make it from peanuts. Alternatively, you can vary the nut – almonds have a lovely taste – or you can use it as a delicious condiment, for example cashew cream.

You might even get an unexpected visitor. British travel writer Christina Dodwell swapped some of her store of tobacco for fresh camel milk with some camel drivers, and then made gingerbread in the desert one night in Africa.

DESERT GINGERBREAD

Christina mixed a dough of maize flour, chopped root ginger, saccharine, baking powder, salt and fresh camel milk in a pot, which she buried in the campfire's embers. After half an hour the gingerbread was perfectly cooked and she shared it with some camel men who had happened along. The turbaned men sat down with her in the desert darkness and then sang in reverence to her horse – they had never seen one before.

Travelling magically is about following principles, not a recipe. Christina did not have all the ingredients for her meal and was prepared to swap and then improvise. By not being scared of some strange men suddenly appearing she gained a wonderful memory. Follow the third principle, 'go local' in your diet; you will learn about new foods, they will raise your vibration and you will feel better. Gradually your tastes will change and you will come across some great food choices to make when you are back home.

Tuning into some local variety may mean going vegetarian or vegan, one meal at a time.

Veganism and vegetarianism

··

Alas for those who never sing
But die with all their music in them
Oliver Wendell Holmes

One thing that deserves to be made more of in travel books is the advantages of eating vegetarian and vegan food. Vegetarians don't eat meat or fish, but they may eat dairy products and eggs; vegans don't eat food from any animal source.

Eating local veggie and vegan food is often very easy and almost always cheaper. It's worth noting that by being a vegetarian or vegan, you'll be avoiding almost all food poisoning – the toxin that causes botulism lives in pork, tapeworms hide out in pork and beef, and campylobacter thrives in dead chicken. Food poisoning is rare in vegetarian food and virtually unknown in vegan food. Also, crucially, cases of gastroenteritis are very rare. As gastroenteritis is the most famous cause of illness in certain countries, bear this in mind as you tread your path.

Now we'll look at a little-known advantage in vegetarian and vegan food – the power of kindness. For it's easy for us to help animals not die with 'all their music in them!'

The power of kindness

Any kindness that I can show to any fellow creature, let me do
it now; let me not defer to neglect it, for I shall not pass this way
again.
Etienne de Grellet

When physicist Albert Einstein said we must 'widen our circle of compassion' to include all earth's living creatures, he was referring to the power of kindness. For eating meat is fundamentally unkind to animals, even if they are raised organically, and it is important to treat others the way we wish to be treated. Many of our great people were vegetarians such as Leo Tolstoy, Mahatma Gandhi, Leonardo da Vinci and Albert Einstein. They were also beings of genius, with the ability to make connections where others do not. The fabulous thing about practising kindness is that it ricochets back to you, and serves you in turn.

Vegetarianism and major religions

In what torne ship soever I embarke
That ship shall be my embleme of thy Arke
John Donne

If you follow a vegetarian or vegan diet you will be in tune with the fundamental teachings of the major religions. All major religions encourage vegetarianism. Hinduism states that not eating meat makes you lighter and more spiritual, and members of the highest caste, Brahmins, must be vegetarians. In the Sikh holy book, Guru Granth Sahib wrote to his people, 'You say that the One Lord exists in all, so why then do you kill chickens?' According to the Prophet Mohammed, the whole earth is a sacred prayer carpet. The inviolate Hadiths (laws) of Islam forbid cruelty to animals, saying 'it is a great sin for man to imprison those who are in his power' and 'there is a meritorious reward for kindness shown to every living creature'. The Old Testament, source of faith for Christians and Jews, says in Isaiah 11:8–9, 'a suckling babe shall play over a viper's hole, and over an adder's den a weaned child shall stretch forth his hand. They shall neither harm nor destroy in all my holy mountain; for the knowledge of God shall fill the Earth as the water covers the sea.' The sonorous saying indicates that when we become sufficiently full of spirit, then humanity shall resemble the Ark of God.

Your health and your vibration

May the idea of what is pure, extended even to include the
morsel of food in the mouth, become ever more filled with light
Johann Wolfgang von Goethe

A vegetarian diet is kinder to your health. For example, according to an Oxford University study of 1985, vegetarians had only a third of the risk of getting heart disease of the meat eaters who consumed more animal fat, half the risk of an appendectomy and lower death rates from cancer. And it's kinder to your vibration. You will no longer be eating the fear that pervades every cell of the animal in the moments before he or she is killed. As the Hindus say, you will become lighter.

The effects are profound. Dr Janez Drnovsek, the former Prime Minister and President of Slovenia, enjoyed a peaceful life after a terminal diagnosis of cancer, living years longer than the doctors had expected. He changed his diet to a raw vegan one and his belief system to one incorporating a spiritual reality. We shared some hours of empathy over lunch in Brdo Castle near Ljubljana and he told me always to follow my inner voice. When we raise our consciousness we know what we should eat, what kind of treatment will help us and what will not. Then you don't need help from 'people with a lower level of consciousness, who may offer a little rational knowledge'. For 'everything is connected. Better quality food is somehow connected with a higher level of consciousness. It is a parallel process, if we can do one we can do the other.' So you and the earth will be helped.

So many people worry about their diet, their weight and their health, and so on, yet the solution is simple. Raise your vibration. Then allow your inner voice to dictate what you eat and drink. When you allow your vibration to change, it's simple, even effortless, to change your diet to a healthier one. For example, I usually want to eat healthily and my weight remains fine without me even thinking about it. Yet if I don't want to, and eat chocolate or chips for example, then I do, without guilt. My weight remains fine. My intuition is guiding my body straight and true.

Let's look at how we can raise our vibration even further through our food choices.

RAISING YOUR VIBRATION

It is rare that anyone reverences himself enough
Quintilian

Our vibration is raised either choice by choice, or all at once as happened to Paul in Part 2, Chapter 8, 'Three qualities for true expansion', when he changed his belief system in an instant. We'll now see three examples of raising your vibration choice by choice, for you *are* worth reverencing. You can choose to eat and drink raw food, juice and water. You may feel worse for a bit, while you are detoxing, but then you will feel better. Don't doubt each choice makes a difference to the world. It does.

Raw food

Allow your vibration to be raised by returning to the food that is closest to the source – raw. The original crystalline vibration of the food is undamaged by cooking, so it can do us more good. Try salad, fruit, nuts, nut milk, whatever you find. The fresher and more local the better. There are many weblogs of people who swear their vibration has been raised by eating raw, and the before and after photos tell a story.

Fresh juice

You could get fresh juice from a young coconut straight from the tree, or mango juice on a tropical beach. Juice can be made out of most fruit and vegetables, and a celery and ginger juice on a city street can taste just as good as the examples above. More and more places now offer freshly squeezed juice and it's easy to make your own – some people travel with portable juicers. A fresh juice every day will effort-lessly help you raise, then maintain your vibration.

Water

Our most important liquid is water. About 80 per cent of our body weight consists of it. We need to drink as much as possible, even more than the recommended 2 litres (3½ pints) a day when we are going through transformational spiritual experiences, and we certainly need to make sure we always drink our daily 2 litres. But there are so many health warnings about even water now.

What do you do when you travel? It is important to make ethical choices about where you get the water from, but sometimes they are diffi-cult to make, particularly in a strange environment. I do not normally recommend taking water purifying tablets as they can adversely affect you and the environment, so that leaves us with four main choices:

1. Buy water in plastic bottles and drink from them when unavoidable, as they contribute to a massive amount of land-fill. Check the seal is intact.
2. Collect water yourself and make sure it is boiled for at least three minutes in certain climates.
3. If you do drink tap water then leave it for half an hour if you can, so the chlorine added to it in many countries will evaporate.

4. Drink local water, but be sensible. Drinking from a fresh spring is likely to be safe and will build up your immunity, but drinking from a dirty tub at a market is not likely to be.

Generally I recommend taking your own fresh (or boiled) water with you in a bottle or flask that you then reuse. There are some beautiful sources of water around and it's fun finding them, such as 'the fairy springs' at Glastonbury, England. Even if you decide to drink tap water, be happy and grateful before you drink and take a moment to put that energy into your water and your food before you eat – scientific studies show that the water responds. Japanese scientist Masura Emoto has shown in a series of experiments that water given love, changes its vibration to give a beautiful holographic pattern. So water you send love to will help you even more, as the power of vibration is immense. Allow your waters to flow and your vibration will jump up.

INTO ECSTASY

A true pilgrim, working with love, moves the earth energy through the landscape . . . helping to vivify the Earth and create patterns of light
Philip Rawson

Raising your vibration propels you higher and higher. Your atoms zing and you feel instantly in tune. Your intuition will become so strong that you will be able to pick up a newspaper and know the outcome of the main news stories of the day. Some people are even able to predict the main news stories, so that reading the newspaper becomes boring. Your consciousness is more exciting. Your experiences snowball and your life becomes extremely – well, interesting is a word that always applies. That's for a period until you reach a new white plateau, a higher one than you were on before. Then your life will become interesting again, and the path continues, winding ever upwards, creating a pattern of your light. And so it goes on. The road of silver. The road to your magic.

When you reach your shining core you will know a magical life. The ordinary laws of cause and effect won't apply to you – at least sometimes. Your life is far more extraordinary than you have ever believed possible. Dr Michael Werner, a Swiss scientist, provides a fabulous example.

Michael receives light

The only precondition for being nourished by light is to have trust in it

An anonymous scientist

Michael Werner is fit and well having eaten only a few handfuls of food since 2001 and hardly drunk at all. He passed a rigorous scientific test sitting in a room in a Berne hospital for ten days without eating or drinking. He was under constant surveillance, and was absolutely fine at the end. He said that the observers couldn't seem to understand him when he mentioned he'd been like that for years. Dr Werner said he now feels healthier and more energetic, more sensitive, more internally stable, and has developed a better relationship with his wife and children. He has chosen to carry on with his work as managing director of a research institute, while feeling much freer inside.

'Living on light' is a very interesting concept, and maybe more. As Dr Werner's experiment has been scientifically validated, it seems our usual models concerning the process of receiving nourishment may be very limited. For tremendous things are possible when our vibration is raised. For example, he reported that he receives all he needs from the ether, 'that subtle dimension of reality in which there proceeds the divining, wishing and imagining of possibilities which is the preliminary stage of manifestation'. According to Huna, the ancient religion of Hawaii, the ether is the silvery *aka*, the sticky, shadowy substance whence all things come into being. It's the word for a foetus, as well. Our energy helps our intentions grow, and they eventually arrive in our world, the world of day, in a process many call 'manifestation'. And then, if our minds are in alignment, and it's for our highest good, our desires can even stay. By acting in integrity, and 'walking our talk', we become a creator, just like a god or goddess. As an interesting note, the Hawaiian word for god or goddess is *akua*, separated from *aka* by the letter u, which means 'quality of', as in light. To improve our quality of light all we need to do is raise our vibration.

TAKEAWAY

> *Hawvlan lachma d'sunkanan jaomana*
> *(Give us this day our sacred wisdom)*
> **Alternative translation of the Lord's prayer**

In food terms, a takeaway usually refers to a meal 'to go'. So what do we take away from this chapter where we have seen how we can raise our vibration through food, by taking in substances as close to the source as possible? It helps us reconnect to our source, our sacred wisdom.

Reaching our inner core becomes easier with practice. Remember your power to choose is vital, and one choice at a time will take you to a new place. For we are part of a bigger system, and we can give our consciousness – and our money – to an ethical system, or a less ethical one. Choose wisely. Try local. Try veggie. Quaff down fresh juice. And if you sometimes slip back, then don't beat yourself up. For what brightens sometimes fades. There will be times when you need to lower your vibration, particularly when you are travelling and not leading a stable life. You are just 'too sensitive' to your environment, as if your skin is so thin it's transparent. If this happens, eat lots of stodgy food such as rice and potatoes, until you are ready to move along your silvery road once more, and travel further into your brightness. We are each a work in progress, so do give yourself a break. You are doing your very best, after all, and who can do more than their best?

Grow at your own pace, and soon your choices will take on a momentum of their own and become effortless. You will quite simply feel, and look, much better. You are resonating on a higher level of vibration, part of the circle of compassion you have helped to create.

Your care for the earth is reflected in the higher, brighter world around you. It's time for the next chapter, 'When do you accept hospitality?'

CHAPTER 12

When do you accept hospitality?

*A sojourning Bishop in New Zealand was offered a
woman for the night by his Maori hosts. At his offended
look they offered him two*
From an Anthropological book

In this chapter we view hospitality as a gift. It is part of the greater
system of gift-giving we explore throughout this book. You will already
be familiar with it in your life, for it is one of the principles on which
the universe works. When a gift is given, a gift needs to be returned,
and we'll explore the importance of this in the next chapter.

These two chapters carry on from Part 2, Chapter 2, 'Where to stay',
and further explore the section on staying with locals. For, very often,
the locals you meet will invite you to stay in their home. Sometimes
it will be a great idea to accept their invitations; at other times there
could be disastrous consequences. How do you know when to distinguish between them?

In this chapter we'll look at individual standards for accepting
hospitality which, of course, vary from person to person and culture
to culture. Accept it not from a feeling of lack, but from a sense of
being in the right place at the right time. For that will create manifestation from your Higher Self rather than your subconscious mind.
We will learn about the Law of Trust, the outcome of the first power,
the power of asking for help. We'll also look at how long to stay for
and when to move on, another great invocation of the Law of Trust.
Finally we'll look at a new definition of hospitality, one which was
once ours and remains in many native peoples and faiths. The earth

as our mother. For in truth we are not separate and she gives us the deepest gifts we can know.

Cultural questions

....

The great thing about climbing lesser hills is that they give you fantastic views of the greater ones
Donnie Munro

Many cultural questions come into play when we decide whether or not to accept hospitality. A travelling Inuit, for example, may traditionally have a warm welcome when he arrives at the igloo where he spends the night – his host's wife. Likewise the male visitor to Thailand may find a woman included in the price of his hotel room. Or, like the unwary Bishop in the example above, he may be offered two. So just how do we know what is expected of us, and how do we decide if it's acceptable?

The anthropologist Marcel Mauss famously said that there is no such thing as a free gift. But how do we know what's implied? You need to look at the culture. If, for example, your offer is from that Hong Kong silk trader who tried to sell you the contents of his factory, or who wants his daughter to marry a Westerner, his motives may be very mercenary – but then there's nothing wrong in marrying for money in Chinese culture. Unless you are seriously interested in either of his proposals it is probably best for you to refuse. If you are a woman travelling in the Mediterranean and that young man who has been following you along the street and eyeing you up and down invites you to come home and meet his family, you may not want to take his invitation at face value. Again, you may be considered to have more money than sense, and there may be reports of other women of the same nationality as you sleeping around – so beware.

INDIVIDUAL STANDARDS

God is present in every act of service. All life turns on this law
The Bhagavad Gita

Everyone has different standards of course, both culturally and individually. Sauce for the goose is not necessarily sauce for the gander. What is acceptable to me may not be acceptable to you and vice versa. Not only must you decide what is acceptable but you must also learn to recognise it, as not everything that's included in the invitation will be explicit, a lot will depend on context.

Basically you need to trust the invitation. If you are not sure ask your intuition and try the Hand Exercise from Part 1, Chapter 2. If a man invites a woman, he often makes it clear he wants to sleep with you, but leaves it up to you to initiate things. In such cases, I have found it absolutely imperative to send the right signals, such as in the subjects you talk about, the responses you give and even where and how you sit. If in doubt, err on the side of caution. It will probably be helpful if you wear conservative clothes so as not to attract too much attention. Of course, this is true for any circumstance not just travelling – the lessons learned in travelling magically can be applied to life and vice versa.

ACCEPTING HOSPITALITY

A river without islands is like a woman without hair
Mark Twain

Accepting hospitality in local homes is one of the delights and learning experiences of your trip, where you can meet people in many different ways. The growth of the Internet means there are many websites which can hook you up with locals (see Resources). Each one has slightly different standards and verification schemes. If you go couchsurfing for example, you can meet locals and sleep on their couch. Nothing is required in return, except for you to be considerate and polite, and your host will often show you around their area. Again, you do need to follow your feelings, which are getting honed as you have so many decisions to make on a daily basis now.

Yet I would still recommend meeting people 'on the ground', if possible, so you are aligned with their vibration. This is because being on the same wavelength is vital – it's indefinable and very personal. You either click with someone or you don't. Making this decision is far easier when you are travelling alone, for you and your friend may have different reactions, and then you might not know which one to follow. There may be nothing wrong with a particular place or family, it is just not for you, just as a country may not be. But when it's right, it's really right. Even though you may not meet people you click with that often in your home society, you will meet them surprisingly often when you travel. When you think about it, it's not unexpected, as the number of people you meet goes up exponentially. So you are far more likely to meet people you have empathy with, and empathy transcends cultural barriers. In fact, it happens so often it's relatively easy to practise the Law of Trust. When we practise the Law of Trust then we allow our intuition to discern what's best for us to receive.

The Law of Trust
All is best, though oft we doubt
John Milton

It took me a few years of magical travel to decide that I would stay with people only when I click with them. Otherwise, I would rather avoid emotional and spiritual contraction and pay for a room. I then took a trip up and down the west coast of America, Canada, Alaska and Hawaii. To my surprise I only paid for six nights' accommodation out of the entire three months I was there. My decision had freed my energy to attract some glorious experiences into my life.

A lady I met saving a cat in front of a Russian cathedral in Sitka, Alaska, took me in, helped me to deal with some family issues and gave me a bag of opals I still treasure. Once, when I was hitch-hiking around Hawaii and feeling rather poor, which I wrote about in Part 1, Chapter 12, 'What about money?', I invoked the power of asking for help as I stood by the side of the road with my green rucksack. Then my very next ride led me to a guy in Kauai, Hawaii, who allowed me to sleep in his lounge that was full of the exact books I needed for my rather 'out there' research on Hawaiian cosmology, and encouraged me to swim on his private beach with its own waterfall. Another man, on the remote Alaskan island of Angoon, the fortress of the brown bears, invited me to stay in 'the best beach house in Alaska', his many-windowed house overlooking the sound. There I participated in the funeral feasting of the two clans, the Raven and the Eagle, for the highly respected traditional chief Jimmy George who had just passed on.

On that trip, I received hospitality beyond my wildest imaginings and never once did I feel uncomfortable. I see myself as learning the Law of Trust then, knowing that my vibration would bring the right people to me. But of course when we learn to accept we also need to learn to decline, hence the next section.

HOW LONG DO YOU STAY FOR?

Ka to he ra, ka rere he ra
(A sun sets, a day is born)
Maori proverb

Next comes the question 'how long do you accept hospitality for?' In general do not prolong your stay for longer than you have been invited.

This is one area in which a direct question is difficult, as politeness may force many a family to say 'you are welcome' even though their younger daughter may be coming back that day and needs her bed back. So be very careful, and try and interpret what the family *doesn't* say as well as what they do say.

If your love affair is running out of steam, do you stay for longer and try and reawaken it? This is another tricky area, fraught with potential for miscommunication. Generally the answer is 'no'. Move on with dignity, and leave a way of getting in contact, so if your sometime lover wants to see you again he or she can do so. Trust the universe and move on.

MOVING ON

....

'I am very cold'
Sign on a fridge in India

Being in the wrong place means that you are missing in the right place. Trite but true. So you are doubly in the wrong place.

There is nothing worse than tiptoeing around a household where you are not quite welcome, wondering what to say, when to say it, and if you can make a mug of tea. In this situation you should not stay, and I say that in full awareness that you are saving money by being there. Your time and your spiritual growth is precious, so leave. Leave so that you can find somewhere better. Who knows, there might be a conversation waiting for you in a local hostel, or a perch on a nearby campground. Magical travel involves having the courage to move on.

You sometimes have to say no and leave, even when it's awkward and unexpected, to keep your self-respect. We might be in a place where we hoped we were welcome, but were not. This might even be the case if we are staying with relatives.

Laura's story

Anak dipangku dilepaskan, beruk di rimba disusukan
(A child in the lap is let go, a monkey from the forest is nursed instead)
Indonesian proverb

Laura went to stay with her father's new family in Cornwall. It was a bit of an effort for her, as she hadn't been invited to her father's wedding and hardly knew her half-sister, whom she hadn't even met until she turned eight. But she still believed in the importance of family, and so she did her best. Her stepmother gave her lots of subtle insults when her father wasn't around, and he didn't believe her when she tried to tell him. The last straw for Laura (and we each have our own) is when she visited at Christmas for the first time. Everyone received Christmas presents except for her, even though she had carefully chosen presents for all the family. Her father said his wife bought the presents and it was nothing to do with him. It crossed her unspoken line and she has not returned since.

Other people are free to create their own way too, and sometimes all we can do is respect ourselves. So it's vitally important to be able to say no, just as important as saying yes, and one should go with the other, as we have already seen in Part 2, Chapter 7, 'The power of saying no'. Remember you *do* have value and treat yourself accordingly, even if others don't.

Now we have the chance to look at a type of hospitality which is always unstinting in its generosity – our earth. For hospitality comes not only from humans, but also from the rest of nature, and ultimately, earth. Our green earth looks after us all.

SHARING TRUE HOSPITALITY

Treat the earth well. It was not given to you by your parents. It was loaned to you by your children
Kenyan proverb

Our earth's great hospitality can best be understood in sacred terms. We are precious guests in an eternally giving world. We do not own it, although culturally specific ideas of land ownership and private property may make us believe we do. My anthropological studies have shown me that no indigenous society treats nature as being owned, rather that we humans and all our relations comprise a portion of the magic circle. We each hold a small fragment of the enchantment. When we see the world with a sacred eye, we will realise that we are always the recipient of unstinting generosity.

In the Resources I have included a section of stories of people who went into the wilderness – and were rewarded beyond their wildest dreams. For example, Marie Tieche:

The lure of the wild
We all have our own White South
Sir Ernest Shackleton

Englishwoman Marie Tieche was living and working in the Arctic town of Spitsbergen after leaving her unsatisfactory marriage in Hampshire, England. She had a bedsit in her new home, and was doing a few different jobs to keep body and soul together. She went to a bar one night, and met a German scientist, Hauke. That night he invited her to come for a year with him to a very remote hut, where there was no possibility of leaving if it went wrong. Soon afterwards she agreed. Why?

'A new chapter. I hoped it would be a good tale, not too much sadness. I wanted the new me in there, not the old one, not someone else's. The real me. I wanted to set myself free, to stretch myself, assert myself, expand my horizons. I couldn't change my past, but I could change my future just by being myself.' When she was there, she found she was, slowly and subtly, becoming different. 'The sun had coloured the rocks around the hut beautiful shades of peach, doing nothing to dispel the feeling of separation from the rest of the world, but intimating warmth. An invitation to a new, basic life. Shared with nature. Shared with Hauke. In England I'd felt trapped in a big world, like a bird in a golden cage. I had so much – was it too much? Was it too little? Too much in the material sense, too little of life's basics. Friendship. Companionship. Conversation. Contact. Love. Hope. Would the wide, open spaces, the wind, the sea, the long dark nights, the discomfort, the aloneness, fill the empty caverns I felt inside me? I wanted it to take away the loneliness, to fill the void. To heal.'

THE WISDOM OF THE WILD

....

> *We do not receive wisdom, we must discover it for ourselves,*
> *after a journey through the wilderness*
> **Marcel Proust**

One of the great things about the wilderness is that it forces you to reduce your life to your basics, and so you have both more time and more space to perceive what is really important. Marie found a white, pure space inside her, and did not want to leave the hut at the edge of the northern ocean of snow she and Hauke had made into their home. She had overwintered further north than any other woman before, and went on to write a bestselling book, *Champagne and Polar Bears*, about her experience; certainly one powerful way to give back what she had learned. Perhaps most importantly she opened her heart.

It is very likely the time and the space provided by enforced isolation gave Marie the opportunity to do so. Having the courage to spend time in the wilderness lends a far deeper texture to our lives than the shallow pleasures of drink, drugs and television. The journey into the wilderness is no longer a journey into the heart of darkness, it is the journey into *our* heart, the heart of light.

So in this chapter we have moved from seeing hospitality as a gift we can choose to accept or decline, to viewing it as a greater quality. For ultimately, the wilderness lies not only outside, but also within. Travelling magically is a way through. Wisdom is a gift, as Proust put it, to be discovered for ourselves. The greater wisdom is the wisdom of the heart.

CHAPTER 13

What do you give back?

Give, and it will be given unto you
Luke 6:38

We must always ask this question, as the successful receiving of gifts such as hospitality demands giving something back. Every action demands a reaction. Damming your energy leads to it atrophying and results in less wonderful things happening to you. When you give back though, your world continues to sing, then you receive again, and give again. You rapidly find yourself in a new loop on the silver spiral of your soul.

In this chapter we shall examine the Law of Balance, which you need to follow after the Law of Trust. Then we shall look at what you can give in return for accepting hospitality, from the more usual factors such as money or immediate help to something more long term. Giving and receiving, then giving back again quickly and receiving again, is known as being 'in the flow'. I look at a wonderful example of an inveterate traveller who lives her life that way. Then finally I explore how we need to give back to our green earth, whose hospitality we have learned to accept at the end of the last chapter. The circle is complete.

THE LAW OF BALANCE

> *When your life takes a new direction that is part of your growth.*
> *Balance is taking place*
> **Catherine Ponder**

When you follow the Law of Trust you will be given amazing things. The energetic Law of Balance states that what is given to you, you must return. It does not always need to be to the same person, or in the same dynamic, but generally we always need to strive for a little more, a little more justice, a little more love.

If you are a giver, for example, the mother taking care of the children, then learn to receive gracefully – know that you will pass on your good elsewhere even if not to that person, that time. If you are a taker, more typically a successful male who takes his good fortune for granted, then stop taking and start giving. Of course these categories are not prescriptive and the gender categories are only a guide, not a given.

But isn't your trip a fabulous chance for you to experiment with being someone different? Draw some balance into your life. Follow the Law of Balance. Give back.

WHAT YOU CAN GIVE

> *Give what you have. To someone, it may be better than you dare*
> *to think*
> **Henry Longfellow**

True giving always invokes a response, and now it's time to move on to what to give back. We all have something to give. You may offer your body, only if you are both free and you really want to. Don't do it because you are expected to – it's better to stay somewhere else. You can give practical help, such as babysitting, looking after the animals, teach English (as Alexandra did in Egypt in Part 2, Chapter 2, 'Where to stay') or help with the house. Of course you should also give kindness.

You can give presents. Sometimes giving money is best. It may be appropriate, especially in underdeveloped countries, to pay your host family. You may pay directly, or you may pay later. For example one Fijian family I know put up an American visitor for three months in their traditional home on Vitu Levu, the main island, for free. David had very little money at the time, but went back to home, got a job and later paid them several thousand Fijian dollars, enough for one of the daughters of the family to get a nursing degree. That was a very satisfactory outcome for all concerned, and one completely in resonance with spiritual principles. There are so many ways to give.

Some very special gifts are the ones only you can give, the result of your life experiences, the reason you are attracted there in the first place. As amazing as it may seem, you will find that you are exactly the right person to deal with the place, and the situation, you're in. The guy with the spectacular beach house in Alaska needed someone who knew Russian for his work in publishing – I studied Russian for years. The guy in Hawaii needed feedback that his brilliant research on Hawaiian astronomy was worthwhile – I was in a position to give him that. Odd talents, yes, and I didn't have to worry how I would give – the universe showed me.

If you're not sure what your skills are, don't worry. Travelling will help bring them out. Singing, dancing and playing music, for example, are useful almost everywhere you go. Your talents will attract people who need them. If you've got good handyman skills, you'll meet someone who needs a handyman. If you're an accountant you'll encounter someone who needs help with their finances, and so on. That's the way the universe works.

Rita Golden Gelman gives many fabulous examples of what to give back when staying with a local community in her book *Tales of a Female Nomad*.

Reciprocity in Bali

I move through the world without a plan, guided by instinct, connecting through trust and constantly watching for serendipitous opportunities
Rita Golden Gelman

Rita started travelling magically when her husband suddenly asked for a divorce when she was 48. She decided she did not want a life where her grown children gave her reason for living and she hunted for another man, like so many women of her age. So she made a different choice, a magical choice.

Rita has travelled widely around the world for years and years, going wherever it felt right. She said, 'I have no permanent address, no possessions except the ones I carry, and I rarely know where I'll be six months from now.' She often stays with local families in native villages and learns new languages, new recipes and most importantly, a new way of being. For Rita, as for Saki, having an address concealed who she really is.

In Bali, Rita was offered a fabulous house to stay in, the artists' village of Ubud. It boasted marble floors, wood carvings, exquisite art and had a lily pond in the lush garden. No mention was made of payment by the owners, a family of artists. 'That night, as I listen to the croaking frogs in the lily pond outside my window, I think about what I can do to reciprocate. I have been given this exquisite place to live in, without even a hint of their wanting anything in return. But life has taught me the doctrine of reciprocity, and I have found that it is alive and well and operating all over the world. Kindnesses must be returned.' She gave help with the English language, as well as writing a catalogue about the mythology of the sculptures the Balinese family were selling. Rita is an author of over 80 books, so that was no problem, and she welcomed the chance to learn more about Balinese and Hindu mythology. So the doctrine of reciprocity helped both Rita and the Balinese family. She said she has learned to 'listen to the spirits, the inner one that is a part of me and the ones from the other, invisible, world'. When you follow spriritual laws, everyone will be helped.

Years later Rita is still going, continuing to live, love and learn from different cultures in the world, moving lightly along the silver road to her magic. There's much to learn from Rita's example. Her grown children are supportive and enjoy visiting her in the places she goes to. They do not say, 'Oh God, I have to visit her', rather, they want to visit her – for Rita is happy in herself, and her children also love to see the countries she finds herself in. She's showing them a great example of what's possible when you travel without your kids. She is living in the flow.

The final section on what to give back, follows on from the lore and the wisdom of the wild in the last chapter. The earth gives to us so very much. How can we best give back to her?

GIVING TO THE EARTH

....

> *Namé samé kadri chhé*
> *(Thanks beyond the sky and earth)*
> **Dzongkha proverb**

At the end of the last chapter we looked at how spending time in the wilderness can help replenish our spirit. Now, at the end of this chapter, we see ways of giving back to the earth who holds us. How do you give back to the earth, the sun, the rain, the flowers, the creatures and the world that do so much for you? There are many ways.

You need to be calm and balanced in yourself. Take time. Slow down. Connect to the deep, slow heart of the earth. Notice the beauty of your surroundings: the way the water glistens on a leaf, the dampness of grey snow, the depth inside the pool and the brown wood of your table. Allow an attitude of gratitude for all of the weather, the compassion of the rain, the warmth of the sun, the touch of the wind and the shivering grace of a rainbow.

And when you feel the grace, or you wish to feel the grace, do a quick meditation for all life.

Meditation for all life

1. Focus on your breathing – in-out, in-out, in-out.
2. Become vibrantly aware of your surroundings: What do you see? What do you hear? What do you smell? What do you touch? What do you feel?
3. Allow gratitude to flow through your whole body in a stream from the crown of your head to the soles of your feet – from the heavens to the earth.
4. Send thanks to every element, the whole earth and the totality of creation for supporting you.

Meditate as often as you can, as it helps the earth and it helps you reach your Higher Self, the land of your delight.

More practical actions also help you access your Higher Self.

Pick up litter. Don't make more. Make love tenderly (and discreetly) outside if you'd like to and it's appropriate. Recycle. Look after the land and water. Give money to a charity you believe in if you work too hard to help directly. Make it a regular tithe, not just a one-off. And then there are things all of us can do. Change to green electricity or go off-grid. Switch off. Buy less. Help someone who wants help. Regularly feed a homeless human or animal.

Feel genuine response-ability. Count your blessings. Do all of this with love and without anger, for then the love vibe you give will multiply. And don't you want more of the power of love in your life?

SPIRALLING THE CIRCLE

> To give is why I am on this road. In giving, I receive. It is an endless circle of bestowing and accepting
> **Joseph Dispenza**

We have seen how giving and receiving is part of an endless circle. There are so many ways to give, from your skills and your talents, to a deeper part of yourself. In these uncertain times we have looked at the necessity of giving to the earth too. So when you receive hospitality do give back. And when you do give, give with love.

For example, when you reciprocate hospitality back in your home country, be sure to make your guests feel genuinely welcome. Western culture does not teach the value of this the way Islamic cultures do. Therefore you will be drawing on the feelings that were invoked while you were travelling, and you need to recreate to use them back home. For example, you can also offer hospitality when you find yourself with a spare couch, keeping up your 'travelling vibe' that way. Everyone's lives will benefit, particularly your own, as giving from your heart is a great opportunity to create from your heart. Your heart creation is the most important one of all.

For, most vitally, we must learn to love. We talk about the importance of loving ourselves throughout the book. Of course loving others is one way to get there, and we explore it in the chapter on making love later in this section, as well as more impersonally in this chapter. Learning to love is how we change the circle into a spiral, one taking us ever higher.

Our love needs not to be reserved for 'romantic love', or 'family love' as love is so often construed as in the West. For that limits it. Our love must include our earth. And what better way of learning to love a very small, special portion of the earth, which then radiate out to the rest, than camping?

CHAPTER 14

The point of camping

Earth was his couch, his covering was the sky
Virgil

Camping helps you reconnect to the earth. Through it, you can learn not only about the earth's true value, but your own. For lying on the soft skin of the earth will teach you many lessons such as acceptance and trust. And just like travelling magically it will show you what's really important. Camping needn't be part of your magical trip, but do at least consider it.

For example, just because you would not normally camp in your home country, does not mean that you would not enjoy it in the country you're visiting. The warm feeling of sitting around your campfire at night and the freedom of waking up in your tent by the ocean beats even the friendliest hostel. If you're not used to it, don't worry, various courses exist to teach you the basics of going into the wilderness, including those for women only or ones for people who want to specialise in cold-weather travel – for example, learning new skills such as mountaineering. Tents are wonderful for they enable you to bring your home with you and put it up wherever you are. How cool is that?

In this chapter we'll look at what to bring and at the two main types of camping. Then we'll go more deeply into one of the themes of travelling magically – the rewards that your new connection with nature brings.

WHAT TO BRING

Here are some tips on the equipment you will need if you do decide to camp:

- ✧ Tent
- ✧ Backpack
- ✧ Sleeping bag (in most situations, a cheap nylon one is fine)
- ✧ Air mattress or foam pad
- ✧ Torch (you don't need to take spare batteries, see Resources)
- ✧ Candles/matches
- ✧ Small stove (if you don't make a fire)
- ✧ One or two light pots or billycans
- ✧ Set of light crockery
- ✧ Inflatable pillow or sweatshirt stuffed with clothes
- ✧ Lantern

It's definitely worth practising camping in an environment you know before venturing into a strange one, if you are not used to it. Remember too in most countries there is the option of hiring or borrowing a tent and your gear. If you do bring gear, and know you won't be camping again, then you can always sell it or send it home. And do check you've got the best tent for the conditions. For example, if there are lots of insects, make sure your fly sheet works. If you are doing lots of hiking then make sure your tent is as light as possible – but if you are travelling by car, then you can afford to have a heavier tent with a bit more space. A vestibule is worth it to stow your gear, which may be wet and smelly, so it doesn't have to be in the tent with you. With a bit of practice, you'll soon have a system for putting up your tent, making your fire and preparing your food that works.

HOW TO CAMP

There are two main choices: organised camping, for example on a campsite, and wild camping, where you pitch your tent in a wilderness. Organised camping is even cheaper than a local hotel, and it is usually just as easy to meet people, for example in the shared showers or kitchen – they are great places to start your camping experience.

However, wilderness camping is free and you will be in tune with the environment and yourself. It's likely to leave you with even more special memories.

Comparisons – campsite or wild

Campsite	Wild
Allotted area	Choose your own site
Shops are often available	Bring your own stores
Other people around	More likely to be deserted
Shared facilities – bathroom, kitchen	Create your own
Small charge	Usually free

Here are some camping tips I wish I'd known about.

Camping tips

✧ Choose your camping spot well before sundown, so that you have time to set up.

✧ Find a flat spot, or at least ensure your head is above your feet.

✧ You need to check your nearest water source to ensure you won't get flooded if it rains. For the same reason avoid hollows.

✧ Avoid insect nests, and try and ensure you're not in the path to their nest or you'll be overrun.

✧ Follow the rules of the area you are in – for example in 'bear country' keep your food well away from your tent.

✧ Follow sensible local advice.

✧ Check you're doing minimal damage to the environment, for example be careful of unusual flowers under your tent, as you want to cause as little damage as possible.

✧ Learn how to build a fire pit (safely, in certain environments) and cook with an open fire instead of bringing gas and stove with you

✧ Reconsider the use of toilet paper. Leaves and ferns do just as well, as does a long, flat stone or your hand which can be washed in water afterwards.

✧ Don't fish or hunt or cause destruction.

✧ Leave nothing but footprints.

Rewards

....

> *You must do the thing you think you cannot do*
> **Eleanor Roosevelt**

There is always fear involved when we do something we have never done before. Perhaps that's particularly the case with camping if we grew up in an unfamiliar city environment and are used to seeing nature as something separate from us. Camping certainly scares me but no time as intensely as my first camping trip on the West Coast Trail in Canada – talk about a baptism of fire. As with any emotion, which means 'movement away from', go into it, allow it to travel away from you through its own force, and let the earth support you.

Confronting your fear brings huge rewards. I still get scared, but love the feeling of being in a remote area, with my lantern burning on the hook inside the tent, reading or writing or simply contemplating how glad I am where I am. By making your home on a mountain or the edge of a cliff, it will be like no one has ever been there before. What a great metaphor for your power to create home wherever you are. In the case of camping it reconnects us to the primordial part of ourselves, and the deep, slow heartbeat of the earth. Your connection will enrich every part of your life.

It certainly refreshed parts of Jill Frayne's being she couldn't normally reach, as described in her book, *Starting Out in the Afternoon*.

Jill gets to know her country
Wisdom sits in places
An Apache

Canadian Jill Frayne took a trip to northern Canada and Alaska when she was in a time of transition. Her daughter was graduating and her relationship was breaking up. She travelled around by car and kayak, camping on the way. 'I had a glimpse of something this summer. There was the exhilaration of the views, the extravagant layout for the senses each day, but I also got an inkling of the join, the non-difference. There were a few seconds somewhere – maybe in the Yukon or

Atlin or on that high plain out of Haines – a few seconds when my whole being relaxed, when I was held in the land, not separate and apart but in it, just another sentient creature, another form of shrub or mountain.' She went on to say that because she feels no difference between her and the land, she is not afraid to die. 'I can go home. If I am endless and inconsequential, a flake of mountain that thins and blows away, where is the loss? The mountain is always coming and going.'

What an amazing result to issue from a summer away – to have lost your fear of death. Now Jill has a new home, a remote cabin in the woods, and goes on kayak trips with her new boyfriend. She has got to know her country and herself in a deeper way, a spiritual way.

MERGING WITH THE EARTH

This we know. The earth does not belong to man. Man belongs to the earth
Chief Seattle

Jill's sense of oneness is what indigenous people regularly perceive. For example, Richard Nelson describes the traditional Koyukon view of the Athabaskan peoples of northern Canada in his book *Make Prayers to the Raven*, 'all that exists in nature is imbued with awareness and power'. We have lost this sense and that is why camping is particularly important for us in the West. For relatively effortlessly and for a small expenditure, camping enables us to regain our sense of the sacred. Even if we don't know what's happening, while we're wet and cold and miserable. Trust me that earthmerge is occurring, working slowly and surely to enable you to experience more truly and on a deeper level.

Of course, another way of experiencing oneness is to visit a sacred site – an experience we sometimes know as the mystical. Now we'll see when it's a good idea to do that.

CHAPTER 15

When to visit the sacred

Spirit of place! It is for this we travel
Alice Meynell

In this chapter we will see that the sacred is truly everywhere in our earth of many cultures and colours. Yet some places are recognised as being especially sacred. The power of the sacred can catapult us towards our greater joy and happiness better than almost any other method, save for opening our hearts.

We need to know two things about the sacred. How to find it and how to experience it. As the sacred is wherever you are, it is not always appropriate to visit a special place. Where you are at is always more important than the place. For you do not need to visit a recognisably sacred place to find enlightenment – thank goodness. Nor do you need to go abroad to visit the sacred, although many people do. Every country has its own recognised sacred places. In this chapter we shall look at when to visit the sacred, and also when not to. Then, if it is appropriate for you to visit, we'll move on to the next chapter which includes five steps to having a mystical experience.

A sacred place may be a church, a temple, an island, a crystal, a city, a bay filled with leaping dolphins, a mountain or a rock. You may seek and find the sacred in a tree, a waterfall, a volcano, or any other force of nature – there are many gateways. For example, The Green Cathedral in Forster, New South Wales, Australia, seems to grow out of the forest. The trees arch overhead in the forest clearing, and the pews are hewn from tree trunks. The atmosphere inspires awe. The world's biggest crystal lies in Kauai, Hawaii. Someone had a dream about where it was buried in the Arizona desert. The dream was acted on, the crystal unearthed and now its gleaming bulk shines in the middle of a temple in Hawaii. Ultimately there are as many examples of objects being sacred as there are objects. For, in the end, everything is sacred.

Yet the deep harmony of the sacred must be heard, and once heard, experienced. Sometimes getting away from our familiar routine, even our familiar belief system, will help us do that.

WHEN TO VISIT THE SACRED

When the mountain calls you,
You cannot refuse
Filipino shaman

Visiting a place with a vibration higher than your own will help you, when the time is right. That is why so many religions stress the importance of pilgrimage and visiting the sacred, in accordance with the fourth principle of magical travel, opening to the mystical. Islam encourages its followers to go to Mecca, Catholics to their shrines such as Lourdes and Hindus to Benares, City of Light. Many of us go on our own pilgrimage, to the place that lures us.

Do you hear the call of the sacred? Are you ready for something more to happen in your life? You need or desire a new person, quality or sense of meaning. For visiting the sacred will shake you up, and after the experience you will never be the same again. Your atoms will be rearranged and you will be made anew.

In vibrational terms you are moving up to a higher level, therefore attracting more experiences with opportunities for spiritual growth. If you're feeling really stuck, visiting the sacred is an excellent way to propel you on that accelerated route. So when you hear the call – respond to the call. You will respond like magic to your right place, which may be for a moment or a lifetime or more – and every part of your life will improve. Whatever is true, or becomes true for you, trust that your intuitive guidance will bring you to the right place for you to expand your learning at this particular point in your development. As ever, follow your feeling.

Let's look at the procedure for choosing where to go.

Choosing your sacred place

Different places on the face of the earth have different vital efflu-ence, different vibration, different chemical exhalation, different polarity with different stars: call it what you like, but the spirit of place is a great reality
D.H. Lawrence

There are as many ways to choose a sacred place as there are creatures on earth. You may have always wanted to go there, or it is a place that you have only just heard about. It may be famous or unknown. In the sea or on the land. In this dimension or in another one (at least according to the Hawaiians, for whom sacred sites, *wahi pana*, exist both physically here on earth and in the dimensions around us). It may be in the city or a remote area. It may be in your country or in another one. Whatever the reason, you will be lured to the spirit of a place by its vibration. Maybe you will just be attracted to its name, which does encode the very vibration of a place, or 'something about it'.

Why do you get different feelings in different places? We need to look at a concept new to the West but found in every indigenous culture around the world – the spirit of place. I believe it is found everywhere for a reason. Perhaps the spirit of place does really, truly exist? The science of place is found in every single culture on earth. We know it as Feng Shui or Geomancy. For, if places have their own power, then it is important to build on them correctly. Perhaps that's why there are house diviners all over the world known as an *uranai-shi* in Japan or *akuhikuhipu'uone* in Hawaii. For places contain energy. There are many stories about the forms energy can take, which have become part of cultural myths. It may be the Green Man in England, the Rainbow Serpent in Australia or even the Loch Ness Monster of Scotland. The sacred melody of somewhere like Glastonbury is so strong that millions of people hear it. As to whether or not to respond, well, that depends on your internal music.

It's now time to look at when not to visit the sacred. For just as Richie discovered in the Orkney Islands, it's not always right to go to a sacred place when you think you should.

WHEN NOT TO VISIT THE SACRED

Living the new spiritual awareness is the matter of passing through a series of steps or revelations
James Redfield

Unusually for a travel book, I'm going to say that there are times when not to visit places. Just as visiting the right place in the right way at the right time will really improve your energy and your life, getting it wrong can destroy it. So you need to make an informed decision from your Higher Self, so that you can move through your series of steps or revelations at the correct pace. Visiting the sacred isn't like being at school or university – there is no overarching right or wrong upon which you can be examined. However, there is a 'curriculum' that you design yourself – within a wider framework that can't be changed – the need to treat our earth with respect. There are three reasons not to visit the sacred:

1. It is the wrong place for you.
2. It is the wrong time for you.
3. The place doesn't want you to visit.

These concepts aren't necessarily easy to understand, so we'll see how they work.

The wrong place for you

There are many stories about people whose visit to a place had disastrous consequences. Interestingly, those same stories are found all over the world and I found a few of them in researching my Ph.D. in the meanings of the sacred. Take the warnings seriously.

297

Hank gets covered in sand
Okea pili mai
(Clinging sand)
Hawaiian proverb

Having paid a lot of money to get to Hawaii, Hank wanted to go to a temple to say he had been there when he got home – maybe not the best motivation. Hank was rather out of touch with his feelings, but went into that sandy temple on the Big Island even though he didn't really want to. He was a little scathing of it (after all the humble grouping of stones by the sea wasn't what he had expected), and after that nothing seemed to go right for him. His hire car wouldn't start, his girlfriend dumped him and he just wanted to get back to mainland USA as soon as possible and lick his wounds. He didn't associate his problems with the temple of course, but he certainly never wanted to return to Hawaii.

Sometimes a place is wrong for you, because you don't have enough personal power or *mana*, as was the case for Hank. It would take a lot of work for him to be ready to visit that temple in Hawaii. Don't visit a place when it is the wrong place for you, even if it is right for your friend, or you really want to go there. If it feels wrong follow your feeling. You'll never know the hassle you will have saved yourself.

The wrong time for you

Sometimes the place is still wrong for you, but only because there's something you need to do first – it's a case of getting the timing right. Richie needed to find forgiveness before visiting St Magnus's Cathedral, as we saw in Part 2, Chapter 5. Or it may be the wrong time because there is somewhere else you need to be, someone for you to meet, or a rest for you to take. Or you may not even know why it's the wrong time. You don't actually need to, just like you don't need to know why it's the wrong guy or girl for you (it might help you to, but you don't need to). Just follow your feelings and visit only at the right time.

The place doesn't want you

There are a few reported cases of the spirit of a place not wanting humans to visit. You do need to follow the feeling you pick up. For example, many mountains almost never want humans to visit. This is because our vibration is usually not high enough, as the place is so sacred and wants to maintain its purity. Some people say this explains why bad weather conditions, and so on, stop some mountains being climbed. For really, why on earth are the wishes of humans more important than the wishes of places that may have been there for millions of years? The short answer is that they are not – respect the sacred.

Once you have travelled past these obstacles you need to ask for permission – and listen to the answer.

PERMISSION TO VISIT

Asking permission from the spirit of the place to visit recognises that we humans are only guests on the earth. That humble attitude goes a long way to helping to restore the sacred balance of earth that humans have done so much to destroy recently.

The exercise of asking permission is a simple one and should be done before you enter.

1. Stand near a point of entry, relax and close your eyes.
2. Connect to the earth by shooting the energy downwards from your feet towards the earth's heart.
3. Start to hum. Don't worry about the note, allow it to come out. For each place has its own melody and you are 'tuning in'.
4. Imagine you are holding a wand and strike it on the ground, calling out to the spirit of place to emerge.
5. Take some time and see what sort of impression you get of the spirit of the place; its shape, colour, gender, name and feeling.
6. Now silently formulate your desire to enter the sacred place and send it out to the spirit.
7. Breathe deeply and wait for a sign.

CLIMBING THE MOUNTAIN

....

You can always climb higher within
A peace message

The sign you receive might be in the way the wind blows, it may be a shiver, or the flight of a bird, or a silent 'yes' or 'no' in your mind. Of course you must always follow the answer you get. If it's a 'no' you need to respect the wishes of the place at this time. By doing your thing, going with the flow and following the signs you will be in the perfect frame of mind to allow in the greater magic. You don't *need* to go to a sacred site to do so; although it could help you, it could also hinder you. That will be the case if you go to a place you are not ready for, because you feel you 'should', as Hank did. It would also be the case if Richie had gone to the cathedral when he wasn't sufficiently integrated. Relax. It doesn't need to be today or tomorrow if the timing doesn't feel right. There's always work to do on yourself first, for we each can always climb higher within.

If the answer you receive is a 'yes' then great, the next chapter awaits.

CHAPTER 16

Opening to the mystical

Within and around the earth
Within and around the hills
Within and around the mountains
Your power returns to you
Tewa prayer

The fourth principle of magical travel, be open to mystical experiences, is vital, as my research indicates a mystical experience is the one people most want to take away from their magical trip. After you have been scooped out of your ordinary reality with the silver spoon of bliss, you can never be the same again. Your life is tipped up and over on to the side of light.

So who can experience the mystical, and how can we precipitate this state? People often think mystical experience is restricted to 'special people', they are prophets or shamans or otherwise 'marked out'. But in fact this isn't the case. Absolutely anyone can have a mystical experience. However, there are also things you can do to make it more likely. One is to go to a sacred place – as long as the time is right – which we saw in the last chapter. The process of asking for permission cannot be missed, for it is vitally important.

Then, there are five easy steps to having a great experience in a sacred place. The first is to respect the place, the second to raise your vibration, the third is to relax, the fourth to respond to your intuition and the fifth to receive your experience. If you do have a mystical experience you may feel various emotions, which are sometimes overwhelming, or you may just want to sleep. It hits all of us in different ways at different times. The chapters dealing with taking rest and coping with change will hopefully cover most circumstances, as will the final Part 'Coming home again', which gives tips on integrating your change and living in a very special world. We'll see an example of it in Louisa's experience at the end of this chapter.

Finally, a mystical experience cannot be guaranteed, for it depends on more factors than mentioned here. But at least, in following this advice you won't be making any mistakes and you will be allowing the energies of the sacred to waterfall down into every pore of your being in whatever way is most appropriate for you at the time. Let's now see the five steps in more detail:

FIVE STEPS TO A MYSTICAL EXPERIENCE

> Take the first step in faith. You don't have to see the whole staircase. Just take the first step
> **Martin Luther King**

1. Respect the sacred
2. Raise your vibration
3. Relax
4. Respond to your intuition
5. Receive your greater good

Respect the sacred

Every place is sacred. Every place has its own sound – breath if you like – and chant, as well as being underlaid by a kind of harmonic map to the sacred energies of the site. Much of this knowledge has been lost, although certainly not all. The indigenous people are often the guardians of the sacred traditions. They may try to persuade you only to visit at a certain time or in a particular way, or at a certain time of the month. Other sacred places, such as Stonehenge in England, may be guarded by police, and then you're under different laws. In fact, as long as you follow the guidance about when to visit a place and strictly adhere to the advice below you have every right to be there.

✧ Bring a token gift with you to offer to the spirit of the place, such as water or a chant
✧ Talk very little, if at all
✧ Move carefully
✧ Don't take drugs or substances to enhance your experience. You don't need to
✧ Don't impinge on anyone's energy
✧ Don't disturb a creature
✧ Damage nothing
✧ Don't move or remove anything at all. Stones, for instance, should not be removed from their place
✧ Don't take photographs

There may be exceptional circumstances in which it's appropriate to take photographs, but only if you ask for permission first. The rewards of visiting the sacred correctly are immense.

Miranda flourishes

Rather than you controlling the garden you become the garden
Kala Ambrose

Growing up in North America in a family that didn't travel, Miranda never thought she'd go to Cambodia, but a little voice inside prompted her to do so. Her visit to the temples of Angkor Wat enabled her to experience the stones merging into the sunshine and she became part of a dancing, higher reality in which there was only love. She later realised it was her first mystical experience.

The next step is to raise your vibration.

Raise your vibration

Just as every soul thrums to its own drum, so every place has its own melody. You will be lured to the spirit of a place by 'something about it' – even though you will not know why. Your experience there will depend on the way your tone interweaves with the resonance of the place, and that's why it's easier to enjoy mystical experiences in certain sites. You can help them along by raising your vibration. This discreet exercise can be done within a sacred place, or anywhere, at any time.

Raising your vibration

1. Close your eyes.
2. Stand square and centre yourself on planet earth.
3. Know that you are you, and that you are here, at this place, for a reason.
4. Experience a feeling of joy surging through you from the heart of the earth, below the ground.
5. You are now filled with light and delight.
6. Open your eyes and look at the world anew.

Raising your vibration is a very simple and effective exercise. I wish I'd known it when I started travelling – it would have saved me so many spaced out feelings. It's easy to do, and the effects are very noticeable. For when you quaff the elixir of joy then it's so much easier for the light to rush in.

Bob finds joy

Here in this body are the sacred river: here are the sun and moon, as well as the pilgrimage places. I have not encountered another temple as blissful as my own body
Sahara Doha

Bob from Australia went to visit some Aboriginal rock carvings in his country. He didn't feel very much at all as he looked at them by the pool in the rainforest; even though he intellectually recognised they were sacred, he felt disconnected. Then he did the exercise above. As he connected to the earth he suddenly felt a surge of joy throughout his body. He looked around and the world was sparkling. The carvings meant something to him now. They seemed to spark to life and he had visions of generations of aboriginies at that site by the clear water. He knew he would never forget that place, that day, that rock, that light. Bob's vibration had been raised.

Relax

Let go of your expectations and relax, because nothing is less condu-
cive to fulfilling the fourth principle of magical travel – having a
mystical experience in a sacred site – than the idea that you 'should'.
It's exactly like having an orgasm, in that you need to let go to allow
the blissful feelings to flood in. You don't need to think, you don't
even need to hope, you just have to let go in faith and trust. I wrote
a similar sentence in my first book *The Sacred Power of Huna* about
the experiences leading to the cosmic orgasm, another name for the
mystical. I said there we can reach it through making love. We can also
reach it through visiting the sacred. Meanwhile you need to have some
uncontrolled time in the sacred – relax.

Remember what I said at the beginning of the chapter that you can
have an experience of enlightenment anywhere. They have occurred
on motorways, in diving boats, in crop circles and even on operating
tables. The important thing in en-lighten-ment is the sight, not the
site. Here's an example bestowed on someone who certainly wasn't
expecting it. He told me about it along a high and lonely road fringed
by white mountains, when he picked me up as I was hitch-hiking.

Barry and the deer

*The real reason for going to a sacred place however, is not just to
get high. The purpose is to come into harmony with the greater
unity of all life*
James Swan

Barry was a Kiwi bush hunter from the South Island. Just like many
of his compatriots, he liked to shoot deer. One day, he shot one, but
not very cleanly and followed her trail of noise and blood through the
trees. He sat down next to her as she looked into his eyes when she was
dying. He felt a great sense of love as he looked into the peaceful well of
her eye and wondered why he had not known before that every creature shares the same spark of life. He realised that we are all connected
and decided, out of the bottom of his heart, never to extinguish again
the spark of another creature who shares his desire to live.

Barry certainly didn't believe in mystical experiences until he had one. He was busy 'doing his thing' and relaxed in the sense that he had absolutely no expectations.

When you *are* relaxed, then it's easier for your guides and angels to contact you. For example, when you meditate or go to sleep then it's a great opportunity for them to impart what you need to know. It is usually recommended that you rest quietly and calm your mind in a sacred space for at least 15 minutes if possible. Be open to your guides. It's time for the fourth step, respond to your intuition.

Respond to your intuition

During your uncontrolled time in a sacred space, you will be drawn to one place rather than another. Follow it. The vibration in a sacred place is not uniform; in a temple, for example, the altar has a different, usually higher resonance than the outside walls. That is why where you go within the site is important. Allow every single step to be guided. Don't do anything because you 'should'. As ever, follow your intuition and not your expectations – your heart and not your mind.

Your guides might be the weather, or birds and animals on the site, or something even more abstract; and by 'guides' I don't mean tour guides. Many tour guides will have great knowledge about the place, but it is best to wander about on your own and pick up things directly, unless you have time to make several visits. Then it's fine to get some received knowledge from the guide's conscious mind. But don't do this *instead* of following the guidance of your Higher Self, as tour parties tend to do. After all, you know where best to go, and the place does have the power to speak to you directly when you know how to relax and listen.

The Temple of Tikal
Everything whispered and everywhere was green, a deep, dizzying green
Claire Scobie

When I visited Tikal in Guatemala, a huge complex of hundreds of temples in the jungle, I was overwhelmed by the amount of choices. Should I go to this temple grouping or that one? There wasn't time for them all. In the end I followed a couple of wild turkeys I saw in the jungle, because I was attracted to their plumage, which was iridescent in the sunlight. They took me to a particular site with a huge plaza in the middle, where I felt at peace. Then the flashy flight of a toucan through the trees led me to the top of Temple Number 5, where there was already someone meditating and where the view was incredible. Then it was time for the Perdido Mundo, the Temple of the Lost World, where the blossoms flamed above the canopy of jungle and I knew why I was there.

Allow your Higher Self to guide you and it will bring you something incredible.

Receiving your experience

Now it's time to receive whatever experience is there for you. For what's for you, won't go past you.

Quite possibly the ultimate experience, much talked of by sages, poets and philosophers from times immemorial, is the mystical. Mystical experiences are the best feeling we can have on earth. They bring a feeling of lightness, of rightness, of brightness. They bring a feeling of union, of communion. They bring feeling. Feeling so intense there is no room for anything else. If you are meant to have one, of course, as there are times when it's best for you to simply relax and enjoy. It's not for us to say. It's simply for us to pray. And prepare. For we can certainly reach a state where we are likely to have them.

Skye waterfall

Siubhal a' chait a chaidh don eas dhut!
(The way of the cat that went to the waterfall to you!)
Gaelic proverb

A waterfall stands and falls in the most sacred valley on Skye, once inhabited by Druids and visited by seekers of the sacred from all over Europe. Today there are black-faced sheep grazing by the ancient remains of their temples in the quiet green valleys by the silver sea. The cliffs slip in and out of the mists, and just like Hawaii, Skye is full of rainbows.

This particular waterfall is said to be the abode of the fairies. I take students on my Huna course there, because it is a special place, a place of power. We offer a blessing to the waterfall then do a short exercise to raise everyone's vibration. Whenever the student feels ready, he or she goes alone to the waterfall and relaxes under the fall of water and asks to receive the correct experience, the silvery power of asking for help. Then he or she responds intuitively as the power of the water merges with the power of the student; some huge openings of the spirit of the *haumana*, or student, have occurred under the spray.

The five steps: respect of the sacred, raising vibration and then the power to relax, the power to respond and the power to receive have all been followed. On top of that, the students have also been doing a course on how to raise their consciousness. The result throws open the silvery portal to your Higher Self, the space from where magic regularly happens. The ending of our journey is always the continuation. You are inhabiting a world of mystery, a world of magic. Louisa Teresa StrongBear wrote a visionary book, *Journey By Night: A Solitary Journey*, about her mystical world.

Louisa's journey into the magic

You have journeyed past the gateway. You have found the door
Louisa Teresa StrongBear

Louisa is a long-haired American woman whose account begins with her leaving her home and her comfy, thick, wool socks and lavender candles to 'find the answer to the question of her life'. She travels alone into the night. Except she is never alone. Louisa has many encounters: Wolf, Raven and Bear and other beings impart their wisdom to her, for Louisa has the ability to learn from many dimensions.

The spectacular lands she inhabits reflect the beauty of her Higher

Self. The Magical Forest is coruscated in light, with rainbows shooting everywhere and music hanging in the air, waiting to sound. 'Low clouds hovered, iridescence pouring out of them: I could see musical notes superimposed over the colours.' She asked about iridescence and immediately received her answer, 'It is the song of the universe. Remember Cloud Song?' The magical forest is the gateway of creation: light, colour, sound.

Louisa goes to many places as she sings her song, and encounters the pieces of her soul. In one encounter, call it a dream, call it reality, from the place of the Higher Self it doesn't really matter for it is all the same, she is told by one teacher: 'When you get there, will you tell them how VITAL it is to remember Magic?' He looked down at my hand, looked up again, and a single tear rolled from his eye. I reached up and dried it with my free hand. 'Cloud Song, the future depends upon it. Tell them to notice colours and the iridescence in the mist.'

Louisa remembered and passed on the message and I am passing it on again in a different context. Louisa also meets with her beloved grandmother, now out of flesh, and is told by her, 'The world needs your light. We are lonely without it. If this were not true, you would not be taking this journey in the first place. Somewhere, in a place of angels, you knew that we were waiting for you. And we are glad that you could make this journey.'

Louisa's leaving home led her to a new home, a land of light. Her multiple encounters with animals and other spirits are characteristic of the shaman's journey, as told in stories all over the world. The encounters we know as 'mystical' experiences have a greater, shining place. The shamanic traditions of indigenous peoples say that every encounter represents a missing piece of the soul, a piece you are learning to remember and draw back in a process called soul-retrieval. Every part of our soul we integrate takes us back to our Higher Self. When we are in our Higher Self we are in contact with our soul. That's how we remember our magic. For the Higher Self is a place of answers, not a place of questions. And when you have the courage to make that journey you and your 'aumakua, your relatives out of flesh, will be joyful. You will draw people around you who share your knowings and who are glad.

Your journey is always a sacred journey. Challenges abound as you pass through the silver gate. It seems like you are tested in every way possible, again and again. The higher the level of your dimensional dance, the more intense your experience. Our spiritual lessons resound.

Yet the journey is so worth it. For magic does not only exist in fairy tales and children's books. The magic is in you.

THE BRIGHTNESS IS WITHIN

One can make a day of any size and regulate the rising and setting of his own sun and the brightness of its shining
John Muir

The home of the mystical experience is within. The author George Leonard said, 'At the heart of each of us, whatever our imperfections, there exists a silent pulse of perfect rhythm – a complex of wave forms and resonances which is absolutely individual and unique, and yet which connects us to everything in the universe.' That 'silent pulse of perfect rhythm' is also known as our vibration. Of course we know how to raise our vibration through several methods we've seen in this book, from exercises to ethical choices we make every day.

So we've seen five steps to having a mystical experience, and a couple of examples. Mystical experiences can be invoked, for example in shamanism courses, as further discussed in Part 3, Chapter 3, 'Valuing your trip'. You then carry with you your gift of knowledge of fire, your passport to a magical world. That sacred knowledge is the one Joseph Campbell spoke of receiving as the result of your quest. We've also seen someone who followed none of those five steps, wasn't particularly enlightened in his habits, yet received one anyway. For the beauty of the mystical is it cannot be controlled or delineated. You have gone on a journey far above all that, a journey to something far greater – your true, magical self. The silvery plane of magic is always there, waiting for you. You just need to believe it is there. Ask for help and open yourself to mystical experiences. Then choose your second power, the power of belief. Then, when you are ready, you will know the third power, the power of faith. Know your life as a prayer. Then you will reach the next loop on the spiral. Accept your new knowledge of the night and integrate it into the light of day. Your day. The day where you help others and still have fun. For the fifth principle of magical travel, integrating your knowledge, is vitally important. That's what we look at in the final section. That's how you make your day last.

The necessity to integrate your experiences means that you often need to rest. We shall explore this in the following chapter.

CHAPTER 17

Take rest

Take rest. A field that takes rest bears a beautiful crop
Ovid

This book is telling you to go out into the world, but it's also saying to take a break from it too. Here we'll see the value of being idle – physically, socially and spiritually. And we'll also look at the regeneration it leads to. So even if you keep yourself busy all the time at home, don't do it on your magical trip. Allow yourself to be idle. Relax and leave your conscious mind behind, and your subconscious mind will also benefit from having the time to recharge – for example, your health will improve. We'll see ways to replenish the springs of your Higher Self, so that you can enjoy inner richness wherever you go.

You need the advice in this chapter whenever your trip gets a little too much for you, whether it's for a moment or a month. And then the next two chapters will help you deal with the changes that are inevitably happening to you.

THE VALUE OF BEING IDLE

The empire is at the fireside
Cicero

The beauty of being idle is that you don't need to wander very far at all. You can take a break from your peregrinations and have time with your best-ever travelling companion – yourself. Stack yourself up with food and drink and then relax and look around the walls of your hotel or hostel room knowing that you need go nowhere and do nothing. You will be doing yourself good – don't let anyone tell you any different.

Philosophical value

By the meadows of memory, the highlands of hope and the shore that is hidden
Algernon Charles Swinburne

The West does not usually value the worth of being idle (some exceptions are mentioned in the Resources). Our society is 'achievement orientated' and someone's value is largely measured in material terms. Weber's *The Protestant Ethic and the Spirit of Capitalism* sums up the place of work in our society – the prime place. We do not have a lot of spare time, and perhaps this is deliberate, for we are not supposed to think too much about the meaning of our life, merely supposed to get on with it, pay our taxes, procreate and do the things we are supposed to do. When we *do* have time, we are encouraged to fill it up with leisure activities to make us rounded personalities. We play sport, music, join the debating team, go out to meet friends, attend parties and weddings, and visit the sick in their homes and hospital. By doing so, we win social approval.

But you lose this approval if you spend time on your own – except, of course, if you are a successful creative person, then it is expected. But of course you do need to be successful, which is a bit of a paradox, as in almost every case you need time on your own to develop the inner resources necessary to succeed. Meanwhile, if you say, 'Sorry, I want to spend Saturday night on my own thinking about the purpose of my life,' people may find you a bit strange. If indeed this is what you intend to do, you may have to lie to be socially acceptable. 'I just want to stay in and read a good book' or 'I think I'm coming down with something' are two possible alternatives.

But isn't it wonderful? Here, while you are travelling, you don't need those white lies as no one knows you. And let's face it, you're not busy in your usual ways. And there are far less social pressures on you – not to mention societal. The importance of lying around and doing absolutely nothing is often acknowledged in non-Western societies, for most of them are based on different values. Cooperation is more important than competition and who you are is more important than what you do. By learning to relax you will fit into these societies better. Relaxation helps you physically as well.

PHYSICAL VALUE

How beautiful it is to do nothing and then rest afterward
Spanish proverb

In general, allow yourself to rest in whatever way feels best for you, at least one day a month, one day a week if you are going through a lot. It may mean staying in your hotel room and reading, or visiting a place alone where you feel calm and good. Don't communicate with others, don't do anything you don't have to, it's your down time and you deserve it. It may last for a day or a week. There may be times when you need far more rest – that's okay, go with it. Why not stay in bed for a bit? You don't need to feel guilty about being idle when you're away, even if you grew up with the Protestant work ethic.

You will also be improving your health, as doctors are now recognising. And, if you keep it up, there will be lasting benefits in your life that would make your magical trip worth it for that alone. You can stave off many illnesses by resting when you feel them coming on. Often getting yourself back into equilibrium will be sufficient to strengthen your immune system – and happily you will never know how much worse it could have been. For relaxing influences your subconscious mind, the building block of your physical body.

SPIRITUAL VALUE

I was tapping into an inner self we all must have had hundreds of years ago, which guided us and told us how to behave
Bridget Amos

We need to understand the process of relaxation on a higher plane. All the culture shock and beautiful sacred moments you are being exposed to shakes you up and moves you on to a higher vibratory level. You are in the process of expanding into your higher light, which is wonderful. But remember nothing in nature expands and expands without contracting – imagine if it did. You are no exception to that rule, so allow yourself to contract. Cry, curl up or just hang out – with yourself. Then spend a few days doing whatever you want. Remember some people never do that in their whole lives. Let all the 'shoulds' go. Be lazy, relax, rest, recover. Treat yourself. You deserve it. For the value of the things of the spirit cannot be measured in money or time. It can only be measured in what you learn. And by giving yourself the space and time to learn, you are performing a very valuable service – to yourself.

REPLENISHMENT

Where can I find a small corner of stillness? Because that's where I like to begin and end
Elizabeth Gilbert

As long as you avoid artificial highs such as drink and drugs, you will find your spirit will gravitate towards the springs it needs to replenish itself. For by letting go of your 'shoulds' and 'musts' you will be allowing it to choose for you. And what wonderful choices you will make. For there are so many places to go now, from spas to ashrams to simply hanging out in nature, as Thoreau famously did in Walden. Do what's right for you and you will feel vibrant and full of life. You will be infinitely healthier and more productive than you were before, because you have allowed yourself to take rest, and then follow your feelings. Without a plan we grow according to the rhythms of nature. Like a plant we grow with both night and day, the sun and the rain.

The next two chapters, the first on dealing with change and the second on how to perform your internal journey will look at ways of doing that more consciously. Expanding you consciousness is vital. For the more conscious you are the less energy and resources you have to expend in getting to the place you want to be, whether that is phys- ical or spiritual. The more knowledge you allow in, the more graceful your journey will become. So now we've taken rest let's look at how we cope with some of the inevitable challenges.

CHAPTER 18

Dealing with change on your journey

Change is never a loss – it's a change only
Vernon Howard

This chapter looks at the process of change. Travelling magically helps you to expand into your Higher Self.

Of course we cannot control the kind of change we are given, and both sudden and subtle change are important. Sudden change feels more major than subtle change, but it is really just different. Some people find that everything changes in a rather abrupt way, as I did after one particularly memorable summer in Hawaii when I discovered that magic really works, and my belief system was blasted away. Others find that change is more subtle. For example, one or two elements of their life change: they recover from a long-term illness or break up with their lover; but these transformations affect everything else, just like ripples in a lake. This chapter looks at the difference between sudden and subtle change and examines how you deal with each of them.

Both sudden and subtle change can have tremendous long-term effects, and whether they do or not depends on you. After a sudden change – which you certainly notice – you will need to retreat for a while, or otherwise integrate it by spending time in a sacred place or making sense of it within your belief system by drawing or writing or composing music, whatever works for you. With subtle change, you don't really notice it but just need to plod on through. You cannot control either one, all you can do is go with the flow and trust that it will all be better when you come out the other side, and it will be. Always remember that magical travel is not an end in itself. It has a purpose and that purpose is to grow.

Sudden opening

The only life worth living is a magical one and this is magic!
Sabrina Dearborn

We've seen some examples of sudden openings, and you may have had one yourself. One way of dealing with them is to go camping and spend some nights on the earth, particularly in a sacred place. It will help you integrate your knowledge; for example, one summer I spent several nights camping with one of my cats on the spiralling green mound of Glastonbury Tor. And not only did we have a wonderful experience, I believe it helped stop a difficult one.

The heart of the earth at Glastonbury

I will pour out my spirit upon all flesh; and your sons and your daughters shall prophesy, your old men shall dream dreams, your young men shall see visions
Joel 2:28

Glastonbury, known as the heart chakra of southern England, is so sacred it seems as though the green fields below the grassy Tor consist of water or vapour rather than solid earth. I woke up late one morning buzzing with information, having had visions of a giant crystal, and a sense that sacred knowledge was being downloaded into me. That's one reason it's a good idea to camp in sacred places, your inner wisdom and the spirit of place permitting. It helps your essence vibrate in time with the place. Even the earth has a pulse, which scientists call the Schumann resonance; it used to beat at 7.8 Hz and now is closer to 11 so the frequency is quickening.

In other words, it is easier for you to dream your dreams and perceive your visions. At the time I was learning a lot of new shamanic techniques, and camping meant that I had no ill effects from 'too much knowledge too soon'. When your wonderful experiences are over and you are alone again, you can feel very empty and, for moments, possibly even worse than before.

THE POWER OF DARKNESS

When it is dark enough, you can see the stars
Charles Beard

Don't despair. Or at least do despair if you want to but know that it will soon be over. Those moments do not mean that you should have listened to everyone else's advice and stayed at home. The terrible time you're having is, perhaps, the inevitable accompaniment to the opening your spirit has been going through – light follows darkness and darkness follows light. You will be experiencing far more of both light and darkness because you have left your familiar trails behind and will be experiencing trials. Nowhere in nature does anything grow in a straight line and you are part of nature. Plants grow through the night and through the day, the moon and the sun, the darkness and the light. You need the shadow, as well as the substance, of growth.

So, after your opening, give yourself some darkness. For, within a few days, all the elements of your personality that you don't like will come rushing out. Emotions in your subconscious, such as anger, fear and jealousy, will become very active. Every action has an equal and opposite reaction, and when you open you will also close. The answer is to rest. Then rest. Then rest. Don't judge yourself, but silently express your feelings, perhaps by keeping a diary. After a few days you may be ready to re-engage, but don't do anything in a hurry. For one week after your mystical experience you need to 'own' your projections. That means instead of saying 'you' say 'me'. That way, for example, you won't say someone else makes you angry, but you will say 'I make me angry.' You won't be 'blocking' any more, and blaming someone else for what is happening to you. They are merely reflecting you.

So you will draw back the light again. As you allow your emotion to flow, it will become motion and dissolve away without leaving a trace, like water in sunlight. Your true inner beauty will not be impaired and you will carry on growing further towards your bliss. All your experience of enlightenment is doing is jump-starting what would have happened eventually. From your new shelf of peace – for believe me it will change again – try and direct your opening. There is more about how to do this in looking inside. Then take the appropriate action.

Things are usually easier if our opening is more subtle, but it can still be very intense.

SUBTLE OPENING

The motions and patterns and connections of things became apparent on a gut level
Robyn Davidson

You may notice how much you have changed only when you meet familiar people again, or return to a familiar place. That's what happened to Australian Robyn Davidson, when she was 27 years old, on her trip across the Australian desert with four camels and her dog. She later wrote about it in her bestselling books *Tracks*.

Robyn crosses the desert
We travel not for travelling alone
By a greater heat our fiery hearts are fanned
Robert Louis Stevenson

When Robyn bumped into her friend Jenny near Ayers Rock she felt uneasy, 'It seemed that nothing much had in fact happened to me. I had just walked down a road leading a few camels, that's all. But as we sat together that night, in the heavy air of the caravan, my brain started to crack open sideways, spewing forth bits of cement and chicken wire and I knew that the trip was responsible. It was changing me in a way that I had not in the least expected. It was shaking me up and I had not even noticed. It had snuck up from behind.'

> Robyn didn't feel comfortable with the familiarity at the time, and carried on with her trip, thinking about and integrating her life, until finally she was – literally – in a different place. When they reached a beautiful valley she became filled with joy. 'These days were like a crystallisation of all that had been good in the trip. It was as close to perfection as I could ever hope to come.' She had learned what love was.

Robyn's love for the desert led to her deciding to cross it, albeit in an unconventional way. The process of subtle change had led to her having not just moments, but days, of understanding the true nature of freedom. She later introduced both the travel writer Bruce Chatwin, who was inspired to write *Songlines*, and author Salman Rushdie to the Australian desert.

Don't deny the importance of subtle change. For change always leads us to a good place as long as we have the courage to go with it and not retreat back into familiar habits. Your mindset is changing, subtly and unnoticeably, until finally you are at a different bend in your road of light to the place you started out from.

THE POWER OF CHANGE

Change, the strongest son of life
George Meredith

The one certainty in life is change. By making the decision to travel magically you are grasping the change and directing it, for all of the principles relate to change. Another important lesson is not to control, but to allow. That particularly relates to the first, second and fourth principles of magical travel: follow your intuition, be spontaneous and be open to mystical experiences. For then we ensure that we allow in the best kind of change, the kind that propels us towards the glory of our Higher Self.

The result of change is always growth, and even if we take a few wrong turns along the way, just stick with it. Sometimes, the ones who make it are the ones who don't give up, even when lots of stuff 'comes up' they don't attempt to go back to their old ways, they keep moving.

And now we're going to look at the importance of going within. This is the key to realising the pattern of your life and relationships, so that you can explode into the inner joy that is always lingering.

CHAPTER 19

Going within

Blessed are they that mourn for they shall be comforted
Jesus Christ

Enjoy your 'free time', because you can make it of lasting value in your life. Go within. You have time now to think about those things you don't want to think about. In so doing, you are being very productive, for you are not only examining your inner needs, you are sowing your inner seeds. Doing so correctly will ensure a wonderful future.

In this chapter we shall look at actually how to go within, at the process of both understanding patterns and allowing yourself to feel. Understanding your patterns on a conscious level allows your inner sun to shine, letting yourself feel means that your inner waters freely flow. And finally we shall examine the power of compassion, which means that your emotion no longer contracts and can reign, like a clear and calm pool of water, over the earth it contacts.

WHEN TO GO WITHIN

Pleasant to me is the glittering of the sun today upon these margins, because it flickers so
Irish scribe, ninth-century marginal note

Travelling magically provides you with many opportunities for intro-spection, or going within. For example, you may find that you're forced to wait around a lot more than you are back at home. This may be because of the bureaucracy of the country you're in, or simply because things don't run on time. There may be the long, long bus trips, lasting 14 hours or even three days. However, there are many advantages in being somewhere where there are no opportunities for 'going out' as you understand it. You may be in a village in Zanskar, in the Indian Himalayas, where the population goes to sleep relatively early, or in Israel on Shabbat, the holy day, when everything is closed. You may be in a city such as Montevideo, in Uruguay, which is strange to you, and where you're sure the people would really like you if they only knew you. But they don't. You may feel uncomfortable about going out in a strange city at night on your own, so decide to stay in instead. When you've thought about every crack in the four walls of the hotel room around you, and the ceiling above you, you will begin to think about just why you're there and about the purpose of your life so far.

How to go within

We are required to notice the teacher, the sign, to hear and heed the call or the signal
Caroline Myss

There are two possible paths to going within: the mental way and the feeling way. The 'mental way' means that you use your conscious mind to act as the sun illuminating your patterns. The 'feeling way' indicates that you feel your way through situations and that you prioritise the moon of your subconscious mind. The mental way and the feeling way are two channels leading to your inner pool. Usually the mental way is easier than the feeling, but that's simply because our society values it more. School, for example, encourages you to favour the left side of your brain. If you suppress your feelings and the right side of your brain though, you'll be overly dry and rational, and may not be successful in the ways that truly count. They include having the ability to feel happiness and truly wanting to help others from the deepest part of yourself, a process which brings lasting joy. Some people, especially women, are more comfortable with only feeling and not seeing the wider picture. It's a shame, because then you repeat the patterns and the pain as well as missing out on some tremendous understandings. Balance yourself by activating *both* parts of your brain, not just one, to win the battle of within.

To do that, first ask for your blocks to be removed. You don't even need to know what they are, just ask for them to leave. The universe will respond. But there is one block that you do need to know about: believing that you haven't got enough time for the process. It's never true, as time expands or contracts according to the intensity of your feeling. People who come close to dying, for example, often report their whole life flashes before them in seconds. The intensity of their experience is sufficient to compress important scenes from their life into a very short window.

Even if you are on a quick trip, by allowing yourself to go within you can create all the time you need. The growth of the spirit recognises no time frame but its own.

Understand your patterns

A man has many skins on himself, covering the depths of his heart. Man knows so many things: he does not know himself
Meister Eckhart

To understand yourself ask these questions: who are the important people in your life? What do they mean to you? Why do the same things keep happening to you? What are the patterns in your life?

You need to relax, achieve a meditative state and see what insights arrive. Deepak Chopra said that we think about 50,000 thoughts a day. What are they? God is in the detail. Again, the quieter you can be the better. If you find it difficult to relax, do something that you are drawn to, such as climbing a mountain or stopping at a table in a particular cafe and go within. Record your thoughts in whatever way is best for you. For example, write them down in your journal. Allow whatever you want to be expressed, even if it's unexpected. Poetry, quotes, pieces of music, favourite books or song lyrics. See if you can work out why each one 'springs to mind' at that particular moment. What are you thinking? Feeling? What's the significance of the pattern of the clouds? Or the flight of a bird? One day you'll want to look at your journal again and be surprised at what you 'knew'. Maybe your intuition is already a very powerful force.

While you are doing this you may wish to consider people back at home, who are probably not thinking about you as the swirls and eddies of their particular streams carry on without you. Because the harsh fact is that the hole your absence leaves in most people's lives is pretty easy to wallpaper over. Eventually you will make the connections that you need and you will pierce some of the skins covering the wide inner skies of your heart. You now have one of the most valuable opportunities of your life and the chance to get in touch with the pattern behind it. Allow yourself to do so. Allow yourself to feel.

FEELING

Your pain is the breaking of the shell that encloses your understanding
Kahlil Gibran

Feeling is the most important thing we can ever do. Without it our lives and actions are meaningless.

There are three main ways to allow yourself to feel. The first is to appreciate truly the world around you until you slowly, perfectly, allow your heart to unfold. The second is to physically move around and move until the feelings come up. The third way is a little more dramatic, and that's when some kind of a crisis or illness opens you up, which is talked about in the previous chapter. But if you don't already feel (for example, you are a bit 'dead' and the world seems to lack sparkle and you are drawn to people who *do* express themselves), use your sacred journey as a good opportunity to open up.

The first way is to sit quietly alone and really appreciate the beauty of nature. Open up all your senses; notice, smell, taste, hear and feel the world around you, whether it is a small flower or a lump of rock. Sense the sky. Wherever you are, really be there. Imagine you are in love. You are. With life. With the life in you. And with your new appreciation you need never feel alone again.

Moving is the second way of getting in touch with your feelings, and worth doing if you have been out of touch with them for a long time. When you move, allow your emotions to 'come up' with the movement, such as when you are walking or running. Even if you don't feel connected to your feeling, moving while focusing on the subject of your emotion will ensure that eventually you do become connected.

Of course our feelings aren't always pain free. But whatever you do, don't 'cut them off'. When you allow your feelings to flow your blocks will vanish. Rocks and the water cannot exist in the same space. Rocks are the boundaries containing and separating. Water flows and goes forwards. Rocks are strong, yet water's a life force – pure, full of energy, so no blockages. That's why the waters of your subconscious mind will never overwhelm you even when it seems as though they will. If you need three days to be angry, take three days. If it takes time to mourn the loss of your love, then allow yourself all the time you need. Allow the 'new you' to spread into your appointed channel – your fresh feeling.

Your pain is there for a purpose. As Kahlil Gibran put it, 'Your pain is the breaking of the shell that encloses your understanding. Even as the stone of the fruit must break, that its heart may stand in the sun, so must you know pain.' At certain points you may be hurting so much that you may need to give all your emotions back to the earth, by lying on her canopy, or swimming on top of her watery depths or expressing yourself in whatever way you feel moved. Go outside when you don't know what else to do – it really helps. Some sages say that there is nothing more important than the reconnection to your emotions. Feel so you become real. Your springing feeling means you are far more likely to find and fulfil your mission in life. For by allowing yourself to feel you will become connected to the things of your soul. The result of mourning is morning. The new light over calm water represents the prime result of allowing yourself to go within – inner peace. Then you may truly stand in the sun.

There is only one more key to being truly free, and that is the power to know the rain.

THE POWER OF COMPASSION

> *I am the man that makes it rain*
> **Lone Wolf, Kiowa**

Experiencing the power of your own feelings gives you the chance to develop the most important quality of all – compassion. Compassion is the quality named in Buddhism as being the preserve of all sentient beings. When you truly allow yourself to feel for others you will choose not to hurt them. You feel that we are all linked and hurting them would be hurting yourself.

Compassion is the rain of your Higher Self. Your Higher Self heads the sun and the moon of your other beings. You do not just shine with the sun of your ego or the moon of your attraction. The presence of the sun and the rain means that a new light is created, a beautiful rainbow. You radiate the rainbow of your Higher Self.

Compassion is the single most important quality that you can develop, so your intuition becomes more effective. As long as you continue to go inwards, when necessary and apposite, to reflect on the circumstances you have created, as long as you have the courage to stay with your journey and don't revert to drink or drugs, you will become lighter and lighter. Such is the power of the new light. And eventually you will find that most worthwhile and elusive of goals – inner peace.

INNER PEACE

Atha dipa
Ana sarana
Anana sarana
(You are the light,
you are the refuge,
there is no place to take shelter but yourself)
Inscription under the lid of the golden box containing the
Buddha's ashes

You feel great. You have had the courage to explore your own depths and dive below the skins of your heart. Your inner channels are flowing freely. Your thoughts are becoming less and less, just as in the very first exercises of the book in which you contacted your intuition. But now it's happening without you even realising. You are becoming more and more like many locals in less pressured societies, content to sit and stare into space for hours, not saying very much at all. Feelings flow in and out of your mind like water, with no attached emotion solidifying them into blockages. At your centre is a small, still pool of peace. You know this place.

Your state of grace is considered to be very desirable by people of all traditions through the ages, and they have given it many different names. It may be the Hindu and Buddhist *samadhi* or 'bliss'. Nothing that you used to think was important really is any more. You are accepting of yourself for you realise that you are your own light. You do not need to find approval or justification from anyone. You are accepting and live in a multi-hued world where everyone is entitled to their beliefs. Wherever you go, you bring the light of clarity with you. Congratulations. You are finally achieving what everyone in the West is too busy keeping busy to find, but is truly looking for – inner peace.

CHAPTER 20

Keeping in touch

I came like Water, and like Wind I go
Edward Fitzgerald

There are two main things to realise about keeping in touch: when to do so and when not to do so. You don't need to feel guilty at being out of touch for a while or for even longer, providing you have gone about it in the right way; see Part 1, Chapter 18, 'Clean up your life before you go'. But there are certainly times to keep in touch with others, so let's look at when as well as ways to do so. Then we'll move on and look at reasons to be out of touch and at the benefits it may bring. To get the balance right you need to have the delicacy and skills of a trapeze artist – but this level of subtlety is perfectly possible when you follow your best guide of all, your intuition.

WHEN TO KEEP IN TOUCH

It's always useful to know where a friend and relation is, whether you want them or whether you don't
Rabbit in Winnie the Pooh

People back home may really want you to keep in touch. And you may really care for them and want to keep in touch with them too, even though you also want to raise the energy of your life a notch by travelling. Keeping in touch lets them know that you're okay, and lets *you* know that people do care about you somewhere in the world, even if they don't in this city and on this day. They are probably people you admire, respect and in some way want to become like. If so, your energy is likely to be strengthened, rather than depleted.

WAYS OF KEEPING IN TOUCH

> *I can't see the reason why it can't be done*
> **Kinga Freespirit Choscz**

There are all sorts of ways of keeping in touch. When you are travelling magically it may be difficult for people to get hold of you. For example, when you are in an active phase of travelling magically you will have no address to have letters sent to you – for the second principle is travelling spontaneously. The same goes for telephone calls. So you'll have to do all the work. That's okay. Many times just knowing people care about you will be enough. At other times you'll want to hear back from people, and this is where 'new-fangled' communications, such as email – only in widespread use since the mid nineties – come into their own. For you don't need to be located on earth to receive messages, having an address in the 'virtual sphere' is enough. This has fascinating implications for future thought, and meanwhile it is useful to know that if someone needs to get hold of you in most places, they can. But again, like all technology, it shouldn't be abused, and you certainly shouldn't email *instead* of having new experiences, or even see your experiences in terms of how you're going to report them back, for example, on a blog. That's why I advise using it with caution.

Let's start with old-fashioned ways of keeping in touch.

Old-fashioned ways

> *How could one not write about a country that has met you with an abundance of new things and the joy of living afresh?*
> **Henri Michaux**

Telegram and letter are two old-fashioned ways of keeping in touch. With each of them you have something tangible to touch and keep.

Letters can be an absolute pleasure to receive, especially in these days of technology. But they take a long time to get to their destination and you need an address if someone wants to reply to your letter. If you have an American Express card, then you may use a handy American Express office as a poste restante, or somewhere where you can collect your mail – when of course you know where you are going to be. Postcards are also a popular means of communication, and can be a bit more interesting with just a few carefully chosen words or a quote on them, and some people like to collect the stamps. A word of warning: when you're sending mail in some countries be sure to check that the clerk actually puts the stamps on your letter. If you don't, some workers are so poorly paid that the price of those stamps could make a big difference to their income, and you may never know whether your letter has been sent or not. You can also be a bit creative; for example, when you meet people going back to your country, ask them to call your relatives and tell them that you're well and happy, or give them a letter that they can post when they arrive back.

In more remote areas, a telegram service is often available and is usually fast and reliable, even if it is not cheap. Often used for emergencies, it can still be utilised for other situations, such as sending a 'happy birthday' message. Remember though the contents are not private, unlike a letter.

So both telegrams and letters have their advantages and disadvantages, but at least their 'paper trail' means you have something practical to take out and look at when times get rough.

Telephone

> *I found myself looking at Nova Scotia and thinking about my mortgage*
> *Sarah Ballard*

At the time of writing this book, there are two kinds of telephones, land lines and mobile phones. Land lines are tied to a particular situation in space, and dependent on a particular telephone company to work, as well as a system of wires or 'telephone cables'. If any part of these is cut, then the service is lost. Mobile phones are portable, and are dependent on signals – different service providers set up different devices. There are no wires involved. Generally, mobile phones are less portable between countries, but that's usually to do with your service provider. There are several new ways of telephoning springing up and as soon as I write about them they are likely to be obsolete, but you can find out about them in travellers' communities and more details are in the Resources.

International calls can be very expensive, particularly from call boxes and hotels, and some telephone systems aren't always reliable, so don't specify that you'll call at a particular time or day or you could get into trouble. You also need to take the time difference into account. If you are staying in a house with a private telephone, you could ask to borrow it and of course offer to pay the price of your calls (I would recommend giving something extra too for the time and trouble). Try to keep calls short and it's good to be sensitive and aware you are tying up the line, which may be the only one in the house.

What about mobile phones? You can bring your phone from home, but you need to make sure that you are on a tariff that means you can make and receive calls abroad. That will usually be very expensive. Alternatively, you could unlock your mobile phone before you go, then buy a new SIM card in your destination country and use it there. That way you will be paying local prices for local calls. Not many people will have your new number, so at least you will not be receiving calls from people you don't want to hear from. So if you must have a mobile, I would recommend this option.

However, there are certain health risks associated with mobile phones, which are strengthened in times of energetic transition. Also, do you really want to receive a cold call about new windows or your mortgage that could interrupt your experience of communion in a Greek temple? One of the reasons you are travelling is to get away, and so I would not recommend taking your mobile with you. With it, you are just too contactable in the familiar ways by familiar people, and that can easily stop you learning unfamiliar ways to a different kind of contact – your Higher Self.

New-fangled ways

With all technology, we follow the dream of true oneness
René Müller

The evolution of cyberspace has arguably been the biggest single innovation of our generation. By speeding up time (emails can be sent and responded to in minutes) and collapsing space (in that virtual world, it doesn't matter where you are as long as you are 'connected'), everything has changed. It is instantly possible to find out new information about and where to go next. You can change your gender or your age at will, and you can recreate yourself. But as attractive as that cyber-world is, it also has its traps. We will examine it from several angles, and conclude that in the end even the Internet is not as reliable as your inner net. You build your inner net by making connections yourself, between the people, places and languages you love, between this rock and that myth, between that number and this machine. Your inner net is your world. The Internet can be the way to it, but it is not the desti-nation, and like any tool it makes a good servant and a bad master.

We'll start by looking at email.

Email

Those who overcome themselves are strong
Lao Tsu

Electronic mail is the main medium of communication of the Internet. Unlike the telephone, email doesn't depend on people being in to receive a call and the time difference is not important, you just access your emails through a computer. Make sure you get a web-based email address before you depart and don't use your old work or university address as these are not suitable and you may not be able to access your account. If you have access to a computer, telephoning is now very cheap or free over the Internet, and if each of you has a webcam you can actually see and be seen by the person you're talking to. In addition you have access to many 'virtual travellers' communi-ties through your email address.

You can pick up all your messages wherever you are in the world and the system will generally hold them for longer (beware of Hotmail where you lose your account if you don't check it for more than 28 days). Most countries now have email facilities, but not all. For example, in places where electricity is very expensive, or unreliable, email may not be available. Or it might be very expensive or so slow it is hardly worth it. However, this situation is changing rapidly as broadband is reaching into more and more far-flung corners of the world, as well as being standard at most airports, for example. Interestingly, it has never been so easy to be somewhere other than where you are.

Let's look a bit more at the energetic effects. Remember, when you receive and reply to emails, your energy will correspond to the send-er's vibration. If you are having a wonderful time, then your energy will be lowered by the sender's lower vibration. Do you really want to do this to yourself? Use with care. As far as virtual communities go, they can be a great source of useful advice, but make sure you do not plan your trip solely through them, denying your own intuition. As for experiencing your trip through them, that would be even worse. The same goes for other ways of keeping in touch, such as creating a website or blog of your trip. They are not travelling magically. What really is the point of having a blog to tell the world about your experiences so immediately? Your experiences need time to percolate, and you too deserve time away from looking at other people's responses to what you are doing.

But of course you really need to find that caring from inside, and that's why we'll look at the next section, 'When not to keep in touch'. For your dream of true oneness is ultimately to be found in the place that peaceful technology leads you to, not the technology itself, which, if used to the extreme, will actually stop you reaching your goal.

WHEN NOT TO KEEP IN TOUCH

> As for my apprenticeship as a writer, I am sure that my single-mindedness was helped by my being out of touch
> **Paul Theroux**

This is a very important section because there is no better way to ensure you don't travel magically than by constantly keeping in touch with home. We've looked at the temptations of technology throughout this book, now we'll look at good times to be out of touch and at the best reason in the world why you should allow in a new energy.

Good times to be out of touch

> The twenty-first century challenge is how to disconnect
> **Nick Rosen**

Good times to be out of touch include when you don't want to be and when you're having a wonderful time and a terrible time.

When you don't want to keep in touch with someone – tell them. For example, do not promise to send photos and write to people, unless you intend to do so. Breaking your word is bad karma. Anne, from England, was surprised how tolerant people were when she said, 'I'd love to see you again, but meanwhile I've got so much on please don't be offended if I don't keep directly in touch with you.'

When you are having a wonderful time, be where you are. Keep being sparkling and vibrant. Being happy where you are is a great spiritual truth, after all, and one you are creating. Allow yourself to carry on creating this and don't be diverted by other people's expectations or feelings about what you should do, or even by detaching yourself to describe the great time you're having to them.

The same is true for when you're having a terrible time, and even when you're having a mediocre, boring time. You, with your free time (including time for your feelings), may miss people more than they miss you. Now is your chance to contact the inner springs of your resourcefulness. You won't do this unless you are motivated to do so, and, of course, you have plenty of time as you are taking all the rest you need and looking inside. It's a great chance for you to practise your faith too. Don't use the familiar as an excuse not to delve into that most exciting of countries – yourself. And that brings us to the best reason of all for being out of touch.

The best reason
Imagine that the home of your soul is drawing near
Bärbel Mohr

The best reason not to keep in touch with others for a while is to find out who you really are. Those who know you may have already put into a category. Yet you might really be a writer, or an artist, or a therapist, or a doctor, or a storyteller or a trader, but how will you know unless you give yourself the time and space to create? Remember, you need to give this to yourself, no one else will give it to you. That is the point and the purpose of magical travel. You dive down deep into the waters of your soul and by image-in-ing your dreams, you draw them ever closer. There is no greater gift than your soul being directed by the wind of spirit. You came like Water and like Wind you go.

CHAPTER 21

Getting work

Work is Love made visible
Kahlil Gibran

Just like travelling magically, there are an infinite amount of choices in working magically. You don't need to know what you want to do before you set off; indeed when you begin travelling you will meet many people who don't know what they want to do either. But most of them are aware they have options – that's why they are travelling. They can go grape picking in France or pearl farming in the South Pacific, or do almost anything, anywhere. Many books and websites cover the practical aspects of working abroad (see Resources), so I won't go into them here; but I will talk about how you can make your work actually work for you, because there is another way of finding that state of peace – doing your right work.

As ever, take the silver road, the high road in alignment with the first principle of travelling magically, following your intuition. But this is often harder to do with work, for we need to earn money. The first section will explore how you need to make the most out of where you are, even if you know you are doing the wrong job. Then we shall see how you can follow the other principles, travelling spontaneously, going local (for example, finding out about a country's culture through your work), being open to mystical experiences and integrating what you have learned. For you can move on to a whole new level in your chosen career and your life through your expanded intuition, which has been honed by travelling magically.

FOLLOWING YOUR INTUITION

....

*In a moment of synchronicity, events 'just happen' to suit our
personal needs*
Caroline Myss

By following your intuition about where to go and what to do, you
could, seemingly by accident, find a job you love as did English
gapper Roger. He was blessed to find his right career while he was still
young.

Roger finds a new career

*Everyone has talent. What is rare is the ability to follow it to the
unknown places where it leads*
Erica Jong

Before he took up his place to study Economics at a British university, Roger went turtle tagging in Greece. He found it immensely
rewarding, as he loved working outside and felt part of an important
and meaningful project that involved monitoring how many turtles
returned to the beach where they themselves had hatched, to lay their
eggs in turn. Because Roger enjoyed this work so much he changed
his university course from economics to marine biology and developed a career he will love for life.

Roger was really glad he had not gone straight to university and
followed his feeling to go to Greece, even though he had never travelled abroad before. If he had studied economics and then worked in
a bank he would have felt stifled. But among wild creatures he feels
expanded. And his parents are happy now too, seeing their son with
a rewarding career, even if wasn't the one they would have chosen for
him. Most importantly, he's happy.

Following your intuition will always lead to the right thing, even if
it doesn't always happen as directly as it did for Roger. Now it's time to
look at how following the second principle, travelling spontaneously,
can help you find your right work.

TRAVELLING SPONTANEOUSLY

....

> *Don't go where the path is. Go instead where there is no path*
> *and leave a trail*
> **Ralph Waldo Emerson**

Working magically begins with letting go. Probably the most common mistake people make is thinking they have to have everything planned before they leave home. They imagine they have to work for a long time to save the money to have a trip abroad, but there is an alternative. What about working for long enough to get your fare, then going abroad and getting a job when you're there? That way you're still earning money, but you're doing so in a new environment that will make even the most boring job less boring. Plus you'll have the chance to learn other things.

Working in Australia rather than Britain

Let yourself go on the stream of the unknown and accept whatever comes in the spirit in which the gods may offer it
Freya Stark

In my gap year I decided to work in Australia, where I have citizenship, rather than England where I grew up, and stop over in Asia on the way. I worked for four months that autumn for legal firms in London, saving every penny for the flights and spending my lunchtimes dreaming in the travel sections of bookshops (it was a sign I wasn't meant to be a lawyer). Then I set off. In Sydney, I got a very uninteresting job as an office clerk in a very beautiful position overlooking Sydney Harbour. I travelled to work by ferry over the harbour, and the wonderful morning and evening journeys past the beaches of the North Shore, Sydney Harbour Bridge and the opera house, were enough to make the job bearable – just. I still remember its wonderful location; it definitely beat doing the same job in London.

You may not see how you can possibly 'leave a trail' from doing your job – especially if it feels like the wrong job – but trust that by following your intuition the job will be part of your greater purpose. Maybe you are meeting someone you need to meet or learning a quality you need to know. My time in Sydney, for example, enabled me to live with a nice family, consisting of Janice and Glenn and their respective children from previous marriages, for the first time, which, in retrospect, was an important part of my path.

Learning about a country's culture, in following the third principle 'go local', is also valuable.

LEARN ABOUT A COUNTRY'S CULTURE

> *But you who are wise must know that different Nations have different Conceptions of things*
> **Response of the Indians of the Six Nations, 1774**

There are two main ways to learn about a country's culture through working in it. The first is to do what many travellers do, take advantage of easily available, often menial jobs, which you know will be temporary – you are a 'career-breaker'. The second is to select a country because it highlights a particular skill, one you wish to develop. In this case it may become permanent; you are a 'career-maker'.

You can take advantage of the uniqueness of a country by working in industries associated with it. For example, kibbutzim, communal farms, are unique to Israel and you may be fascinated by aspects of life there, such as the way children are brought up communally or the Jewish attitude toward the sacred. It is easy to volunteer to go to one of them, and there is a wide variety of tasks you will undertake that you may not have done before. Starting the working week at 4 am on a Sunday morning may be a bit of a shock to the system, but at least it *is* a shock, with all the possibilities of growth that implies, as we looked at in Part 2, Chapter 1, 'Culture shock'. For after all, you choose how you respond to the shaking up of your system.

Scottish travel writer Alastair Scott has had most jobs you can think of, and quite a few you can't, during his trip around the world which lasted for several years. The variety of choices he made certainly made him richer in experience than if he had stayed in Scotland. For example, he worked on an Icelandic fishing trawler and on a farm in America. You learn what you are prepared to put up with, and, just as valuably, what you are *not*. You will gain a unique cultural insight as well as learning an enormous amount about yourself by being thrown into unexpected situations. At the very least, you will gain a huge fund of stories to entertain people with. And of course there are the careers as travel writer, yachtsman and photographer Alastair developed too. Even though he did not focus on his future career, he found it as a result of his magical travel.

You can deliberately use your work in a country as a 'career maker'. If you want to improve your career skills, as well as earn some money, you are best to devise a strategy. Target your strengths and get some experience in your own country. Then you can decide which country would best help you, and go there. As you may realise from experience in your own country, many of the best jobs are not advertised, they depend on word of mouth. Whether you get them or not may depend on you being there at the time or your attitude when you are there. Both of these things are under your control, and remember your intuition is always there to guide you.

Rhoda in Italy

Enlightenment was not a trophy to be lifted high in one triumphant moment, it was about seeing clearly, and choosing wisely in daily life
Lucy Edge

Rhoda wanted to be an interior designer and was particularly attracted to Italian style and had always loved Italy. Before she had some time out in Italy, she learned a little of the language and did some research on companies she could possibly work for. When she arrived there not only did she feel in love with the food and the architecture and the fashion, she found a job with the company she liked best. She learned a lot – including fluent Italian – and is now known as an Italian interior designer in her home country. Result.

So we've seen two examples of how working within the context of a country's culture can lead to the right career, one indirectly, and one directly. By having the courage to expand you won't go wrong. Now it's time to see how the fourth and fifth principles, being open to mystical experiences and integrating your learning back at home, can possibly help you in terms of work.

OPENING AND INTEGRATING

The higher the frequency of your vibrations, the better you can manifest what you want in life
Bärbel Mohr

Today the world is full of more and more people who have found their right career. The benefit for the planet of so many in alignment is immense. What then can you learn from the fourth principle? Well, there's always more. For your career development can always benefit from the infusion of new energy that results from you doing it in a different place, as long as it feels right to you.

Kim swims with elephants

The Angels have an awareness of patterns and they will help you move
Sabrina Dearborn

Kim is a masseuse, who heard and followed the call to go to Thailand. As well as studying advanced Thai massage Kim did a little work teaching English there. She hung out with other travellers in Bangkok, and visited the markets and the temples and participated in some wonderful Buddhist rituals. Then she travelled magically through the country and enjoyed an amazing experience in North Thailand where she went swimming in a shady pool in the jungle with some baby elephants.

Even though we all resist living on a higher level, when we break through to it, it is so much fun! Kim learned new techniques to use on her clients. She also remembers the elephants' enormous, exuberant energy as she is giving a massage back home. Her regular clients have

341

commented that her massages have got even better. Work and fun blend seamlessly together. For she is open to the angels.

FINDING YOUR RIGHT JOB

> *There are only two ways to live your life. One is as though nothing is a miracle. The other is as if everything is*
> **Albert Einstein**

As your intuition becomes stronger even more ways of making money will open up to you. For you will be in touch with far more 'sources' in the universe. You may find yourself developing a 'portfolio career' doing a bit of this and a bit of that as it suits. Alternatively you may choose to 'downshift' and we'll see in Part 3, Chapter 2, 'Dealing with change at home', the way Aussie Alexa left her high-powered job in computers to become a writer after working in the Antarctic. Of course travelling and working magically can launch you on the road to your right career, and examples are scattered throughout the book.

Finding your right work is only ever a heartbeat away. By letting go, opening up and following your heart you will create it. Travelling magically is not the only path to do so, but it's a bright one. And a lot of fun too, as Kim discovered when she went swimming with the baby elephants. So working magically while you travel is a win-win situation, as long as you are in alignment with your Higher Self. Working with intuition and integrity is love made visible.

Now we'll look at another kind of love, one more usually understood by the word 'love' in the West – making love.

CHAPTER 22

When do you make love?

The world is like a dancing girl – it dances for a little while to everyone
Arabic proverb

Sex is one of the pleasures of life, wherever you are in the world. When you are engaged in it the language of the body speaks for itself. The movements leading towards it speak many languages, the language of love, the languages of lust, the language of flowers, even the languages of money, hope and expectation.

Let's see how the process of 'attraction', from the Latin *tractere* meaning 'pulling towards', can work. In doing so, we'll look at some different aspects. Your looks are less important than you might think, even if slimness is considered desirable in the West, in other countries such as Africa and Polynesia the ripeness of weight is to be praised. Nor is age necessarily a factor, if you do not want to reproduce. But what is likely to weigh very heavily is the economic aspect, which may be connected to your nationality. Let's look at how this has an effect before we look at how to decide whether to make the world dance for you by having sex, and how to deal with any possible commitment. Whatever you decide, you can still have a wonderful time, and create some wonderful memories, as long as you make love in the right way.

ATTRACTION

....

> *Dawn-love it is . . . that first look so quickly felt, so little under-*
> *stood which, if one could only keep it, would outshine everything*
> *in worth*
> **Johannes Wolfgang von Goethe**

The elements by which people are attracted to each other vary hugely around the world, and it is a *cultural*, as well as an individual thing. Anthropologist Tobias Schneebaum had some fun participating in some sexualised contact, such as kissing a headman's penis, during his stay in New Guinea – which he may have chosen because the beliefs and actions there were aligned to his own as a homosexual. One large American woman enjoyed Polynesia because there her rippling weight was valued by men she found attractive. It's as well to be aware of what kind of looks other cultures find attractive before you go there, so you can see where you fit on the spectrum.

Attraction is based on many factors such as looks, the feeling someone gives you – and even ideally, the soul. But attraction isn't always based on things of the soul. Many societies are very practical about sex and it is a means to an end, marriage. Other people's customs affect you directly when you are in their society and you need to be aware of them. Sometimes though, this extra awareness is fun, such as in Tahiti.

For women

> *Women who set a low value on themselves make life hard for all*
> *women*
> **Nellie Clung**

If you're a reasonably attractive woman from a rich country it is possible to get sex almost everywhere you go; the biggest problem is refusing it. Men of many cultures will assume you are on your own not from choice, but because you're really waiting for it. There is a splendid specimen of manhood presenting himself in front of you and offering to show you around, and your refusal may mean you are being coy and playing hard to get. And recently, didn't a Burmese guy, just like him, marry a British girl, beautiful like you, and go back with her to make a fortune in her beautiful country? Just because of your nationality you will be tarred with the same brush in societies where there is little notion of individual choice.

Judgements always bring generalisations. My travelling would have been harder were I Swedish, for example, as the hot and willing reputation of these girls precedes them. Being English can be a problem too as England is considered to be a 'sexy country' with jobs and welfare and, by extension, that makes me desirable too. I have often found it prudent to say I'm from a country such as Iceland, where people are unlikely to have met the natives (particularly a girl who has slept with anyone they have heard of). Iceland also doesn't have a great reputation in terms of jobs, so that makes me less desirable marriage material. I don't wish to be desired for my nationality, but in the world's present socio-economic situation my nationality makes me more desirable. That's also the case for other people from the West, and it's good to be aware of it.

For men

> *Beauty is merely the Spiritual making itself known sensuously*
> **Hegel**

Many societies 'export' their women to marry abroad. They are of economic value to their family for what they can bring in from marrying a foreigner. Men need to beware of in much of the world.

Remember too, you men, that it is highly unlikely that these women want your wonderful body, it is far more likely to be your nationality or your bank account. Without a common language communication can be difficult, so it is unlikely to be your great mind. In countries such as Thailand a Western man with a Thai woman is a common sight, and the sad thing is, he often seems to think she loves him, whereas romantic love is not considered a basis for marriage in Thai culture. She may well be with him until the next bigger (in every way) Westerner comes along. A man may have sex abroad because of his nationality and not his unfailing charm. This may be difficult for him to remember, but he should keep it in mind. He may get a large amount of propositions in certain countries such as Russia where women want to get to the West. He may not be used to saying no, but he should learn quickly. Otherwise he could get himself into a lot of trouble with an unintended wife on his hands, or a furious family, who are prepared to show it.

Remember that sex, in most parts of the world, is a family rather than an individual affair, and in many cultures it is seen as leading to marriage. It is important to be clear about your intentions. I know one eminent anthropologist specialising in New Guinea who is unable to return to a certain tribal area because, in the past, he promised to marry a woman but did not go through with it. If he were to go back to that tribe, he would be killed on sight.

Make sure you act within the parameters of the culture you're in, rather than within your own. You can learn about this from guidebooks, talking to people and just plain observation. You must also watch out for the subcultures. If you find yourself in a Muslim community in a Christian country, for example, sexuality is likely to follow the Muslim rules, not the Christian ones. The community, rather than the general standards of the country, sets the behaviour, and that's the standard you'll be expected to abide by. When in doubt, err on the side of caution.

But you need not practise this caution in every society, as we shall see in the example of Tahiti. There, if a woman or a man wants to have sex with you, it is most likely because they simply enjoy the pleasures of sex without guilt – that is part of their traditional culture.

A POLYAMOROUS SOCIETY

In Europe men and women have intercourse because they love each other. In the South Seas they love each other because they have had intercourse. Who is right?
Paul Gauguin

You may be travelling in a society where there is so much sex that everyone assumes you want a piece of the action. In the hot islands of Tahiti celibacy is virtually unheard of. Many people believe that if they don't have sex several times a week they get the 'filled-up sickness', as they need to let their juices go in the glorious sexual act. Seduction is so easy, it is almost non-existent, but that means almost anything you do can be interpreted as an invitation for sex. I had a difficult time there, for whatever I did, whether it was accepting a drink or asking directions in the street, was seen as soliciting. But I thought I was just accepting a drink or asking directions. I quickly learned not to accept a drink, and when I asked for directions I put a 'closed' expression on my face and refused invitations to go dancing. A 'closed' expression works pretty well anywhere, but it's important to remember refusal must be couched within a culture's terms.

> **In Tahiti, a flower:**
> **Over the right ear means you're taken.**
> **Behind the left ear means you're free.**
> **On top of the head means you're anyone's.**

When you put a flower in your hair be aware of the language of flowers. Remember too that every culture has its own code for offering and accepting sex, even if it is a little less alluring than the Tahitian example. As the visitor to the culture it is your responsibility to be aware of what it is, the chances are no one will explain it to you. So read the guidebooks. Keep your eyes and ears open. Dress appropriately. And above all practise common sense, in deciding when to act.

ACCEPTING SEX

Darling I love your curves, but go slow
Road sign in Kashmir

Sex is a sacred activity, as well as an immeasurably pleasurable one. Most travellers, though, probably don't want to have sex only when it's sacred but because it feels so good. So let's look at how you should act in that scenario.

There will be many times on the road when the person you really click with, you really fancy too. Being together in this context does have lots of advantages. You are free to spend all your time together and to go wherever the wind takes you. The key word here is 'free.' You are free in a way you are simply not at home. Free to do what you want without social approval, or even knowledge. Nonetheless it's important to treat someone the way you would want to be treated yourself, whether it's for a night or a lifetime.

If you decide you might well go for it, here's a checklist of what to look for in deciding whether to accept the offer of sex:

✧ There are qualities about that person you respect and admire, as sex is a fabulous way of joining his or her energy with yours.

✧ Longing should be reciprocal. For example, no payment is involved and you are not having sex out of any sort of obligation, but only because you want to.

✧ You both should be free to explore your connection. Of course you should be both substance-free and bringing your 'best selves' with you. You, the magical traveller, will have dealt with your ex-lovers back home and your intended should be unmarried and not be serious about anyone (or not considered serious by anyone in the culture you happen to be in).

✧ Both of you should be clear about your intentions. If all you want is one night, say it. Do not pretend you want a long-term relationship in order to get sex. If you do it will cause great splintering-of-self. This leads to fission not fusion, and will have great repercussions in your life, not just in that context.

✧ You don't want something long term. If you do, it's better to wait, as in the high-vibe world of travelling magically, even a misplaced word or two can have great consequences, let alone mistimed sexual energy. For that reason alone, take things slowly and allow the energy to percolate and settle, while still spending time together.

The universe works in mysterious ways. One reason you decide to take your trip may be to meet your mate. There will be many signs if that is the case. One of them may be similarity of origin and interests. I am consistently amazed by people who are living close to each other, who share the same interests, may even know the same people, but meet each other a long way away. Tom met his future wife in Southern India and discovered they were living close to each other, one in North America, and the other just over the border in Canada. Coincidences such as this may well be signals from the universe that you are meant to be together. A number of very happy marriages begin through travellers meeting.

You may have a long-distance romance, but I would recommend restricting this to a limited time so that both of you can be free to move on to someone who is there for you in physical reality if you do not decide to make it permanent. At some point you will have to make a choice: do you separate or forge a bond? If you decide to separate from a traveller, this is usually relatively easy as you just move off in different directions, and there is little potential for stalking. However, separating from a local can be somewhat more fraught, as it is likely your standing in their society will be affected too, but that is not something we can go into here. However, you may decide to forge a permanent bond with your local lover, in which case there is a host of things to be aware of.

INTERCULTURAL MARRIAGE

> *Oku faka 'ofa'ofa anoe 'a ko laumatie moho loto he maamani kotokotoa*
> *(How beautiful is your soul! Or I love you!)*
> **Tongan proverb**

There are usually more problems marrying someone from a different background and culture than there are marrying someone from your own culture, as detailed in Dugan Rumano's book on intercultural marriage, *Intercultural Marriages: Promises and Pitfalls*. You need to respect each other's countries and cultures and cherish each other for things to work out. There are many stories, though, of couples who've managed it, and many others of those who didn't. Here are some factors to take into account:

✧ Be careful not to confuse the beauty of where you are with the beauty of the person next to you. People often look far more ordinary in your home context.

✧ There may be an excruciating sense of your wonderful foreign lover not fitting in at home if they come to your culture, and, as a result, seeming considerably less attractive.

✧ Are you prepared to live in your intended's country, or is he or she prepared to live in yours? Adjusting to another country takes effort. In making it, you really should feel you are with the right person.

✧ Don't forget the potential for cultural misunderstandings. For example, the Germans and the British may find they have a different sense of humour. An American male may be used to staying in control. A Japanese girl may subconsciously expect to be protected.

Always remember that your problems are not just the quirks of the guy or the girl. It is their *culture* and you will need to be together for a while to iron out those wrinkles. There are resources to help; Rumano's book identifies 19 problem areas, which are either less severe or absent altogether in monocultural marriages. It's good to be aware of them.

That said, however, there are many stories of people who lead happy lives together; they just happen to have been born to different cultures and countries, but they have each learned to appreciate the beauty of the other's soul.

THE COSMIC DANCE

Shiva rises from his rapture, and dancing, sends through inert matter, pulsing waves of awakening sound and lo! Matter also dances
Ananda Coomeraswamy

By making love in the right way to the right person, you allow the world to dance for you, at least for a while. Your very special time together would not have happened, could not have happened, had you stayed at home. Now it glows among your most treasured memories.

Tim Ward from Canada chose to travel around Asia for two years as a young man in order to study Buddhism and understand the problem of human suffering. Instead he was to experience a sexual and spiritual awakening he documented in his astounding and detailed book *Arousing the Goddess*, which is a course text at Claremont University, California. Having studied the Anthropology of Sexuality for some years at Cambridge University and University of Hawaii, I find it an excellent example of sexuality going beyond the culturally determined through the power of the spirit. A somewhat arresting piece of prose it is included to show how our cultural conditioning can be transcended by magical travel.

Tim flows and flowers

You're like milk in water: I cannot tell what comes before, what after
Mahadeviyakka's song to Shiva, in his form of Lord White as
Jasmine

Tim was surprised to find that the Goddess plays a pivotal role in Buddha's enlightenment – immortalised in the legend of 'The Earth Touching Gesture'. This discovery hurtled him to a life-changing experience of love and passion with a gorgeous blonde anthropologist called Sabina, whom he met in New Delhi. Sabina happened to be studying the statues of the earth touching Buddha, and Tim informally became her research assistant as they travelled around India by local transport, staying in local hotels. Tim saw her as a perfect goddess, and said that Sabina was 'an artist at love'.

One night in Patna, they told each other they loved each other. That was the beginning of their Tantric experience. As Sabina took Tim in her mouth the feeling of impending orgasm spread throughout his body. But instead of exploding, it grew and grew and he lost his erection. Tim's skin seared white hot and his whole body become as sensitive as the tip of his penis, as Sabina moaned beneath him. Then they became suffused with a quiet and tender bliss. The overwhelming electrical force came to them again in a tourist guest house in Bihar. The planet Venus exuded a single white light in the paling sky as they lay together naked once more. Tim's mind shone with the image of a great stone lingam [penis] thrusting out of the earth and the Lord Shiva dancing on burning corpses. Then he passed through the electric fire into 'a calm and tingling awareness, the eye in the centre of the storm'. Sabina breathed with the same rapid rhythm, spasms shook her hips and the jolt triggered Tim's orgasm. His legs arched behind his back. 'I reared and became the motion, the rhythm itself'. Then his shaft felt like a mould being filled with incandescent metal. Tim was about to break through to a universe he had never been to, but then stopped and cried as Sabina softly stroked his hair. She had experienced her breasts filling with milk and had had two orgasms without touching or contact and Tim had had one without ejaculation or an erection. They were both scared. Neither of them had a context for their mystical experiences. That would have helped them cope.

Tim was drawn to the Ramakrishna Mission in Calcutta, where a beautiful long-haired woman was meditating. Aditi told him about the Great Goddess Kali Mahadevi, the source of Tantra. Kali is not just Shiva's consort: 'Before the male priests ever dreamed of Shiva Kali *was*'. Her wreath of fifty severed heads is the same number as the letters of the Sanskrit alphabet. For Kali is also Mother of the Word, singer of the song, the Creator and the Destroyer. When Tim asked Aditi how you get the blessing and avoid the brutality, she told him fiercely he was asking the wrong question. 'The boon is won only when you accept both sides of her, including pain, sorrow, decay, death and destruction. These are not to be overcome and conquered. Run from her horrors and you also run from her blessings. To deny death, to act as if your ego is the centre of things, that must be protected from pain and preserved as long as possible, this is the real death. But embrace Kali as she is, kiss her bloody tongue and feel all four arms embrace you at once, then you have life, you have freedom. This, my young friend, this is Kali's boon'.

To really feel your feelings takes more courage than climbing the highest mountain – and is more worthy of respect. Only then new life pours in. So your world will always dance, whether you are with another or with yourself. Some of you will choose to stay bonded and that's wonderful. Yet even if you do not grow old with your lover, it does not negate the bliss you shared, or the insights you are able to gain if you choose. Declaring their love opened up both Tim and Sabina to cosmic sexuality, yet they were each unprepared for the intensity it set off. Even though Tim no longer saw her as a goddess, but as a real woman with flaws he still wanted to tenderly take care of, they broke apart. Tim, his ego broken open to the sun, continued along the molten path of sexual feeling, so ascending his inner mountain of whiteness. His courage to feel means that today his life and his freedom are held within the arms of a living and loving woman – his wife.

It is time to look at how we too can move on if necessary, yet continue our dance.

CHAPTER 23

Coping with goodbyes

Hearts do not meet each other like roads
Kenyan proverb

Saying goodbye is one of the most traumatic aspects of our 'pilgrim's progress'. In one sense there are no short cuts, you just have to do it. In another sense, we can make it much easier for ourselves. You can choose to believe there is a sense to it, a reason, a greater warp to the pattern than we can perceive with our limited vision. And if you take some time and space for yourself, both taking rest and going inside, and allowing yourself to feel, you will be able to create a new relationship correctly in the future, if that is what you want.

We'll look at a couple of examples of saying goodbye from our Higher Self, and at the importance of correct timing; the point is to move on in faith and trust. Then we'll look at how to get to the same point when someone says goodbye to us, through acknowledging the other person's right to their reality, even if we don't agree with it, and forging forwards into the blazing light of our Higher Self. So these different roads to saying goodbye take us in the same direction, to the place of peace.

Saying goodbye

....

> *Our true business is to be happy*
> **Tenzin Gyatso, the Fourteenth Dalai Lama**

Once it becomes clear that breaking up is necessary, it is healthier to be the initiator as it mitigates 'victim consciousness' in which you feel like a victim. You are taking power, you are taking responsibility and you are deciding the way your life runs. It's great that you have the courage to do that, because hanging on to the wrong thing is not only about hanging on to the wrong thing, it stops the right thing happening and gets in the way of our true business.

Letting go from your Higher Self

....

> *Two roads diverged in a yellow wood*
> *And sorry I could not travel both*
> **Robert Frost**

Say goodbye, not because of your resistance to the inherent problems of weaving a life with another creature, but because you genuinely feel a calling in a different direction. Your soul is calling you to do something else, whether this is to travel or involve yourself in another passion, and you know by leaving this person you will enable yourself to go in that direction. As Robert Frost goes on to say, taking the road less travelled has made 'all the difference'. You can't really imagine doing your soul's calling with this person, and if you try, it feels heavy and tarry.

But this line can be so fine that it becomes a translucent veil. Give yourself some time, some space to feel happy on your own, and then decide. Decide from a position of love, not a position of fear; the exercise on checking your intuition will help you here. When you say goodbye from your conscious mind ('he doesn't earn enough money') or your subconscious ('my God, she's making me feel, AAAARGH!'), you are trying to control the outcome when there is still energy present. You are moving away from love, and when you do that it doesn't work. The guy who doesn't earn enough money will probably end up becoming a millionaire. You will, slowly and surely, experience less and less happiness if you don't create a relationship that makes you feel. Your reasons must be valid on the level of the Higher Self for the correct outcomes to be put in motion.

When you let go from your Higher Self it's a different story. Then the universe works with you and you are both able to move on easily (even if only one of you initially wants to). Jennifer met a Swiss guy Andreas, an architect, in Tivoli Gardens in Copenhagen. He hadn't had a girlfriend for five years, but travelling helped his energy to shift, and he enjoyed remembering what he had forgotten. He came to visit her in New Mexico and wanted a future with her, but she couldn't see it, although she did care for him. She let him go, kindly and thoroughly, and he went back to Switzerland, where he started going out with an old friend. Then he sent a lovely Christmas card to lots of friends, including Jennifer, which publicly thanked her for setting him free to go on to love – a wonderful outcome.

THE RIGHT TIME

The greatest challenge of the day is:
How to bring about a revolution of the heart
Dorothy Day

To bring about the revolution of the heart you need to get the timing right; you need to have learned the lesson of being with the person first. Of course an exception is when you are with your soulmate; then you really need to stick with him or her rather than say goodbye, because you can go farther and faster together – and have more fun on the way.

Carlos was with Sara to learn to get in touch with the true source of his passion through their great sex. When he had completed the lesson, it was time to move on. It was the right thing for both of them, as they did not have enough in common to spend their lives together.

Carlos and Sara

I may not have gone where I intended to go, but I think I have ended up where I intended to be
Douglas Adams

In Italy, Carlos had a really intense time with Sara. They loved each other in Venice, they loved each other in Florence, they loved each other in Sienna. But by Rome Carlos felt the sexual and spiritual energy wane, and although Sara was still very attached to him, he started thinking about getting back to his job in the motorcycle industry. He didn't finish their relationship, but was more loving, acted as if he still felt the same, trying to create the outcome he wanted. It didn't work, and Sara picked up his true feelings and became more and more upset. When they reached Naples in the south he finished it. Any earlier would have been the wrong time, but when Carlos reached a place of peace about his decision, he knew it was time. It was also the right time for Sara, even though she didn't realise it. She went home and got a great new job and a great new boyfriend.

It's amazing the way magic works. Saying goodbye from your Higher Self does have some very positive outcomes, because as long as you carry on acting from your Higher Self (which doesn't need to be all of the time, but at least some of the time) you will *both* create magical new realities. Saying goodbye nicely helps even more, for the love you created together is your plateau of peace, providing you with shelter and succour to draw on in your existence.

And now we'll look at what happens when someone says goodbye to you. A different stimulus can teach you the same things. It's up to you. Always up to you.

SOMEONE SAYING GOODBYE TO YOU

I loved thee once, I'll love no more;
Thine be the grief as is the blame
John Ayton

Sometimes the universe will work through the other person saying goodbye to you. You have to hope that his or her motivations are correct, while remembering that it is not under your control. There may be all sorts of contrary signs, but if only one person understands them, then only one person understands them. Don't try to force someone to grow. Remember that old adage, 'You can lead a horse to water, but you can't make it drink.' And yes, the lines above show that it's very possible for you to get the blame as well as the sorrow. Such is life when we don't act according to our Higher Self.

The next example shows how it's easy to create your reality using the subconscious, even when you don't mean to. The subconscious works on the principle of 'me, me, me, I want, I want' unlike the Higher Self which knows how to let go.

Too much music . . .

Let one song rise from the universe
The Egyptian Book of the Dead

A talented and beauiful young Australian musician, Andrea, met an American businessman, Freddie, when she had just arrived in Los Angeles. He paid for her to share his hotel room and sometimes said he'd take her out for dinner and then changed his mind. Andrea told him exactly what she thought was wrong with him and his life. Freddie's resentment festered, after all he was a successful guy and he hated being told what was wrong with him. One night he went into meltdown and yelled at her that he didn't want to see her again. Andrea dramatically moved out, and now they are no longer in contact.

If Andrea had kept her own room and quietly got on with doing her thing, silently speaking the language that every man understands, although she might not have the guy (repeatedly cancelling dinner is usually a good indication that he has other priorities), she would have kept her self-respect. It's easier when you do not tell a guy you're right and he's wrong, so you can at least forge a ship of mutual respect. It is also a sign that you are learning to trust the universe to teach a lesson so you do not have to.

You must allow someone else their romantic reality, even when you don't agree with it. But it's a hard lesson to learn. To get there we must develop faith in a greater pattern.

An ideal pattern

If the anthropologist needed an ideal pattern to provide an orientation, so did the people themselves
Adam Kuper

On one trip to India I was drawn to the Mount Abu Jain temples of Rajasthan. I was very much enjoying my module in Anthropology and Art and I'd heard that there the stone ceilings were so finely carved the marble held the quality of the light beyond. When I saw a Dutch guy I'd kept bumping into in the more usual travellers' hang-outs of Delhi and Pushkar in this remote area, off the usual circuit, I knew it meant something. So I spoke to him and we immediately clicked.

Leo and I discovered that we were both born at the same hospital in Holland, and our fathers had a similar job. I had left Leiden when I was a toddler and my parents moved to London, and Leo often visited the part of London where I grew up and would stay very close to where I lived. We knew the same people in various parts of the world. Caught in enchantment, together with a scrawny-necked cat called Pushkar, he told me that I felt 'really familiar' and 'almost too good' and that he was falling in love with me. I had a very strong feeling I had never had before – that I would always know him.

If the role of the artist is to release the angel out of stone, then that was accomplished from that white marble. We went to view the temples and saw the lotus-flower ceiling, in which the detail was so fine, on one level it was transparent. Consciousness and life exist on many different levels; that's why the ideal is able to speak to us and say new things at new times. Leo and I were part of the same pattern. Yet there were words. Not all from our centre. Too many words. They did not dispel our shell and we were not to know each other fully. The temple was no longer a glimmering, shimmering whole and the glowing intricacy of the detail showed up at dusk. In the end Leo and I were not able to orient ourselves truly. When he left without saying goodbye, I was devastated. It was as though a giant chasm had opened on the path I needed to take. All I could do was feel and move on, even if I no longer knew where I was going.

To the Taj Mahal

That wayfarer is not there, not there
Rabindranath Tagore

I moved on to the most famous monument to love in the world. I will always remember the sense of peace I received on the lawns of the Taj on Christmas Day. Sitting on a sheet of blue velvet on the crackling grass in front of the floating domes, I read poetry. I felt deeply Tagore's beautiful poem, *Shahjahan*, his ode to the emperor who ordered the Taj to be built, a captive monument to love beyond death. Radiance is a strange word for a building made out of stone but appropriate here. The radiance transformed rock into light, so the Taj seemed insubstantial, floating like a glowing white cloud – a dream in white marble. It felt as though the peace of the world was drawn into those domes, pushing them outwards, bulbous towards the sky. The wide river at the back with its perspectives, the stretch of water at the entrance. Mirroring. One raven flew by me and I saw deep into his eye. Perhaps the slow-wheeling birds were the sera-phim, the messengers. As I wrote in my diary I received new insights about my recent experiences with Leo, the ravens cawing in certain places. A lady walked by, her blue and silver sari streaming and shimmering in the winter sun. Everyone was smiling and laughing. No, the wayfarer was not there, yet it was the most blissful, peaceful and productive Christmas I've ever spent, for I allowed the peace to enter me. The pattern played in place.

I am sure my sense of acceptance on that far-away day, in which I filled a few more of my cells with light, had something to do with helping me to deal with one of my rocks – my assumptions.

A higher parapet

Toeval is logisch
(Coincidence is logical)
Johan Cruijff

I wrote in my diary at the time that there are always swollen domes, inlaid parapets, lessons beyond what we think we need to know. Do not give up faith, although your faith should not be in that particular person, because you don't want to impinge on their free will, but rather in the beneficent workings of the universe to give you what you need. Meanwhile, the energy of your Higher Self may ensure you encounter the other person again, even if it seems impossible.

I bumped into Leo over a thousand miles to the south, when a friend, Janelle, persuaded me to go to Goa. Goa is a magnet for Western travellers (which was one reason why I had to be persuaded) and a huge place. Janelle suggested we hire a moped and we drove for hours over the mountains. We went through several Goan towns and finally, when my legs were screaming in pain, stopped in one called Benaulim at a restaurant called Johnsy's, where she used to go. I was so exhausted that my eyes couldn't even focus, and I went unseeingly across the crowded cafe to an empty bench, where unknown to me, a cat was having kittens under the table. I sat down – right opposite Leo. I was too tired to be shocked, but he was extremely surprised. I let Janelle decide where we went and what we did. It was certainly nothing I could have designed.

But that meeting did not mean Leo was suddenly supposed to

see the light and want to be with me, if being with me would have created more light. He did not. But I did get to say goodbye. And after he quickly disappeared, I was devastated again, but immediately found a sense of meaning again when I spoke to a slim Canadian guy sitting nearby who was talking about how he saw the most beautiful woman in the world in Nepal. Ron told me about his girlfriend back home with tears in his eyes. Later, I waited for him on a nearby sandhill on the beach as the red sun lowered itself plumply into the sea. As we walked and talked along the beach, Ron acknowledged my feelings and told me exactly what I needed to know about my situation. He was my male angel in human form – who also happened to be Leo's long-term travel companion. So the beauty of the beach was not wasted, for even if I did not get to spend more time with the guy, a hard rock inside me dissolved as the lesson seeped in together with the black sky spangled with the hard stars and the rising of the planet Jupiter over the land.

LETTING GO

> *Letting go means letting be, accepting the moment as it is*
> *Which is a very means of opening the heart*
> **Stephen Levine**

That little meeting when my legs were shaking and I had no idea where I was, taught me a lot about the necessity for 'letting be'. If your soulmate tells you goodbye then it will be agonising. But again, you need to allow someone their reality, for it has a right to be there, simply because it is. Let it be.

The need to let go is what William Blake referred to when he said, 'If you love something let it go.' Let go in faith, let go in trust, but let go. No union, however dreamy, can be anchored on dreams alone. Light and the stone cannot hold the same space without sharing an artistic reality, exemplified by the famous Jain temples of Mount Abu. Given that one of you has decided to drop the chisel and stop creating your mutual beauty, you, at least, can still serenely expand through allowing in the greater peace, even if it means you must carve a new parapet on a new blue day.

By doing so you'll be making space for the best possible outcome. Always remember we cannot see what the future will bring and the universe works in mysterious ways, often cloaking its signs. Just because you cannot see the rightness of a particular action or timing does not mean the rightness is not there. Even if you KNOW something's right, you still need to respect the other person's free will. You don't even need to talk about it. Keep your dignity and carry on. Your only role is to carry on doing what's right for you, in the sun and in the rain. By so doing, you'll walk down the road to your heart.

When the road to your heart is open, you'll soon find yourself creating those wonderful, bubbly, connected feelings of love. You will be permanently plugged in and connected to your source. You will become an enchanted creature who has exchanged his or her roots for wings. You will play inside the starry pattern.

Sometimes we do need to slow down and now we'll see some of the reasons we get sick on the road.

CHAPTER 24

Coping with illness

In the midst of winter
I find in myself at last
Invincible summer
Zen Master Dogon

Illness may be a reality of your life on the road. There are so many travellers' tales of malaria, diphtheria and strange internal parasites that remain with you for life. These stories can act as such a dire warning that they can make many people decide not to travel at all, or, if they do, to go somewhere safe. I appear in some of the stories, having been very sick for years as a result of my travels in the tropics and being the poster-book kid for 'Don't go there, you might end up like Rima.'

But any experiences, even the hardest, are what you make them. The crucible of magical travel can lead to some huge shifts in awareness. First I'll look at why we get sick. Throughout this book, I have referred to vibration, and have explained that our vibration attracts experiences to us. I will show how this applied to my own experience with illness. Indeed, there is now a branch of medicine called vibrational medicine that studies the environment of the soul. Getting sick is always part of the journey of the soul, because there are certain lessons to be learned. When they have been learned, the illness can end. So, in the end, there is nothing to fear from illness. And you might end up even being grateful for it.

Illness – random or reason?

···

> *I shall never believe that God plays dice with the world*
> **Albert Einstein**

Illnesses are not just random happenings that strike the unwary traveller. There will be other people breathing the same air as you, drinking the same water, eating the same food, who do not get sick. There are millions of microbes living inside us, which make us sick only at certain times. Why? Our resistance is low, and I am not just talking about physical resistance. We may be emotionally hurt or feeling inadequate in certain aspects of our lives. At other times, there may be a lesson for us to learn, such as the value of appreciating the small things in life. There might be somebody for us to meet we would otherwise have missed. For illness slows us down, and this can be of great value if we are developing too fast. We need to integrate our new consciousness, or else it can run away without us.

I really wish I had known about the possibility of a deeper reason for getting sick, for illness was undoubtedly the hardest lesson of my life on the road. There were times when I was utterly despairing and thought life was pointless. But by living through the pain, and (eventually) finding new realities I realised that illness was not the negative result of my gap-year travel I had thought. I mention my experiences in some detail below because what I have to say applies to others too.

My plague of illness
> *Every living thing can ripen and be saved*
> **Milarepa**

When I first met Liesje, fellow intending Cambridge student, in my old Delhi hang-out Ringo's, it was summer. Monsoon time. Rain poured into the open courtyard and the tables on the roof garden that were so attractive in the winter. Insects appeared, the size of plates. Everything was different. I was different. I was very thin and had what I thought was 'Delhi Belly'. Liesje and I spoke for a while and arranged to meet again in Cambridge in the autumn where I was to go to a couple of parties in her college. We said goodbye and I set off for Pakistan.

Pakistan was a whim, because I'd met a couple of guys who were going there and persuaded me to accompany them – it wasn't safe for a young woman on her own. But when I got sick I held up their travel plans and they left me – alone and 19 in the Karakoram mountains. I made a note to myself, that if I survived I would only travel to a dangerous country with trustworthy people. I nearly died up there in the quiet and dangerous mountains, and when I started spitting blood and couldn't keep water down I knew it was time to go to hospital. I mentioned my attempt to give a sample in Part 2, Chapter 1, 'Culture shock', and one of my worst moments came a little later when I was lying on the examining table, so sick I had almost lost all my faculties, but they were enough to realise that the man who wanted to examine me wasn't a doctor. When the real doctor came things weren't much better. He told me that I was dying, and that I should go home if I could. I got myself and all my baggage back to Delhi in a three-day overland journey, and then back home.

Once in London I checked straight into the Hospital for Tropical Diseases, and rapidly recovered enough to be able to eat and drink. I must admit we had a bit of a party there, as I caught up with several of my companions from India, such as Matt, a kind student who had helped me get home when I was in Delhi, Suzy a nurse who had been working in New Guinea and 'Mad Mary' an Irish nurse. I began to enjoy myself. An injection of vitamin B12 in my buttock meant I could walk again. It had to be one of the best quick fixes in modern medicine. But it was to be my only one.

My illness, tropical sprue, was diagnosed. It is a rare disease and I was only the fifth person in Britain to have caught it. Antibiotics didn't work, so speculation was rife. One doctor said, 'She just couldn't manage India and needed illness as an excuse.' Others said I'd be sick for the rest of my life and would never get out of the wheelchair; in fact I was only in a wheelchair on a very good day, as on most days I was far too sick to get into one. But even that wasn't enough to make me give up university. When I was too weak even to open a folder, let alone take in the contents, I knew it was time to leave. I had met Liesje again at Cambridge, where she at least was hale and healthy. Hence Liesje's remark, 'Poor Rima. She had such a dreadful time in India and [quietly] look what happened to her afterwards.'

Another doctor said I couldn't handle Cambridge and yet another doctor said, 'She got sick because she's depressed' and tried to put me on anti-depressants. I refused and said 'I am depressed because I am sick and had to give up my university career, I am not sick because I am depressed. It is *reactive*, not endogenous depression, and I do not want to take pills, as that would be treating the symptoms, not the cause.' The doctor didn't press it. Sometimes it is best to play these people at their own game. And I realise the lack of an easy fix did cause them problems.

People would approach my mother in the street and say, 'You must really regret letting your daughter go to such a place,' to which, to her credit, she replied, 'No, I don't actually. She was 18 and it was her choice, and I can understand why she made it.' Here I shall skate over the years of my illness; suffice it to say that even in my most despairing moments, and there were many, I didn't regret going to India. For India had helped me live.

I wanted to show that I am not just talking theoretically when it comes to illness. I have been branded in its fires. But the illness did serve to speed up the growth of my soul. For it was time for me to ripen.

LISTENING TO YOUR SOUL

It is not always easy to be sensitive and receptive to India: there comes a point where you have to close up in order to protect yourself
Ruth Prawer Jhabvala

I wouldn't have been ready to listen to my soul when I got sick, but by the time of healing I was ready. For getting sick taught me how to listen.

I intuitively knew that none of the reasons the doctors gave about why I was sick were true, yet I didn't know how to disprove them. I loved India, it had given me the happiest moments of my life. I also loved Cambridge and Anthropology, and was doing well at it until I got too sick to continue. In fact, when I learned how to heal I returned to my degree course and did very well. What was the reason for getting sick? I needed to fit everything into my new quest for meaning, as India had shown me that there are no accidents. I was guided to one of Dr Richard Moss's excellent books, *The I That Is We*, which mentions that often people who are open to a new culture get sick. In a flash I had my answer.

I became sick precisely because I was so open. The more I let myself open, the sicker I became. It was my body's way of telling me to slow down. It explained why the other 'open' travellers I met often seemed to be sick, whereas the 'closed' ones, such as my friend Paul, the British Army sergeant, who thought he had nothing to learn from India, remained in resolute good health. People like him seemed impervious to India's bugs, as well as to her mind-boggling experiences.

The paradox was not such a paradox. I was gaining a lot of spiritual insights, but had no belief scheme to put them in. In other words, one part of myself – the spiritual – was growing, leaving my conscious and subconscious minds far behind. That causes dis-integration, reflected in the disintegration of my poor body. And that's why I had to get really, really sick, before I'd leave India. Therefore I did get really, really sick. I also had to remain very sick or I would have returned. Those spiritual flashes, now I had tuned into them, could not be turned off, so the rest of me had to catch up.

When I changed my belief system, years later in the white mountains of New Zealand, which I wrote about in Part 1, Chapter 18, 'Clean up your life before you go', I took a jump in my healing. For I was prepared to let my more negative, 'rational' system go, and take on board a new one. Was it worth it? Yes! For when I returned to India I went to the same places, ate the same food and even drank the Indian water. I was unaffected, except when my emotions were weak, which was under my control, because by then I knew how to choose what I brought with me. And wasn't the country wonderful without my tummy having a life of its own?

DIS-EASE AND THE JOURNEY OF THE SOUL

We must listen to our soul if we wish to become healthy!
Hildegard von Bingen

We've spoken a little about the journey of the soul throughout the book, about the way our immortal essence may move from incarnation to incarnation, needing to learn different lessons such as letting go, love, compassion and so on, lessons that are speeded up by travelling magically. The importance of the journey of the soul is recognised by certain cultures, such as Hawaiian, Hindu and Tibetan, as well as certain Western doctors. In *Vibrational Medicine for the 21st Century* Dr Richard Gerber defined its study:

> *Vibrational medicine looks at illness and wellness from these many different levels of energy dysfunction that can affect the multidimensional human being. The road to wellness is about more than proper nutrition and exercise. It is about our total energy environment, which includes the emotional-energy environment we create through our consciousness and our attitudes toward people and events in our lives. That energy environment also includes the spiritual energies of the soul that sustain us through the high and low points of our lives . . . To the soul, all of life's experiences, positive or negative, are merely different types of learning experiences chosen by the higher self to provide challenges to the conscious personality or ego as it travels the path to spiritual awakening and enlightenment, the true goal of life.*

Sometimes, once the lesson has been learned, it is time for us to leave our mortal body, and travel to other realms. Some talk of lightness transfiguring patients before they die and the unconditional love they exude. At other times, it will be in our soul's plan to carry on being on earth, having more learning experiences chosen by our Higher Self and hopefully sharing what we have learned. As the soul-truth of illness and dis-ease is becoming recognised, so more and more networks have sprung up, such as the Doctor Healer Network and the Scientific and Medical Network which explore the relationship between disease and consciousness. Members of both include doctors and scientists, some widely respected. Nothing represents the journey of our soul better than the fire of our awakening consciousness. For illness, just like any question, always invokes a response.

RESPONDING TO OUR SICKNESS

Our scientific power has outrun our spiritual power. We have guided missiles and misguided men
Martin Luther King

Medicine can be so much more than the study of symptom and cause. By allowing our illness to transform us we can even be grateful for our disease. In the end, I was glad for my cold winter, for I learned to contact my invincible summer – my soul. I only hoped I could put the lessons to good use. Now I help people, who might be having as difficult a time as I had, to learn how to heal themselves. For we all hold our knowing inside; sometimes we just need a little aid in assessing it.

If our illnesses were to have a place, they live in the moon clouds of our subconscious mind, where our emotions reside. Staying better depends on whether our subconscious falls back into its old habits and that is entirely under our control. It's important to grow our conscious mind too, we need to be very careful of the words we use and not make statements like, 'my illness is killing me'. Change your belief system. Hold a vision of health. When a so-called 'miracle' occurs, which is far more frequently than you might believe, it's a sign that our subconscious has changed; our minds are more integrated and healing is in alignment with the journey of our soul. That's all.

We no longer need to feel scared of becoming sick, or feel a victim when we do. For every illness is part of our soul's journey. We all have the option of being our own healer. By listening to your Higher Self you can see the role your illness plays in your life, and what you can do to get better. Then you can integrate your lessons into your life and help others as you have been helped.

CHAPTER 25

What do you do if it all goes wrong?

He hoʻailona ke ao i ʻike ʻia
(Clouds are recognised signs)
Hawaiian proverb

There will be many times of despair during your travels – far more than you would have had if you'd carried on in your old life. For when your vibratory system is raised things become more intense. But do not despair. For stuff comes up so you can clear it. For come up it will. Wherever you are.

The purpose of life is growth. But just as there is a time for light, so there is a time for darkness. You may be alone and dreadfully sick in your hotel room, or you may be hiking on a remote trail and be so exhausted you can't take another step, while getting burnt by the sun and bitten by flies, or you might have just had to leave that cute person behind. At times like this you'll wonder why you ever left home, and why you didn't choose to be a secretary with a spouse, dog, 2.4 kids and a white picket garden fence.

But you didn't, you heeded the call of your soul. And in the end you will be grateful, I promise. Meanwhile, this chapter will look at two ways of coping with difficulties: giving to yourself and laughing. The purpose of each is to raise your vibration. Then you make a decision about what to do from a higher place.

TREAT YOURSELF

....

Aroha mai, aroha atu
(Love received demands love returned)
Maori proverb

When you are in despair, take the pressure off. Relax. You don't have to decide anything right now. Be kind to yourself.

The occasional treat is very good for your morale. To me, having a quiet room to myself is an immense pleasure after nights of dormitory-style accommodation. Others might prefer to splurge on a favourite meal, or a phone call to someone you want to talk to. You might choose to buy yourself a treat or have a beauty treatment. That's all okay, you're opening yourself up to a lot of new experiences and you're entitled to retreat into the padded comfort of your shell once in a while.

That means doing whatever's good for you: it may be going outside into the mountains, it may be going down to the sea, you may visit a retreat centre or an ashram, or even go parachuting, bungy-jumping or scuba-diving. There's a whole world of experience out there. Give to yourself in whatever way is appropriate for you. Sometimes you may need to take a break in another, easier place or country for a while, and then return to the place you are drawn to, but which has pushed you hard. Give yourself a break. You do deserve it.

Do something that makes you feel good. I have never forgotten meeting a German guy by Lake Matheson in New Zealand, famous for the clarity of the mountain reflection in its peat-brown water. He had spent the last four years cycling around the world. As you can imagine, he had to be extremely careful about the things he put on his bike, as he was aware of any extra weight. Yet he had a little vase on the handlebars, in which he'd placed some hand-picked flowers. It's detail that makes a difference, both to himself and the people he meets. That touch certainly adds to memories. And what, ultimately, is more valuable than a memory? So don't be too hard on yourself.

Laughter, with its amazing power 'to raise your vibrations in a split second' as Ann and Geoff Napier said, provides an alternative way of treating yourself.

Laugh!

....

He who laughs - lasts
Wilfrid Peters

A sense of humour is the most important thing to take when you travel. If you don't have one, get one quick. Practise seeing the light side of situations, because you're definitely going to have to do this when you travel magically, or else you could easily go mad.

There will be many times when you're pushed right to the edge of your personal boundaries and then over them. Our boundary is useful because it it helps us decide what is acceptable to us, and what isn't, but can it be restrictive too? What if our boundary helped us to cope with unbearable situations a couple of years ago, such as an abusive one, but we no longer need it as our vibration does not attract those situations to us any more?

Keeping our boundary may be damming up our energy, always undesirable as it stops us expanding towards the universal. So when our boundary gets pushed and pushed and we just can't stand it any more, remember there is a reason for it. After your boundary has been knocked down, if you want to re-erect it in the same place you may, if you want to move it to a different spot you may. Meanwhile, take it easy. Even when your sense of self is being accosted and everything you hold dear is carelessly trampled on, go ahead and laugh. The beauty of laughter is that you can do it wherever you are, instantly. And it will always raise your vibration.

Laughter is the universal language, understood wherever you go. If you laugh in the middle of bargaining you'll probably get a better price. If you laugh when the bus breaks down, you'll be treated better. If you laugh when you can't get the seat you booked on the train you need to go on, you are beginning to let go of that need. Laughter brings flexibility, the flexibility to allow you to decide what to do next. When things seem unbearable and you just can't believe it, laugh. Remember too that other people have had an even worse time than you. Keep in mind the saying, 'If you don't laugh, you cry.' The choice is yours. So go ahead, laugh.

AFTER YOUR BREAK

....

> *As on so many other stages of my journey, coincidences kept*
> *happening until I accepted them as signposts indicating my next*
> *direction*
> **Lynne Franks**

You've taken your break and are feeling refreshed. But you are still feeling somewhat out of breath. What should you do? Where should you go?

Your terrible time, unless it carries on and on, also does not necessarily mean that you should leave the country you're in. It may mean you need to have even more insights to clear the clouds in your sky, lying on the carpet of your subconscious mind. Follow the coincidences that act as signposts.

Sometimes the signs indicate it's time for you to leave. In this case, they might stop or point you steadily towards home. Additionally, you will feel a longing for somewhere else, even if it's a place you thought you'd never return to – home. So let's go on to the next chapter – when do you go home?

CHAPTER 26

When do you go home?

I can hardly explain to you the queer feeling of living, as I do, in two places at once
Mary Taylor

There is nothing worse than getting home and discovering that you really want to be away again. But then you don't want to stay where you are and don't really want to be at home either. How then do you know what to do? We'll look at some factors: your reaction to the constant change, the possibility you are needed at home, to return might be the right thing for your soul development it's best to move on. You must distinguish between the factors correctly. As ever, the key is your intuition.

HAVE YOU HAD ENOUGH OF YOUR TRIP?

We will sense our inner voice, sense what is right, and what is not
Janez Drnovsek

Travelling gets us in touch with the one constant in life: change. We notice change all the time when we're on the road. There is changing scenery, changing people, changing landscapes. We get used to that constant stimulation and our body adjusts to accommodate it. Then one day, we wake up and that's it – we've had enough. We don't just want, we need, to be back in familiar situations. Scientists say that all animals, including man, have a supply of adrenaline. We use adrenaline in the flight or fight reaction, which is a common response to stress. When travelling, we are literally in flight, perhaps in more ways than one. There comes a time when our reserves of adrenaline are used up and we need to be at home to replenish them.

How do you know when you've reached that situation? You will be constantly sick of everything new and different, and will be hard put to muster even a spark of interest in what used to excite you so much. This can go on for days, weeks, even months and years if you let it. You crave your own language, your own frame of reference and sinking into your own familiar bed at night. You want to be able to walk outside without every sense going on alert, and that is normally only possible where we grew up, in the society we have subconsciously learnt to navigate, where we can do it almost without thought. Taking the Tube in London, for example, takes virtually no thought for me, as I can 'zone out' and still be aware of where I'm going. To many tourists though, going by Tube can be an enterprise that requires immense thought and many questions. What is the difference? Familiarity.

If you have taken rest and spent time on your own, looking inside and feeling, and it still doesn't feel right for you to be away, then trust that there is a reason for it. There may even be a reason for you to return that you don't know about.

Is a voice calling you back?

Surely we aren't all fated to return to our own private Newfoundlands?
Kevin Patterson

Sometimes you're enjoying your trip but you have an accident, or get the type of illness that makes it difficult to continue travelling. This may be the universe saying that it is the wrong time for you. It may be because you need to find more integration first, in which case it's the right thing for you to carry on with your trip, while developing the qualities you need. Alternatively, a person or an animal back home may need your help and this is the universe's way of alerting you. If that's the case you'll feel thick and muggy, because you'll be picking up the signals. Remember that a country is always there, and you can return at a better time; correct timing is the key to unlocking the treasures of the castle. But believe me, the door will stay locked if you're trying to force it open; for example, by trying to stay in a country when you're needed elsewhere.

Because, in the end, we are all fated to return to our private Newfoundlands. And when we do go back, then sometimes we will find a new-found-land that is worth far more. That is because the qualities we have learned on our trip, such as ease of communication, emotional expression and compassion, will now enrich our lives. The range of qualities is huge. For sometimes returning home now is exactly the right thing we need to do for our soul development.

IS RETURNING HOME NOW THE RIGHT THING?

Know that spring or autumn has no unchanging nature
Zen Master Dogon

Your travelling may have given you some great ideas and you can't wait to return home to put them into action. It's impossible for you to carry out your plans where you are. Or perhaps you could, but you'd much rather return home. Suddenly you feel strongly that the longer you stay away the more time you are wasting. You can justify the decision to continue your trip, as there is this particular festival coming up or that bit of money coming in. Basically, however you put it, you simply don't want to be there any more. But your soul does feel fired and inspired by what you really want to do back home. Alternatively, you may simply be sick of your trip and have had all you can take for the moment.

OR IS YOUR VOICE LURING YOU ONWARDS?

Follow the signs, trust the design, you'll reach bright air
Rima Morrell

Some people never want to stop travelling. Hans must have been in his fifties when we met in Greece. His nationality was indeterminate as he seemed to have something to say to everyone in every language, and his only possession was an old khaki bag. He asked for people's addresses but had no address to give them back. He did tell me that if his German lady hadn't died, he'd still be living happily with her in

Germany. Now, he could be anywhere, having learned huge lessons concerning non-attachment and resourcefulness. Even Hans, though, may sometimes have doubts, as he raises his head from his bag, perhaps somewhere in Greece or the North Pole. But he probably has no more than most, and considerably less than some.

Not all of us are meant to have settled lives. You will know where you feel happiest, and for some people like Hans, their soul's country is that starland beyond the bars, the bars being the constraints of society.

HOME NEWS

Movement is only as valuable as your commitment to stillness and vice versa
Pico Iyer

You must always follow your intuition and you are not being a wimp if you return home when the time is right; nor are you 'running away' if you decide to carry on travelling. The most important thing is that you make a decision. For ultimately, as Pico Iyer says, there must be both a commitment to movement and a commitment to stillness. That balance is for each of us to claim.

As far as returning home goes, it is significant that right now you are being drawn to things of your country, such as news broadcasts or special books. It doesn't matter that, not so long ago, you felt you would want to go on travelling this way forever. It doesn't matter what you said in the past, those promises you made to yourself that you'd never go home again. What does matter is how you feel, right here, right now, and your growing realisation that it's not just a passing feeling.

If you've grasped your freedom and flown, but now really relate to that Janis Joplin quote, 'Freedom's just another word for nothing left to lose' then go. Ground your flying bird and go home. You are about to learn to fly in the best way of all – bringing the earth with you. That means living in your Higher Self while being connected to the things of the earth.

PART 3

Coming home again

The journey is the reward
Lao Tsu

CHAPTER 1

Returning home

When an arch locks with a keystone it can stand for all time
Johann Wolfgang von Goethe

You have decided to go home again. Congratulations! You are ready to pass through the remembered doorway. Home may be the right place for you to stay, it may not be. By having the courage to return, you will find out. You will also learn how to integrate your change. That's how you enable the keystone of your Higher Self to stand in place.

First of all though we need to look at some things we may have to deal with. One is finding one foot in one culture, and another in the one you left behind. We'll see an example, then two of 'reverse culture shock' when you feel more attuned to a culture that is not your own. Then we'll look at the way through – integration. For example, we may need to redefine the concept of home, and I give an example of how connecting your minds can improve your home life, for example with your family. I end by stating that home is wherever you are, whenever you are in your Higher Self. The next chapters move on to some practical and spiritual aspects of adjusting to the changes you will find. We are learning to live the fifth silver principle of travelling magically – the integration of our sacred journey into our life.

When you return home it's very common not to know quite 'where you are'. You've brought elements of the culture you've been to back with you, but you are also in tune with some elements in your home culture. You have one foot in one culture and one in another. Magda did.

Magda on the toilet

I do not bring back from a journey quite the same self that I took
Somerset Maugham

After an amazing trip to Asia, Magda from Poland used a Western-style toilet again on the aeroplane back home. It was the first time in months. She had become so used to her bottom not making contact with anything when she went to the toilet that now the seat suddenly seemed quite dirty to her. She decided to put her feet on it and squat, using it a bit like an Indian toilet. She fell in.

Magda's experience is a great example of what happens to many Western travellers when they try to 'bridge the worlds'. Falling into the toilet, metaphorically if not literally, is commonplace. Other common problems to watch out for include drugs and alcohol, which give you a false sense of belonging.

Another common phenomenon now has a name. It is called 'reverse culture shock'. It's what happens when you return to your country, but actually feel more comfortable in the culture you left behind.

I am not in Australia

If you want to know what it is to feel the 'correct' social world fizzle to nothing you should come to Australia. It is a weird place
D.H. Lawrence

When I went to Australia after India I expected to feel at home. After all I had already lived and been to school there. But when I arrived I felt like an alien. I remember being in one family's neat bungalow in a suburb by the sea. The pink furry cover was on the toilet seat, and the place laid for the dog at the dining room table. I felt far more of a stranger than I had in a hut made of painted earth and daubed with magical symbols in the desert of Rajasthan. India felt right. The cows on the road on the way from the airport, the badly painted street signs, the dust-filled sunsets. Australia now felt wrong. When I paid for a ticket on a bus I knew I would have a seat, keep it for the whole journey and the bus would go only to my destination and not somewhere unexpected.

The difference was in me. India had reconnected my soul and I simply could not fit into the place I had previously occupied.

Another example of reverse culture shock happens when you *don't* change.

Richard's story

In order to be perceptive you must do more than simply look around. You must learn to see. And you can only see people and the world properly if you love them
Konstantin Paustovsky

People were nice to Richard in Indonesia when he worked there because of his British nationality, and because they respected his job. He did not realise this and thought it was because they liked him. When he returned home to England he expected the same reaction, and when it didn't happen, he was miserable. At home, people also looked at how he got on with his wife and children. In that sphere he didn't do very well, even his elderly, uneducated mother said to him, 'Why do you talk about peace in the world when you can't have it in your own home?'

Part of another culture's welcoming attitude towards you is because of your culture, not because of you as an individual. Richard didn't realise that. After Indonesia Richard thought respect was his entitlement – it never is. One great determiner of how much you have opened up is how much change you carry with you. Now you, the alchemist, will be confronting your old devils and your hidden fears, in the very place that gave rise to them. There is no more effective way to banish them forever. Several months back home can beat years of living in another country, as the confrontation will be much more powerful on familiar ground. Trying to open up your consciousness is much easier away from home. Integrating it, by contrast, is often easier on familiar territory.

The way through is always integration, integration of our subconscious and conscious minds into our Higher Self. Let's see how it works through the concept of home.

WHERE IS OUR HOME?

Charm'd magic casements, opening on the foam
Of perilous seas, in faery lands forlorn
John Keats

Home exists in our imagination, as well as our reality. It also exists, as we shall see, in our Higher Self.

Home is different things to different people. To an Aborigine it is the 'songline', or features of the landscape stretching over thousands of kilometres, the provider of life, spirit and sustenance. To an Inuit it is an igloo in winter, a camp in summer. To a Crow Native American of times past it was a wooden meeting house, with slats through which you could tickle the parts of those you most desired as they slept. To most Westerners it is a firmly rooted abode made of wood, stone or bricks where the nuclear family lives; but to some it could be a commune, a monastery, a barge or a tepee.

Wherever our home is, its greatest importance is in what it represents. Home is a mirage that we carry with us wherever we are. It hovers above us when things get bad, it provides comfort in times of trouble. 'At least,' we can say to ourselves, 'people don't eat guinea pigs there.' So be prepared for home to mean something different to you now. It is far easier to change our conscious mind after we return from our silver journey, for we have been exposed to other places, other ways of doing things.

The effect of home in our subconscious mind is even stronger. Home is our past, where we feel our deepest roots and where we learned the beliefs that we unconsciously live by. However, in virtually every family, these beliefs are not as healthy as they could be. In other words they do not work toward our highest good, and their very familiarity stops us questioning them. How then do we integrate? The answer is to continue to choose the things you do want, and leave behind the baggage you don't want. Like Tony.

The greenstone door

Tatau pounamu
(Greenstone door)
Maori expression for enduring peace

The child of successful London parents, Tony was bullied by his father. He was told that he was useless and would never amount to anything. Then, when he was 17, in a probably not unrelated decision, he left home and started travelling around the world. Tony spent seven years on a commune in India, and then lived in the USA, ending up in Seattle. He had some counselling, and finally felt ready to see his father again.

They met on top of the Space Needle, Seattle's most famous landmark, one day at sunset. As they dined in the revolving restaurant, watching the city whirl by, Tony pointed out the areas where he'd lived: Queen Anne, Capitol Hill, Magnolia. He felt his father acknowledging him for the first time. After he had asked his father some questions about his life and his father replied, he realised that the wall that had divided them for 20 years was paper thin. When he stuck a finger into it – such as by asking questions and really hearing the replies – it collapsed, just like the Berlin Wall.

Now Tony has returned home to the United Kingdom and is part of the family again, going round for Sunday dinner and on family holidays and others are benefitting from Tony's experience. He has also found his career – as a therapist – and his parents are supportive. Tony loves to help people as he once needed help. He has made his peace and the abuse has ended.

Through counselling Tony was able to select the beliefs he wanted, and through travel he learned he was worth something after all. Thus he empowered both his conscious and subconscious minds, allowing the door of his Higher Self to spring open and the contact to his family to be remade.

Families also make their own choices, and Tony's could have chosen not to talk to him again. Then, all you can do is to hold on to your high vibration, trusting you'll meet the people you need, knowing that you are no longer contributing to the cycle you grew up in. By moving on to a new level, you break the curse for everyone. By going home you'll be helping more people than yourself, even on the subtle, invisible levels where you may not be acknowledged, but you nonetheless make a difference.

When you know how to integrate your minds then you can approach the green land of your soul.

THE SOUL-LAND

The flowers appear on the earth
The time of the singing of birds is come
And the voice of the turtle is heard in our land
Song of Solomon 2:12

On the way to our Higher Self we are always guided. In Part 2, Chapter 4, 'Travelling spontaneously', I mentioned one of the signs, a green tortoise, I followed on my magical trip up the coast of America. The tortoise represents the earth and land in many cultures, including the Native American and Hawaiian. The colour green contains the qualities of growth and consciousness. The sea-going equivalent, the 'green turtle', happens to be the last creature in *The Hawaiian Oracle*. My book and cards set out the place of animals as guides in the Hawaiian tradition. Signs always lead us to our Higher Self. Here we are bigger than culture shock, even reverse culture shock. The world is our home. Honu Kahiki, the green turtle, guides you to your Higher Self.

Why then does the turtle continue to swim through the far seas, which are often rough? Hawaiian traditions say every creature on earth is heading for the lost island of paradise, Kane Huna Moku, our true homeland, which lies in the direction west. On this fair island there are springs: the waters of emotion overcome the judgement of the conscious mind. On the island too stand the inner gardens of the moon: our subconscious mind is now balanced and fertile. When we are integrated, we reach the shining isle, appearing out of the silvery mists. The time of the singing of the birds has come to our land.

CHAPTER 2

Dealing with change at home

People want to be settled. Only so far as they are unsettled
is there any hope for them
Ralph Waldo Emerson

Often people on a high vibration find their first experience of culture shock when they return home, not when they go abroad. They are so in tune with their soul purpose that they only choose to visit countries where they are intuitively comfortable. But on returning home you have to deal with the changes within you, as well as the changes to your home or country. Bringing a new kind of awareness to a place is knowing it for the first time. The very familiarity of your environment seems to highlight the dislocation between your present and past experiences.

CHANGES IN YOUR WORLD

The real voyage of discovery consists not in seeking new worlds,
but in having new eyes
Marcel Proust

We all have the image of an unchanging home. But in fact it is not like that, and why should it be? It is only our own vanity that makes us think the world revolves around us after all, and that vanity comes from our subconscious mind. When you get home after a long trip there may be some redecoration that you may not have been told about, babies born, trees cut down and politicians elected. In other words, life on the beach goes on, whether you're part of it or not. If your parents have lived in the same house for a long time, do you remember how much bigger it seemed when you were smaller? As you grew, the house shrank, though of course really it didn't change at all. After a shorter trip the changes you perceive may still be immense even if they are not there physically. Truly a case of having 'new eyes'.

Home can also seem much worse or much better. To Mark it seemed much better.

Mark returns to New Zealand

To look and to see are two different things which rarely coincide
Alexander Blok

When Mark arrived back in New Zealand from his big OE (his overseas experience) that lasted for four years he was delighted. He was shocked by the changes in Auckland airport, but glad to be back among languages and cultures (English and Maori) he recognised as his own. Hills had never seemed so green and sheep so white. After his time in England he really appreciated the villages with their lack of distinction between rich and poor. His country went from being an oppressive place he wanted to leave to being a beautiful spot where he wanted to raise his family. Everything was better for him. Mark doesn't need a Huna exercise.

But Lara does, for to Lara her homeland seemed far worse.

Lara sinks into Canada

There is no truth. There is only perception
Gustave Flaubert

When she returned to her home city of Toronto after her wonderful trip around the world, Lara had a terrible time. She felt strange and ungrounded and disconnected from everyone around her. The television programmes she'd previously enjoyed she couldn't be bothered to watch, reading bored her and she had nothing to say to anyone anymore. For no one understood what she'd been through, and, indeed, she couldn't really formulate it to herself.

Home was different because her *perception* was different. A spiritual truth and a cornerstone of Huna, the ancient wisdom of Hawaii. Change your perception, change your world. How can we practically do that? There are two Huna exercises to help us 'tune into' our new perceptions of our country. The first is for when you feel almost too disconnected – you are 'spacy'. The next is for when you feel heavy and bored. Let's look at the simple techniques to deal with your situation.

Feeling light

You are 'spaced out'. It's almost like you are on drugs, but of course as a magical traveller you will not be, you will be high on magic. The sky will seem really, really blue, the clouds super white and, indeed, more interesting than the town at your feet. You will feel disconnected from people, but not really too bothered about it, although somewhere within you are aware it is important. Lara found this happened to her when she returned to Toronto, she got lost in parts of the city that she had previously known quite well. It was like she was listening to a strange call, and felt a bit 'up with the birds'. She needed to ground herself, and the following exercise helped her.

Grounding exercise

1. Remove your footwear and stand with your bare feet on the earth.
2. Take several deep breaths: in-out, in-out, in-out.
3. Visualise your place in space as seen in the solar system, then on a map of the world, then your local area.
4. Hold still for a moment.
5. Notice the sensations around you: the touch of the wind, the way the light is, the feel of the earth under your feet.
6. Feel some energy running from the bottom of your feet towards the centre of the earth, connecting you to it as if with a pipe made out of white crystal.
7. Stand like that for a few minutes.
8. Enjoy.

This exercise will help you become more solid, so that you are better able to cope with the changes you will inevitably encounter. To all the exciting space-cadets out there, do it as often as necessary. Remember, you need to be integrated. It is no good only part of your becoming en-light-ened, it needs to be all of you so that you are not split and can bring all of yourself with you into the light.

Feeling too heavy

John had the opposite problem from Lara, he felt really heavy when he got back from his trip to Alaska.

John adjusts to New York

Only in quiet waters do things mirror themselves undistorted.
Only in a quiet mind is adequate perception of the world
Hans Margolius

John had a great time in Alaska, but now found his New York world very restrictive. Suddenly the buildings seemed too tall and the concrete exceptionally hard. He felt stifled and out of touch with his essential nature. He felt his reality was being defined by other people, his colleagues, his friends, and so on. This was difficult after his time away during which he tuned into being the creator of his own experiences. He still used to wear his outdoor gear going around the city at night, and he found he could not enjoy his favourite neighbourhood cafes and bars the way he once had. Something needed to change, but what? John still defined himself by his job and he wasn't ready to give that up; so he decided to change his attitude, and 'lighten up'. I taught him the huna 'lightening exercise'. Soon John's body began twitching and sparking whenever he sat in position. He loved the exercise, and his world in New York became really exciting, and his sex life improved too. His lightness led to far greater openness in his home city.

The following exercise appears deceptively simple but works like a dream. Do it on a daily basis.

Lightening exercise

1. Sit quietly in a chair, just in front of a wall.
2. Make sure your head is tipped back touching the wall behind you at an angle of 45 degrees. This position encourages blood flow to your head.
3. Spend several minutes in that position, asking for your being to be flooded in light.
4. Enjoy the feelings of lightness you receive.

So whether you feel too heavy or too light, there is always something you can do to change your 'state of being'. You are making your soul more alive, pulling it towards the lodestone of your own North Star. Magnetising your soul means that you manifest a genuine state of well-being (the source of which is your soul) rather than a superficial feeling of contentment (the source of which is your ego). But, of course, there will also be changes in you. The changes you encounter are challenges, and it's great you have the courage to grasp them head on, rather than just have them just happen to you. You will take a giant leap forward in the evolution of your soul, and that is so worth it.

CHANGES IN YOU

> *Things do not change. We change*
> **Henry David Thoreau**

How have you changed? What can you do about it? Do you explore your own town in a different way, or do you up sticks and relocate?

The golden rule is to do nothing fast. For your changes need time to percolate. For the truth is that people will pick up the changes in you, as we simply can't hide the fact that our vibration has changed. For example, one result of your heightened vibration is that your world has speeded up. Things happen much faster to you than they used to. Friendships change relationships end quickly, and everything is different now.

Yet the world has no standards by which to value your change.

That's not your fault. People's expectations of you are the same, but you are not. For example, you may find yourself being more assertive. When your neighbour visits you and lights up her cigarette and says, just as she always has, 'You don't mind do you?', instead of pretending you don't, as you always have before, you might say, 'Yes, I do mind actually.' At first, your neighbour will be surprised, but she may end up respecting you for it. As something that has expanded does not fit easily into the space it previously occupied, if you try to force yourself back into the comfortable groove you lived in previously, it may cause problems. It is important not to take on other people's negative ideas and expectations, especially in your delicate time of transition.

You can protect yourself with the following exercise. Do it whenever you're around people you don't resonate with or if you are in a challenging environment.

PROTECTING YOURSELF

The white bubble exercise

1. Stand or sit calmly.
2. Imagine you are completely surrounded by a pure white bubble. You are a white island in a greater sea. No feeling from outside can come in unless you let it.
3. Sit quietly and realise that the allowing is always your choice, for your bubble is always protecting you, whenever you want it to.
4. Therefore nothing can disturb you that you do not allow. You are the creator of your feelings.

Inside your buoyant bubble you are ready to expand and interact with the world, your new world. You will have friends, everywhere, among the 2 per cent who are willing to embrace your new ideas, although, of course, you won't always be around those people.

Your priorities have changed. Your old job may have been held open, but you may not want it. There may be the same old parties with the same old people. After a few perfunctory enquiries about your trip, the conversation may move on to other things. They may be things you used to be familiar with but now don't really care about. You may have to pretend, until you can move on. For example, you may decide you need to change your home or your job as a reflection of your spiritual shift.

RELOCATION

··

*'I went a little farther,' he said. 'Then still a little farther – till I
had gone so far that I don't know how I'll ever get back.'*
Joseph Conrad

Sometimes we can't go back – and nor do we want to. For example, we are very drawn to a particular kind of landscape after we travel, just as during our trip. Luckily countries often offer many kinds of landscapes. Britain, Australia and New Zealand each offer snowy mountains, forests, islands, remote beaches and pastoral landscapes, for example. You can easily find somewhere to suit you.

If you do choose to go and live in a city – you have a great project that needs people around, or you simply want to be there – choose somewhere with green spaces and only live with people you like. The rules for who to travel with also apply to who you live with. In fact you can never leave your guidance behind. Many people prefer to live on their own at this point.

People go and live in the countryside surprisingly often after travelling magically – perhaps because the vibration of nature is more aligned to your new vibration. I would recommend renting instead of buying, as your vibration is changing so fast. It will also give you time to decide where you really want to be. Many travellers move to caravans, chalets, even caves at this point. It's as if their desire to simplify, to reduce life to its essentials, has carried on after their trip. They also very much appreciate the value of time, and do not want to work too hard again – so their lifestyle now can often be called downshifting.

DOWNSHIFTING

....

The true harvest of my life is intangible – a little star dust
caught, a portion of the rainbow I have clutched
Henry David Thoreau

When you downshift you consciously decide other values are more important than your society's definition of 'success'. That is why downshifting is often associated with travelling magically, as each of the five principles are based on the same view. In fact, when you are guided by your intuition you will leave shared values behind. That's inevitable. For you will be seeking your own sky. Indeed, if there's a common theme to what happens after travelling magically, then it is probably downshifting. Alexa Thomas, for example, the girl who went to be a cook in Antarctica, decided she didn't want to return to her job in computers in Sydney and became a writer instead. Travelling magically does change you, so you don't necessarily want your old life back.

But there's an exception; and this is when your old life made your soul sing. For example, I returned to the same university to do the same degree, after my experience of travelling magically, with great verve and enthusiasm. I still loved it. I just loved it even more. That's because I was already doing my right thing. So parents, please don't worry that your children travelling magically in their year off will get put off their degree. If it's the right thing for them they definitely will not. And if it's not, isn't it better they find out now rather than in the future?

When you downshift, just like when you relocate (which is why they often go together), you simplify. And when you simplify then it becomes easy to value what's truly important. Now we'll see how to value your trip.

CHAPTER 3

Valuing your trip

True wealth is wealth of experience
Bill Gates

Remember your experiences are the most important things that you bring back from your trip. But how on earth do you share them with people? You have three choices: deny the trip ever happened, share your experiences inappropriately (I don't recommend the first two) or share them appropriately. Then we'll explore a couple of ways of valuing your trip, such as writing about it, or engaging in some sort of further study, at home or abroad. But it's only worth it if it helps the growth of your soul, if it feeds your true wealth of experience. For the corollary of valuing your trip is valuing yourself, the subject of the final section.

DENYING YOUR TRIP

The new space . . . has a kind of invisibility to those who have not entered it
May Durly

Don't pretend your trip never happened. Denial, even though it seems like the easiest option – it will get your partner off your back, and she will no longer feel threatened by the beautiful women in your photos – is actually the hardest. The things you don't want to cope with are still there and will merely reappear in another form. New hills will alter the smoothness of your inner landscape. You *have* made your trip and it is part of what makes you who you are today. To deny that is to deny an important part of yourself. Funnily enough, you'll find that in future years people won't thank you for it and they'll put you down in subtle little ways. And, maybe even more importantly, they'll respect you less as you didn't have the guts to stand up for your experiences. If you can't talk to people around you, why don't you keep a diary, write a book or join an Internet discussion group?

Don't be too hard on yourself. You've had the bravery to step forward into a world where few people go, and which even fewer know. The new world does indeed have a kind of invisibility to those who have not entered it. Let's now look at how *not* to share your experiences, and then at how to share them.

SHARING INAPPROPRIATELY

> As awareness increases the need for personal secrecy almost proportionately decreases
> **Charlotte Painter**

Don't be disappointed if your experiences are not appreciated by people back home, as 98 per cent of the population wish to remain stuck in their old habits. They may put you down because your new freedom threatens them. People don't necessarily want to hear, for really hearing you might remind them of all the things they haven't done in their own lives. However, this is more than likely to be subconscious, and all you'll experience is them shutting off from you without you knowing why. Don't judge yourself, as it's not your fault. Isn't it great you are not 'there' any more?

Sharing inappropriately involves babbling about your trip, miracles and insights to anyone who isn't ready to hear about it – most people. Actually, it's quite hard to share magical experiences. How exactly do you share your experience of enlightenment in eastern Russia anyway, or your sense that you had found God in France, or even that you really wanted to get married in Uruguay? This isn't your fault, but our Western society does not value the miraculous, except in one particular man, over two millennia ago. Indeed, if you go on about your experience of magic too much people may start saying that you need to see a shrink. Keep it up and people will say you are mad, and maybe try to cart you off to the nearest asylum.

Vibration is key, and sharing inappropriately does a great deal of damage. You have raised your vibration but others may not have raised theirs. Don't give others knowledge they're not ready for. Share only in appropriate ways, and, even then, recognise that others might not want to hear.

SHARING APPROPRIATELY

> *The only difference between the genius and the average person is that the genius has already found his inner light, while the average person hasn't*
> **Walter Russell**

Don't expect people to understand and to validate all of your experiences. One or two might if you're very lucky, but most won't. Say as little as possible if you don't want your relationships disrupted too much, and don't babble. The story of each experience is like a growing foetus: it needs to be nurtured gently in the dark until it is ready to emerge into the light. Just like the baby-to-be, if your stories are thrust into the world too soon, they will die. Give yourself some time to be the custodian of your experiences before you share them with a wider audience. You will know when the time is right, but it is likely to be months rather than days, which means that blogs are not a good idea at this point.

If you share your experiences in a more formal context, such as giving a talk or a slideshow, you will need to tailor it for your audience.

SHARING IN A FORMAL CONTEXT

> *In telling the tale of my travels*
> *I am made complete*
> **Freya Stark**

Telling the story of your trip will help you. But do remember your experiences are not a miracle to others, only to you. It is your job to convey them in the best way possible. When you are invited to give a talk about your trip, why not accept, even though you may not be used to presenting? It will give you more confidence and make you realise you have something unique to share. You should be paid something for your time – even if it is only enough to cover your expenses and a bit extra. Here are some guidelines:

The presentation

✧ Don't overload the presentation with too much information.
✧ Illustrations provide a focus for your words. Don't show more than about 20 in an hour-long talk, or the audience will get saturated.
✧ Allow the truth of your experience to shine through and don't flip through them too fast and stop talking for some seconds.
✧ Make sure your talk is appropriate for your audience. If you are speaking about botany in the Himalaya and you once had an amazing experience with a plant there, focus on the botanical descriptions to your audience of gardeners.
✧ Drop your magical experience in very casually as part of your talk. Anyone who is on your wavelength can grab you at the end. In my experience of giving talks, at least one person in every audience usually understands a deeper meaning, and will be keen to speak to you privately. Meanwhile the rest of the audience will have had a nice talk, with no pressure to comprehend a belief system they have never experienced. Signs are as effective in teaching, as they are in so many other contexts.
✧ Do thank the organiser at the end and make sure you leave plenty of time for questions.

SHARING IN AN INFORMAL CONTEXT

Talking about those places restores colour to the night
Laurie Gough

Most of your sharing will occur in an informal context. Sometimes it's best to downplay your experience, at other times to give people what they want. Downplaying your experiences means that a bigger barrier won't be erected between you and your loved ones. They probably won't understand what you've been through, which could leave them feeling inadequate – so then they might try to put you down in return. Giving people what they want is a good way for you to practise an important lesson, the lesson of humility.

Downplaying

> ### *Steve and Jane*
> *Blood has fingers and it opens tunnels under the earth*
> *Pablo Neruda*
>
> In New Zealand, I met a couple from Yorkshire, Steve and Jane, who had unbelievable adventures wherever they went. They got chased by a gunman for hours in the mountains in Colorado, attacked by birds while on a boat in New Zealand and almost drowned in Fiji. But they just said what was expected of them, they had a great time.

Indeed they did have a great time – they just had a little more than that and decided to keep quiet. Their friends and family still wanted to know them.

Give people what they want

I asked one American billionaire the secret of his success. He told me that there were two secrets: one was to follow his intuition (well, we know about that one), and the other was to give people what they want.

Let's see how that works:

✧ Tell your mother who loves knitting about the types of jumpers women knit in Nepal. Show her some pictures of the designs and explain how they each have an intrinsic meaning.
✧ If your brother is really into cars, describe some of the rides you've had, and amazing vehicles you've seen. Give him a few ideas.

You may think you have not had a direct effect, but believe me you have. For you have talked to people on a level they feel comfortable with, and, that, together with your profound vibratory change, will spark immense changes in them. They will not feel threatened, and you will not be preaching. A win-win situation.

Another way of valuing yourself is to do what's right for you. In the last chapter we looked at how you may feel the need to relocate or downshift, the physical move representing your spiritual shift. In the following section we'll see how experiences such as writing about your trip, further study and all kinds of courses from scuba-diving to drum-making can be the loci of that shift. Your magical experiences represent a part of your soul, one you are reclaiming to help you grow, to help you know.

WRITING ABOUT YOUR EXPERIENCE

> *To you has been given the magic to write the stories which will arch across time to touch the souls of kits unborn*
> **Richard Bach**

Even if you've never written before you may get the urge to write about your experiences. As ever, follow the call and allow your writing to flow from your soul.

There are some excellent writing courses led by professional writers, who will help you with your writing, as well as giving you some contacts. Lucy Edge, author of *Yoga School Drop-out*, a book about her search for enlightenment in India, found a travel writing course at the Arvon Foundation in the UK propelled her into writing and publication – and a new life.

What do you write about? Well, it might, of course, be the country you went to and your experiences there. You may decide to research it more deeply. Or your writing may come out in poetry, in a visionary novel or even in a form that doesn't exist yet. If it feels right to you to write, then write. It will take you to a higher place in the plane of silver. The product of your Higher Self will inspire others, as so many stories in this book have inspired me.

Today's traveller is very lucky, for there are so many ways to publish your experiences, from paper to the web. There are some very well-respected websites for travel writers (see Resources). I am recommending this way rather than blogging, because you will need to craft a story about one or more of your experiences on the road. The perspective you need to develop is good for you and good for your art. The best writing is subtle, resonating through the ages, with the ability to be interpreted in many different ways. Very few blogs are of that quality. Sometimes it's good to be forced to work a bit harder to bring out a golden piece of your soul. So your soul will be polished.

You may be so fascinated by what you find that you want to study other cultures and belief systems in a more formal way.

ANTHROPOLOGY

Everything objective conspires to make us think of the bird world as a metaphorical human society: is it not after all literally parallel to it on another level?
Claude Lévi-Strauss

Anthropology, the study of mankind and the knowledge of the world around us, is the subject of choice here. You can do an evening course or a university one. You will get a fascinating reading list, and have so many interesting topics of conversation, dinner parties will never be the same again. You will gain an effective context for your experiences, for you can compare them with what others have said in, and about, other cultures, everywhere. I feel enormously privileged to have been able to study it. New worlds open up, whether they are of myth in New Guinea, poetry in the Arctic or kinship laws in Africa.

Anthropology is based on mental constructs, although there are branches of it such as Affective Anthropology which study the emotions and Reflexive Anthropology that considers your own role in interpreting other cultures. However, as yet in Anthropology – I hope the situation will change soon – there is no place for validating your spiritual experiences. If you would like them to be honoured in the context of other cultures, then you may want to consider shamanism.

Shamanism

....

> *'Eli eli kulana o 'Aina'ike*
> *(Profound is the knowledge of the sighting of the new land)*
> **Hawaiian proverb**

There are now a number of shamanic courses available and I have recommended a few in the Resources. Many of them are intensive. Others cover the same information in a period of weeks or months, and still others last for a year or more. In these courses you study the ancient wisdom of the culture concerned. In a good course, you will also learn 'techniques of ecstasy', which at least in Huna ancient Hawaiian wisdom covers subjects like 'rising in love' and integrating your subconscious and conscious minds. You are likely to have some very special experiences of your 'new land', for as we have seen in Part 2, Chapter 16, 'Opening to the mystical', they can be induced.

The danger here is in going too far the other way into an unboundaried experience, so for that reason I would highly recommend those run by teachers with an academic background in the subject they are teaching, as it does show a certain rigour. As in any course I would only learn from people who offer written feedback sheets, so students can fill them in without pressure and say what they really think. Please don't learn from those who use drugs or psychotropic plants, or advocate their use in their courses, even though they may be indigenous. The world is different now and you do not need them to have a spiritual experience as we have seen throughout this book. Indeed it will be much harder for you to reach a state of integration and function effectively in the world.

One last warning. Be careful of shamanic teachers – usually male – who feed off the women in the group's sexual energy. They will be easy to spot as they use inappropriate sexual remarks and touching, maybe under the guise of 'letting down your boundaries'. Remember you decide your physical boundaries, no one else.

Make your decisions from your Higher Self and you will always be fine.

OTHER COURSES

....

> *As Above,*
> *So Below*
> **Ancient proverb**

Other courses you might want to do include activities you might have enjoyed on your trip, or ones you would like to learn more about in the future.

How about kayaking, sailing or scuba-diving? You can learn at home or learn abroad. Do whatever feels right to you. Learning abroad is often likely to be cheaper, and if you book with the course organiser directly and don't go on a tour, then it will be cheaper still. All the courses mentioned in the Resources include the contact details of the organiser, rather than an agent, for this reason. Or how about going powder skiing in Canada or learning to make a drum in Hawaii or jewellery in Mexico? The world is your oyster.

You may decide you prefer an evening course in maybe a language or an interest of yours in the local area; no problem, most areas offer plenty of courses, and ones run by local authorities are particularly good value.

You may decide to go to university for the first time, or return there, and commit to a long course to help you grow. You might even want to learn about an area you never felt comfortable with such as maths, languages or computing – learning about the unfamiliar is good for your soul. You might even be inspired to learn about techniques for survival in the wilderness – courses in self-sufficiency abound. I remind you of the quote at the beginning of your magical trip, 'Whatever you do or choose to do, begin it. Begin it now.'

For, if your intuition leads you to do a course, following it will lead to you valuing the person who must be important to you – you. Because, if you don't love yourself, how then can you truly love anyone else? You gave yourself the gift of a magical trip. Now give yourself another gift. Appreciation.

VALUING YOURSELF

....

The most important things are the things you don't see
Ben Okri

Don't give yourself a hard time for not having more or different magical experiences, or even if you are not sure you've had any at all. Don't worry. Enlightenment comes to us all at a different pace. Trust that you had exactly the experiences you were meant to have. Meanwhile you need to value yourself sufficiently to acknowledge the magi, magician, in you. You know anything is possible. After all you have been in some really tough scrapes, and you got yourself out of them, didn't you? You know that others love you, but you are also aware that they have a certain investment in you staying as you are. If you really want to shine, you need to have the courage to go beyond that boundary. It is the people who love us the most who can hold us back the most, and although you love them too, your greatest responsibility is to yourself. You realise that everyone's interests can best be served by you going after your highest good.

By placing your intuition at the centre of your life, you are recognising your experiences have a purpose. Even if you are not acknowledged by the people around you, you need to acknowledge yourself. Keeping in touch with your intuition will help this happen, as you will be filled with a 'buzzy' feeling and have a sense of connection and purpose, as if you're in love. You are truly rich, in the sense of having a wealth of experience. And you recognise the most important thing of all: in the end, all we have is love. And the most important love is the love you feel towards yourself. If you ever feel you're in danger of losing it, there's one certain way of getting it back: that's to have another wee trip into the magic.

CHAPTER 4

Riding off into the sunset again

My soul, there is a country, far beyond the stars
Henry Vaughan

There are as many options in the world as there are opinions. But you still can't get that great place and those great people out of your head. What do you do?

Riding off into the sunset might be really tempting when you get back. But check it out first. Make sure your urge really is from your Higher Self, for you'll be saving yourself a lot of time and money if it isn't. Getting in touch with your Higher Self through your intuition is not a one-step process, it needs to be done again and again as we've seen throughout this book, but the more we do it the easier it becomes. So we'll look at when to go. Then we'll look at how to ride off into the sunset. One way is to travel magically again. Another is to do something more structured, such as volunteering or a charity challenge. Yet another is to move to a new country. What's best for you?

WHEN DO YOU GO?

I will love the light for it shows me the way
Og Mandino

Only travel when your Higher Self tells you to. As ever, first of all we need to confirm the desire isn't from one of our other minds. Don't forget to check it with the Hand exercise (see Part 1, Chapter 2).

Meanwhile we'll look at some examples of travelling again from each of our minds, our subconscious mind, conscious mind and Higher Self.

Your subconscious mind

So think as if your every thought were to be etched in fire upon the sky for all and everything to see, for so in truth, it is
Book of Mordred

Be careful your desire doesn't occur from your subconscious mind, the home of many lurking terrors.

Your ego lives here. Your wants live here. That is not a place you want to create from. If you feel superior to your country and your society when you return and think something like, 'It's all so small and I'm so big now', then ego-spot. Your familiar people don't really understand what's happened to you and they never will. In fact they don't deserve the new you. Another warning sign, and we talked about how to discuss your experiences in the previous chapter. You are not being particularly spontaneous if you decide, over your dinner of spaghetti on your first day back, that you're taking off again – you're just being scared. For the subconscious is also the place of our fear.

It may be the right thing for you to travel again, but give yourself time to come to the correct decision. Sometimes a place will call us and call us. But the call is from our subconscious, our mind of desire, not our Higher Self. Don't mistake it. And don't make John's mistake of thinking it's not important. It is and will affect every area of your life.

John dances with dolphins, but . . .

My own yearning for the Highlands was in those days as tormenting as an unconsummated love affair
Gavin Maxwell

John grew up in Croatia and Australia, then moved to Britain. He sees Britain as a place away from his childhood, one where he chose to be as an adult. He feels at home there and chooses to get involved in spiritual practices. Whenever he returns to his homeland, Croatia, he returns to the patterns of his family. Sadly his family patterns include battles, such as court cases. But every year now, for the past seven years, John has chosen to spend the summer in Croatia making money doing property development. But as beautiful as his houses by the sea are, and however much the dolphins dance for him, he simply doesn't feel the sense of spiritual connection he does in Britain.

A very talented guy, John is aware of what he is missing but hasn't been able to create it yet; I don't think he will until he resists the familiar call of his homeland and his family. I want to state this is nothing to do with Croatia, for many it is the country of their dreams, it is merely to do with John's *reaction* to Croatia. The spiritual push he needs to overcome the strength of his family patterns is found in Britain, not Croatia; every time he returns to Croatia, he reactivates his old patterns.

Sometimes a country is wrong for your present level of vibration, even if it was right in the past. It will call you and call you, but it will not be for your highest good. The challenge lies in resisting the lure. Let's continue the journey through our minds.

Your conscious mind

> No pessimist ever discovered the secrets of the stars, or sailed to an uncharted land, or opened a new heaven to the human spirit
> **Helen Keller**

Your conscious mind is a wonderful configuration of your thoughts and expectations. We've looked at the importance of our thoughts in a number of chapters, particularly Part 2, Chapter 19, 'Going within', now it's time to view our expectations. Our expectations are unhelpful, for they are about what we *expect*, rather than what is, and they propel us away from being right here, right now.

It's very likely we held expectations about our return to our country. Let's say throughout your trip you held a candle for a particular girl or guy. But you get home and they don't even call you or respond to your message. You are devastated and want to run away again. Hold your horses. Remember you are a different person now, this person may not be in your best interests. Also remember the first power, the power of asking for help. Ask. Then detach your energy and carry on in your life and see what happens. If he or she wants you they'll be attracted to the new you, if they don't they won't. Whatever happens, you don't need to do anything, except stick around for a while. After all, every night there will be another sunset, unless you go all the way down to the South Pole of course, when there is only one a year.

How about if you do decide to go away again? Surely your expectations aren't so disruptive then? Well, yes they are actually. You need to let go of them to find the place you need to be. For the place your Higher Self wants for you will not always be the place you think it will be. In fact it might even be the place you think it won't be.

Bryan and Riechelle find their right country

We need to learn to set our course by the stars, not by the lights of every passing ship
Anonymous proverb

Bryan and Riechelle left their native America as they were uncomfortable with the values there. Devoted Christians, they lived for four years in Belize, but nothing quite worked out. They got burgled and mugged several times and felt people didn't respect what they were trying to do for God. Bryan always said the one place he didn't want to go was Guatemala, he'd heard so many bad things about it. Guess where Bryan and his wife are living now? You guessed it. Guatemala. They love it. They raised money to buy land and built a beautiful home in the Rio Dulce area, adopted three local children and set up programmes to bring medical care to remote areas of the jungle. They have many more plans to help others. Everything flows. When I stayed with them in their lovely home they told me they'll die in Guatemala – it's their home now.

Bryan and Riechelle don't need to ask the eternal question, 'where now?' By following their Higher Self, they found their right place. If you choose you can follow your Higher Self more directly, and avoid some trials of the silver path. Why not choose to do so?

Your Higher Self

> *My purpose holds*
> *To sail beyond the sunset and the baths*
> *Of all the western stars, until I die*
> **Alfred Tennyson**

If you do decide you want to travel again and it's for all the right reasons, then go for it. You are seeking the lands beyond the sunset. Where do you go then? Do you return to the same place or go to a different one?

Go to a new country when you want a big change. Going to a new country shakes up your old preconceptions and beliefs and allows the unexpected in. That keeps you open to the wonderful, uncontrollable stream-of-consciousness we call life. For life is after all, all potential manifest, one particular course has been chosen out of an infinite number of possible streams. When you choose the highest then the rewards are infinite.

Elizabeth finds the best thing of all – inner peace

> *In every woman there is a Queen. Speak to the Queen and the Queen will answer*
> **Norwegian proverb**

Elizabeth Gilbert had had a tough few years. Then, at 30, she realised she didn't want her life anymore. Her condo in Manhattan and house in the country left her cold and she walked around with a deep well of meaninglessness inside her. Nor was she willing to have a baby to fill herself up, for it didn't feel right. Elizabeth's divorce was very difficult. She was left with only three constants. Her job as a writer, her love of travel and her ability to make friends.

Elizabeth decided to go away for a year – to Italy for four months to rediscover pleasure, to India for the next four to contact her spirituality and to Bali, for the final four, to seek balance. She found it all. She discovered the 'best pizza in the world' in Naples, and experienced transcendental bliss in an ashram in India. In Bali she studied with a traditional healer and developed equilibrium amidst the exuberant external foliage. Elizabeth recorded her experiences in a diary which became the basis of her mega-bestseller *Eat, Pray, Love* (hey, I'm not just advising you to keep a diary for no reason).

When travelling we can follow any of a rich mosaic of roads of all colours and sizes. But the only one of core value is the silver road to your magic. For by travelling it you will reach both your heart and your Higher Self. Elizabeth's unwavering emotional courage and willingness to take risks led her deep inside. Her diary enabled her to view both her journeys, inner and outer, and discern the patterns. Elizabeth said she was 'not rescued by a prince', but was the administrator of her own rescue. That is the power of her heart. Her inner bravery led to outer rewards that must have been beyond her wildest dreams. An appearance on Oprah, a book selling millions. Not only that but more and more American CEO are now leaning towards allowing their employees to take sabbaticals; after all, their employee could be holding the next *Eat, Pray, Love* inside them. Oh yes, and she got married again and most importantly of all, she knows how to go inside and find the pocket of peace which is always there, the pearl beyond price. That is the power of Elizabeth's Higher Self. What is the power of yours?

So we've seen the power of creating through our subconscious mind, our conscious mind and our Higher Self. Of course decisions taken from our Higher Self are so much more powerful at every level. Do ensure every decision is taken from there, whether it is to go or to stay.

The last dilemma we need to view is a common one. You KNOW you should be in another country, but your commitments keep you in the one you're in. What do you do?

FEELING STUCK

....

> *I am the master of my fate*
> *I am the captain of my soul*
> **W.E. Henley**

How about if you know you do want to get away from your Higher Self, but you're stuck elsewhere? There are two things you can do. Change your world or change yourself. Let's start with changing your world.

Your kids are in school and you can't take them out, your ex-wife won't let you take them away, you're taking care of an elderly parent or have another reason to be in a place. You were really happy when you were travelling magically, particularly when you remember a certain country, where your memories seem to shine, but you just don't feel that way now you're back. What do you do? Situations change. To call in desired change, invoke the three powers in the invocation of silver.

Invocation of silver

- ✧ Sit quietly. Surround yourself in shining silver light.
- ✧ Invoke the power of asking for help.
- ✧ Allow your plea to hang in the air in front of you for a while.
- ✧ Surround it by a circle of silver stretching up to the sky. That is the power of belief.
- ✧ Surround *that* by a silvery cloud infusing everything. That is the power of faith.
- ✧ Let your prayer float away now.
- ✧ Trust that the best outcome will be set in motion.

Your prayer will be heard. And if it's in your best interests, your blocks will be removed so you can go away again. Now carry on with your life.

Your second option is to change yourself. Remember that your vibration is the most important thing. For in a sense, your desired country exists only in relationship to you. You create your country. Therefore you can create your bright country wherever you are. You don't have to go back to the place where you were happy, you can choose to be happy now. For wherever you go, you bring your Higher Self with you.

I discover my Higher Self doesn't belong to a country

Only when the sun and moon are one
And all our beams turn into streams
Then the long path will be done
Rima Morrell

New Zealand gave me an enormous amount of exactly what I needed, when I needed it. Wanaka's fabulous lake, inspiring mountains, golden sunsets and crystalline air will live inside me forever as the place where I learned to relax, let go and let the magic in. I remember the sunlight pouring into my living room, and looking out of the large windows on to the shining strip of lake and the steep mountains sprinkled with sugary snow. The bedroom had the same view, and I could also see the steep slopes of brown mountains closer by as I washed up in the kitchen. I associate the overwhelming sense of beauty and harmony I felt there with the place. And I still love a crackling fire and the Kiwi accent, and support the All Blacks rugby team.

A few years later I had a crisis in which one of my closest friends was killed and I was no longer sure of the direction my life was taking. I went back to Wanaka, but as the popular ski season was approaching, I was told that I wouldn't get a place that would fit my needs. But lo and behold I did. The very same cottage became free, so I was back and installed there. But why did I not have those same feelings? Now, the town seemed small and provincial, and the gossip petty. The beauty of course was as overwhelming as ever, and my view exactly the same, but I did not appreciate it the way I once did. What had changed? I had. Although I loved walking across the alpine meadows starry with flowers to the swimming pool in the mountains, I actually missed dirty streets. In other words I was ready to return to the stimulus of London, and I learned to find London a kind and interesting city.

What was going on? A place gives us a particular quality we need. When we have learned the lesson we are free to leave. In New Zealand I learned about the life of the spirit. When I learned to express the spirit in my life I was free to be anywhere I wanted. I realised the power was in me, not the place. Exactly the same happened when I lived on another beautiful island – Hawaii (my soul has definitely done well in this life, living in places of overwhelming physical beauty). I had to be there because the call from my Higher Self was very strong. I wrote about my experiences in my first book, and did the research for my Ph.D there. Having done that, I could leave. For the point of the experiences wasn't to stay in the place, it was to integrate, and then share them.

How then do you decide whether to return to the country of your dreams? Your intuition is the key. Look at why you want to return. Is your decision taken from your Higher Self, or another part of your mind? Can you create a new country for yourself in a place where you have been happy? Or are you better off letting bygones be bygones? If you create battles when you're there, then it's still resonating with your subconscious. But if you simply get a bit bored, and don't feel much energy, then you simply don't need to be there anymore. Always remember you are bigger than your country. So you need never feel stuck.

Now we've seen whether to take off, it's time to look at how to go. We've already seen many examples of travelling magically. It might feel right for you to take off that way again, or you might want to explore another alternative such as home exchange. You might have become so sure of what you want that doing something more structured actually feels more freeing. Take note of how you feel when you read those words. Does your heart leap or does it sink? If it leaps, let's explore two increasingly popular ways of having a structured journey, voluntary work or charity challenges; we have already seen tips on jobs in Part 2, Chapter 21, 'Getting work'.

Voluntary work

....

> *One way to learn compassion is to cultivate the wish to help*
> *others. This simple gesture automatically opens the heart*
> **Tarthang Tulku**

Voluntary work has become increasingly popular. There are so many
things you can do to help. You can teach English in the Arctic, or help
with refugees in sub-Saharan Africa. You can count elephants in Sri
Lanka or plant trees in New Zealand. And you can do many of these
things in your country too, on either a part-time or an intensive basis.
Voluntary working on an intensive basis usually requires moving to the
centre, which usually has accommodation, although it may not be of
the standard you are used to. Many organisations and charities are very
short of workers and also don't have a regular income (the organisers
may have to work elsewhere for example to bring one in), so your effort
is very valuable. It may also be important to you to do something you
believe in, which will help you grow into your Higher Self.

Many organisations have sprung up to cater for people's desire to do
voluntary work. They often charge thousands for the privilege. Don't
use these agents, but contact the charity or organisation directly. There
are several advantages for you. The first is that you will not be sent
somewhere, but will choose somewhere, so you are far more likely
to find a place aligned to your vibe. On the higher levels of creation
– which you are now on – that is vitally important. The second is that
any money they charge will go directly to that organisation, so they
can utilise it more effectively. It is entirely fair for schemes to charge
a reasonable amount for the provision of accommodation and facilities, and to cover their costs, but you shouldn't be paying any more
than that unless there is a significant amount of training involved. You
certainly don't need to pay for an agent's nice office in the developed
world. So the third advantage is, it's far cheaper. If you want to give
your money away, why not give it to the charity? Utilise your efforts as
effectively as you can.

Maryam's story

Stay the course, light a star
Change the world where'er you are
Richard Le Gallienne

When Maryam returned to London after a holiday in the Caribbean she felt she was in the wrong place. She was financially secure, her daughters were settled, her divorce had gone through some years ago but she was restless. She decided to return to the Caribbean which she had really enjoyed and ended up doing some voluntary work teaching in a school on her favourite island. They were delighted to have her, and she was glad to be there. Maryam felt a sense of light-ness rather than heaviness when she woke up in the morning.

Maryam rode away into the sunset. How about you? Perhaps you're not that keen to do regular work any more and would like a bit of a challenge? Well, there's a new category, the 'charity challenge', which may be perfect for you.

CHARITY CHALLENGE

We are a way for the cosmos to know itself
Carl Sagan

Charity challenges are great, for they raise money for your favourite charity, as well as publicising a cause, and ensure that you undergo a personal challenge. When you relate your challenge to a cause and bind them with the power of your spirit, for example by visiting a place that's sacred to you in the appropriate way, then the breakthrough is enormous. Tess illustrated that.

Tess climbs her inner mountain

Only when you reached the top of the mountain could you see and understand all that the other person saw and believed
Pali Jae Lee

Tess Burrows had always dreamed of mountaineering, but didn't start doing it until she was well into her fourth decade. She was also passionate about the Tibetan cause, and found a way of bringing them together in designing a challenge so a group of people could climb the highest mountain in the world. (Everest is the highest when measured from sea level, Chimborazo in Ecuador when measured from the centre of the earth, as the earth is an obloid spheroid not a round globe.)

The group prepared very carefully, adding messages of peace to the sponsorship form and gathering offerings to be left on top of the mountain, including a crystal shaped like a six pointed star and messages of peace to be read out. The group of four were all necessary for the success of the expedition. Tess, her boyfriend Pete, G.T. and a young Tibetan, Migmar, started off climbing the mountain together.

Tess and Mig made it to the summit, together with their guide Pepe, 'a strong, gentle, angel-like presence, a guide in the true sense of the word'. Pete and G.T. were very experienced mountaineers, Mig had never climbed before and Tess was nearing fifty. Yet both Tess and Mig resounded with a passionate belief which kept them going when their bodies were giving up. At the white summit, after they had been brought to their knees in humility again and again, given everything they had and then more, they buried the crystal in the powdery snow and left the prayer flags flying. 'If you had been watching our planet from space that day, you would have seen the colours flying from a bright star at her furthest point . . . The blues, whites, reds, greens and yellows, blowing, again and again . . . Messages from the mountain . . . spinning into a whiteness and purity ablaze with light.'

Tess gained meaning and motivation and said she learned to 'climb her highest mountain within – myself'. Migmar Tsering was later honoured by the Dalai Lama who said his 'indomitable spirit' and 'undiminished determination' represent the best of Tibet. Money was raised for two causes, and they stamped the earthly vibration of peace at the white place where the earth and the sky meet. British actress Joanna Lumley said, 'Now the peaceful crystal shines from Chimborazo.' Such is the dazzlement created by moving into your Higher Self.

The last choice for creating a big change in your life is a more final one – emigration.

EMIGRATION

Second star to the right, and straight on 'til morning
Anonymous

Emigration is making the choice to settle in another country – maybe one you went to on your trip – permanently. More and more people are now choosing to change the country and society of their birth. For not only do we now live in a more mobile and flexible world, we are aware that we do. Of course we've always had the options, but we now *know* we've got options.

There are many tried and tested trails for emigration – such as the one taken by the hundreds of thousands of Australians and New Zealanders who come to Britain and the Brits who go the other way. Yet however many have gone before, emigration always takes personal courage. For it is not easy settling into a new job, a new society, a new banking system and leaving your friends and family behind. Sometimes though it is easier than staying where you are. For every day a little bit more of you dies inside. You are simply in your wrong place and have even lost the motivation to do the invocation of silver we saw earlier in the chapter. How then do you set off?

> If you too want a big change then make something happen. If you want things to happen even faster, then face your fear. If you hate the cold, go to a cold place and learn to like it. If you can't bear insects, go to a humid jungle. By doing what you dislike you will learn to integrate it. That will be of great benefit to your life.

Go away when you need change in your life. If you want a big change then *be* the big change. The bigger your step the further you will go and the more you will learn. Look at Dorian and Bridget.

Dorian and Bridget make their mark on the North

The First Nations people of the Yukon believe that our lives are a story. At the end, what will your story be?
Bridget Amos

Dorian and Bridget had a good, easy life in Polperro, Cornwall. But Dorian wanted to have a life 'studded with experiences'. He told his wife over a meal of chips who said, 'If you think about something too much, you just talk yourself out of it and never do it. We're only here once. Let's go get some action! Can you pass the salt please?' The next month they'd decided to go to Northern Canada, one of the few untamed wildernesses left in the world, with the freedom to 'live deliberately', as Thoreau said. Dorian ceremoniously burned his suit and tie, and they exchanged their watches for large sheath knives.

But Dorian and Bridget didn't know very much about the wilderness. They'd intended to spend their first night camping, but felt scared, so they slept in the Vancouver ferry terminal instead. The first time they went canoeing they didn't know which end was the front. Dorian made a waterproof tent which didn't work and their first weeks of camping on Victoria Island were miserable. 'We were tired, irritable and introverted. Our learning curve over the last two weeks had been vertical and we just weren't enjoying ourselves. Everything was a struggle from getting a drink of water to feeding the dog.' Then, one night in British Columbia, they finally slept well under canvas and woke to songbirds and clear skies and splashed about in a nearby river. 'We were really free, for a moment, a minute, a memory. And even this smallest taste of freedom was worth losing floodlit ferry terminals to feel.'

After that Dorian and Bridget began learning about a new world, a slow, silent and magical world, step by step like a toddler. They developed camping routines and finally felt comfortable with leaving time behind. After some weeks by a lake they met an old-timer in the Yukon who thought very hard when they asked him what day it was, crossed his eyes and stuck his tongue out and finally said, 'Monday was some-time last week.' They became aware of the importance of being, not doing, their joy brought on by the simple things in life, warming their limbs in front of a fire, the coming of dawn, the call of a raven.

They found their right place more easily than they expected, after canoeing 500 miles down the mighty Yukon river, Bridget in her little black cocktail dress. They survived (just) and moored in the shallows below Dawson City, just before midnight when the sun was shining high. They loved Dawson, home of the Sour Toe cocktail (it includes a real big toe with blackened toe nail dipped in your drink), where gold is still legal tender from the gold-rush days and the mountains and forests push up against the town. They ended up buying some land and built a cabin among the spruce trees, without running water, electricity, mirrors, clocks, lock or telephone. They spend night after night reading to each other over candlelight, and the only letters they receive are from friends and family, not bills. For many months a year they live in a forest gripped by winter and stillness, where the snow muffles every sound. 'The stars are so big you can almost touch them and they really do shine. The moon and the constellations cast a bright silver light across the wilderness and throw dark blue, contorted shadows onto the sparkling snow.' Bridget had a baby, and breastfed him in the cabin, and they would take him camping, the only heat a stove in the wall tent. Then, when they got a neighbour, they staked out land further down the Yukon river to build another cabin, as well as laying claim to a goldmine.

Dorian and Bridget left their country and found a life of adventure, one they created themselves. If travelling magically ultimately is a process of learning spiritual lessons, then so is emigrating. Dorian said extra time with his family, and the challenge of coping with new situations together, made him be with them in spirit as well as body. 'I want my son to know and love me for who I am, not what I do. I want my wife and my life intertwined and inseparable.' Bridget said, 'Happily gone is the neurosis of caring what others think and how they perceive me, all the boring body image issues. Bye bye. What a waste of time. I know for certain that on the day those issues won't be important, so instead I appreciate life. I am sitting here breathing in and out, and for that I am truly grateful. Today is a gift and if this is all I have gained from living up here it is enough, because it has freed me from fear.' She went on to sum it up, 'I have arrived here, exactly where I need to be, to learn what I want to learn and to be content. I haven't been able to escape me, but instead I am now someone I don't want to escape from.'

A FEW MORE THOUGHTS

> *Glanzen wie dem Besten*
> *Der Mond und die Sterne*
> *(As to the best*
> *The moon and the stars lend light)*
> **Johann Wolfgang von Goethe**

Emigrate only if it will help you move into your Higher Self, the best of you. But remember you can't leave the rest of you behind, you must learn to integrate it. For in the end, however far you go you bring yourself with you. You are being unrealistic in expecting all your problems to be solved by moving. But you do feel there are more opportunities for opening and expansion in a particular country, you like the people and the type of nature, you know the language or you are prepared to learn it. If you want children or have them already, you've already thought about things like the language your children will learn to speak, and the culture they will grow up in, and are happy with your decision. Be aware as well, that having parents not from that country will affect your kids, sometimes in a good way – independence of thought, sometimes more negatively, for example, it might be harder for them to fit in. Taking everything into account, you feel you would be happier if you left.

Use your intuition to find the area you wish to settle in, but do take practicalities on board too. Factors such as public transport, the type of local community and so on deserve to be considered. I do not recommend buying a home before you go, as it's best to find it where you are, and do check the local laws and network with other expatriates – in the Valencia region of Spain local developers can legally expropriate or compulsorily purchase part of the property you have bought, for example. Be aware and do your research before you buy. If you like a country but you are not sure whether you want to move there in the future, then please don't buy a home there. 'Second homes' disrupt the local economy, and buying one abroad will mean your energy will become 'stuck' to one particular area of one country, and will affect the way you change and grow. Prioritise your growth.

SAILING AWAY

If you sail for Kahiki you will discover new constellations and strange stars over the deep ocean
Percy Smith

This chapter is the last one on change. In it, we've seen several ways of changing your life. You know that you're ready for something when the horizon is luring you and your blood is sparkling. You can certainly do this literally if you so choose, for example by crewing on someone else's yacht. But you do need to ensure your decision to sail into the glowing pink sunset is made from the right place.

We've seen ways of deciding whether your decision is made from the Higher Self or one of your other minds, and an example of each. We've seen the magic that happens when you are inspired to journey by your Higher Self and how it radiates out to every part of your life. We've seen a couple of more structured ways of travelling – volunteering and doing a charity challenge, and how helping others can help you. We've also looked at a more permanent way – emigrating, and at the advantages it can bring to help you learn your spiritual lessons more aptly. We've also seen what happens when you return to a place and it's not from your Higher Self. Sometimes our experiences were very specific to a time in our lives, a time where the quality of the place brought out certain things we needed then. Maybe we could have kept its image unsullied and shining in our minds, by not returning.

Do decide according to your Higher Self. Choose countries which embody the qualities you want to develop. Of course you might not know what they are – in which case, don't worry, the universe will bring them to you when you decide according to your greater guidance. Your intuition will always guide you straight and true. For in the end, as Bridget Amos so aptly said, 'What matters at the end of your life, is your story.' Choose to write it whatever way feels best to you. But do choose. And do write it.

Now it's time to move on to the next chapter on other ways of integrating your change.

CHAPTER 5

Integrating your change

Utopias are often only premature truths
Lamartine

Integrating your change is your most vital task, for the rest of your life. It means not only walking your talk, but talking your walk. It means being as well as doing. Feeling as well as thinking. Letting go as well as initiating. All the stuff you have been doing on your trip you need to carry on doing. What fun.

In this chapter we will see how you can bring your new world with you. In the next sections we shall look at how to live with integrity and intuition. Integrity and intuition are the paths to accessing that rainbow country of many colours, your Higher Self. Your Higher Self is embodied in your soul purpose.

BRINGING YOUR NEW WORLD WITH YOU

Fly like a bird . . . and bring the earth with you
A New Zealander

Travelling magically you have found a world of magic and meaning. A world of spirit and sensing. A world of rhythm and revelation – your world. It is not an artificial world, reached by the false gods of the senses such as drugs, alcohol, sex and food, or a shallow world which needs to be continually recreated. It is a deep world. A true world.

You created it. Your challenge is now to utilise your wonderful feelings in the reality of your day-to-day life. You can easily access them again through the few simple techniques I've shown you in this book such as raising your vibration in Part 2, Chapter 16, 'Opening to the mystical'. By walking your talk back at home you will truly fly like a bird and bring the earth with you.

LIVING WITH INTEGRITY

> *The true man sings*
> *Gladly in the bright day*
> **Celtic song**

One Hawaiian definition of integrity, *kupono,* is a wonderful one: unity of thought, word, feeling and action. Your subconscious is standing upright and you are in tune with the magic of your Higher Self. Wrap every action with meaning. For example, when you buy a plant for your loved one, make sure that:

✧ Your thoughts are kind
✧ Your words are loving
✧ Your feelings are loving.

Keep up this unity of thought, words, feelings and actions for a day or more. How quickly your world will change to reflect you. Walk your talk and you will walk in rainbows.

> **Do this in every area of your life. What matters is your kindness. What matters is that you have the courage to know. What matters is that you have the courage to grow. What matters is that you have the courage to love.**

There are people living in integrity all over the world. It might be the dustman down your street, or the mountain guide who refuses to accept money for the extra help he gave. It might be the teacher doing her very best for her kids and family back home. Some people are better known: Nelson Mandela who led a country to freedom, the Dalai Lama who keeps the flame burning for his country, Tibet, in exile and his old friend, Dr Janez Drnovsek, who went from the traditional pomp of his office to a life of humility, moving out of the Presidential Palace in Slovenia to a house in the mountains. Dr Drnovsek talked of the importance of finding your inner balance before you help others, saying raising your consciousness is the answer to the problems of the world. In a life where there is such pleasure in simplicity, there is no need to be complicated.

It reminds me of the story of the Mexican fisherman.

The Mexican fisherman

A great inner revolution in just a single individual will help achieve a change in the destiny of a nation and rather, will cause a change in the destiny of humankind
Daisaku Ikeda

Living in a small hut by the sea, the Mexican fisherman caught fish that provided him with enough for his present needs, but with nothing left over. He was quite satisfied until he met an American businessman who suggested he got more boats, employed other fishermen and made a profit from them. He could move to America and start a fishing empire, have a large house, a big car and all the status he ever wanted. Then, when he became really rich, he could retire to a cottage by the sea and lead a simple life.

The fisherman was not attracted by this proposition; he was already leading a life of ease and grace in his cottage by the sea. A simple man, yet one filled with the silence of ages. Through his happiness, unselfishness and sense of community he was able to influence those around him. The world of integrity is a deeply satisfying one. Your integrity creates your home in the world from where you truly stand and sing amid the glory of the bright day.

LIVING WITH INTUITION

....

I arise today
Through the strength of heaven
Celtic invocation

Living with intuition is bliss, you will know you are always protected, so you cannot put a foot wrong. Your world will be much more resonant and you will know that you are always home. So you will truly be residing in the land of magic, one you no longer need a ticket and a passport to access.

You are always guided

A cold sun rises to the rim of the white world, bringing light wind
Peter Matthiesen

When you live with your intuition you are always guided. It may be to go this way or that way. It may be to take a break, or pick up that book and find a meaning. It may be to go to that workshop or on holiday in that place at that time. It may be to write a letter or spend a night in by the fire. There is a sense of purpose about your actions and you are full of bliss.

Your world is much fuller

Suddenly everything feels alive, radiates energy, emanates Being
Eckhart Tolle

You notice the black, shiny-feathered bird that feeds at the edge of the windy lake, and his mate that follows him by the edge of the silvery water and calls to the bird flying above. The lacing of the branches of the tree is portrayed in the silent water. The first bird flies upwards. It is all significant – it all holds meaning. You create the meaning. The more you find, the more alive you will be.

You are always protected

I am held on all sides by countless wings of light
Tess Burrows

Always know that you will be safe. Make sure you walk down the right streets, and remember your guardian is always with you – whether this guardian is your intuition or an angel. Jeanie wanted to go down an alleyway on her visit to London, but had a funny feeling about it, so she took the longer route by the road. She thought nothing more of it, but in the local paper some days later she read that a poor girl was raped in that very alleyway later that night. Intuition? Or Jeanie's angel? It doesn't really matter, what does matter is that she followed that little voice, for her soul did not need to learn a difficult lesson.

You know you are always at home

Owl on a snow-thick limb
Shifting soft feathers
Snow falls on snow
Zen Buddhist saying

Travelling magically undoubtedly helps your challenges to happen faster. That's great, for your challenges are lessons your soul has chosen. You come into contact with the qualities you need, which may be represented by you being drawn to a particular country.

For example, growing up in Britain during the cruise missile era, the liberals around me didn't like America. I took on their colouring. However, when I went there I absolutely loved it, and I still do. I can look at it as a whole, see it and still love it. Maybe America represents to me the qualities I found there, such as openness, freedom and love.

Now your greater speed means you have the chance to rise into a higher vibration, so you can share more of your light. Our true home, the soul, never leaves us once our vibration is raised. Now I've got to the happy state where wherever I go I meet someone I know, or someone who knows people I know. I might be in the wild mountains of Georgia in the Caucasus, or in a back alley in Kathmandu or walking across a bridge in Sydney. I have no need to feel isolated any more. That's not to say I don't, but somewhere I know I will soon meet someone I have a deep level of connection with. Other magical travellers report the same thing. We are all catapulted up into a higher level of reality, where, wherever we go, we are always at home, like a roosting bird.

We need to express our new reality through doing our soul purpose. It doesn't necessarily matter where you are or what it is, but it has to be the right thing for you, and it must help others.

YOUR OUTER JOURNEY LEADS TO YOUR SOUL PURPOSE

....

The knowledge of God shall fill the Earth as the water covers the sea
Isaiah 11:9

Your magical journey is not just memories. Your experiences provide a wealth of valuable resources to change your reality, and to help others change theirs. After your trip you will almost certainly have more of an idea of what you really want to do. You have accessed your Higher Self. The radiant rainbow of our Higher Self is formed when the sun of our conscious mind is leavened by the waters of compassion flowing from our heart. The moon of our subconscious mind is no longer visible in the bright day, for her power is integrated within the Higher Self like the rainbow, which arches over and unites. Indeed this chapter brings the concepts discussed in Part 1, Chapter 1, 'Travelling with intuition', together. Intuition, the Higher Self, the journey of the soul and vibration all effortlessly combine. Living according to our Higher Self means we are living a soft and radiant life – a rainbow life.

Now we'll look at a couple of examples of people who found what they were meant to do by taking the road of silver.

Tony and Maureen Wheeler influence millions to travel

No snowflake falls in an inappropriate place
Zen Buddhist saying

The Lonely Planet empire of guidebooks started with Tony and Maureen Wheeler's overland trip to India, which led to them writing and publishing a budget guide book about it. Millions of people have travelled and become more open to other cultures as a result of following their advice. If you go where you are meant to be, your great journey will influence others.

Karen incorporates a special culture in her life's work
We have no art. We just do everything as well as possible
A Balinese on art

Karen Kingston, like many of us, fell in love with a country. In her case it was the Indonesian island of Bali. Unlike many of us though, she knew what to do with her attraction to the culture. She started a business incorporating the Balinese principles of space-clearing as well as the principles of Feng Shui. She is not only a successful businesswoman and the author of several books, but she has also helped thousands have a clearer and cleaner energy. What a wonderful way of incorporating her love for a culture into her life.

The silver road that lies open before you always leads to a new ledge of light, a higher state of consciousness. That gleaming place is the goal of magical travel and the five principles meet and merge at this high point, suffusing you in a cloud of silver.

By starting off with the first principle, your intuition, you have learned to follow it in everything you do, for you know it guides you straight and true. Then you are open to the second principle, being spontaneous. That way you always do what is right for you now and are not held up by the past. You have learned from the third principle, go local, and are open to new ideas and other ways of doing things, so you can more effectively follow the first and second principles and allow your knowledge to expand. The fourth principle, be open to the mystical, illuminates your rainbow existence. And you know how to weave the fifth principle, integration, into the magic. So you have created a bright, silver-threaded tapestry of light and excitement, your life. Your life unfurls from your high point on the mountain, infusing your world in a waterfall of molten light. So many are coming into contact with the true and shining beauty of your soul.

YOUR SOUL PURPOSE IS ALWAYS TO HELP

....

The love of a single heart can make a world of difference
Immaculée Ilibagiza

With your higher state of awareness you must always help others. There is nothing more important. Your soul purpose will always help. More and more people recognise this now. For example, the young prodigy Akiane Kramarik has a clear connection to her source. She said, 'I want my art to draw people's attention to God, and I want my poetry to keep their attention on God.' The satisfaction that you get from doing your right thing is sustaining. For once you know how to access the inner springs of your soul, you will always be refreshed, rejuvenated and at peace. Your love will truly make all the difference.

CHAPTER 6

At home in the magic

*Mon secret. Il est très simple. On ne voit bien qu'avec le
Coeur. L'essential est invisible pour les yeux
(Here's my secret. It is very simple. One cannot see except with
the heart. What is essential is invisible to the eyes)*
Antoine de Saint-Exupery

Movement may begin with outer travel but is only properly measured by our inner travel. For the silver road of magic we choose through following our intuition always leads to one destination – within. For we know now that home is not necessarily our country, or even another country, and nor is it to be found in another person. Our home is in opening to our Higher Self: that's how we return to the true source of our magic, our soul. And of course we reach the rainbow country of our Higher Self through opening our heart. Our intuition guides us to the countries, circumstances and people we need for our heart to open. A vital and necessary journey.

THE HIGHER SELF IS ALWAYS WITHIN
When I open my heart I find the way, a gap through the wall of mountains. Through me I allow the world to unfold. I have the magic of earth, wind and flame.
The Egyptian Book of the Dead

> When we reach a certain level of vibration, we have found our way through the gap in the wall of mountains. We are there, on that high level. Allow the world to unfold through you, hold within you the magic of earth, wind and flame. Hardly anyone on earth has achieved this state, although many traditions believe we are surrounded by guides and angels who have already got there. The way through the wall of mountains is to open our heart. Then we can bring the wonderful qualities of the sacred with us all the time, wherever we are. The magic is no longer in the place, it is in you.

BEING IN YOUR POWER

Home is where the heart is
English proverb

When you are truly in your power, you will be happy. For you are in touch with your true source, your inner one. It is as though we each have our own enclosed space or walled garden – *paradeiza* in Persian, from where the English word 'paradise' comes. In order for our garden to flourish it must contain water, the water of our emotion. Happiness is a well, something that is always there and can be drawn on as and when you need it. Two streams replenish the well of happiness: the stream of the heart that feels everything, and the stream of the radiant mind, which understands everything. Your inner well of tranquillity remains calm despite the flow of experiences, insights and new understandings. From it rises your inner spring of silver, the expression of your soul purpose in the world.

You know when to speak up and when to be silent. You know when to love and when to let go. You know when to work and when to have fun. Your streams increasingly merge. You have forged your own path, while allowing others to be who they are. You always desire to help and do so when it's appropriate, sometimes you help just by being who you truly are. You are bubbling with creativity that you express in a focused way. You look much younger than you are, without the need for any surgery, as the power of your inner self is enough to renew your cells. When rocks are in the way of your silver streams, you reach in and remove them so that you are transformed – again. You have found what is essential and invisible to the eyes.

Once you have seen with new eyes, and reconnected to your shining sky within, you are motivated to live in new ways, ethical ways, ways in tune with the growth of your spirit. You learn anew that home is where your heart is, and you know to create your homeland, your heartland, wherever you are. For with your new awareness you only ever choose to be in the right place. Your awareness is honed by your courage in shrugging off your shackles and setting off across the bright seas towards the shining skies, following the calls of the birds lured by the rainbow light. At the end of your journey there is only ever you, a truer, brighter, happier, more loving, more magical you.

AT HOME IN THE MAGIC

A man travels the world in search of what he needs and returns home to find it
George Moore

We have come home. Home to the heart of magic. Our true selves. So many people's experience of coming home is a happy one – 'Home again, home again, let us all sing.'

Wherever your home is, I wish you peace, one of the most blessed qualities. Indeed that is how you will recognise your home, by the feeling of peace you associate with it. The shimmering island, poised in the silver sea, is not a place but a state of grace. There, where your outer land meets your inner, is a union of clarity and balance and feeling. For ultimately peace is inside us. To access it we need to do the right thing for our soul's growth. With your elements in alignment, you will no longer need to travel, except to share or to help.

Wherever you are you will be 'at home' with yourself; at home in the magic. You have taken the road of silver that leads to the lodestone of your being, your core of silver and gold. You have let go of the people and concepts you needed to release. Your horizon has expanded so that you are aware of far more of the world. You know how to create the desired land within and you reach out to other hands in love. Your life provides continual lessons for you to learn from every direction, and you quickly and joyfully do so. Your journey will always continue, forging the silver path to your true home, the peace in the heart of the magic.

Resources

INTRODUCTION: WHY TRAVEL THIS WAY?

Disillusionment with Western values

Emile Durkheim, *Suicide*. Free Press, 1997. Famous sociological description of disillusionment in Western society and its causes.

Inspiration

Graham Greene, *Travels With My Aunt*. Vintage Classics, 2006. A retired bank manager leaves his boring life in Highgate, London to travel around the world – and changes rather a lot. An intoxicating read.

Make the Most of your Time on Earth: A Rough Guide to the World. Rough Guide, 2007. Over 1,000 inspiring ideas of things you can do in interesting places to add some exciting memories to your life.

The Travel Book: A Journey through Every Country in the World. Lonely Planet Pictorial, 2005. Coffee table book covers each of the 230 countries in the world – where do you really, really want to go?

PART 1: BEFORE YOU GO

Chapter 1: Travelling with intuition

Your hero's journey

Joseph Dispenza, *The Way of the Traveller: Making Every Trip a Journey of Self-Discovery*. Villard Books, 2003. Gentle book with much advice for your inner and outer journey.

Joseph Campbell, *The Hero with a Thousand Faces*. Fontana, 1993. Lovely book from popular mythologist details the role of the hero in societies around the world – and how it is not out of anyone's reach.

Following your intuition

J.C. Beaglehole, *The Life of Captain James Cook*. Stanford University Press, 1974. Fascinating biography of world's most famous explorer – perhaps only because he had the courage to follow his intuition and 'go where no man had gone before'.

Your Higher Self

Max Freedom Long, *Growing into Light: A Personal Guide to Practising the Huna Method*. DeVorss and Co., 1955. Practical exercises for dealing with problems and growing into your Higher Self according to Huna the ancient wisdom of Hawaii.

Jean Shinoda Bolen, *Crossing to Avalon: A Woman's Mid-life Pilgrimage*. HarperCollins, 1994. Inspiring tale of a professor of psychiatry and Jungian analyst who finds a spiritual awakening through travel.

James, Sean and Tim O'Reilly (eds), *The Road Within. True Stories of Transformation and the Soul*. Travelers Tales, 2002. Compilation of tales about how adventures in the outer world lead to the development of inner wisdom.

Chapter 2: Accessing your intuition

Exercising your intuition

Shakti Gawain, *Developing Intuition: Practical Guidance for Daily Life*. New World Library, 2002. This book, from a manifestation expert, does exactly what it promises.

Sonia Choquette, *Trust Your Vibes Oracle Cards: A Psychic Tool Kit for Awakening your Sixth Sense*. Hay House, 2004. Set of 51 oracle cards with accompanying guide that help you choose what ability to develop next. Particularly useful for beginners.

Cosmic ordering

Ask for what you want: www.baerbelmohr.de Website in German and English offers true stories on the results of following your intuition.

Bärbel Mohr, *Cosmic Ordering: The Next Adventure – Instructions for overcoming doubt and manifesting miracles*. Omega-Verlag, 2005. Better than her more famous first book, true stories of manifestation.

How to travel

Rolf Potts, *Vagabonding: An Uncommon Guide to the Art of Long-Term World*

Travel. Villard Books, 2003. Vagabonding is the American word for travelling without structure, this lovely and simple guide helps you do it.

Chapter 3: When do you go?

General advice

Country information: www.lonelyplanet.com/destinations Brief information on most countries, forums answer your questions.
Weather around the world: www.weatheronline.co.uk Offers 5-day forecasts.

There's a season for everything

Events in various countries: www.whatsonwhen.com
Arts exhibitions and shows: www.artrepublic.com/wow For those interested in the arts.
Gretel Ehrlich, *This Cold Heaven: Seven Seasons in Greenland.* Fourth Estate, 2003. Prize-winning poet muses on the significance of ice, among other topics, in her tale of seven winters in Greenland – her favourite season there.

Festivals

Festivals: www.bugbog.com/festivals Festivals and carnivals organised under different categories including Arts and Heritage.
World Party: The Rough Guide to the World's Best Festivals. Rough Guides Ltd, 2007. www.worldparty.roughguides.com Describes which festivals to go to find what you're looking for.

Chapter 4: Year off, life off or fortnight off?

Very little time off

Rachel Weiss with Julie Adams, *Are We There Yet?: Rach and Jules Take to the Open Road.* Allen & Unwin, 2005. Two Australian women have a lively two-week adventure in their country. Amusing and well written.
The Lonely Planet Guide to Experimental Travel. Lonely Planet, 2005. Director of the Laboratory for Experimental Tourism gives advice on how to enjoy the unexpected while you travel, even if you only have an afternoon to spare.

A year off

UCAS, Student Helpbook Series, *A Year Off . . . A Year On?* Lifetime Careers

Publishing, 2005. For younger people. Guide for British students with good information on the university admissions process.

Resigning from your job: www.i-resign.com Sample letters and suggestions on spoof website.

The Career Break Book (Lonely Planet) Lonely Planet Publications, 2004. Superb guide to the practicalities of taking time off, particularly career-breaking adults.

Never too late

Marco Polo magazine: www.marcopolomagazine.com Dedicated to adventure travellers over 50.

Some special advice for Australian seniors: www.smarttraveller.gov.au

Ruth Barton Davis, *The Hitchhiking Grandmother: The Adventures and Spiritual Journey of a Northwest Woman Who Hitchhiked Across America and Europe after 50.* Pilgrim Way Press, 1992. Grace Small starts hitching around North America and Europe when she is a grandmother, dressed in a proper suit, hat and gloves – and discovers even more faith.

Joan Rattner Heilman, *Unbelievably Good Deals and Great Adventures That You Absolutely Can't Get Until You're Over 50.* McGraw Hill. Latest edition. Largely American focused, but money-off savings include luxury and economy travel all around the world.

A life off

Richard Branson, *The Autobiography.* Virgin Books, 2007. Interesting autobiography of one of Britain's most unusual – and successful – businessmen.

Somerset Maugham, *The Moon and Sixpence.* Dover Books, 2006. A stockbroker deserts his family and goes to Paris and Tahiti to fulfil his dream. Memorable novel based upon the life of painter Paul Gauguin.

Vicki McKenzie, *Cave in the Snow: A Western Woman's Quest for Enlightenment.* Bloomsbury, 1999. Autobiography of a Western woman who became a Buddhist and spent 12 years (between 33 and 45) alone in a cave in the Himalayas. She remains in India and is a champion of the right of women to achieve enlightenment.

Timothy Ferriss, *The 4 Hour Workweek: Escape 9-5, Live Anywhere, and Join the New Rich.* Crown Publishers, 2007. Practical guide written by a young American to doing not so much work – wherever you may be.

Chapter 5: Assessing your risks

Travelling for the differently abled – guides

Candy Harrington, *Barrier-Free Travel: A Nuts and Bolts Guide for Wheelers and Slow Walkers*. 2nd edn. Demos Medical Publishing, 2005. Valuable guide to problems the disabled will encounter and how to overcome them.

Going to America?: www.disaboom.com Useful advice for disabled travellers to America, as well as disabled organisations there.

Disabled travel: www.accessatlast.com British-based site gives advice for Europe and USA.

Access arrangements: www.everybody.co.uk Features accommodation in Britain. A useful guide to access arrangements and disabled facilities on major airlines.

Airport porter service: www.maclellan-skycaps.com Prebook at Heathrow and Gatwick, free for those over 65 or those with special needs, otherwise reasonable cost.

Freeing your mind and spirit

Janine Shepherd, *Never Tell Me Never*. PanMacmillan, 2004. Left a virtual paraplegic after being hit by a truck while she was training for the Olympics, Australian Janine went on to fly, walk and have children.

Nicola Naylor, *Jasmine and Arnica*. Eye Books, 2001. Beautiful account of blind woman from London who goes to India alone to study aromatherapy – and how she grows her 'third eye' or sixth sense and rediscovers her love of life.

Jason Roberts, *A Sense of the World: How a Blind Man Became History's Greatest Traveler*. Eye Books. Story of the extraordinary travels of a nineteenth-century blind naval officer, Robert Holman.

Chapter 6: Finding a culture to suit you

Magazines

Wanderlust: www.wanderlust.co.uk Magazine for passionate travellers, useful website.

Geographical: www.geographical.co.uk Magazine with beautiful pictures and a cultural focus, published by Royal Geographical Society.

Music

Various artists, *Rough Guide to North African Café*. Rough Guides, 2007. One of many CDs of world music by Rough Guides – see which songs stir you.

Tourist office

Tourist office for the country: www.towd.com Tourist board offers useful, albeit official, information.

Shows

The Times travel show: www.destinationsshow.com Held in London in February and Birmingham in March, many stalls and talks.

The *Telegraph* travel show: www.adventureshow.co.uk Held in London in January, many stalls and talks.

Career break show: www.onelifelive.co.uk Held in London every March.

Travel bookshops

Daunt Books: www.dauntbooks.co.uk Marylebone (London) branch arranges books by country.

www.stanfords.co.uk Virtual home of map shop whose incarnations are in Covent Garden, London, as well as Bristol and Manchester. Best to buy maps before you go, as countries may inaccurately represent their features for political or other reasons.

Guidebooks

Different series have different strengths. Here is an overview:

Lonely Planet www.lonelyplanet.com Wonderful series, packed full of useful information for the independent traveller, also tells you to leave it behind sometimes and just take off on your own. Best for Asia, but the only series to cover every country in the world.

Footprint: www.footprintguides.com Best guides for South America. Inspiring and entertaining series good for 'flashpackers', with many ideas for activities.

Rough Guide: www.roughguides.com Good for young people, often a 'party element'. Africa is particularly well covered.

Trailblazer guides: www.trailblazer-guides.com Detailed and accurate guides for the expeditioner. If they cover the region you are going to (such as Central Asia), then they are worth getting.

Blue Guides: www.blueguides.com Good for cities, archaeology and culture.

Bradt Guides: www.bradtguides.com Excellent series of guides to unusual destinations or unusual guides to mainstream ones.

Let's Go: www.letsgo.com Started by Harvard students, good budget guides with special seniors sections.

Time Out: www.timeout.com Detailed city and walking guides; particularly good for those with very little free time.

Other types of books written by 'outsiders'

Examples of travel books are given throughout the book. Here are some series I'd recommend:

Travelers' Tales: www.travelerstales.com Quality series of travel anthologies based in USA on various subjects such as women, families and spirituality.

Summersdale Publishers: www.summersdale.com Publishes broad range of travel literature, usefully divided by both theme and country on website.

Eye Books: www.eye-books.com Inspirational and life-affirming books based on inspiring experience, many concern lessons learned while travelling.

For examples of titles on Anthropology please see the 'Anthropology' section in Part 3, Chapter 3, 'Valuing your trip'.

Books written by 'insiders'

Milan Kundera, *The Unbearable Lightness of Being: A Novel*. Harper Perennial Modern Classics, 1999. Excellent account of a love affair in the former Czechoslovakia.

Gabriel Garcia Marquez, *Love in the Time of Cholera*. Vintage Books, 2007. Proponent of magical realism explores love in many forms in Latin America.

Chinua Achebe, *Things Fall Apart: A Novel*. Anchor Books, 1994. An Ibo man finds it difficult to adapt to the forces of modernisation sweeping Africa and the world.

John Kennedy Toole, *A Confederacy of Dunces*. Grove Press, 1987. Brilliant comic novel about New Orleans and the life of a section of the underclass.

Robert Van Gulik, *The Haunted Monastery: A Judge Dee Mystery*. University of Chicago Press, 1997. Atmospheric detective tale set in Imperial China, haunting imagery.

Jane Austen, *Pride and Prejudice*. Penguin Classics, 2007. Iconic comedy of manners in a gentle England.

Australian Ballads and Henry Lawson Short Stories. Viking, 2003. Selection of most popular writings of Australia's cultural icon.

Barry Crump, *Gold and Greenstone*. Beckett Sterling, 1993. Iconic tales of the New Zealand bush by a true Kiwi.

Keri Hulme, *The Bone People*. Picador, 2001. The worthy Booker Prize winner is not one of the easiest reads here, but well worth it, dipping and whorling like the spiral shell of the Maori author bringing the sounds and scents of Aotearoa (Maori name for New Zealand) to the reader.

Witi Ihimeara, *The Whale Rider*. Heinemann, 2005. One young Maori girl reconnects to her culture and saves her village. Subject of a popular film.

Ethical ways to get your books

Green Metropolis: www.greenmetropolis.com UK-based website where you can buy many travel, guide and other books for only £3.75, including postage. Some money goes to replant trees.

Cygnus Books: www.cygnus-books.co.uk Free book club sells cheap books in the Mind, Body, Spirit category. Inspiring monthly magazine.

Languages

Phrasebooks and dictionaries to download: www.travlang.com

Phrasebooks to download: www.bootsnall.com/tk/books/lingual.shtml

Chapter 7: Planning an ethical path

Ethical travel

Guide to ethical travel: www.ethicaltraveler.com Tips for ethical travel, says travellers can be a positive force for change.

Assessing tourism: www.tourismconcern.org.uk Fights exploitative tourism, and suggests ways to change it.

International Centre for Responsible Tourism www.icrtourism.org Under 'Resources' there are many ebooks to download, on subjects like environmental impact and responsible travel.

Green Tourism Business Scheme: www.green-business.co.uk Assesses tourist-related businesses in UK and Europe.

Ecological conscience: ecoescape.org Directory of green places to stay and visit in the UK, stories of sustainable escapes.

What don't you want?

Amnesty International: www.amnesty.org Information and campaigns on human rights abuse, get information on your destination.

Human Rights Watch: www.hrw.org Defends human rights, and exposes
violations in individual countries.

Free Tibet campaign: www.freetibet.org Information on Tibetan cause,
including travelling there.

International Fund for Animal Welfare: www.ifaw.org Campaigns to make
a better world for animals and people, details of programmes in place in
individual countries.

Chapter 8: Where do you really, really want to go?

General

www.vagabonding.net Rolf Potts's website has lots of useful tips.

Jenny Diski, *Skating to Antarctica*. Virago, 2005. Autobiographical account
about the power of whiteness and why the author wanted to go to
Antarctica.

Mairi Hedderwick, *An Eye on the Hebrides*. Canongate Books, 2000. Well-
loved author of the Katie Morag children's books, who lives on the
Hebridean Isle of Coll and describes a six month trip to every island in
the archipelago in this whimsical and well-informed account.

Ideas about islands: www.islandsmag.com

Chapter 9: When do you fly?

When to fly

Johnny's website: www.johnnyjet.com Probably the most extensive website
on flying on the net.

Eric Leebow and John E. Discala, *You Are Here: Travelling with
JohnnyJet.com: The Ultimate Internet Travel Guide*, Yahbooks Publishing,
2003. Over 3,000 useful websites.

Long-term forecast: www.farecast.com Charts lowest fare between departure
and destination cities, allows you to see cheapest time of year for travel.

Compare airlines: www.airlinequality.com Useful website where passengers
write about their experiences of the different airlines.

Be a courier (major city): www.courier.org Suitable for those travelling
alone with hand luggage only who want to visit a major gateway for a
short time. Membership site.

Private jet broker: London-aircharter.com London Air Charter Centre offers
discount on 'empty legs' of private jets within Europe.

Antoine de Saint-Exupery, *Wind, Sand and Stars*. Harcourt Brace, 1967. In this exquisite treatise, a mystical Frenchman uses flight as a symbol of human aspiration.

Tips for booking (UK and USA)

Immediate flight: Farecompare.com Updates 6 million fares between 77,000 city pairs three times a day. See Top deals list.

Want something cheap?: www.sidestep.co.uk Another useful price comparison website.

Know your destination, not your place: www.flycheapo.com Find out which airlines fly to the European city you want to go to, with links to each airline and airport.

Last minute flights (USA): www.travelocity.com

Last minute seats: www.airhitch.org

The Kasbah: www.kasbah.com Cheap flights from the UK and USA.

One-way flights: www.opodo.com

Cath Urquhart, *The Times Holiday Handbook: The Essential Trip-Planning Guide*. Navigator Guides, 2006. The detailed description of using the Internet and choosing between airlines is useful if you haven't done it before.

Tips for booking (Australia and New Zealand)

Cheap flights from Australia: www.flightcentre.com.au

Cheap flights from Australia/New Zealand: www.atlas-club.com.au

Before you go

The extra things: www.holidayextras.com.uk Book airport parking, hotels, lounge etc. in UK before you set off.

The best seat on the plane: www.seatguru.com Shows you the design of most major airplanes, so you can choose the best seat.

Sleeping in airports: www.sleepinginairports.net Travellers give recommendations on the quietness and safety of different airports.

Your carbon footprint

Calculate your carbon footprint: www.earthday.net/footprint Helps you calculate how much energy you use on a daily basis.

Climate Care: www.climate-care.org Calculates emissions from your individual trips and helps you offset them.

Trees for Flights: www.treeflights.com Plants trees to offset carbon.

Chapter 10: How else can you travel?

See Part 2, Chapter 3, 'How do you get around?', below, for additional tips.

Driving

International driving licence: international-license.com When an international licence is necessary and how to obtain it.

Off-road vehicle tips (UK): www.frogsisland4x4.com Includes advice on preparing family vehicles.

Buying a used vehicle in UK: www.autotrader.co.uk *Autotrader* magazine widely available in UK newsagents.

Motor insurance

The AA: www.theaa.com Exhaustive insurance site including Internet-based route services for the UK and Europe.

The RAC: www.rac.co.uk Another big site; check extra breakdown insurance overseas here, and includes lists of things you need to drive legally in different countries.

Hitch-hiking

Best hitch-hiking website: www.digihitch.com There are some practical tips for drivers here.

Kinga's and Chopin's website: www.hitchhiketheworld.com Accounts of their journey and some useful questions.

Kinga Freespirit Choxzcz, *Led by Destiny*. Bernardinum, 2004. Brave Polish vegan girl hitch-hikes around the world with her boyfriend Chopin. They discover it is an even more magical place than they know.

Simon and Tom Sykes, *No Such Thing as a Free Ride? A Collection of Hitch-Hiking Tales*. Cassell, 2005. At last an anthology of personal stories about hitch-hiking by over 90 contributors including Sir Ranulph Fiennes, George Monbiot and Mike Leigh, as well as an MP, a Nobel Prize winner and the creator of Dungeons and Dragons.

International public transport by land

Public transport details worldwide: www.routesinternational.com Buses, trains etc. all over the world. Includes an excellent disabled section.

Terry Tarnoff, *The Bone Man of Benares: A Lunatic Trip Through Love and the World*. Bantam Books, 2005. Original hippie trip which lasted for eight years in the 1970s. Try now without the drugs.

Rory Maclean, *Magic Bus: On the Hippie Trail from Istanbul to India*. Penguin Books, 2007. Absorbing account of the author's travels along the original 'Hippie trail' between Europe and India.

Travel by rail

Excellent advice on rail and shipping transport around the world: www.seat61.com Named after the founder's favourite seat on Eurostar.

Inter-railing in Europe: www.Interrailnet.com Choose different passes to travel around Europe.

Budget rail travel Europe: www.bugeurope.com Excellent advice on rail travel, including which discount cards you qualify for.

European Rail Timetable Independent Travellers. Thomas Cook Publishing, latest edition.

Christopher Portway, *World Commuter: Great Journeys by Train*. Summersdale, 2001. Christopher's first long rail journey was as a prisoner of war. Since then he has made many more – including courting his wife by train and is a spectactular journey.

Booking directly

Each of these sites is the operator's, which is usually cheaper, and includes advice on discounts.

The Ghan, www.railaustralia.com.au Booking The Ghan across Australia.

The Canadian, www.viarail.ca The Canadian takes you from Toronto to Vancouver and is a spectactular journey.

Many classic rail journeys in India: www.indiarail.co.uk Can book by this office in UK as well as in Indian rail stations, which is an experience.

Scotland: www.firstscotrail.com Book beautiful journeys across Scotland.

Trans-Siberian Express: www.seat61.com/Trans-Siberian Information on booking directly at ticket offices in Moscow to Beijing in China or Vladivostok on the eastern side of Russia (from where you can take a ship to Japan).

Travelling by boat

Yachts

Joshua Slocum, *Sailing Alone Around the World*. Shambhala Publications, American classic account of the first person in recorded history to sail single-handed around the world.

Kevin Patterson, *The Water In Between: A Journey At Sea*. Penguin, 1999. A young Canadian doctor, depressed after the wrong love affair ends, buys a sail boat and goes all the way to Tahiti, while speculating on the nature of travel and his own life.

Greg Becker, *The Seagoing Hitchhiker's Handbook: Roaming the Earth on Other People's Yachts*. High Adventure Publishing, 1994. Guide to ports, yachts and what you need to say to get a job and get taken along.

Cargo boats

Travel around the world: www.strandtravel.co.uk Describes regular and freighter cargo boat sailings.

Glenda Adams, *Dancing on Coral*. A & R Classics, 1987. Beautiful novel describing the voyage to England so many Australians took in the 1950s, and how it becomes a voyage of self-discovery.

Cruise ships

Cruising Association (UK): www.cruising.org.uk No fee, will take novice crew and you can go around the world from the UK.

Cruise ship job finder: www.cruisejobfinder.com Three hundred and fifty thousand people work in the $30 billion industry. This site will help you be one of them, with jobs in all sorts of categories from booking agents, to casino hosts, beauty therapists and sound and light technicians.

Leading Cruise Agents Alliance: www.thelca.com Contact for most UK cruise specialists.

Polluting nature: www.cruisejunkie.com Compares the emissions of various ships.

International motorcycling

The Motorcycle Diaries, Walter Salles (dir) DVD, 2004. Based on the book by Che Guevara, this film shows panoramic shots of South America on his trip around the continent as a young student with a friend, interspersed with his awakening social conscience.

Ted Simon, *Jupiter's Travels: Four Years Around the World on a Triumph*. Jupitalia Productions, 2005. Solo trip around the world of 78,000 miles in the 1970s. Many fascinating tales from Ted's trip in this classic account.

Cycling

Bettina Selby, *Riding the Mountains Down: A Journey by Bicycle to Kathmandu*. HarperCollins, 1985. When Bettina was 47, she no longer had to provide for her family and could do what she wanted. Very well-written account of her trip alone across the world by bicycle.

Anne Mustoe, *Lone Traveller: One Woman, Two Wheels and the World.* Virgin Publishing, 2002. Well paced and well informed account of a retired British headteacher's second trip around the world. Usefully divided into topics based on things she's learned.

Walking around the world

Ffyona Campbell, *The Whole Story: A Walk Around the World.* Orion, 1997. British girl (almost) walks around the world and faces up to what she has missed. Well worth reading, both for seeing where determination can get you, and for an honest account of facing up to an inner battle.

Chapter 11: Who do you go with?

Women going solo

Journey woman: www.journeywoman.com Interesting reports from women on the road.

Marybeth Bond, *Gutsy Women: Travel Tips and Wisdom for the Road.* Travelers' Tales, 1997. Useful stories and advice from this excellent series.

Travelling with yourself

Paul Theroux, *Fresh Air Fiend: Travel Writings.* Mariner Books, 2001. Excellent stories of Paul Theroux's life in travel as well as reflections on other travel writers.

Wilfred Thesiger, *Arabian Sands.* Viking Press, 1985. Classic narrative from British adventurer in the Arab world.

Freya Stark, *The Journey's Echo.* Ecco Press, 1988. Excerpts from Freya Stark's books. Adventurer who travels on her own through the Middle East.

Pali Lee and Koko Willis, *Tales from the Night Rainbow: The Story of a Woman, a People and an Island. An oral history as told by Kali'ohe Kame'ekua of Kamalo, Moloka'i 1816–1931.* Night Rainbow Publishing. 1990. Moving account of Native Hawaiian spirituality, including the inter-connectedness of humans, animals, colour and all of nature, indicating that we're never really alone.

Soulmates

Antera, *Twin Flames: A True Story of Soul Reunion*. Twinsong, 2003. Auto-biographical account of how this rather close Californian couple met and merged.

Ulli Springett, *Soulmate Relationships*. Piatkus Books, 2003. Excellent guidance on this challenging topic.

Kevin J. Todeschi, *Edgar Cayce on Soulmates: Unlocking the Dynamics of Soul Attraction*. A.R.C. Press, 1999. Practical guide to the different types of soulmate relationships and how we can learn from them, as shown by Edgar Cayce's readings

Chapter 12: What about money?

Travelling without money

Barter instead of money: www.letslinkuk.org LETS communities exchange goods and services from vegetables to massages, to provide a higher quality of life for all concerned.

LETS (NZ): www.letsnewzealand.org.nz New Zealand site features similar exchanges

Saving money before you go

Pay less: www.moneysavingexpert.com Very valuable independent site featuring excellent money saving tips in Britain, as well as for travel abroad.

Martin Lewis, *The Money Diet*. Vermilion, 2006. The book of the website. Superb tips on everything from cheap spectacles to reducing your household bills.

Saving on bills

Power-cost calculator: The Owl on sale in B&Q superstores, UK. Plugs into any socket and displays how much electricity you are using and the hourly cost.

Fuel bills: www.uswitch.org Compares your household bills and finds the cheapest provider.

Saving on water bills in UK: www.waterwise.org.uk Energy saving tips and suppliers for your water.

Other kinds of saving

Shopping.com. Compares prices etc. for specific category, and has users' reviews.

Getting a weekly lodger: www.mondaytofriday.com Ideal for those who work away from home, but want their space back at weekends, or for someone who only needs somewhere during the week.

Ethical investing of your savings: www.trilliuminvest.com

Give and get for free: www.freecycle.org 'Changing the world one gift at a time.' In local groups around the world, people offer, or state, what they want, one good at a time by email. What comes around goes around.

Recycle now: www.recyclenow.co.uk Information about ways to recycle online.

Travelling with money

Financial advice USA: www.motleyfool.com Planning your finances.

ATM locators

Mastercard/Cirrus/Maestro locator worldwide: www.mastercard.com

Visacard locator worldwide: www.visa.co.uk

Credit cards

The Post Office: www.postoffice.co.uk The only UK credit card that is presently free to use abroad. Must be British citizen to apply.

Pre-payment cards

Load with currency before you go: www.which-prepaid-card.co.uk Comparison site for prepayment cards.

Chapter 13: What about your place?

Storage

Storage (UK): www.safestore.co.uk

Storage (Au): www.selfstorage.com.au

Finding tenants

See also houses and flats in Part 2, Chapter 2, 'Where to stay'.

www.freetranslation.com Will translate your text or advertisement in to other languages.

Advertising in UK: www.gumtree.com All major cities represented in popular room-, flat- and house-finding website that many backpackers use.

Vegetarian accomodation: www.vegcom.org.uk Free guide to accomodation for vegetarians and vegans in the UK.

Advertising in NZ: www.gumtree.co.nz Accommodation in various New Zealand cities for singles and sharers.

Advertising in Australia: www.gumtree.com.au Accommodation in Australian cities for singles and sharers.

House and pet sitting

Petsitters UK: www.animalaunts.co.uk House and animal sitters in UK and internationally.

Petsitters UK: www.dogsit.com National Association of Registered Petsitters, holds large register of contacts.

Homesitters: www.homesitters.co.uk Home and petsitting services.

Before you go

Australia: www.australiapost.com.au Will forward mail for up to one year, domestic and international.

New Zealand: www.nzpost.co.nz Will forward mail for up to one year, domestic and international.

UK: www.postoffice.co.uk Will redirect post for up to two years.

Gas safety certificate: www.gassafety.co.uk Make sure you get this before you go if you're renting your place.

Chapter 14: What do you do about the kids?

Travelling with children – general tips

St John's Ambulance first-aid course for babies and children (UK): www.sja.org.uk Learn how to deal with common emergencies.

More reviews on travelling with kids: www.kidscantravel.com Practical advice and ideas for activities including walking in various regions of the world.

Stories on the web: www.talesmag.com Tales from a Small Planet has quality stories from expatriates, including children.

The young child

Dervla Murphy, *Where the Indus is Young: A Winter in Baltistan.* John
 Murray, 2003. Interesting account of the author's travels in Pakistan with
 her six-year-old daughter.

The older child

Dan Glick, *Monkey Dancing.* Public Affairs, 2003. Heart-warming book
 about family relationships and the power of travel after tragedy (bereave-
 ment and divorce).

Niema Ash, *Travels with my Daughter: Forget Convention . . . Follow Your
 Instinct.* Eye Books, 2002. Unconventional trip with Niema's 15-year-old
 daughter; includes accounts of her meetings with 60s rock stars.

Travelling as a family

Laura Manske (ed.), *Family Travel: The Farther You Go, The Closer You Get.*
 Travelers' Tales, 1999. Stories about families gaining deeper roots and
 stronger wings through travelling together.

Victoria, Sergei, Valya and Igor Boutenko, *Raw Family: A True Story of
 Awakening.* Raw Family Publishing, 2002. Inspiring book about this happy
 family, with details of the trek along America's coast.

John, Marie-Christine and Rebecca Ridgway, *Then We Sailed Away.*
 Time Warner, 1998. Family leave their adventure centre in North-west
 Highlands and sail to the South Pacific and Antarctic.

Thoughtful Alaskan family travel the world: www.worldhop.com

Travelling as a single parent

Michele Jamal, *Volcanic Visions: Encounters with Other Worlds.* Arkana, 1993.
 A Californian lady 'wakes up' – and how – in Hawaii, while her son also
 has some interesting experiences.

Marybeth Bond, *Gutsy Mamas: Travel Tips and Wisdom for Mothers on the
 Road.* Travelers' Tales, 1997.

Resources for children to take on their trip

Very young children

*Let's Get Going! Travelling with Kids. Songs, Stories and Lullabies for Relaxed
 Road Tripping!* Lovely selection of songs on this CD, ending with
 'Somewhere Over the Rainbow'.

Dance Along with Mr Boom, Moonbeam Music: www.mrboom.co.uk

Scottish children's entertainer sings some self-composed songs on cosmic themes.

Paul McCartney, Geoff Dunbar and Philip Ardagh, *High in the Clouds.* Dutton Juvenile, 2005. Wirral the squirrel searches for sanctuary in this beautiful book with ecological theme.

Young children

Hugh Lofting, *The Voyages of Dr Doolittle.* Signet Classics, 2000. Dr Doolittle sets sail for Spider Monkey Island opening up a world of natural history on the way.

Heather Forest, *Wisdom Tales from Around the World.* August House, Inc., 1996. Short stories from different world faiths shine a light into the wisdom of each continent.

Lewis Carroll, *Alice's Adventures in Wonderland and Through the Looking Glass.* Signet Classics, 2000. Fabulous account of Alice's adventures that children (of all ages) will enjoy.

Older children

W.E. Johns, *Biggles Goes to the South Seas.* Armada, 1975. Swashbuckling series about the adventures of a pilot in many countries of the world.

Christobel Mattingley, *New Patches for Old.* Puffin Books, 1980. Perceptive tale of a 14-year-old British girl who emigrates to Australia with her family, and how it affects her growing up.

Madeleine l'Engle, *A House Like a Lotus.* Laurel Leaf, 1985. Young American girl goes to Greece and learns about the nature of love and compassion.

Oscar Wilde, *The Complete Fairy Tales of Oscar Wilde.* Noriana Books, 2007. Deceptively simple tales on eternal themes such as love, art, faith and loss.

Carolyn McVickar Edwards, *In the Light of the Moon: Thirteen Lunar Tales from Around the World Illuminating Life's Mysteries.* Marlowe and Company, 2003. Myths full of grace, arranged according to the phases of the moon.

Herman Hesse, *Siddhartha.* Bantam Classics, 1981. Young man goes wandering in a quest to find the meaning of life.

Travel insurance for single parents and families

www.travelleronline.com Free annual travel insurance for children, but you must join the WEXAS travel club.

NatWest: www.natwest.com Offers cover if child travels separately from you.

www.simpletravelinsurance.co.uk Covers children up to the age of 22 if in
continuous education.

Leading Edge: www.leadedge.co.uk Policies aimed at single parents travelling with children.

Schooling

Education Otherwise: www.education-otherwise.org British site on home-
schooling.

Home education in Australia: www.hea.asn.au Australian site promoting the
practice of home education.

Home education in New Zealand:
http://homeeducationnz.co.nz/homeschool.html New Zealand site on
home-schooling.

Council of International Schools: www.cois.org

Chapter 15: Travelling with your animal

Animal communication

Dawn Brunke, *Awakening to Animal Voices: A Teen Guide to Telepathic
Communication with All Life*. Bindu Books, 2004. Excellent guide to
animal communication applicable to people of all ages and stages.

Widening your categories

Yi Fu Tuan, *Dominance and Affection in the Making of Pets*. Yale University Press, 2004. Readable study by a geographer of how power relations
impact our relationship with our pets.

Jeffrey Masson, *The Nine Emotional Lives of Cats: A Journey Into the Feline
Heart*. Ballantine Books, 2004. Study of the author's life with his cats,
detailed descriptions of going on walks with them.

Philip Pullman, *The Golden Compass*. Scholastic Books, 2007. Brilliant
first book of the 'Northern Lights' trilogy starts in Oxford then explores
worlds beyond our own.

Ted Andrews, *Animal Speak*. Llewellyn, 1994. Superb guide to many creatures of North America and how they can act as our totem or guide.

Richard Adams, *Watership Down*. Scribner, 2005. Beautiful story of the
migration of a band of rabbits to a safer home.

Travelling with your animal

Worldwide travel guide for pet owners: www.pettravel.com Superb advice to guide you through the maze of different regulations and carriers.

Service Animal Registry of America: www.affluent.net/sara Under the Americans with Disability Act, any animal ordinarily trained may be a service animal, therefore you may be able to bring your animal anywhere you go in America if you have special needs.

Rory MacLean, *Stalin's Nose: Across the Face of Europe.* Flamingo, 1993. Hilarious book about a trip around Eastern Europe in a van – with his aunt, her dead husband and her pig, weeks after the fall of the Berlin Wall.

Spud Ponsonby-Taylor, *Small Steps with Heavy Hooves: A Mother's Walk Back to Health in the Highlands.* Summersdale, 1998. What do you do when you're a single parent with a dog and a diagnosis of cancer? Do your passion, in this case walking.

Clare de Vries, *I & Claudius.* Bloomsbury, 1999. Excellent tale of Clare's road trip across America with her beloved cat Claudius.

Dog Gone Classical Music: Mozart. Audio CD, 2006. Mozart interspersed with nature sounds, very calming, for dogs and everyone else, also cat equivalent.

Where to stay with your animal

Travelling in USA: www.petswelcome.org Hotels that welcome you travelling with your pet (usually a dog), throughout America.

Pets Welcome! Farm Holiday Guides, 2007. Tips on where to stay with your dogs in Britain, including narrowboat holidays.

Cabins in woods (UK): www.forest-holiday.com Pet-friendly cabins in partnership between the Forestry Commission and the Camping and Caravanning Club in secluded woodland settings.

Self-catering cottages www.denekin.com Almost any animal welcome when you stay in the cottage on our animal sanctuary in Scotland.

Leaving your animal behind

See Part 1, Chapter 13 'House and pet sitting' for recommendations.

Restrictions on travelling with animals

Pet passport scheme: www.passportforpets.co.uk Gives details on certain animal movement to and from the UK without quarantine, but with rabies injection and microchip.

Quarantine rules (UK): www.defra.gov.uk
Quarantine rules (Au): www.travelbug.gov.au
Quarantine rules (NZ): www.maf.govt.nz

Pet insurance
This is relatively easy to find on a good website such as
moneysavingexpert.com, except if you have an older pet.

RSPCA: www.rspca-petinsurance.co.uk Decent pet insurance, including pet
over the age of 10, does not cover homeopathic treatment.

Marks and Spencer: www.marksandspencer.com Pet insurance for older pet,
includes homeopathic insurance.

National Farmers Union: www.nfuonline.com Best for insuring multiple,
non-traditional pets.

Side effects of vaccination and microchipping
Information network: www.wddty.com Information on side effects of vaccinations for animals.

Information network: www.vetpathology.org American College of
Veterinary Pathologists offer details of experiments linking microchips to
cancer.

Finding an animal abroad
Mark Shand, *Travels On My Elephant*. Penguin, 1992. Prince Charles's
brother-in-law buys an elephant, rides her through India, learns to recognise her special qualities then sets up a foundation.

Christina Dodwell, *Traveller on Horseback in Eastern Turkey and Iran*. Long
Riders Guild Press, 2004. This respected explorer shows what is possible
for a woman on her own.

Rescuing animals
Born Free Foundation: www.bornfree.org.uk You can report abuses of
animals here.

Karin Muller, 'Rescue in the Exotic Animal Market' in *Women in the Wild:
True Stories of Adventure and Connection*. Travelers' Tales, 2003. Karin
buys baby monkeys from a market in Vietnam to save them from a
terrible end, and gets other travellers involved.

Chapter 16: Preparing for a safe trip

Official advice from your government

Please note these websites are not exclusive, and contain useful information even for non-citizens of the country.

For UK citizens: www.fco.gov.uk/travel Go to section called 'Before you go' for checklist.

For NZ citizens: Foreign office (NZ): www.safetravel.govt.nz Section called 'Before you go' gives valuable advice.

Visas

Find your embassy: www.embassy.com And check visa requirements for any country in the world.

Medical notes

John Hatt, *The Tropical Traveller*. Penguin, 1993. Excellent advice for those travelling to tropical countries. Out of date, but information is still useful.

Before you go

Hospital for Tropical Diseases (UK): www.thehtd.org Excellent medical advice from the experts.

Medical Advisory Services for Travellers: www.masta.org Health briefings tailored to your journey, private travel clinics across UK.

Travel health clinics (Australia): www.travelclinic.com.au

National Travel Health Network: www.nathnac.org Funded by Department of Health to promote high standards in travel medicine, up-to-date information about diseases and how to stay healthy on your travels.

Information network: www.whatdoctorsdonttellyou.com Information on side effects of vaccinations fur humans.

When you're there

Travel health Online www.triprep.com Recommended clinics and hospitals around the world.

International Association for Medical Assistance to Travellers: www.iamat.org Non-profit organisation offers lists of English-speaking doctors and inspected clinics and hospitals in many countries.

Travel insurance
Warnings from your government

If you go to a country on these lists, your insurance is likely to be invalid.

Foreign Office (UK): www.fco.gov.uk/travel Latest travel warnings for British subjects. Includes several leaflets, including what you do in various emergencies and on the support you can and cannot expect from the consulate.

Foreign affairs (Australia): www.smarttraveller.gov.au Check out latest travel advice for Australians. Section on dual nationality and how it may affect the support given to you if you are not travelling on your Australian passport is particularly useful.

Foreign affairs (New Zealand): www.safetravel.govt.nz Excellent travel advice designed for Kiwis.

US Department of State: www.travel.state.gov Official travel warnings for Americans.

Companies specialising in 'gap year' travel

STA Travel: www.statravel.co.uk Student insurers are usually cheap and reliable for everyone.

Boots: www.boots.com Additionaly offer of £1,000 'incarceration cover' for parents to visit you if jailed overseas.

Endsleigh: www.endsleigh.co.uk Endsleigh offers a smaller excess than many other policies

Special needs (pre-existing medical conditions)

Freedom Insure: www.freedominsure.co.uk Travellers with pre-existing medical conditions.

Free Spirit: www.free-spirit.com Travellers with pre-existing medical conditions.

British Insurance Brokers Association: www.biba.org.uk Broker will help you find the best policy for special needs.

Special needs (older people)

Insurance advice for the over-50s (Australia): www.nationalseniors.com.au

The Post Office (UK): www.postoffice.co.uk Insures 60–74 year olds, usually for single trips.

Bon Voyage (UK): www.bon-voyage.co.uk Insures up to the age of 90 including pre-existing medical conditions, when flights or accommodation are booked in conjunction.

Annual multi-trip policies: www.nationwide Offers rare multi-trip coverage
for 65–80 year olds, although only within Europe.

When don't you need insurance?

Health care coverage in Europe: www.ehic.org.uk If you are British and
going to Europe you should have the free European Health Insurance
Card available from the post office.

Chapter 17: What do you take?

Clothing

www.onebag.com Useful advice on packing light.
Greenfibres: www.greenfibres.com Fairly traded organic fabrics.
Millets outdoor stores (UK): www.millets.co.uk Very cheap outdoor gear.
Many high street branches.
Ethical shoes: www.vegshoes.com American based, will send abroad if you
order six weeks in advance.
Vegetarian shoes (UK): www.vegetarian-shoes.co.uk Brighton based store
delivers animal friendly shoes and clothing worldwide.
Croc shoes: www.crocs.eu If you live in Europe get your Crocs here.
www.crocs.com Crocs are cheapest here but must be shipped to an
American address.
List of international size changes for clothing and footwear: www.safariquip.co.uk
Bourgeois Bohéme: www.bbohéme.com Vegan shoes and ethical fashion
with compassion. Informative newsletter, London showroom.

Cosmetics

Image consultants: www.colourmebeautiful.com Helps men and women
find the colours that suit them best.
Lush: www.lush.co.uk Fabulously creative and ethical cosmetics including
excellent solid shampoos.
Plant-based wipes: www.urchin.co.uk Hypo-allergenic, environmentally
friendly wipes make more 'sense' than the individually wrapped ones.

Technology

See Part 2, Chapter 20, 'Keeping in touch', for advice on using technology
when you're away.

Taking electrical items abroad: www.kropla.com Advice on plugs, voltages, phones, international dialling codes, Internet roaming codes etc.

Solar technology UK: www.solartechnology.co.uk Or avoid the need for plugs and voltages altogether by using solar technology, which recharges only by the sun – and even cloudy days have some sun.

Portable solar chargers for electrical equipment: www.wavemaker.co.uk This type of thing is particularly useful for your magical trip.

Chapter 18: Clean up your life before you go

Decluttering your body and soul

Decluttering: ebay.co.uk Sell your stuff with unwanted associations here.

Karen Kingston, *Clear your Clutter with Feng Shui*. Broadway, 1999. Helps you get rid of your stuff in accordance with ancient Chinese principles.

Jon Sandifer: www.fengshui.co.uk Former chairman of Feng Shui Society and founder of Macrobiotic Association offers personal consultations combining expertise in varied oriental disciplines.

Australian life coach: www.radiantcoaching.com.au Just the coach to help you on a big project. Deanna Sorensen has walked alone and unsupported across Australia and says ordinary people can do extraordinary things.

International Coach Federation: www.coachfederation.org.uk Personal and business coaches. Over 12,000 members worldwide.

To help you set off

Jude O'Neill and Bridget Fonger, *The Lazy Woman's Guide to Just About Everything*. Quality Books, 2001. If you feel quite stuck, as though you can't lose control, get this book about a year to six months before you want to go and put the tips into motion.

Susan Jeffers, *Feel the Fear and Do It Anyway*. Ballantine Books, 2006. Excellent book with specific exercises to help you do what you are scared to do.

Steve Davey, *Unforgettable Islands to Escape to Before You Die*. Firefly Books, 2007. Some motivation for you. Great photographs and six pages of description of 40 islands.

PART 2: WHEN YOU'RE THERE

Chapter 1: Culture shock

Useful information

Language translator: http://babelfish.altavista.com Translates between English and other languages. Invaluable for foreign websites.

Time and date: www.timeanddate.com Works out the time, date, sunrise, sunset, dialling codes etc.

Useful information on over 250 countries: www.izoxzone.com Free download with everything from dialling codes to maps.

Currency converter: www.xe.com Get the latest rates on this site.

Adjusting to a country

Cultural etiquette: www.ediplomat.com Designed for diplomats, the site is still useful, giving advice on etiquette in many countries.

Craig Storti, *The Art of Crossing Cultures*. Intercultural Press, 2001. Useful tips from an American cross-cultural educator on how to deal with culture shock, as well as looking at how you come across.

Culture shock

William Sutcliffe, *Are you Experienced?*. Hamish Hamilton, 1997. Funny novel about two backpackers' culture shock in India.

Sean Doyle, *Beyond Snake Mountain*. Indus, 1991. An Australian man's experience in Pushkar that includes detailed descriptions.

E.M. Forster, *A Passage to India*. Penguin Books, 2000. Deserved classic illustrating the potential for misunderstanding in Anglo-Indian relations.

Christopher Koch, *The Year of Living Dangerously*. Penguin, 2005. Excellent book about an Australian journalist who goes to Indonesia at the time of the 1960s coup and the ensuing culture clashes.

J. Maarten Troost, *The Sex Lives of Cannibals: Adrift in the Equatorial Pacific*. Broadway, 2004. Hilarious story about what happens when Dutchman Maarten and his American girlfriend go to live on a remote island in the Pacific.

Adjusting yourself

Margaret Fay Shaw, *From the Alleghenies to the Hebrides: An Autobiography*. Birlinn, 1999. Autobiography of a Canadian archivist of Gaelic who ends up living in the Hebrides and buying an island.

Greg Dening, *Islands and Beaches. Discourses on a Silent Land: Marquesas 1774–1880*. University of Hawaii Press, 1980. We all bring our worlds with us. Fascinating tales of cross-cultural encounters between sailors and natives and the effect on each, by an Australian historian who is also a lyrical writer.

Chapter 2: Where to stay

Hotels

www.priceline.com Name your date, price and select your star rating – when you get to your destination airport you will be allocated an unused room in the hotel of your rating. Great for your first couple of days.

Find your hotel: www.expedia.com Choose different hotels from a limited selection. You can specify single occupancy but it usually makes no difference to price.

Discount hotel bookers (US only): www.quikbook.com Pay the hotel directly in local currency – unusual on a discount booking site, but it gives you more security and usually cheaper.

Where to stay worldwide: www.i-escape.com Some more expensive escapes for a treat. Older market.

Hostels and backpackers

Youth Hostels: www.iyha.org The flagship group. Safe hostels of an international standard, private rooms as well as dorms, cooking facilities. All ages.

Hostels worldwide: www.hostelworld.com Can specify whether you are travelling alone on the website.

Hostels Europe: www.europesfamoushostels.com Travellers choose best hostels of Europe. Mostly for young people.

Pod space in London: www.easyhotel.com Founder of EasyJet offers cheap minimum rooms – 'pods'.

Pod space at airports: www.yotel.com Somewhere to sleep and shower at Heathrow, Terminal 4; Gatwick South; and Schiphol, Amsterdam.

Independent feedback on accommodation

Genuine customer reviews: www.tripadvisor.com Hotels and hostels with a rating composed of all the reviews over the last six months.

For backpackers: www.bug.co.uk Probably the most comprehensive review of hostels on web.

Virtual Tourist: www.virtualtourist.com Over a million members, largely younger, share travel tips including best accommodation, packing lists, local customs and warnings.

Renting flats and houses

See Part 1, Chapter 13, for finding tenants.

Advertising in UK: www.loot.com Newspaper has many properties to rent, covers London and northern England.

Rent-a-home.com.au Daily rates for fully furnished flats or holiday homes for a week or more. Some last minute availability.

Renting in Australia: www.cracker.com.au Australia's biggest website has many classifieds.

Renting in New Zealand: www.trademe.co.nz Huge website with rental rooms and flats, and much else.

Animal sanctuaries

Our holiday cottage on Skye in north-west Scotland:
www.denekin.com Stay on our animal sanctuary by the sea, healing winds, sacred waterfalls, midnight sun, spiritual library, clifftop walks, animals welcome.

Cottages and cabins to rent in Best Friends Sanctuary: www.bestfriends.org Self-catering in Red Rock country in beautiful Utah, on the USA's biggest sanctuary.

Alan Rabinowicz, *Jaguar: One Man's Struggle to Establish the World's First Jaguar Preserve*. Island Press, 2000. Story of a biologist's struggle to establish a jaguar reserve in Belize, where you can now rent cabins.

Going local

Dixe Wills, *Places to Hide in England, Scotland and Wales: You Can Run and Now You Can Hide*. Icon Books, 2006. Quirky and eccentric guide to free bridges, caves and trees to hide in.

Barbara Tedlock, *Time and the Highland Maya*. University of New Mexico Press, 1992. Anthropologist's excellent guide to some complex meanings of time among the Maya – helps dispel the myth that 'primitive' peoples are unsophisticated.

Kapawi Lodge Ecuador: www.kapawi.com Ten-day walk from nearest town, or reach by jungle flight and canoe. Kapawi Lagoon is the largest community based project. Seventy per cent of employees are Achuar, and in 2011 the lodge will be handed over to tribe.

Laurie Gough, *Kite Strings of the Southern Cross*. Travelers' Tales, 1999.
Beautiful, beautiful book on Laurie's travels in the Pacific, although take her statements about Hawaii with a pinch of salt.

Chapter 3: How do you get around?

See also Part 1, Chapter 10, 'How else can you travel?', for tips.

Driving within a country

Association for Safe International Road Travel: www.asirt.org Safe driving advice for different countries, including those with poor safety records.

Terence Stamp et al., *The Adventures of Priscilla, Queen of the Desert*. Stephan Elliott (dir.), DVD, 2005. Two drag queens and a transsexual go on a road trip in the Australian desert on a bus called *Priscilla*.

Ridesharing

Ridesharing website: www.freewheelers.com Offer or request lifts worldwide here.

Ride Amigos: www.rideamigos.com Share cabs and carpool in major American cities.

Within a city (UK): www.citycarclubs.co.uk Reasonable membership and fees, covers many cities in the UK.

Ridesharing website (NZ): www.carshare.co.nz Free service linking drivers and passengers in New Zealand.

Ridesharing website (Au): www.shareyourride.net Links drivers and passengers in Australia, New Zealand and America.

Riding across America

Driving free cars (USA): www.autodriveaway.com Transport cars from one city to another. Must be 33 or over. Foreigners need passport with exit visa and Motor Vehicle Drivers Record from home country.

Jack Kerouac, *On the Road*. Penguin Books, 1999. In print since 1957, this is the classic of the Beat Generation. Read it and your trip won't be the same.

Susan Sarandon et al., *Thelma and Louise*. Ridley Scott (dir.), DVD, 1991. Two friends have their liberating adventure turn into something more in this feel-good chick flick.

Laurie Gough, *Kiss the Sunset Pig: The American Road Trip with Exotic*

Detours, Summersdale, 2006. In this exquisite account Laurie returns to her past realising she was really seeking the sense of possibility in the girl she used to be.

Nikki and David Goldbeck, *Healthy Highways: The Traveller's Guide to Healthy Eating*. Ceres Press, 2004 (supplement 2007). The lawyer and nutritionist co-authors of the bestselling *Supermarket Handbook* have produced this excellent guide to natural and organic cafes and restaurants, while driving across America, so you will *not* become a 'supersize you'.

Hitching within a country

Tips: www.digihitch.com Superb hitch-hiking website. Features tips for both drivers and hitch-hikers.

Contact others: www.couchsurfing.com (go to 'Groups and hitch-hikers'). Many hitch-hiking groups enable you to share experiences.

Will Ferguson, *Hokkaido Highway Blues: Hitchhiking Japan*. Soho Press, 1998. One day Will decides to follow the progress of the cherry blossom north, hitch-hiking all the way.

Tony Hawks, *Round Ireland with a Fridge*. Ebury Press, 2007. Comedian decides to hitch around Ireland with a 'cool friend', a fridge, for a bet.

Joe Bennett, *A Land of Two Halves: An Accidental Tour of New Zealand*. Scribner, 2005. English teacher, resident there for ten years, goes hitch-hiking to get to know his adopted country.

Local transport within a country

You get the best information when you are in a place, so don't worry if you can't find much out on the Internet.

Peter Moore, *Swahili for the Broken-Hearted: Cape Town to Cairo by Any Means Possible*. Bantam Books, 2002. Inveterate Aussie traveller goes through Africa by local transport and hitch-hiking.

Coaches in Europe: www.eurolines.com

Alain De Botton, *The Art of Travel*. Hamish Hamilton, 2002. Literary guide that gently reflects on the nature of travel.

Alistair Caldicott, *Batting for Pakistan: Guns, God and Cricket*. www.alitravelstheworld.com, 2006. Author travels overland through Pakistan in this incisive social commentary.

Cycling and walking within a country

Cycling and walking, UK

www.ordnancesurvey.co.uk Free downloadable guides to map-reading and details of maps.

Cycle network: www.sustrans.org.uk Sustainable transport charity offers National Cycle Network map for free.

London cycle network: www.londoncyclenetwork.org.uk Find out where the cycle paths are.

www.visitbritain.com/getactive See Walkers Welcome and Cyclists Welcome schemes.

Walking: www.countrysideaccess.gov.uk Details of countryside access in England, links to Wales and Scotland.

Long distance walking, cycling and horse riding trails in England and Wales: www.nationaltrail.co.uk

Long distance paths in Scotland: www.walking.visitscotland.com

www.ramblers.org.uk Britain's biggest walking group includes many local branches. Includes information on walking festivals.

Walking in NZ

Guide to tramping: www.tramper.co.nz Excellent system of long distance footpaths interspersed with inspired huts to stay in.

Pilgrimage

Camino de Santiago: www.csj.org.uk Official website for pilgrimages.

Very small boats

Canoeing and kayaking in Britain: www.bcu.org.uk Recreational canoeing and white-water kayaking.

Sea kayaking: www.seakayak.co.uk Sea kayaking in UK. Contact for international links.

Canoeing and kayaking in New Zealand: www.rivers.org.nz Recreational canoeing and white-water kayaking.

Kiwi Association of Sea Kayakers: www.kask.co.nz Sea kayaking in New Zealand.

Jill Fredston, *Rowing to Latitude: Journeys Along the Arctic's Edge*. North Point Press, 2002. Jill and her husband 'disappear' for months each summer. In this interesting and reflective account, beautiful wilderness descriptions answer the question 'why?'

Dolphin spotting in Scotland: www.geminiexplorer.co.uk Cruising and boat
  hire in north-east Scotland, the sunniest part of Britain.
Whale watching in New Zealand: www.whalewatch.co.nz Maori-owned
  company in Kaikoura will tell you legends while searching for whales.

Swimming

Tips on swimming trips, mainly in Europe: www.swimtrek.com One
  mode of magical travel you can't do alone. Group provides boating
  support.
Charles Sprawson, *Haunts of the Black Masseur: The Swimmer as Hero*.
  University of Minnesota Press, 2000. Cultural history of swimming.

Chapter 4: Travelling spontaneously

The significance of signs

Gill Edwards, *Stepping into the Magic*. Piatkus, 2006. Excellent tips on how
  to move towards your desire.
James Redfield, *The Celestine Prophecy*. Bantam Books, 1996. Classic book
  on the importance of following signs, in parable form.

Interpreting signs

Denise Linn, *Secret Language of Signs: How to Interpret Coincidences and
  Symbols in your Life*. Wellspring/Ballantine, 1996. Lovely, deceptively
  simple book containing much useful information.
Donni Hakenson, *Oracle of the Dreamtime: Aboriginal Dreamings Offer
  Guidance for Today*. Connections, 1998. Powerful book and card set based
  on Aboriginal spiritual beliefs – one way of making a decision is to draw
  a card and interpret it according to the accompanying book and your
  intuition.
Clifford Geertz, *The Interpretation of Cultures*. Basic Books, 2000.
  Lively anthropological classic looks at cultures in terms of the meanings
  the natives 'guarding other sheep in other valleys' ascribe to them.
Robert Graves, *The White Goddess*. Faber and Faber, 1999. Fascinating
  exploration of Celtic mythology and how signs lead to meaning, from one
  of Britain's famous poets. By his own account, written from his intuition.

Chapter 5: It's all in the timing

Synchrony

Ranulph Fiennes, *Mad, Bad and Dangerous to Know*. Hodder and
 Stoughton, 2007. Sir Ranulph's autobiography describes a rather
 exciting life.

John Lynch et al., *Sliding Doors*. Peter Howitt (dir.), DVD, 1998. Explores
 what happens both when a girl gets – and doesn't get – on a particular
 train home.

Synchronicity

Carl Jung, *Synchronicity*. Routledge, 1985. Masterly account of how
 'synchronicity' serves to illustrate the deeper processes of our lives.

Robert Hopcke, *There Are No Accidents: Synchronicities and the Story of Our
 Lives*. Riverhead Books, 1998. Compelling true stories of synchronicity,
 organised under themes such as love, dreams and work.

Mihaly Csikszentmihalyi, *The Flow: The Psychology of Optimal Experience.
 Steps toward enhancing the quality of life*. Harper & Row, 1990. Investigation
 of ways being in 'the flow' enhance experience.

Chapter 6: Meeting people

See also Part 2, Chapter 12, 'When do you accept hospitality?'

General advice

Meeting people: www.craigslist.org Originally USA based, now stretches to
 the rest of the world.

Meet in real space: www.meetup.com Choose your group according to city
 and interest.

Meeting older people: www.retiredbackpackers.com Good site for older
 backpackers, includes travel tips.

Lionel Blue and Jonathan Magonet, *Sun, Sand and Soul: A Little Bit of
 Heaven on Holiday*. Hodder and Stoughton, 1989. Heartwarming guide,
 includes anecdotes on learning from people.

Chapter 7: The power of saying no

The law

Fair trials: www.fairtrialsabroad.org Helps British citizens believed to have
 been wrongly imprisoned overseas.

Prisoners abroad (UK): www.prisonersabroad.org.uk Supports British prisoners abroad, their families and returning prisoners.

Sally Field et al., *Not Without My Daughter*. Brian Gilbert (dir.), DVD, 2001. Fictionalised account based on the story of Betty Mahmoody, in the book of the same name, who falls in love with an Iranian man in America and marries him. They go to Iran for a holiday, he announces they will stay and she cannot leave without her daughter. This is the story of their escape.

Sex

Sexual health: womenonwaves.org Dutch website that lists family planning, sexual health and women's rights organisations worldwide.

Protecting children everywhere: www.ecpat.org.uk End Child Prostitution, Child Pornography, and the Trafficking of Children for Sexual Purposes. Children's rights organisation campaigns against child exploitation.

Louisa Waugh, *Selling Olga: Stories of Human Trafficking and Resistance*. Phoenix 2007. Evelyn Waugh's granddaughter has researched harrowing true stories of human slavery in Eastern Europe and Britain, the world's fastest-growing organised crime.

Patricia McCormick, *Sold*. Hyperion, 2006. Novel about young Nepali girl Lakshmi who looks forward to leaving her village, and her anguish on discovering she is about to become a child prostitute. Based on extensive interviews with a few of the half million children who are sold into sex slavery according to WHO (World Health Organisation). Good present for a man going to certain countries perhaps.

Drugs

Sandra Gregory and Michael Tierney, *Forget You Had a Daughter: Doing Time in the Bangkok Hilton – Sandra Gregory's Story*. Vision, 2003. Sandra's autobiography of her time in Thai and British prisons after being caught drug smuggling in Thailand as a young woman. She later turned her life around and got a degree from Oxford.

Rock 'n' roll

For festivals see Part 1, Chapter 3, 'When do you go?'.

The power of saying yes

Danny Wallace, *Yes Man*. Ebury Press, 2005. Brilliant story of what happens when Danny takes the words of a stranger on a bus, 'say yes more', literally and says yes to everything for a year.

Chapter 8: Three qualities for true expansion

Immaculée Ilibagiza, *Left To Tell: Discovering God Amidst the Rwandan Holocaust*. Hay House, 2006. Inspirational account of a refugee in a country at war; a girl who learned to forgive horrific brutality, including the murders of her own family by people she knew.

Chapter 9: Travelling ethically

Inspiration

Paulo Coelho, *The Alchemist*. HarperCollins, 1992. Fabulous tale of a boy who is drawn to the desert and gains the wisdom necessary to find his treasure.

Chapter 10: Spending your money

Choose carefully

M. Mauss, *The Gift: The Form and Reason for Exchange in Archaic Societies*. Routledge, 1990. Anthropological classic on the spirit of objects and the reasons why they are exchanged.

Jeff Greenwald, *Shopping for Buddhas*. Lonely Planet, 1996. The author travels to Nepal looking for the 'perfect Buddha', then realises he's putting the material ahead of what's really important.

Ethical shopping

Fairtrade: www.fairtrade.org.uk Organisation that monitors the provenance of goods ensuring fair trade for all.

Ethical Consumer magazine: www.ethicalconsumer.org When you join you have online access to ethiscore.org, so you can check sources before you buy certain objects.

Duty: www.hmrc.gov.uk Advice on paying duty for goods brought into Britain.

Duncan Clark, *The Rough Guide to Ethical Shopping*. Rough Guides, 2004. Useful guidance on the issues involved.

Ken Finn, *My Journey with a Remarkable Tree*. Eye Books, 2005. Ken follows a beautiful tree from the Spirit Forest of Cambodia, to its end in a garden centre in North London in this beautiful account.

The power of relationship

Bronislaw Malinowski, *Argonauts of the Western Pacific.* Waveland Press, 1984. Important account from one of the founding fathers of Anthropology of the economic and cultural systems of the Trobriand Islands.

Following spiritual laws

Catherine Ponder, *The Dynamic Laws of Prosperity.* DeVorss and Co., 1985. Money as part of a greater spiritual system. Christian focus with biblical quotes and plenty of practical wisdom to help you change your belief system.

Chapter 11: Your food choices

Eating big

Supersize Me: A Film of Epic Portions. Morgan Spurlock (dir.), DVD, 2004. Excellent story of the film maker who ate only junk food for a month – and how big he grew.

John Robbins, *Diet for a New America: How Your Food Choices Affect Your Health, Happiness and the Future of Life on Earth.* Stillpoint Publishing, 1987. The son of the founder of Baskin Robbins ice cream gives a stark picture of how the choices you make affect the earth. Many environmentalists' Bible.

Eating small

Farmaround: www.farmaround.co.uk Covent Garden based firm delivers fresh fruit and vegetable boxes to London and the North of England.

Ann Vanderhoef, *An Embarrassment of Mangoes: A Caribbean Interlude.* Broadway Books, 2003. Canadian couple in their forties leave Canada and sail around the Caribbean, where they are never happier. Gorgeous recipes and descriptions of local food eaten in context.

Alison Johnson, *A House by the Shore and Scarista Style.* Time Warner, 1998. Alison and her husband go from Oxford to the outer Hebridean isle of Harris, where they open a hotel. She reproduces many local recipes.

Christina Dodwell, *An Explorer's Handbook: Travel, Survival and Bush*

Cookery. Hodder and Stoughton, 1984. This book deserves to be much better known. Some brilliant recipes and brave stories.

Richard Mabey, *Food for Free*. Collins, 2007. Foraging guide to plants of England. Some lovely pictures, *and* will save you money.

Tarla Dalal, *Swadisht Subzian*. Sanjay & Co., 2005. India's no. 1 cookery author gives you recipes from different regions of India in this excellent book.

Vegetarianism and veganism

Vegetarian Society: www.vegsoc.org Committed to providing advice on all aspects of vegetarian lifestyle from recipes to courses.

Veggie resources: www.happycow.net Probably best guide on the net to vegetarian resources including food and accommodation worldwide.

Vegetarian Guides: www.vegetarianguides.co.uk Guidebooks for vegetarians and vegans in Britain, Europe and elsewhere, including places to eat and stay.

Rainforest Action Network, www.ran.org Campaigns for alternatives to dependence on oil, while being respectful of indigenous rights.

Raising your vibration

Janez Drnovsek, *Thoughts on life and consciousness*. E-book translation of Slovenian bestseller. Simple and powerful guide to awakening your consciousness involving a daily programme of thoughts.

FRESH network: www.fresh-network.com Europe's largest living and raw food organisation.

Vegan raw business: www.shazzie.com Site includes very interesting seven-year blog of the spiritual effects of transitioning to raw food diet.

Masaru Emoto, *The True Power of Water*. Pocket Books, 2005 or DVD. Classic research from a scientist, unforgettable pictures of the crystalline dimensions of water and how they are affected by our intent.

Natalie Savona, *The BIG book of JUICES and Smoothies: 365 Natural Blends for Health and Vitality Every Day*. Duncan Baird Publishers, 2007. Simple and delicious recipes. An added benefit is the analysis of nutrients and tips for juicing for specific ailments.

Kate Magic Wood, *Raw Magic*. Rawcreation Limited, 2008. Transformative recipes show you in this high-vibe book how to use food to propel you into ecstasy.

Michael Werner and Thomas Stockli, *Life from Light: Is It Possible to Live Without Food?*. Clairview Books, 2007. True story of a Swiss chemist's life without food. Recommended, particularly for scientific-rational types.

Chapter 12: When do you accept hospitality?

Organisations to help you stay with local people.
See also Part 2, Chapter 6 'Meeting people'.

Free accommodation in return for cultural interaction: www.couchsurfing.com
Excellent non-profit organisation facilitates contact between travellers and local community by offering a free couch to travellers. 'Changing the world one couch at a time.' Vouching and identity verification system (through credit cards) ensures relative safely, and detailed profiling means you can pick and choose who you want to stay in your home. Presently mainly younger travellers.

Hospitality club: www.hospitalityclub.org Free membership and stays in private homes all over the world; you are asked to reciprocate.

Servas: www.uservas.org An international host and traveller network, Servas believes that peace in the world comes about through cultural interchange. For a not inconsiderable yearly fee everyone – host and traveller – is interviewed in their home country and you are given a letter to bring to your host. Then you are able to stay free with locals for two nights, and expected to spend your evenings with them in cultural interchange. Presently mainly older travellers.

Share hospitality: www.welcometraveller.org Mainly for the older traveller. Requires a small honorarium for each stay. Special interest groups such as crafts and running are catered for. Disabled access can be specified.

The lure of the wild
Marie Tièche, *Champagne and Polar Bears*. Summersdale, 1998. Compelling story of an Englishwoman living in the Arctic, who gets a very special invitation from a man she meets in a bar to spend a year in a northern hut alone with him, with no way of leaving. She accepts . . .

Chapter 13: What do you give back?

Reciprocity

Rita Golden Gelman, *Tales of a Female Nomad: Living at Large in the World.* Crown, 2002. Author sets off across the globe after a failed marriage. Inspiring tales from her time with local communities, tips on keeping in touch with children and friends – 15 years later she is still happily travelling.

Random Acts of Kindness: www.actsofkindness.org Fascinating website
    dedicated to examples of the difference small acts of kindness make in
    people's lives. Events listing brings different communities together.
Caroline Myss, *Invisible Acts of Power: Channeling Grace in Your Everyday
    Life*. Free Press, 2004. True stories of giving and an interpretation of the
    relationship to the chakras of the body.

Giving to the earth

John Seed, *Thinking Like a Mountain*. New Society Publishers, 1988. Famous
    depiction of native spirituality and views about the environment from
    Chief Seattle of the Suquamish.

Chapter 14: The point of camping

General advice

Advice on packing light: www.backpacking.net
Women-only wilderness trips (USA): www.callwild.com Call of the Wild is
    the world's longest-running travel company for women. Wilderness trips,
    mostly in America, teach camping skills to empower you.

Campsites

Information on overnight sites: www.campingandcaravanningclub.co.uk
    Membership club giving details of campsites at home and abroad.
Information on overnight sites: www.ukcampsite.co.uk Details of campsites
    in UK.
Jonathan Knight, *Cool Camping*. Punk Publishing, 2006. Advice on selecting
    the best campsites in England (or Wales or Scotland). Includes the down-
    sides of each site, such as road noise, which is invaluable.

Rewards

Jill Frayne, *Starting Out in the Afternoon: Mid Life Journey into Wild Land*.
    Vintage Books, 2003. Fifty-year-old Canadian lady goes into the wilder-
    ness for the first time.
Richard Nelson, *Make Prayers to the Raven: Koyukon View of the
    Northern Forest*. University of Chicago Press, 1986. Sensitive study of
    the Kuyokon of Northern Canada focuses on their relationship to their
    environment.

Chapter 15: When to visit the sacred

General advice

Martin Gray, *Sacred Earth: Places of Peace and Power*. Sterling, 2007. World pilgrim has spent over 20 years visiting the world's power places following a vision. Can get with DVD from author's website, www.sacredsites.com

World Heritage List: http://whc.unesco.org Identifies parts of the world's heritage most in need of protection, good information on certain sites.

Famous sacred sites: www.sacred-destinations.com Features sacred destinations divided by categories, including travel tips and links to articles about them.

Where to go: www.sacredplaces.info Guide to over 50 of the world's sacred places by Druid leader Philip Carr-Gomm, spiritual/ecological focus.

Deepening your understanding: www.sacredland-org Organisation promoting links between sacred places, indigenous wisdom and environmental justice.

Chapter 16: Opening to the mystical

Experiencing the sacred

Rima Morrell, *The Sacred Power of Huna: Spirituality and Shamanism in Hawaii*. Inner Traditions, 2005. Describes my journey into the sacred, interspersed with deep understandings of Hawaiian knowledge of ancient wisdom, possibly the deepest on earth.

James Swan, *Sacred Places: How the Living Earth Seeks Our Friendship*. Bear and Co., 1995. Book about the sacred features many accounts of mystical experiences.

T.C. McLuhan, *Cathedrals of the Spirit: Messages of Sacred Places*. Perennial, 1996. Guide to how many people – and you too – can find the sacred within and without.

Louisa Teresa Strongbear, *Journey by Night: A Solitary Journey*. Author-House, 2006. Magical fable about shamanic experiences, written as though every word has been dipped in silver.

Chapter 17: Take rest

Philosophical value of being idle

Max Weber, *The Protestant Ethic and the Spirit of Capitalism.* First published in 1904, this book by the famous German sociologist on the links between the Protestant work ethic and the rise of capitalism is surprisingly easy to read.

Marie-Louise Franz, *Time: Patterns of Flow and Return*. Thames and
Hudson, 1979. Excellent study of the nature of time and how it changes.
Jungian psychotherapist looks at mathematical, philosophical and religious contexts.

Retreats

Vipassana centres: www.dhamma.org Ten-day silent retreats all over the
world. Free as funded by donations from people who have benefited.

Directory of transformational retreats: www. places-to-be.com

Yediburunlar Lighthouse, Turkey, www.yediburunlar.blogspot.com Mountain
retreat offering gourmet organic and locally sourced vegetarian food, swimming pool, stunning views and complementary guided hikes along the
Lycian Way.

Spas

Thailand: www.thesanctuarythailand.com Detox sanctuary in Koh Phangan,
programme of talks.

Mexico: www.riocaliente.com Space to reclaim and restore authenticity of
self, which can get lost in the modern world, amidst natural hot springs.
Interesting programme of speakers.

Szechenyi, spa in Hungary: www.budapest.com Once Europe's largest spa.
Pools have jets cascading down from statues. Budapest, Hungary where
spas are for everyone.

Chocolate sauna: www.atlantis-vodnomesto.si/eng Imaginative spa with
swimming pools and many kinds of saunas including chocolate ones in
Ljubljana, the capital of Slovenia.

Spa show, www.spashow.co.uk Held in London in November.

Ashrams

Sri Aurobindo Ashram: www.sriaurobindoashram.org Established in
Pondicherry since 1926, teaches the development of consciousness on
the physical, pranic, emotional, mental and spiritual levels. No obligatory
practice.

Auroville: www.auroville.org Auroville commune in Southern India, offers
university-accredited spiritual courses as well as chances to meditate in
peace, and an opportunity to choose from over a hundred settlements to
stay in.

ShantiMayi: www.shantimayi.com Small ashram near Rishikesh in the

Himalayas, where the guru is a Western woman of the Sacha lineage offering many spiritual opportunities for growth.

Anne Cushman, *From Here to Nirvana: The Yoga Journal Guide to Spiritual Travel in India*. Riverhead Trade, 1999. Useful guide for people seeking ashrams and yoga schools.

Lucy Edge, *Yoga School Drop-out*. Ebury Press, 2005. Fashionable London advertising executive Lucy goes to India. Excellent description of different yoga schools and ashrams on her well-observed inner journey.

Other

Beach resort in Southern India: www.saivishram.com No alcohol and vegetarian food in this resort, which offers secluded cabins by the Arabian Sea. Plenty of outdoor activities, so good if you want to experiment with how fun life can be without certain things.

Henry David Thoreau, *Walden*. Digireads, 2005. Classic musings by a man who lived in his cabin in the woods, and extols the value of simplicity.

Caroline Sylge, *Body and Soul Escapes*. Footprint Handbooks, 2007. Thorough, thoughtful and well organised guide to spas, healing retreats and yoga centres worldwide. For anyone who needs a break.

Chapter 18: Dealing with change on your journey

Creating change through travel

Robyn Davidson, *Tracks*. Picador, 1998. Beautifully written and deep account of this lone woman's camel trek across Australia.

Bruce Chatwin, *The Songlines*. Penguin, 1988. Another travel classic, provides a thoughtful look at the Aboriginal culture of Alice Springs from this well respected travel writer.

The philosophy of change

Lao Tsu, (trans.) Stephen Addiss and Stanley Lombardo, *Tao Te Ching*. Hackett, 1993. Beautifully translated edition of this classic work by a Chinese sage on the impermanence of all things.

The Bhagavad Gita As It Is. With Introduction, Translation and Authorized Purports by His Divine Grace A.C. Ghaktivedanta Swami Prabhupada. The Bhaktivedanta Book Trust, 2002. Hindu classic and inspiration for hundreds of millions all over the world, discusses the nature of the soul.

Mark Dyczkowski, *The Doctrine of Vibration: An Analysis of the Doctrines and Practices of Kashmir Shaivism*. Motilal Banarsidass, 1989. A book to help you realise the impermanence of all things.

Fritjof Capra, *The Tao of Physics: An Exploration of the Parallels Between Modern Physics and Eastern Mysticism*. Wildwood House, 1975. Tremendous book showing links between science and the mystical – and the nature of impermanence.

Coping with sudden opening

Esther and Jerry Hicks, *The Astonishing Power of Emotion: Let Your Feelings Be Your Guide* (with CD). Hay House, 2007. The authors of the popular DVD *The Secret* discuss the concept of vibration (left out of the DVD against their will) and how changing your vibration alters your reality.

Rescue remedy: www.rescueremedy.com Highly recommended in liquid form for stressful situations.

Hazel Courteney, *Divine Intervention*. Cico Books, 2005. *Sunday Times* journalist Hazel survived a 'spiritual emergency', in which she became telepathic, highly activated and aware of the true state of nature, and even mobile phones.

Chapter 19: Going within

Understand your patterns

The New Golden Treasury of English Verse, chosen by Edward Leeson. Pan Books, 1980. Even if you don't normally read poetry, this selection of some of the best poetry in English is endlessly illuminating about the human condition.

Sam Keen and Anne Valley-Fox, *Your Mythic Journey*. Jeremy P. Tarcher, 1989. Advice on writing in terms of understanding your life as a myth.

Julia Cameron, *The Artist's Way: A Course in Discovering and Recovering Your Creative Self*. Pan Books, 1997. Account of how raising your vibration leads to greater creativity.

Lee Carroll, *Parable of Kryon*. Hay House, 2000. Simple and effective stories about ways to lead a fuller life.

Feeling

Lency Spezzano, *Make Way for Love*. Psychology of Vision Press, 1995. Heartwarming true stories about the process of opening your heart.

Cilla Conway, *The Devas of Creation: Connecting with the Energies of the Universe.* See www.devasofcreation.com Seventy-two beautiful cards, each embodying a quality such as 'water' and 'seed', encourage your intuitive interpretations.

Chapter 20: Keeping in touch

Phones

Advice on mobile phones for travelling internationally: www.kropla.com

Free calls, domestic and international, over the web: www.skype.com Both parties must have the software.

Free calls without a PC: www.jajah.com Can call free from country to country by entering your home number and the number of the person you want to call.

USA mobile: www.celltradeusa.com Can get mobile number for shorter time with no activation fee, useful for temporary residents in USA.

Email

Yahoo email: www.yahoo.com Unlimited and free web-based email; you can access wherever there's an Internet connection.

Locations for using wireless Internet: www.wififreespot.com

Internet cafes worldwide: www.cybercafes.com

Virtual travellers' communities

Virtual Tourist: www.virtualtourist.com World's biggest online travel community.

Travellers Contact Point: Travelerscontactpoint.com Many tips for Australia, New Zealand and UK.

Bootsnall Travel: www.bootsnall.com Resource for independent travellers.

Chapter 21: Getting work

Worldwide

Jobs for travellers: www.anyworkanywhere.com

Jobs for gappers and older travellers: www.payaway.co.uk

International recruitment: www.adecco.com Huge job recruitment site with 6,600 branches in over 70 countries and territories.

International recruitment: http://globalgateway.monster.com
Recruitment agency offering temporary and permanent jobs on five continents.

Dave's ESL cafe: www.eslcafe.com Best resource for teachers of English as a second language.

Vacation Work Publications: www.vacationwork.co.uk Offer other guides and notice boards for working abroad.

Susan Griffin, *Work Your Way Around the World*. Vacation Work Publications, latest edition. Long-standing working travellers' 'bible', this gives you many tips and tricks.

Alastair Scott, *Scot Free: A Journey from the Arctic to New Mexico*. John Murray, 1986. (See also 2 others in the series.) Fascinating work-life encounters from this Scotsman's five-year trip around the world. Written in lively accessible style.

UK and Europe

Jobs in UK: www.reed.co.uk UK's biggest job site for temporary and permanent jobs.

Jobs in Europe: www.jobs-in-europe.net

Work permits: www.workpermits.org Advice on how to get work permits for the UK. Useful for Australians, New Zealanders and others.

Asia, Australia, New Zealand – and further

Working in Asia: www.jobsdb.com JobsDB offers job opportunities across Asia.

Working in Australia: http://seek.com.au Huge and well-organised site; offers jobs in many categories.

Working in New Zealand: www.seek.co.nz Australian subsidiary; site still offers a good range of jobs.

Working in the Antarctic: www.rayjobs.com You must be a US citizen to qualify for these support jobs to the scientists – 60 per cent of the janitors on McMurdo Base have a Ph.D.

Chapter 22: When do you make love?

Attraction

Tobias Schneebaum, *Where the Spirits Dwell: An Odyssey in the Jungles of New Guinea*. Grove Press, 1994. A gay anthropologist travels to New Guinea and participates in certain rituals.

Elaine Hatfield and Richard Rapson, *Love & Sex: Cross-Cultural Perspectives.* Allyn and Bacon, 1996. Fascinating study of attitudes to passion, jealousy and rejection all over the world.

Accepting sex

Booklist: www.beaumode.net/romancebooks Comprehensive list of books about cross-cultural romance.

Don George (ed.), *Wanderlust: Real-Life Tales of Adventure and Romance.* Villard, 2000. Real-life stories of romance on the road, including some by well-known travel writers.

Marguerite Duras, *The Lover.* Pantheon, 1998. Classic tale of the love affair between a young French girl and an elegant son of Vietnam.

Intercultural marriage

Dugan Rumano, *Intercultural Marriage: Promises and Pitfalls* (2nd edn). Nicholas Brealey, 2001. Cross-cultural trainer and journalist identifies 19 trouble spots, such as religion and male–female roles, either less severe or absent in monocultural marriages, and gives advice.

Douglas Kennedy, *A Special Relationship.* QPD, 2003. Gripping novel about a marriage between an Englishman and an American woman that goes disastrously wrong.

Laura Rowchowdhury, *The Jadu House: Intimate Histories of Anglo-India.* Transworld, 2000. Enjoyable account of the anthropologist's Ph.D. research in India, including her marriage to a Bengali scholar.

Joana McIntyre Varawa, *Changes in Latitude: An Uncommon Anthropology.* HarperCollins, 1990. Honest account of an older Australian lady's marriage to a younger Fijian man, and how she must change to settle on his island.

The Cosmic Dance

Tim Ward, *Arousing the Goddess: Sex and Love in the Buddhist Ruins of India.* Monkfish Books, 1996. Deep Budhist philosophy merges with Tim's description of tantric sex in this wonderful book which deserves to be on every college curriculum.

John Hamwee, *Love's Energy: How to Stay in Love.* Frances Lincoln, 2001. Excellent guide to dealing with the strong energies set free by falling in love.

Chapter 23: Coping with goodbyes

Saying goodbye

Phyllis Krystal, *Cutting the Ties that Bind: Growing Up and Moving On.*
Weiser Books, 1994. Quality advice and exercises to help you move on.

Jonathan Raban, *Passage to Juneau: A Sea & Its Meanings.* Alfred Knopf, 1999.
Beautifully written, almost meditative book, as this well respected travel
writer sails from Seattle to Alaska and learns his family is to split up.

Chapter 24: Coping with illness

For practical advice, see above Part 1, Chapter 16, 'Preparing for a safe trip'.

Listening to your soul

Caroline Myss, *Sacred Contracts.* Bantam Books, 2002. Discusses the way
illness may be in our soul contract.

Richard Moss, *The I That Is We.* Celestial Arts, 1982. One of my favourite,
favourite books. Advanced study of why we get sick.

Richard Gerber, MD, *Vibrational Medicine for the 21st Century: A Complete
Guide to Energy Healing and Spiritual Transformation.* Piatkus Books,
2000. Guide to many alternative systems of medicine from a medical
doctor.

Responding to our sickness

Scientific and Medical Network: www.scimednet.org Mainly
professionals and scientists are members of this interdisciplinary
forum. Explores the frontiers of science, medicine, spirituality and
experience. UK based, but hosts international conferences and has a
regular magazine.

Scientific and Medical Network in New Zealand: www.geocities.com/fsmn_nz
New Zealand branch based in Auckland offers monthly meetings.

Doctor Healer Network: www.doctorhealer.net UK-based organisation
brings doctors and healers together in regular meetings and conferences,
finding points of contact between them.

Patch Adams, *Gesundheit.* Inner Traditions, 1998. Ways in which laughter
and somewhat unconventional medicine can make you feel better.

Herbert Benson and Miriam Clipper, *The Relaxation Response.* Harper
Paperbacks, 2000. Great book giving tips for relaxation and the medical
evidence for it.

Louise L. Hay, *You Can Heal Your Life*. Hay House, 2002. Simple and very effective exercises and techniques to cure aches and pains.

Chapter 25: What do you do if it all goes wrong?

Practical advice

Find your embassy: www.embassy.com Location of embassies throughout the world.

Other people are having a worse time than you ...

Redmond O'Hanlon, *Into the Heart of Borneo*. Penguin, 1985. Like the book below, guaranteed to make you feel better, for at least you are not in the author's predicament.

Eric Newby, *A Short Walk in the Hindu Kush*. Picador, 1981. Hilarious travel classic; tale of author's journey to Afghanistan.

Seeing anew

Gavin Pretor-Pinney, *The Cloudspotter's Guide*. Sceptre, 2007. Lovely guide to the clouds in the outer sky.

Chapter 26: When do you go home?

Is a voice calling you back?

Newspapers etc.: www.worldnews.com Network of online newspapers and radio stations for all regions.

www.live-radio.net/info.shtml Live radio broadcasts for every country in the world in real time.

www.planet.lv/misc/chartz International pop music charts arranged by country.

Home news

For examples of books about a culture, which may include your own, see Part 1, Chapter 6, 'Finding a culture to suit you'.

Google Earth: www.earth.google.com Shows you pictures of your favourite places – and the sky above them.

PART 3: COMING HOME AGAIN

Chapter 1: Returning home

Reverse culture shock

Jamie Zeppa, *Beyond the Sky and the Earth: A Journey into Bhutan.*
Riverhead Trade, 2000. Superb and honest account by a young Canadian
teacher who agreed to work in the remote Himalayan kingdom of Bhutan
for two years. At first she hates it, but ends up becoming a Buddhist and
falling in love with the country and a man, and experiencing reverse
culture shock when she returns to Toronto.

Craig Storti, *The Art of Coming Home.* Nicholas Brealey, 2001. Written for
the corporate market, the tips on coping with reverse culture shock are
nonetheless useful.

Where is our home?

Global Ecovillage Network: http://orgs.takingitglobal.org Sustainable
villages all over the world based on values of community, ecology and
spirituality in different degrees.

Diggers and Dreamers (UK): www.diggersanddreamers.org.uk UK-based
communities seeking members.

Willing Workers on Organic Farms: www.wwoof.org.uk Host farms in
UK and all over the world offer opportunities to live and work for a
while.

Steven Feld and Keith Basso (eds), *Senses of Place.* School of American
Research, 1996. Anthropological essays on the way places are known,
imagined, yearned for, held, remembered, lived, contested.

The greenstone door

Family therapy: www.deep-field-relaxation.com Tribal cultures talk about
each person as a thread in the greater family tapestry. Clif and Galina
Sanderson's excellent system for healing family patterns through love.

The soul-land

Rima Morrell, *The Hawaiian Oracle: Animal Spirit Guides from the Land of
Light.* Connections and New World Library, 2006. My book and card set.
Choose a card and open the accompanying book, which guides you to
the mythological value of different Hawaiian creatures, and the way their
qualities illuminate your path home.

Chapter 2: Dealing with change at home

Changes in your world

Marshall Berman, *All That is Solid Melts Into Air*. Penguin, 1998. One of my
favourite geographical books on the ills of modernity.

Eckhart Tolle, *The Power of Now*. Hodder and Stoughton, 2001. Deceptively
simple guide to seeing through form and accepting what is.

Changes in you

Relocating

Ghillie Basan, *The Moon Is Our Nearest Neighbour*. Little Brown, 2001. Couple
move to the remote Highlands, do up a croft and learn to make a living.

Lynne Franks, *Absolutely Now!*. Century Books, 1997. PR guru lets go of
her husband, home and commitments, moves to Majorca and finds some
answers.

Downshifting

Chris Sangster, *The Downshifter's Guide to Relocation*. How To Books, 2005.
Very useful practical guide from someone who moved from London to
the Scottish Highlands on the 'how-tos' of downshifting.

Alexa Thomson. *Antarctica on a Plate*. Summersdale, 2005. Enticing story of
this successful young Australian's life change as she downshifts by going to
Antarctica to work as a chef – while camping.

Sarah Susanka, *The Not So Big Life: Making Room for What Really Matters*.
Random House, 2007. Architect gives excellent advice on downshifting
your life, including dreams, meditation and spirituality, as well as more
practical matters.

Chapter 3: Valuing your trip

Sharing in a formal context

Globetrotters travel club: www.globetrotters.co.uk Opportunities for giving
talks in inspiring organisation, branches in London and Toronto.

Royal Geographical Society: www.rgs.org High-quality talks by top
explorers in central London and one of the world's top geographical
libraries. You must join to access the facilities.

Guide to public speaking: www.toastmasters.org Groups all over the world
help you develop your skills. Excellent programme and encouragement.

Writing about your experience

Popular website where you can contribute: www.virtualtourist.com

Opinionated writing on travel and other topics: www.hackwriters.com

Quality writers on different topics and countries: www.salon.com

Regular competitions, stories and chance to participate in a book:
www.travelerstales.com

Community of professional travel writers: www.travelwriters.com

Connections for professional writers: www.writersmarketplace.com

Arvon Foundation: www.arvonfoundation.com Offers week-long writing
courses at several residential centres in Britain.

Irish Writers Centre: www.writerscentre.ie Intensive courses in Dublin.

Anthropology

David Pocock, *Understanding Social Anthropology.* Adarsh, 2004. Solid
introduction to the principles of social anthropology.

Gregory Bateson, *Naven: A Survey of the Problems Suggested by a Composite
Picture of the Culture of a New Guinea Tribe Drawn from Three Points of
View.* Stanford University Press, 1958. Lively study of a New Guinea tribe
which practises transvestism.

Margaret Mead, *Coming of Age in Samoa.* Harper Perennial Modern Classics,
2001. Controversial study which explores the nature of sexual freedom
among teenagers in the South Pacific.

Thor Heyerdahl, *Fatu-Hiva: Back to Nature.* Nal Books, 1974. Little-known story
of his time with his first wife on an island in the South Seas. His curiosity about
the Polynesian culture inspired him to develop the Kon-Tiki expedition.

Katy Gardner, *Songs at the River's Edge: Stories from a Bangladeshi Village.*
Virago, 1992. British anthropologist spends years in a Bangladeshi village
and evocatively records the culture she finds.

Shamanism

Shamanism helps us become more conscious through raising our
consciousness by contacting all of nature.

Courses in Huna, Hawaiian shamanism: www.hunalight.com Learn
Hawaiian wisdom in London (weekly courses) and Skye (intensive
courses every June).

Courses in Shamanism, bushcraft and survival skills: www.anamcara.org
Many courses in retreat centre close to Inverness.

Druidry: www.druidry.org The Order of Bards, Ovates and Druids offers
training programmes and camps in Britain's sacred tradition.

Celtic shamanism: www.hallowquest.org.uk Celtic scholars Caitlin and
John Matthews also offer training programmes and courses in the ancient
wisdom of the British Isles.

Further study

Courses in London: www.floodlight.co.uk Official guide to all adult education courses in London.

The Open University: www.open.ac.uk Courses, distance based or with
classes that lead to a university degree, for those without qualifications.

Official university entry (UK): www.ucas.co.uk University and college
admission service in Britain.

Official university entry (Au): www.uac.edu.au University and college
admission service in Australia.

New Zealand qualifications authority: www.nzqa.govt.nz Links to tertiary
education courses in New Zealand and Australia.

Craft

Your local directory (found at your library) will have details of things going
on in your area. If you wish to go away:

Portland Sculpture and Quarry Trust: www.learningstone.org One–four
week, stone-carving courses in the local Portland stone, held in a Dorset
quarry.

Jewellery making in Mexico: www.instituto-allende.edu.mx At the
Instituto Allende in San Miguel de Allende, jewellery making in gold,
silver and precious stones; traditional Mexican weaving and intuitive
painting.

Eco retreat in Canada: www.eco-retreat.com In Kw'o:kw'e:hala (British
Columbia) let Raven clan practitioners teach you basket and hat making
from cedar bark or make your own drum. Relax in the wood-fired sauna,
in the outdoor hot tub under the trees and around the nightly camp fire.

Hawaiian culture: www.ocet.wcc.hawaii.edu Learn Hawaiian drum making,
wood carving and other things at Windward Community College in
Hawaii.

Self-sufficiency

Permaculture: www.permaculture.org.uk Courses in sustainability.

Greenwood Centre, Shropshire: www.greenwoodcentre.org.uk Short courses
in everything from felt making for yurts to basket making and coppicing.

Woodland skills: www.wholewoods.co.uk Craft weekends in the woods in Ashdown Forest, Sussex include making an earth oven and family bushcraft.

Islay bushcraft: www.islaybushcraft.co.uk Survival courses on this southern Hebridean island include spending the night in a cave. Family friendly.

Foraging Ireland: www.greenbox.ie/ecobreaks Three-day wilderness therapy sessions where you learn open-boat skills and sail to Lough Allen island to camp.

Willing Workers on Organics Farms: wwoof.org.uk Free, short-term placements on organic farms in UK and around the world offer opportunities to learn practical skills.

Water skills

Royal Yacht Association qualifications: www.sailingcourses.co.uk At Adrenaline Sailing School in Hampshire you can sleep on the boat while you learn.

Youth Hostel Association: Courses in techniques for kayaking and surfing: www.yha.org.uk

Scuba diving: www.redseacollege.com Get your PADI qualification on the Red Sea; many additional courses in activities, such as underwater photography and night diving.

Skiing

Green Resort Guide for skiers: www.skiclub.co.uk Ski Club of Great Britain Guide shows environmental measures ski resorts are taking.

Powder skiing in Canada: www.skifernie.com Steep and deep two-day camps to improve your powder riding.

Skiing and skywatching: www.abisko.nu Learn to ski cross country, then watch the northern lights from the observatory in northern Sweden where you can stay overnight, before a morning sauna.

Spiritual

Courses on Holy Island: www.holyisland.org Learn meditation, feng shui etc. and other skills on Holy Island, off Arran, Scotland.

Retreat, meditate and learn yoga in the Scottish wilderness: www.shantigriha.com Couple with doctorates, living in the UK's most remote community at Scoraig in Scotland, offer courses and ever-fresh food. Interesting spot, too, for all those interested in renewable energy. Five miles from the road so extremely peaceful.

Courses in animal communication: www.livingark.com Come to our sanctuary and learn how to sense what the creatures are saying to you and widen your world.

Thai massage: www.thaiyogamassage.infothai.com Learn Thai yoga massage in Thailand and worldwide.

Tantra and yoga: www.agamayoga.com Month-long courses in energy awareness, *kundalini* work and tantric sexuality in India, Thailand and elsewhere.

Other

Perfume making: www.aromasciences.com Develop your own scent on these one-day courses in Ullapool, north-west Scotland.

Music: www.scratch.com Courses in DJing in America.

Circus skills Australia: www.nica The National Institute of Circus Arts, a government-accredited institution, provides training in circus skills. Learn everything from trapeze to juggling.

Yoga and surfing: www.samudra.com.au Retreats where you learn yoga and surfing on the beach; held in Australia and elsewhere.

Chapter 4: Riding off into the sunset again

Travelling again with your Higher Self

Elizabeth Gilbert, *Eat, Pray, Love*. Bloomsbury, 2006. Brave woman leaves her husband and spends a year around the world looking for, and finding, herself. Extremely well written account.

Astrocartography: www.thedreamtime.com This ancient science produces a map based on your birth place and time and helps you choose where is the best place for you to live by the extrapolated movements of the planets. Worth checking out even if you don't believe in astrology; all you need is your date, place and time of birth – many have been surprised by the results.

Home exchange

Teacher Home Swap: www.teacherhomeswap.com Exclusively for teachers.

Home Swap: www.homeforexchange.com American site, reasonable membership fee.

Home Base Holidays: www.homebase-hols.com Reliable service based in
UK.

International home exchange: www.ihen.com US based site, covers many
countries.

Volunteering

All of these programmes only have modest fees, if any.

Survival International: www.survival-international.org Promotes the rights
of indigenous people. Volunteering opportunities in London.

NZ Trust for conservation volunteers:
www.conservationvolunteers.org.nz Opportunities for Kiwis and others
to help preserve some of New Zealand's most beautiful places.

Volunteering in Australia: www.volunteeringaustralia.org Largely corporate
website, featuring many opportunities within Australia.

Businesspeople volunteering outside Australia: www.abv.org.au Short-term
mentoring of projects in Asia and the Pacific; you receive an allowance.

Foundation for Sustainable Development (USA): www.fsdinternational.org
Grassroots programmes in sustainability where your speciality, such as
finance, can be utilised. Seven different categories including finance and
women's empowerment.

Helping street children in India: www.ChildrenWalkingTall.com No charge
for volunteers in this project in Goa, India, but helpers are expected to be
self-funding.

Aiding disabled children in Mexico: www.pinapalmera.org Working
towards social integration, disabled volunteers welcome, no fee, nominal
charge.

Teaching in the Arctic: www.frontiersfoundation.ca Volunteers in this
Canadian organisation must have a strong desire to learn about another
culture, living expenses paid.

Teaching in the Sudan: www.svp-uk.com Sudan Volunteer Programme
organises people to teach English there, modest living expenses.

Working with animals in Britain: www.livingark.com Our charity offers
opportunities for working with animals and developing a spiritual focus.

Indigenous projects worldwide: www.workingabroad.com Offers projects
with a conservation and indigenous focus for a minimum of two years.

Volunteering: A Traveller's Guide to Making a Difference Around the World.
Lonely Planet, 2007. An excellent guide to finding an organisation, going
it alone or setting up your own charity.

Charity/aid work

Charity Challenge: www.charitychallenge.com Organises fund-raising expeditions for UK charities.

Nick Stanhope, *Blood, Sweat and Charity*. Eye Books. 2005. Handbook to realising personal change through undertaking charity challenges.

Tess Burrows, *Cry from the Highest Mountain*. Eye Books, 2002. Excellent account of a spiritual challenge to raise awareness for Tibetan causes.

Emigrating

Resources

British Expats (UK): www.britishexpats.com Offers stories, blogs and meetings for British citizens living abroad.

Australian Expats (Australia): www.expatsaustralia.com Jobs and a virtual community, mainly for professional Australians.

American Expats (USA): www.americanexpats.co.uk Useful advice for Americans living in the UK.

Living and working abroad: www.escapeartist.com

NZ News UK: www.nznews.co.uk Excellent, free London-based weekly newspaper and website for Kiwis in Britain.

Examples

Bryan and Riechelle Buchanan's site: www.junglemedicmissions.org Describes the Buchanans' great medical work helping Mayans in remote areas in Guatemala.

Dorian Amos, *The Good Life: Up the Yukon Without a Paddle*. Eye Books, 2004. Very brave couple emigrate to Canada. They end up in the Yukon despite being unfamiliar with the great outdoors, and Dorian rediscovers his love for his life – and his wife.

Dylan Nichols, *What Are You Doing Here?* Pen Press Publishers, 2007. Irreverent look at the life of some of the over 200,000 Australians in London – some useful tips.

Clive James, *Unreliable Memoirs*. Picador Books, 1981. Vivid life story of Australia's favourite comedian – now England's cultural icon.

Effects on children

David Pollock and Ruth Van Reken, *Third Culture Kids: The Experience of Growing Up Among Worlds*. Intercultural Press, 1999. Many examples of children who have grown up in countries which are not their parents' own – 'third culture' kids – and how it affects them.

Sara Taber, *Of Many Lands: Journal of a Traveling Childhood*. Foreign Service Youth Foundation, 1997. Dr Taber, a specialist in cross-cultural human development, reflects on her experiences growing up in many lands, and this lovely workbook provides space for you, or your kids, to do the same.

Sailing away

Professional Yacht Deliveries Worldwide: www.pydww.com Offers opportunities for newly qualified yachtmasters to gain experience by delivering yachts worldwide.

Crewing in UK: www.crewseekers.co.uk Largest crew agency in Europe, boats travel all around the world.

Chapter 5: Integrating your change

Janez Drnovsek, *Vom Wesen der Welt*. Verlag Hermagoras, Mohorjeva, 2006. Lucid look at the changes we need to make to help our world. Presently only available in German.

Akiane and Foreli Kramarik, *Akiane: Her Life, Her Art, Her Poetry*. W. Publishing Group, 2006. Beautiful pictures and poetry from this ten-year-old girl. Shows what is possible when someone follows her inner voice.

..

Index